150TH ANNIVERSARY CIVIL WAR CHRONICLE

Foreword:
William C. Davis

Consultant:
Richard A. Sauers, Ph.D.

LEGACY

Foreword writer **William C. Davis** is an award-winning historian who has written and edited many Civil War titles, including *A Way Through the Wilderness, A Government of Our Own: The Making of the Confederacy,* the six-volume series *The Image of War,* and *Touched by Fire.* He was nominated for a Pulitzer Prize for *Breckinridge: Statesmen, Soldier, Symbol* and *Battle at Bull Run.* As a consultant, he has contributed to *The Blue & the Gray, The Civil War Wall Chart,* and *Great Battles of the Civil War.* A professor in the history department at Virginia Tech University, he is a frequent lecturer and consultant on the Civil War.

Consultant and contributing writer **Richard A. Sauers, Ph.D.,** earned his doctorate in American history from Pennsylvania State University. He is the author of more than two dozen books on the Civil War, including *The Gettysburg Campaign, A Caspian Sea of Ink: The Meade-Sickles Controversy,* the two-volume set *Advance the Colors! Pennsylvania Civil War Battle Flags,* and *A Succession of Honorable Victories: The Burnside Expedition in North Carolina.* He is coauthor of *The Blue & the Gray.* His articles and reviews appear regularly in a variety of Civil War publications.

Contributing writer **Martin F. Graham** is the coauthor of several Civil War books including *The Blue & the Gray, The Civil War Wall Chart, Great Battles of the Civil War, The James E. Taylor Sketchbook,* and *Mine Run: A Campaign of Lost Opportunities.* He specializes in Civil War and World War II history and has contributed to *Civil War Quarterly, Civil War Times Illustrated, World War II, America's Civil War,* and *Blue & Gray Magazine.* He is past president of the Cleveland Civil War Round Table.

Contributing writer **George Skoch,** former associate editor for *Blue & Gray Magazine,* has written and edited numerous articles and books about the Civil War. He is coauthor of *The Blue & the Gray, The Civil War Wall Chart, Great Battles of the Civil War, The James E. Taylor Sketchbook, Mine Run: A Campaign of Lost Opportunities,* and *Lone Star Confederate* (winner of the SCV/SGR Book Award for 2003). He has contributed to *Civil War Times Illustrated, America's Civil War,* and *Civil War Book Exchange & Collector's Newspaper.* He has also created maps for scores of military history books.

Contributing writer **Clint Johnson** has written seven Civil War books including *Bull's-Eyes and Misfires: 50 People Whose Obscure Efforts Shaped the American Civil War, In the Footsteps of Robert E. Lee, In the Footsteps of Stonewall Jackson,* and *Civil War Blunders.* He is a frequent speaker at Civil War round tables and can be found on the Web at www.clintjohnsonbooks.com.

Legacy Publishing is a division of Publications International, Ltd.

ISBN-13: 978-1-4508-1479-9
ISBN-10: 1-4508-1479-4

Manufactured in China.

8 7 6 5 4 3 2 1

Library of Congress Control Number: 2010938664

Contents

CHAPTER ONE

The Road to the Civil War 10

When European powers colonized North America, they also imported African slaves to augment the labor force. Focused primarily in the South, slavery became a cornerstone of the new American nation founded in 1776. Compromise after compromise on the issue did not prevent the United States of America from tearing apart in 1860.

CHAPTER TWO

1861: The War Begins 60

The election of President Abraham Lincoln caused a crisis in the South—11 states felt threatened enough to leave one Union and form another, the Confederate States of America. Neither North nor South expected a long conflict when the shooting started.

CHAPTER THREE

1862: The Year of Battles 112

Casualty counts rose at an astonishing rate as names such as Shiloh and Antietam entered the national awareness. The North could not find a winning commander, and an underrated general named Robert E. Lee took control of the Army of Northern Virginia.

CHAPTER FOUR

1863: The Turning Point 176

The war continued to grind on as neither side could gain the upper hand. The Confederates invaded the North but were stopped in Pennsylvania at a hamlet named Gettysburg. General Ulysses S. Grant, who was winning battles along the Mississippi, was brought east to face off against Lee's Army of Northern Virginia.

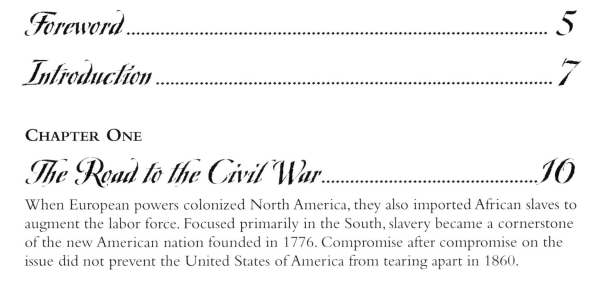

Foreword

America went to war with itself in 1861. The issues seemed cloudy and confused, but virtually everyone involved knew that the war had something to do with slavery. Slavery defined power in 1861—who would have power and who would not. And once slavery brought on secession, the act of secession itself all but guaranteed conflict: Now there were two presidents, each constitutionally obligated to preserve his nation. Ironically, the fighting that ensued saw people sacrificing their hopes and futures for largely the same ideals—honor, defense of home and country, and liberty.

This war was a war between brothers, and the participants fought and killed one another with alarming intensity. The rapidity with which they engaged in reunification after the war, however, shows that neither side ever really learned to hate each other. Or, perhaps after just having fought a war that all but gutted the nation, these warriors were simply too exhausted to hate. Nearly two-thirds of a million people lost their lives. Hundreds of thousands were missing limbs, scarred by injuries, or wracked with incurable diseases. The true cost of the war, however, can never be calculated for the simple reason that it affected not only those who fought and suffered

Private Arnold of the 22nd Regiment New York National Guard Infantry strikes a heroic pose.

or died, but also the potential they did not live to fulfill, the future they were unable to influence. What might the nature of the United States in the 20th century have been had there been no war? It is impossible to know, for nothing escaped the 1860s unchanged.

Americans have always viewed "their war" through the concerns, prejudices, and aspirations of their own times, often losing the real story of the conflict in the process. As the war faded into the past, it came to be viewed in the North as both a triumph of patriotism over disloyalty and a crusade to end slavery. The South, forced to deal with the emotional and psychological impact of defeat, created the "Lost Cause" myth. Postwar Southern leaders tried to replace their protection of slavery and their hopes for its extension as root causes of secession with a lofty stand for constitutional principle and what they believed to be states' rights.

A century after the war, however, viewpoints changed, and historians began to see that while slavery had everything to do with secession, it had relatively little to do with why soldiers actually fought. Instead, it has become apparent that Northerners overwhelmingly felt a spiritual commitment to the idea of the Union and wished to avenge secession's insult to the flag. Meanwhile, however much they universally approved of slavery, Southerners actually went to war to protect their homes and hearths from invasion. And in the fierce determination and morale of people on the home front, North and South, Americans today are seeing a fuller picture of a war that involved the minds and spirits of entire populations.

Right into the present, our conceptions—and misconceptions—of the issues and events of the Civil War continue to influence our lives and public affairs. Abraham Lincoln is somehow shaped into being a standard-bearer for candidates on all sides in presidential elections. He is probably quoted—and misquoted—as much as any other human in history. Statues of Lincoln are still erected to honor his memory, even while people elsewhere actually pay tribute to John Wilkes Booth for his "patriotic" act in murdering the President.

Whole cultures have also grown around the Confederate flag, itself now an embattled banner, as it has become a symbol for a mixed, even contradictory, fraternity of disparate elements such as sincere conservatives concerned about the growth of government; survivalists, neo-Nazi extremists, and various "militias"; avid history buffs; and even average citizens who display it as a self-proclamation of individuality. On the other side of the issue, civil rights groups are equally vehement in condemning the flag and its display as symbolic of racism and oppression. All groups misrepresent the real meaning of the flag for their own ends in the way people of all eras use the past to serve their current needs. Others do the same thing with the personalities of the Civil War. The whole concept of the hero faces serious challenges to its definition. Citizens of some places seek to remove the names of Northern and Southern leaders from schools, to prevent statues from being erected, or to take down those statues already standing.

In short, our conceptions of the Civil War still shape our views of ourselves today. Indeed, the way Americans look at this conflict—its issues and consequences and the myths we have created—says very little about the war itself but a great deal about how we wish to see ourselves. Americans can gain an understanding of the nation we are today by looking for their reflection in the Civil War.

William C. Davis

Introduction

$\mathcal{T}$he Civil War is arguably the premier watershed event of American history. The seeds of civil war were sown in the 17th century with the founding of English colonies in the New World. Within a few years of the establishment of Jamestown, African slaves began to be imported to work in the fields. As the colonies grew, so did the role of slavery. During the founding of the United States when the nation adopted a constitution, that great document legalized slavery and stipulated that five slaves were equal to three whites for computing representation in Congress.

Over the years, Northern states gradually abolished slavery. In the South, however, the institution continued to grow; in some states, black slaves outnumbered white residents. Many people abhorred slavery, however, and emancipation societies soon advocated the end of that institution and the equalization of rights for all Americans. As the country grew, frequent ideological clashes between North and South resounded in the halls of Congress and across the nation as sympathetic Northerners helped slaves to freedom and fought against restrictive laws intended to help slave owners reclaim their property.

By the 1850s, the political equilibrium between North and South was evaporating. Fighting erupted in the Kansas territory as both sides attempted to influence voters into deciding for or against slavery. A new political party—the Republican party—was formed to oppose the institution. Even though the 1860 Republican presidential candidate, Abraham Lincoln, indicated he would do nothing to destroy slavery, hotheaded Southerners believed otherwise. When Lincoln won the election against a splintered Democratic party, South Carolina announced it would secede from the Union. By the time Lincoln was sworn in as the nation's 16th President, a new Southern Confederacy had been formed by the seceded states of the Deep South.

It was not long before open warfare erupted. South Carolina troops bombarded the Union garrison of Fort Sumter in April 1861. Four years later, in April 1865, the South was broken, both militarily and economically. But the cost had been high. Roughly two-thirds of a million Americans lay dead, and more than a million had been maimed and wounded.

Photographer James F. Gibson captured this June 1862 mix of Union captains and lieutenants during the Peninsula Campaign in Virginia.

A group of Union soldiers lie dead at Gettysburg. In addition to the absence of shoes (doubtless taken by needy Southern troops), their pockets have been rifled. The bodies show the effects of bloating and rigor mortis. The entire battle area was permeated by the smells associated with unburied bodies of both people and animals.

These Columbiad guns of the Confederate water battery at Warrington, Florida, photographed in February 1861 before the start of the war, are situated across from Union Fort Pickens at the entrance to Pensacola Bay. Fort Pickens could have replaced Fort Sumter as the flash point for the war, but an uneasy truce was maintained between the fort and Confederate forces around the bay. Fort Pickens remained in Union hands throughout the war.

The war, which began as a war to preserve the Union, was turned into a war to free the slaves when Lincoln issued his Emancipation Proclamation on January 1, 1863. And even though the war did free the slaves, once the period of Reconstruction ended in 1877, African Americans were largely forgotten and relegated to second-class status for decades.

Civil War Chronicle presents an integrated view of the Civil War, its causes, and its legacy. Designed for general readers, this book presents a chronological approach to the war and its background, beginning with the foundation of English colonies in America. The stage for war is set in the first chapter by examining slavery and both its proponents and opponents. The major political battles that took place across America are included to show how divisive the issue of slavery was in the nation.

The chapters focus on a year or period concerning the war. The narrative takes the reader through the major campaigns and battles, looks at the important generals on both sides, and examines the home fronts of both North and South and what took place behind the lines. Political decisions and actions that affected the war effort are also addressed.

Although the fighting ended in 1865, the effects of the war continue to resound today. Examinations of these effects are provided in the final chapters, beginning with the era of Reconstruction (1865–77), in which the defeated South essentially became an occupied region subject to the voting whims of a Republican-controlled Congress.

Following the disputed presidential election of 1876, the U.S. Army withdrew from the last states it continued to occupy. Essentially, the national government abandoned African Americans until the civil rights movement of the modern era. The war's legacy in other areas up to the present day is also examined: the impact of veterans in politics and the rise of the pension system, the war's vast literature, heritage tourism, battlefield parks, and the African American struggle for recognition and equal rights.

Throughout this book, sidebars provide details of important battles, leaders, events, and inventions related to the war. Modern photography was developed just prior to the conflict, and many photographs in this book allow the reader to see how period photographers such as Mathew Brady captured the first modern war with their cameras. Wartime and postwar artwork from diverse artists who worked for some of the popular weeklies of the day, such as *Harper's Weekly*, as well as those who gained fame later, such as William Trego, show how Americans both viewed and remembered the conflict.

These engineers of the 8th New York State Militia are captured by the camera during the first year of the war. Engineers played a vital role on both sides of the conflict, working out the logistical details for battle, maneuvering, and travel.

The timeline running across the bottom of the pages includes important battles and engagements. One estimate of the number of encounters between soldiers in blue and gray includes 76 battles, 310 engagements, 46 combats, 1,026 actions, 29 assaults, 6,337 skirmishes, 299 operations, 26 sieges, 64 raids, 727 expeditions, 252 reconnaissances, 434 scouts, and 639 affairs—over 10,000 incidents in all. The timeline also provides a quick chronological look at war-related events in politics, the major changes in generals, wartime elections, and other related matters. In fact, the timeline extends from Jamestown to recent years, tracing the major actions that led to war as well as the era of Reconstruction and postwar milestones as diverse as the deaths of the last true veterans, the establishment of battlefield parks, the experience of African Americans—including the election of the first African American president, and other nationally important dates.

The Civil War is the most written-about event in American history. Some bibliographers have estimated that the war has spawned on average one book per day since April 1861. This vast literature includes official records of the conflict, memoirs, biographies, battle and campaign histories, unit histories, political tracts, home-front accounts, pictorial works, monument-dedication booklets, statistical compendia, encyclopedias, and a host of specialized studies ranging from discussions of the role of women in the war to prison accounts, weapons analysis, and reenactment studies. This new general history of the war, its causes, and its legacy may inspire readers to delve more deeply into this crucial American event. Local libraries and bookstores will help you in finding more titles of interest. The increasing fascination with the Civil War is indicative of the overall importance of the conflict in the course of American history. This book can serve as a beginning.

The Road
TO THE CIVIL WAR

THE NATION CANNOT ESCAPE THE PROBLEM OF SLAVERY

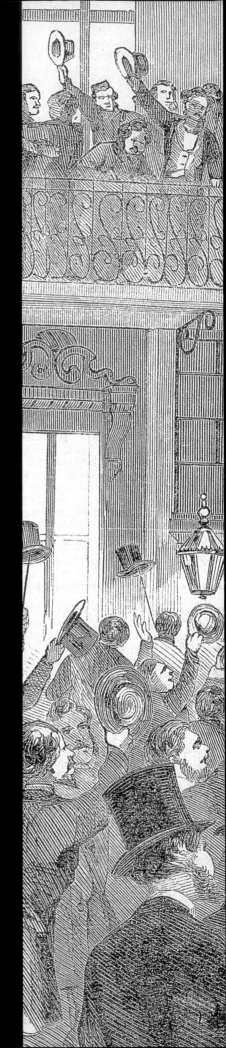

A cheering crowd gathered outside St. Andrew's Hall in Charleston, South Carolina, awaiting the result of a vote that was never in question. Inside, 169 delegates from every corner of the state debated their continued allegiance to the United States of America. That nation had just elected a president who, many Southerners insisted, opposed the institution of slavery and intended to do away with it.

Celebration overwhelmed the city of Charleston, South Carolina, on December 20, 1860, after the state's secession from the United States of America was announced. The revelers in this period woodcut gather outside the Mills House Hotel, one of Charleston's finest, which was located across the street from St. Andrew's Hall (later called Secession Hall), where legislators had voted to secede.

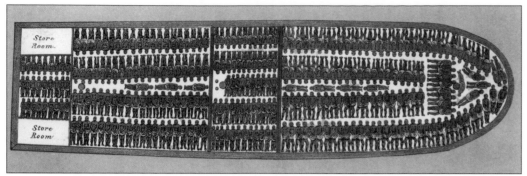

On the afternoon of December 20, 1860, word quickly spread that the vote had finally been taken. The delegates unanimously voted for South Carolina's independence. The ordinance of secession read, "We, the people of the State of South Carolina . . . do declare and ordain . . . that the union now subsisting between South Carolina and other States under the name of the United States of America is hereby dissolved."

This diagram of the slave ship Brooks was circulated by abolitionists throughout Britain to show the crowded conditions that typically existed on such vessels. Bare wooden planks were stacked between decks to store the greatest number of slaves, with little more than two feet normally left between planks. Built in 1781, the Brooks transported human cargo for almost 25 years. It carried as many as 740 slaves at a time until laws reduced the allowed capacity to about 450.

Within weeks, six other Southern states followed South Carolina's lead. The delicate balance that held the United States together for 73 years had collapsed. Diarist Mary Chesnut of Charleston wrote, "We are divorced, North and South, because we have hated each other so."

Abraham Lincoln's election alone did not trigger these events. Tensions between Southern and Northern legislators had simmered since the nation began. Instead of deciding slavery's fate as a national issue, the Founders gave each state the right to decide. This compromise between those opposing the "peculiar institution" and those favoring it launched an internal struggle for control of Congress that ultimately led to secession and war.

The Growth of Slavery

The roots of slavery in North America can be traced back to Jamestown, Virginia, England's first permanent settlement. In 1619, Dutch traders sold "20 and Odd" Africans to colonists for supplies. These Africans were indentured servants who would work off their debt to earn their freedom. But the trend moved

Born a slave, James Armistead was granted permission to enlist in the American Army during the revolution. He served as a double agent for General Marquis de Lafayette and fed the British false information about the status of the Revolutionary Army. Following the war, he was freed as an award for his military service, and he assumed the name of his benefactor. This portrait was painted by John B. Martin.

1607
MAY 13
England's first permanent settlement in North America is established in Jamestown, Virginia.

1619
AUGUST
The first Africans are imported into Virginia. They are sold as indentured servants.

1641
Massachusetts becomes the first colony to legalize slavery.

away from servitude toward slavery as the colonies made the institution legal. In 1670, Virginia's House of Burgesses declared, "All servants not being Christians imported into this colony by shipping shall be slaves for their lives."

By 1700 over 25,000 blacks were held captive throughout all of the colonies. Not limited to Southern territories at this time, a growing number worked on farms and as domestic help throughout the North.

The low cost of slave labor enabled Southern plantations to grow crops economically. It was much cheaper to clothe and feed slaves than to purchase and maintain the equipment or pay the number of workers that would otherwise be necessary to produce the same crops.

A New Country

While slavery spread throughout the colonies, the British colonists themselves began to bridle against what they saw as too much control of their affairs from Britain. Representatives from the 13 colonies met in Philadelphia to chart the course of a new nation. The Second Continental Congress adopted the Declaration of Independence in 1776.

Delegates from the 13 states met in Philadelphia in 1787 to draw up a Constitution for the United States. Friction developed between those wishing to eradicate slavery and those demanding it be maintained. A compromise was reached, and three points relating to the issue were included in the Constitution. One provided that slaves were to be counted as three-fifths of a person in the census, giving Southern states greater representation in the new Congress.

1664
To limit the opportunities for slaves to gain their freedom, Maryland defines slavery as life-long servitude.

1688
FEBRUARY 18
In what is regarded as the first antislavery protest in the colonies, Francis Pastorius and the German Friends at Germantown,

Pennsylvania, declare that slavery goes against Christian principles.

As British author and lecturer William Makepeace Thackeray toured America in 1852 and 1853, his secretary and cousin, Eyre Crowe, took notes and sketched some of the memorable scenes they encountered. Crowe published his memoir of the trip and produced a number of paintings, including this trip to the Richmond Slave Market. "On rough benches were sitting, huddled close together... young negro girls with white collars fastened by scarlet bows."

Written by Thomas Jefferson, it read in part, "We hold these Truths to be self-evident, that all Men are created equal, that they are endowed, by their Creator, with certain unalienable Rights, that among these are Life, Liberty, and the Pursuit of Happiness." While Jefferson, George Washington, and other leaders of the new nation expressed belief in equality and liberty, they were slave owners themselves.

Organized opposition to slavery developed early after its introduction to the colonies. The Quakers were one of the first organized groups to take up the antislavery cause. Their pacifist approach was a model for the abolitionist movement that followed. Adding to the moral argument against slavery, the practice was losing economic viability in the North. After the American Revolution, cheap immigrant labor made slavery impractical in the region. Northern sentiment began to shift against slavery.

1739

SEPTEMBER 9
Promised freedom in Spanish Florida, slaves revolt south of Charleston, South Carolina, killing masters and seizing weapons. Stopped by the militia before reaching Florida, the Stono Rebellion leaves scores of whites and blacks dead in the bloodiest colonial uprising.

1775

APRIL 14
The Pennsylvania Society for the Abolition of Slavery, the first antislavery organization in the colonies, is organized by Quakers.

Slave Life

"I was born and bred on the plantation of Old Mars Robert English, one hundred miles from Charleston. My younger days were happy ones. I played with the massa's children until I became seven or eight years old, then I had to go into the field with the other black folks and work hard all day from earliest dawn till late at night. We ate twice a day, that is, when we got up in the morning we were driven out into the fields and were called into breakfast at noon by the blast of an old tin horn.

"All we got to eat then was three corn cake dumplins and one plate of soup. No meat unless there happened to be a rotten piece in the smoke house. This would be given to us to make our soup. Why the dogs got better eating than we poor colored folks. We would go out into the fields again and work very hard until dark, when we were driven in by the crack of the overseer's lash and frequently that crack meant blood from some unfortunate creature's back, who, becoming weary had shown signs of faltering."

Slave John Jackson

The Confederation Congress, in its final session in 1787 before a new constitution replaced the Articles of Confederation, passed the Northwest Ordinance, which set the rules of government over the Northwest Territories, land north of the Ohio River and east of the Mississippi. One significant regulation was "neither slavery nor involuntary servitude" would be permitted in the territory or in any state later established from it. This ordinance was carried over when the Constitutional Convention met later that year to draft a new constitution.

Slavery was the most controversial issue facing the Constitutional Convention of 1787. Attempts to eradicate it failed due to its importance in the nation's economy, particularly in the South. Instead, heated debate led to a number of compromises in the U.S. Constitution. Three articles specifically addressed slavery. One provided that, in the census used to determine the number of congressional representatives from each state, a slave would count as three-fifths of a person. Another called for the importation of slaves to end in 1808, 21 years later. The third article provided that escaped slaves must be returned to their masters, even if they have crossed state lines. These acts legitimized slavery as an acceptable institution in the United States. The Founders, facing a number of important issues head-on, decided to skirt this one, passing its confrontation down to succeeding generations.

Southern legislators quickly realized their ability to preserve slavery depended on opposing attempts by their Northern counterparts to reduce or eliminate it entirely. To maintain this delicate balance, Southerners had to fight every attempt by Northern legislators to admit "free" states to the

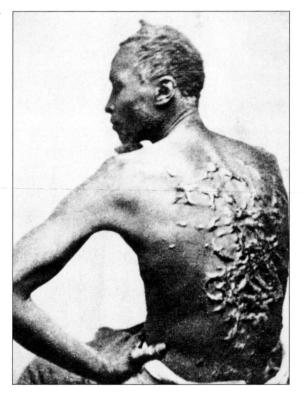

This escaped slave's bare back, scarred by lashes from a whip, shows the extent of plantation justice to a photographer in 1863. The master had power of complete discipline over his slaves.

1776
JULY 4
The colonies declare their independence from Great Britain. The Declaration of Independence proclaims, "All men are created equal."

1777
JULY 8
Vermont, not yet a state, abolishes slavery in its constitution.

1780
MARCH 1
Pennsylvania legislates the gradual abolition of slavery.

An Escape Attempt

"As soon as I was convinced that it was them, I knew there was no chance of escape. I took refuge in the top of a tree and the hounds were soon at its base, and there remained until the hunters came up in a half or three quarters of an hour afterwards. There were two men with the dogs, who, as soon as they came up, ordered me to descend. I came down, was tied, and taken to St. Louis jail. Major Freeland soon made his appearance, and took me out, and ordered me to follow him, which I did. After we returned home I was tied up in the smokehouse, and was very severely whipped. After the major had flogged me to his satisfaction, he sent out his son Robert, a young man eighteen or twenty years of age, to see that I was well smoked. He made a fire of tobacco stems, which soon set me to coughing and sneezing. This, Robert told me, was the way his father used to do to his slaves in Virginia. After giving me what they conceived to be a decent smoking, I was untied and again set to work."

*Slave **William Wells Brown**, on his recapture*

Union. As the country gained more and more territory, that proposition became more and more difficult. The possibility of secession was often threatened if legislative compromise was not enacted. An early triumph by Southern legislators was the Fugitive Slave Act of 1793. The Constitution had granted slaveholders the right to retrieve escaped slaves, but this new law made their prerogative more explicit. Slaveholders were now empowered to enter any state and, after proving ownership, retrieve their runaway "property." This law also denied blacks the right to testify on their own behalf or to receive a jury trial.

King Cotton

The year 1793 saw another significant development in strengthening the hold of slavery over the South. Cotton was emerging as the South's most important cash crop, but demand by Northern textile mills outpaced the South's

Prior to the invention of the cotton gin, cotton was considered too labor intensive to be viable as a cash crop. One slave could take up to ten hours to separate a pound of cotton from its seed. With the advent of the cotton gin (short for engine), the production of cotton exploded. One planter could produce up to 1,000 pounds of usable cotton per day.

1781

MARCH 1
The Articles of Confederation are ratified.

1783

The Supreme Judicial Court of Massachusetts effectively abolishes slavery in that state.

1784

Connecticut enacts legislation for gradual emancipation of slaves.

Rhode Island passes a gradual emancipation law.

capacity to produce. While visiting Georgia in 1793, Eli Whitney, a Northerner, solved this problem by developing the cotton gin, a device that separated cotton seed from fiber. Cotton production virtually exploded throughout the South. Along with this, however, came a dramatically increased need for slaves to grow and harvest the crop.

Yet even so, the practice of slavery continued to be a much-debated issue throughout the South as well as the North. Most slaveholders had not chosen their dependency on slavery but had inherited it along with the plantations they ran. Even if they wanted to free their slaves, most could not afford to do so and still run profitable farms. They were economically trapped by slavery, and they fought in any way they could to maintain its existence. As Northern sentiment grew against the practice, Southern proponents did not hesitate to claim their own treatment of slaves was much more humane than what factory workers received from ruthless Northern manufacturers.

Growth and Expanding Borders

As slavery grew, so did the country. In what was popularly called the Louisiana Purchase, the United States acquired an 800,000–square-mile tract of land from France in 1803. Several new territories were created from this vast expanse extending from the Gulf of Mexico to the Rocky Mountains. The untamed area also provided fertile new ground to which proslavery and antislavery forces could import their struggle.

The importation of slaves ended in 1808, as called for in the Constitution, but the sale of slaves between and within states continued. If the Founders intended to abolish slavery by ending the slave trade, they failed. By 1800, more than 80 percent of slaves had been born in America. The number of slaves increased from 1.2 million to almost 4 million during the half century before the Civil War.

Although the importation of slaves to America was banned by Congress in 1808 and made punishable by death in 1820, the sale of slaves within the United States continued until the Civil War. This invoice from 1835 was typical, although a note at the bottom details an unexpected $40 addition to the sale: "I did intend to leave Nancy child, but she made such a damned fuss I had to let her take it."

1785
FEBRUARY 4
The Manumission Society of New York is established. Among its founders are Alexander Hamilton and John Jay, future Chief Justice, of the U.S. Supreme Court.

1787
JULY 13
The Northwest Ordinance prohibits slavery in the Northwest Territories. It includes a fugitive slave law to prohibit slaves escaping to freedom in the territories.

SEPTEMBER 17
The U.S. Constitution prohibits the importation of slaves after January 1, 1808; includes a clause requiring the return of fugitive slaves to their owners; and stipulates that five slaves are equal to

Slavery was effectively abolished in the North by 1820. Congress was split between 11 free and 11 slave states when citizens of the Missouri Territory petitioned for statehood. Admitting Missouri as a slave state would tip the scale in favor of the South, an unacceptable situation for Northern legislators. The issue was resolved when Maine petitioned to enter the Union as a free state, thus maintaining the balance. But what became known as the Compromise of 1820 or, more popularly, the Missouri Compromise, contained additional provisions. Slavery was barred from the rest of the Louisiana Territory north of the 36°30′ line. This legislation allowed Congress to settle into a period of relative peace before the enticement of continued western expansion drew the country into conflict with Mexico.

THIS MOMENTOUS QUESTION, LIKE A FIRE BELL IN THE NIGHT, AWAKENED AND FILLED ME WITH TERROR. I CONSIDERED IT AT ONCE AS THE KNELL OF THE UNION.

Thomas Jefferson on the issue of slavery

Americans pushed west into the Louisiana Territory and beyond. Mexico had encouraged Americans to settle in its province of Texas. A number of settlers, including many slaveholders, jumped at the opportunity, but they clashed with the Mexican government. Among other points of friction, when Mexico abolished slavery in 1829, freeing all slaves in the country, Texans refused to follow suit. Conflict continued to grow until 1835, when Texans revolted against the military government of General Antonio Lopez de Santa Anna. It took less than a year for the Texans to defeat Santa Anna's army, which led to the creation of the Republic of Texas. Texas President Sam Houston sent a delegation to Washington, D.C., requesting annexation of Texas as a state or recognition by the United States as an independent nation.

According to international law, Texas was still part of Mexico, but President Andrew Jackson recognized its independence in 1837. Eight years later, it was annexed as a slave state. But tensions that existed between Texas and Mexico were transferred to the United States. Following a clash of cavalry troops in April 1846, the United States and Mexico erupted into war the next month. Gaining combat experience were a number of soldiers who would figure prominently in the Civil War 15 years later. The Mexican War ended in February 1848 with Mexico conceding 500,000 square miles of land to the United States for 15 million dollars, new territory for slaveholders and abolitionists to contest.

three white Americans for the purposes of determining representation in Congress.

1790
FEBRUARY
The Society of Friends (Quakers) petitions Congress to abolish slavery.

1793
FEBRUARY 12
Congress passes the Fugitive Slave Act.

The Compromise of 1850

In response to the debate over the status of those territories, Congress passed five bills, popularly called the Compromise of 1850. California was admitted as a free state; slave trade, though not slavery itself, was banned in the District of Columbia; the borders of Texas were officially set; other territories purchased from Mexico were permitted to organize without restrictions on slavery; and a new Fugitive Slave Law empowered Northern authorities to return escaped slaves to their masters. The Fugitive Slave Law further provided that any person assisting in a slave's escape would be subject to six months in prison, levied a $1,000 fine, and forced to reimburse the slave owner for the slave's market value. This act caused much Northern dissension. Joshua Giddings, a representative from Ohio, issued this challenge: "Let the President drench our land of freedom in blood; but he will never make us obey that law."

Bales of cotton are piled as high as possible on the deck of the Mississippi steamer Henry Frank. *Because of the number of ships laden with cotton that left New Orleans for Northern industrial ports, the city was considered King Cotton's capital.*

OCTOBER
Eli Whitney applies for a patent on the cotton gin.

1799
New York enacts gradual emancipation legislation.

1800
AUGUST
The Gabriel Plot, a significant slave revolt in the area of Richmond, Virginia, is discovered and suppressed.

Architect of the Missouri Compromise and the Compromise of 1850, Henry Clay earned the title "The Great Pacificator." As speaker of the House in 1820, Clay crafted the Missouri Compromise, resolving the bitter conflict over the status of territories from the Louisiana Purchase that threatened to splinter the nation. Again 30 years later, as senator from Kentucky, the 73-year-old Clay helped persuade Congress to settle its dispute over territories acquired after the Mexican War. Clay retired from the Senate before the Compromise was finalized. His ability to find common ground between opponents was missed as secession approached.

1803
The United States buys the Louisiana Territory from France.

1804
New Jersey passes legislation for gradual emancipation.

1808
JANUARY 1
As required by the Constitution, the importation of slaves into the United States is abolished.

Abolitionists

By this time, the abolitionist movement was highly visible throughout the North. Three of the most famous and outspoken proponents of the movement were an escaped slave, a Boston publisher, and a New England author. Frederick Douglass, the son of a slave and a white man, escaped to the North in 1838. He became an abolitionist lecturer three years later. Evading capture and a forced return to slavery, he fled to Europe until he was able to buy his freedom. Not only a renowned speaker, Douglass also published an abolitionist newspaper, *North Star*.

William Lloyd Garrison also published an abolitionist paper, *The Liberator*. He believed Congressional laws sanctioned slavery and once burned a copy of the Constitution in protest. Preferring moral persuasion to brute force, he opposed the Civil War until after the Emancipation Proclamation.

Harriet Beecher Stowe wrote the most famous abolitionist work, *Uncle Tom's Cabin*. Published in 1852, it became an immediate best seller, introducing thousands in the North to what quickly became stereotypical depictions of the evils of slavery. Some radical abolitionists felt the book did not go far enough to denounce the practice, while most Southerners condemned the book as grossly exaggerated. "I estimate the value of antislavery writing by the abuse it brings," Garrison wrote Stowe. "Now all the defenders of slavery have let me alone and are abusing you."

Another outgrowth of the abolitionist movement was the Underground Railroad, a loosely organized series of safe houses that successfully ushered thousands of escaped slaves to freedom in Canada. The number of "conductors" employed in this network continued to grow over the years, particularly after passage of the Fugitive Slave Law of 1850. The Underground Railroad is said to have helped 75,000 blacks escape to Canada.

To publicize and illustrate the plight of slaves in the South, the American Anti-Slavery Society began publishing the Anti-Slavery Almanac *in 1838. It contained abolitionist poems, essays, news articles, and drawings. The society was established in 1833 by leading Northern abolitionists, led by William Lloyd Garrison. Its members demanded the immediate, uncompensated emancipation of slaves. By 1840, the year this issue was published, the society had about 250,000 members in almost 2,000 local chapters.*

The Kansas-Nebraska Act

Since the passage of the Constitution, any territory attempting to enter the Union as a state had been met by debate over slavery. Illinois Senator Stephen A. Douglas realized if this continued, it would slow western expansion. He became the leading proponent of the popular sovereignty movement, which held settlers in each territory should determine that territory's stance on slavery. Douglas and his followers believed acceptance of this doctrine would unite a severed nation under a unified cause. He may also have reasoned that if successful, he could ride his movement into the White House in 1860. As a test in 1854, he introduced the Kansas-Nebraska Act, which nullified the part of the

1816–17
The American Colonization Society is formed, with Henry Clay and Francis Scott Key among its founders. Its purpose is to help free blacks and slaves emigrate to Africa.

1820
MARCH
Congress enacts the Missouri Compromise: Missouri is admitted as a slave state, Maine is admitted as a free state, and slavery is banned in the remaining territory of the Louisiana Purchase north of 36°30′.

Slavery

Sprawling plantations built adjacent to massive fields of cotton, tobacco, and other cash crops sprang up across the South in the decades before the Civil War. The rapid development of the Southern agrarian society created a small group of landed gentry, made up of less than 25 percent of the white population, who controlled large groups of black slaves. The cost of purchasing the number of slaves necessary to work the fields was often greater than the cost of the plantation and the land. The price of a single strong field hand in 1860 could run as high as $1,800.

Although the life of a slave on most plantations was not as severe as its worst depictions in the Northern press, blacks were treated more as property than as human beings. They had few civil rights, they were denied legal standing in court, and they were prohibited from testifying in court against whites. Teaching slaves to read or write was prohibited by law. Slave marriages and divorces were not a matter of legal record and required the master's permission.

Some laws did exist to protect the personal rights of slaves. Limits were set on the number of hours per day masters could force them to work, and slave owners were required to give adequate care. Slaveholders who killed a slave could be hanged. While these laws against slaveholders could be strict, most jurisdictions gave owners full control over the handling of their slaves. On some plantations, slaves learned to read and write and were allowed to choose their own mates.

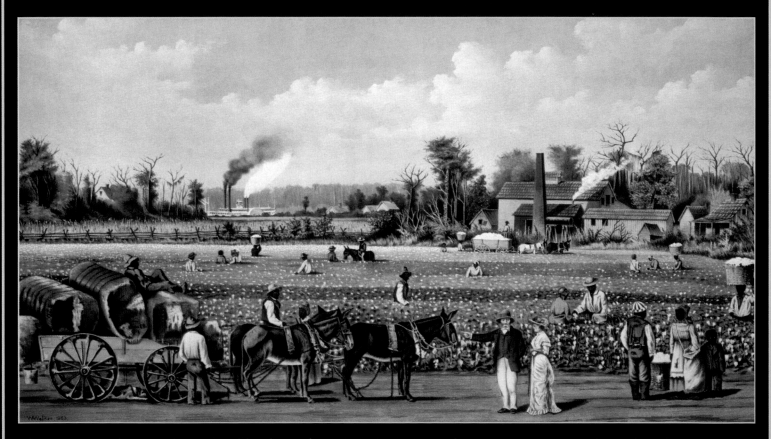

This painting depicts plantation life along the Mississippi River. The cotton crop was planted in the spring. Harvesting and preparing the crop for sale normally extended into the early winter months.

Missouri Compromise prohibiting slavery north of the 36°30′ line. The act passed Congress, but it ignited a bloody conflict in Kansas.

Proslavery and antislavery forces fought, sometimes savagely, for the future of the Kansas Territory. One participant in the fight was fanatical abolitionist John Brown. He led four of his sons in an attack on a small proslavery settlement along the Pottawatomie Creek in eastern Kansas. Five settlers were hacked to death in front of their families. Brown's violent attack on the institution of slavery did not end in Kansas. In October 1859, he and 21 followers briefly held the U.S. Arsenal at Harpers Ferry, Virginia. They intended to arm thousands of slaves they believed would flock to Harpers Ferry to join the rebellion once they learned of it. But a small contingent of U.S. Marines commanded by Lieutenant Colonel Robert E. Lee stormed the firehouse, trapping Brown and his followers inside. Ten of the raiders were killed, and seven, including Brown himself, were captured. The abolitionist leader was executed for murder and treason two months later.

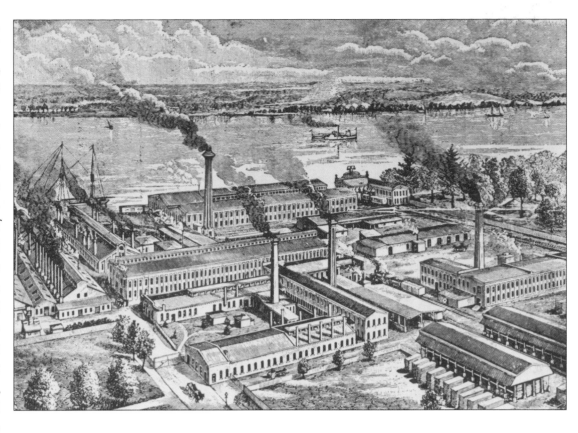

This factory in Philadelphia belonged to Henry Disston & Sons, one of the growing number of Northern businesses producing consumer goods. Manufacturing was supplementing agriculture in parts of the North. The company claimed this plant to be the world's largest producer of saws.

A Slaveholder

"His Plantation was considered a model one and was visited by planters anxious to learn his methods. He was asked how he made his Negroes do good work. His answer was that a laboring man could do more work and better work in five and a half days than in six. He used to give half of Saturdays to his Negroes unless there was a great press of work, but a system of rewards was more efficacious than any other method. He distributed prizes of money among his cotton pickers every week during the season, which lasted four or five months."

Susan Dabney Smedes, *on her father Thomas Dabney's Mississippi plantation*

1821
The first settlement of free blacks and former slaves is established at Cape Mesurado in what will become Liberia.

The antislavery journal *Genius of Universal Emancipation* begins publication.

1822
MAY 30
A plot by free black Denmark Vesey to lead a slave insurrection is revealed to authorities in Charleston, South Carolina.

Although he had freed the slaves on his family's tobacco plantation, Roger Taney, the 79-year-old Chief Justice of the U.S. Supreme Court, wrote the controversial majority decision in Dred Scott v. Sanford in 1857. He not only ruled against Scott's freedom but also wrote that Congress did not have the right to ban slavery in the territories of the United States.

Dred Scott sued his deceased master's estate for his freedom on the grounds he had lived with his master in the free state of Illinois and the free territory of Wisconsin. The U.S. Supreme Court ruled against Scott because they found that slaves were not citizens and could not, therefore, file a suit in a federal court. Even though Scott lost the case, a new master later freed him, his wife, and their two daughters.

After the passage of the Kansas-Nebraska Act of 1854, hundreds of Missourians illegally voted in favor of a proslavery legislature in the Kansas election. Labeled "Border Ruffians" by abolitionists, they were employed to drive "free-soilers" from the territory. They participated in the sacking of the antislavery stronghold of Lawrence, Kansas, on May 21, 1856. Fighting for control of the state would continue for three more years and cost about 200 lives.

The Dred Scott Decision

Several Northern states tested the validity of the various fugitive slave laws, but the greatest judicial test of a slave's rights did not result from an escape from bondage. John Emerson was an army surgeon who owned a slave named Dred Scott. In 1834, Emerson took Scott from Missouri, a slave state, to Illinois, a free state. Emerson then took Scott

1827
MARCH 16
Freedom's Journal, the first black-owned newspaper, publishes its first issue.

1828
Vice President John C. Calhoun anonymously writes *The South Carolina Exposition and Protest*, laying out the case for state nullification of federal law.

1831
JANUARY 1
William Lloyd Garrison publishes the first issue of *The Liberator*.

Slave Insurrections

From the moment the first African was enslaved in the American colonies, the threat of violent rebellion was ever present in the minds of slave owners. When few incidents surfaced over the years, control over slaves became lax, which resulted in unsupervised interaction between slaves on their own or on neighboring plantations.

In 1800, Gabriel Prosser raised an army of 1,000 fellow slaves in Virginia. He intended to capture the arsenal at Richmond, seize weapons, kill whites, and establish an independent black state with himself as king. Heavy rains on the appointed night washed away key bridges along their route, delaying them. Before they could regroup, the slaves were exposed. Virginia Governor James Monroe ordered the state militia to round up the conspirators. Prosser and about three dozen of his followers were executed.

Stricter laws were quickly enacted to curtail the unsupervised movement of slaves. In 1831, Nat Turner, acting on what he believed were religious visions, led the most violent slave uprising. Turner and seven followers murdered their master and his family. Gathering slave recruits as they wandered the countryside, their killing spread. They terrorized Southampton County in Virginia for almost three days and were finally stopped by a force of state militia and armed citizenry. The official count of the dead stood at 55. Turner escaped and hid for six weeks before being captured. He was eventually hanged with 16 of his followers.

Slave insurrections were not limited to black participants. An increasing number of whites joined in black revolts, the most famous being John Brown's raid on Harpers Ferry, Virginia, in 1859.

While incidents of slave uprisings were relatively rare, isolated incidents of rebellion added to the establishment of strict controls over slaves. The most publicized episode was the massacre of more than 50 whites in Virginia by a band of slaves led by Nat Turner. This drawing depicts Turner's arrest in October 1831.

This image shows John Brown, after his conviction for treason, being led from the courthouse to the gallows on December 2, 1859. He had become an extremely polarizing figure, despised across the South but revered and beloved by blacks and abolitionists in the North, as depicted here. To many in the North, Brown was considered a martyr to the antislavery cause.

AUGUST 21–23
Nat Turner leads a slave revolt in Southampton County, Virginia.

1832
JANUARY 6
The New England Anti-Slavery Society is founded by, among others, William Lloyd Garrison.

1832–33
South Carolina threatens to nullify Congress's Tariff of 1828 in what came to be called the South Carolina Nullification Crisis.

Politicians with Southern sympathies made up the majority of James Buchanan's Cabinet in 1856. The intentions and actions of Secretary of War John B. Floyd and Secretary of the Interior Jack Thompson were suspect during the Fort Sumter crisis in December 1860, leading them and Secretary of the Treasury Howell Cobb to resign. Floyd was later relieved of command in the Confederate Army after he abandoned his troops at Fort Donelson, Tennessee, in February 1862.

to the Wisconsin Territory, which had been designated as free due to the Missouri Compromise. Years later, master and slave returned to Missouri, where Emerson died in 1843. Scott sued Emerson's heirs for his freedom. Two issues faced the Missouri district court: Did Scott, a slave, have the right to sue in a federal court, and was his status as a slave changed when Emerson willingly took him to a territory where slavery was banned? That court ruled in Scott's favor, but the judgment was overruled by the state supreme court. The U.S. Supreme Court, a majority of whom were pro-Southern justices, eventually ruled in 1857 that since Scott was a slave, he was not a citizen of the United States and therefore could not present suit in federal court. The Court could have stopped there, but it did not. It further stated that the Fifth Amendment guaranteed no citizen could be "deprived of life, liberty or property without due process of law." Since slaves were property, their masters had the right of possession even in free territories and states. Further, the court ruled that Congress

AMERICA WILL NEVER BE DESTROYED FROM THE OUTSIDE. IF WE FALTER AND LOSE OUR FREEDOMS, IT WILL BE BECAUSE WE DESTROYED OURSELVES.

Abraham Lincoln

had had no authority to regulate slavery in federal territory as it had done in the Missouri Compromise and the Kansas-Nebraska Act. Southerners lauded the decision as a reaffirmation of their rights, while many in the North condemned it. William Cullen Bryant wrote, "Hereafter, wherever our . . . flag floats, it is the flag of slavery."

1833
Abolitionists from across the country meet in Philadelphia to form the American Anti-Slavery Society.

1834
Slavery is abolished within the British Empire.

1835
Trustees of Oberlin College vote to admit black students.

FEBRUARY
The abolitionist *Anti-Slavery Record* first uses the name "Liberty Bell" in reference to the famous bell in Philadelphia.

Cotton Gin

Although Northern textile mills increasingly demanded cotton, the manual resources required in preparing it made it uneconomical to grow. After harvest, it took a slave as many as ten hours to remove one pound of cotton lint from the sticky seed. Due to lack of adequate labor, cotton crops would often decay in the fields.

Eli Whitney, a Northern tutor and amateur inventor, learned of this problem in 1793 while in Georgia. Whitney later wrote, "All agreed that if a machine could be invented . . . it would be a great thing, both to the Country and the inventor."

Within ten days Whitney developed a prototype of the cotton gin, a device that used toothed cylinders to separate the cotton fiber from the seed through wire screens. With the gin, planters could produce as much as 1,000 pounds of cotton per day. Cotton production expanded dramatically throughout the South.

Cotton Gin

An improvement upon the log cabin in which Abraham Lincoln was born, this was the Lincolns' home in Springfield, Illinois, the only house they ever owned. It was common practice during 19th-century political campaigns for supporters to flock to the candidates' homes for impromptu speeches, so this became a busy place during the 1860 presidential election. This had one-and-a-half stories when the Lincolns purchased it in 1844; they added the second story in 1856.

Depictions of Abe Lincoln splitting rails were numerous during the period of the 1860 presidential election. To garner support for Lincoln, Republican delegates came up with tales of his humble beginnings, which have since grown into legend. One of the most popular stories had Lincoln splitting rails to make fences in rural Illinois.

1836
MAY 26
Congress adopts a gag rule against abolitionist petitions.

DECEMBER 19
A stricter gag rule is enacted by Congress. Such rules would be enacted regularly between 1836 and 1844.

1837
NOVEMBER 7
Abolitionist editor Elijah P. Lovejoy is murdered by a mob in Alton, Illinois.

Lincoln and Douglas

Riding on his popular sovereignty movement, Stephen A. Douglas ran for reelection to the U.S. Senate in 1858. His opponent was a lawyer with little statewide or national exposure, Abraham Lincoln. "A house divided against itself cannot stand," Lincoln declared in his nomination speech. "I believe this government cannot endure, permanently half slave and half free. I do not expect the Union to be dissolved. . . . It will become all one thing or all the other." Opposed to the expansion of slavery through popular sovereignty, Lincoln participated in a series of debates with Douglas. Lincoln lost the election, but he became a national spokesperson for the antislavery movement.

Two years later, Lincoln was nominated by the Republican party as its candidate for president. He was again pitted against Douglas, who ran as a Democrat. In trying to nominate a candidate, however, the Democratic party split along regional lines. Southern Democrats ran their own candidate, John C. Breckinridge of Kentucky. Lincoln won the day by carrying all but one Northern state. He lost in every Southern state, some of which did not even place his name on the ballot.

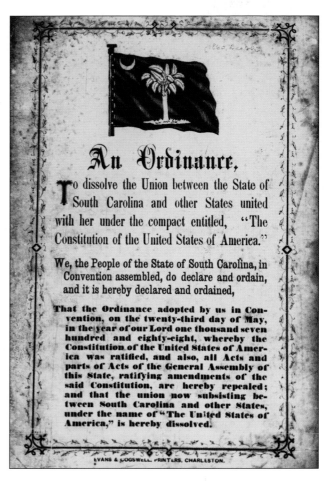

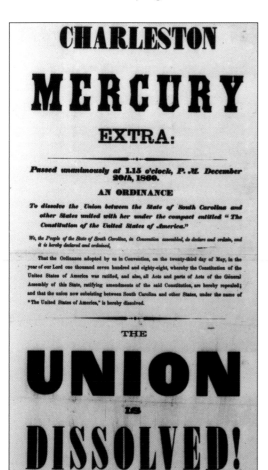

This election embittered many in the South and ended any attempt at further compromise. Creating a new nation became the only alternative in the minds of these disenfranchised citizens. The secessionist zeal that led to South Carolina's vote for independence from the United States on that December afternoon in 1860 began a series of events that made war inevitable.

Word passed quickly after South Carolina voted to withdraw from the Union. This broadside, an extra edition from the Charleston Mercury, *was printed within minutes of the decision.*

By a vote of 169 to 0, the secession convention, meeting in Charleston, South Carolina, voted to leave the United States on December 20, 1860. "The cheers of the whole assembly continued for some minutes," wrote a delegate, "while every man waved or threw up his hat, and every lady waved her handkerchief." Six more Southern states followed South Carolina's lead by February 1, 1861.

1839
The antislavery Liberty party is formed by moderate abolitionists.

1841
MARCH 9
The U.S. Supreme Court announces its decision in the *Amistad* case.

1842
The Supreme Court rules in *Prigg* v. *Pennsylvania* that states cannot hinder the recapture of a runaway slave by an out-of-state

The Underground Railroad

Since many of the Founders were slaveholders, it is understandable that they included a provision in the Constitution requiring escaped slaves to be returned to their masters. This stipulation was followed in 1793 with the federal Fugitive Slave Law, which granted slave owners the authority to enter any state to capture their "property." As a result of this law, Canada became the only haven for men and women trying to escape a life of servitude.

Sympathetic whites and free blacks provided shelter whenever possible, but it was difficult for runaway slaves to identify those willing to help from those equally willing to return them to their life of bondage. It is believed that Isaac T. Hopper made the first attempt to organize temporary havens in 1787. By 1836, this secret network of safe houses extended throughout the North. Traveling primarily by night, fugitives would move from house to house, where they received asylum and security during daylight hours. To preserve the secrecy of the network, railroad terms were used as code. Sympathizers, called "conductors," would escort escapees between safe houses, called "stations." This network therefore became known as the Underground Railroad.

Religious groups, particularly the Quakers, were active in establishing and maintaining this loose collection of way stations in almost every Northern state. Even though the network ran into the Deep South, most successful escapes took place in the uppermost slave states. The majority of refugees who succeeded in reaching Canada were young, single men.

Levi Coffin, a Quaker, assisted more than 3,000 slaves to freedom and became known as the "president of the Underground Railroad." Harriet Tubman, a fugitive slave, returned south 19 times to guide blacks out of captivity. Others who participated in sheltering runaways along the Underground Railroad included William Lloyd Garrison, a newspaper editor and staunch abolitionist, and renowned feminist Susan B. Anthony.

Although the Fugitive Slave Law of 1850 called for six-month prison sentence and a $1,000 fine for anyone convicted of aiding a runaway slave, the traffic along the Underground Railroad dramatically increased in the decade before the Civil War. Exact numbers were never kept, but it was estimated that as many as 75,000 blacks traveled through the network. That figure may be highly exaggerated, however, since no more than 1,000 slaves were reported missing in any single year.

Situated in Manhattan's Greenwich Village, this small two-story house served as a headquarters for the Underground Railroad. Created as a means to assist escaped slaves to freedom in the North and Canada, the Underground Railroad was a series of abolitionist-owned "stations." "Conductors" guided the runaways by night from one station to another along a preestablished path.

The Samuel Colt Factory, the world's largest privately owned armory, was built in 1854 in Hartford, Connecticut. More than 1,000 persons were employed here. Colt supplied the federal government with more than 40 percent of the revolvers used during the war. Prior to the First Battle of Bull Run, Colt also sold revolvers to the Confederacy.

Born a slave on a Virginia plantation in 1815, Henry Brown escaped in a most unique fashion in 1849. With the assistance of a friend who sealed him in a box, Brown was shipped to the office of an antislavery campaigner in Philadelphia. He made the 350-mile journey in 27 hours via railroad car, steamboat, and horse cart. His exploit made him a sought-after antislavery lecturer. The memoir of his remarkable experience was published in 1851.

The organized African slave trade began about A.D. 700 when Arab traders established slave markets throughout the central part of the continent. An estimated four million slaves were traded in the Middle East before Portuguese merchants began exporting Africans to the Spanish colonies in the Americas. This painting depicts the control of the Middle Eastern cultures in the trade by presenting slave drivers wearing turbans.

master; however, states are also not required to assist in that slave's recapture.

1844
The Methodist Church splits into Northern and Southern branches over the issue of slavery.

Congress revokes the gag rule in regard to antislavery petitions.

This illustration by Henry Howe shows what life may have been like on a slave ship. The deck hands are stowing captured blacks into the prow as cargo. Conditions aboard ship were horrendous. Many ships restrained captives in leg irons throughout most of the journey and provided a minimum of food and water. A large number of captives died during the Atlantic voyage. Captains stuffed as many onto their ships as possible to ensure a profit.

Eli Whitney's great claim to fame was as inventor of the cotton gin, but he did not receive great profit from it. The gin itself was quite simple, and instead of waiting for Whitney to manufacture them, Southern planters pirated the design and built their own. After fighting the planters unsuccessfully in court, Whitney returned North and developed a process to create interchangeable parts for manufacturing, revolutionizing Northern industry as he had Southern agriculture.

Right: When the first Africans were brought onshore to the North American colonies by Dutch traders, it is unlikely anyone involved recognized the significance of the event. These Africans became indentured servants, eligible to work off their captivity, but it would be only a short time before that option was unavailable to most. Howard Pyle created this picture, imagining how the moment may have happened.

Slaves wrestle with bales of cotton along the New Orleans levee. More cotton passed through New Orleans than any other Southern port. By 1795, the South was exporting 8,000 tons of cotton per year.

1845
MAY 10
Baptists in the South organize the Southern Baptist Convention in response to a split with Baptists in the North over the slavery issue.

1846
MAY 13
Congress approves President James K. Polk's request for a declaration of war against Mexico.

AUGUST
Representative David Wilmot of Pennsylvania writes a proviso prohibiting the spread of slavery into any territory the United States might obtain from Mexico

Frederick Douglass

The son of a slave and a white man, Frederick Douglass escaped to the North in 1838. Self-educated, he became an eloquent spokesperson for abolition.

"In thinking of America," Douglass wrote, "I sometimes find myself admiring her bright blue sky—her grand old woods.... But my rapture is soon checked when I remember that all is cursed with the infernal spirit of slave-holding and wrong; When I remember that with the waters of her noblest rivers, the tears of my brethren are borne to the ocean, disregarded and forgotten; That her most fertile fields drink daily of the warm blood of my outraged sisters, I am filled with unutterable loathing."

Douglass traveled to Europe, where he wrote his autobiography to silence skeptics and raised $600 to purchase his freedom. Returning to the United States, he published a weekly abolitionist newspaper, the *North Star*, and assisted the federal government in raising black regiments throughout the war. He served as U.S. Minister to Haiti from 1889 to 1891.

Douglass was an extremely successful writer and speaker. "I appear this evening as a thief and robber," he told Northern audiences. "I stole this head, these limbs, this body from my master, and ran off with them."

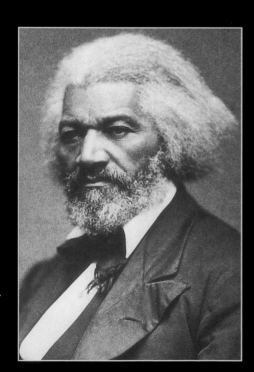

Slaveholder Presidents

Slavery was so pervasive in American culture that it was taken as a matter of course that a man of wealth would own slaves. In fact, of the first dozen presidents, ten—all except John Adams and his son, John Quincy Adams— owned slaves while in office or had owned slaves before taking office. George Washington, Thomas Jefferson, James Madison, James Monroe, and John Tyler all came from Virginia plantation aristocracy. William Henry Harrison did too, although he moved to the free-soil Northwest Territories and changed the status of his slaves to indentured servants. Andrew Jackson and James K. Polk both became wealthy as Tennessee lawyers; Jackson was even a slave trader for a time. Zachary Taylor owned a Mississippi plantation. The one Northerner among these Southerners, Martin Van Buren of New York, owned one slave before the practice was outlawed in that state. These ten are not the only slaveholders to hold the office of the president. Two presidents after the Civil War, Andrew Johnson and Ulysses S. Grant, had owned slaves before that conflict.

George Washington

Thomas Jefferson

James Madison

James Monroe

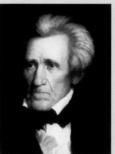

Andrew Jackson

Martin Van Buren

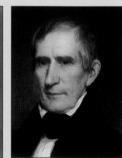

William Henry Harrison

John Tyler

James K. Polk

Zachary Taylor

This design of a slave on bended knee—beseeching God or perhaps his master—became a popular antislavery symbol. It was often accompanied by the motto: "Am I not a man and a brother?" Josiah Wedgwood, British manufacturer of pottery and ceramics and member of the Society for the Abolition of the Slave Trade, created a medallion of similar design that was sometimes worn as jewelry.

In 1787, black members of the St. George's Methodist Episcopal Church of Philadelphia were segregated to the church's gallery. While kneeling and praying outside of the gallery one Sunday, they were forcibly removed. These segregated congregants left the church and formed the Free African Society, which later split into Episcopalian and Methodist factions. The leaders of five churches met in 1816 to form the African Methodist Episcopal Church. Richard Allen was the denomination's first bishop.

The American Colonization Society was formed at the end of 1816 and beginning of 1817 by an odd combination of abolitionists and slaveholders to repatriate free blacks to Africa. A few years later, the first group of free blacks sailed to the coast of Africa and set up a colony that would later develop into the nation of Liberia. The total number of people who left the United States for Africa throughout the society's history was close to 20,000.

and appends it to a military appropriations bill. The Wilmot Proviso is excised in the bill's final version.

1847
Senator Lewis Cass of Michigan first proposes the idea of popular sovereignty.

1848
The Free-Soil party is formed in Buffalo, New York. The Free-Soil presidential candidate is former President Martin Van Buren.

This illustration from The American Anti-Slavery Almanac for 1840 shows two mothers and their children being whipped by an overseer while working in the field. The division of labor along gender lines became less evident the farther south one went, and women with small children were often forced to work the land. Children typically joined the others at work at about the age of ten.

South Carolina's John C. Calhoun, senator, vice president, and holder of various Cabinet posts, was a rival of Andrew Jackson and an early Southern advocate of secession. Angry over Congress's Tariff of 1828, South Carolina legislators voted to nullify the act, a stand backed by Vice President Calhoun. President Jackson called it absurd that "a faction of any state, or a state, has a right to secede and destroy this union." On the verge of war, the situation was diffused when Congress passed the Compromise Tariff of 1833.

Artificial waterways such as the Erie Canal, shown here shortly after it was completed, helped to widen Northern territories for expansion and production by making transportation far more efficient.

FEBRUARY
The Mexican War ends. Mexico transfers 500,000 square miles of land to the United States.

1849
JANUARY 22
John C. Calhoun, senator from South Carolina and the spokesperson for a caucus of Southern members of Congress, reads an address listing the major acts of aggression the North has committed against the rights of Southerners.

Slaves plant sweet potatoes at the Pope Plantation near Hilton Head, South Carolina. Although staged for the photographer, this picture presents a view of various tasks assigned to slaves on a typical plantation.

The McCormick reaper, patented by Cyrus McCormick in the 1830s, combined into one machine all the steps necessary to reap a field, giving agricultural productivity a huge boost. By 1865, as families moved west to claim new land, this and similar new technology allowed for quick westward expansion.

This 1830s sketch of wooden-masted ships depicts the bustling port of the Long and Central wharves in Boston Harbor. Boston remained an important Northern port throughout the Civil War.

DECEMBER 22
Fractured by the slavery issue, the House of Representatives elects Howell Cobb of Georgia to be speaker of the House after almost three weeks and 63 ballots.

1850
JANUARY 29
In an attempt to smooth over the sectional crisis, Henry Clay of Kentucky introduces a series of resolutions to the Senate.

FEBRUARY–APRIL
In what came to be known as "The Great Debate," the Senate deliberates over Clay's resolutions.

This serene image of blacks waiting to be placed on the auction block is far from typical. Although owners made sure their slaves were scrubbed and well dressed, the blacks themselves were rarely as relaxed as those depicted here, particularly when loved ones accompanied them to the block. Faced with separation and an uncertain future, they found auction a terrifying experience.

This painting depicts the auction of a woman while potential buyers examine a slave family. William Wells Brown wrote of a man separated from his wife at such an auction. The husband's parting words were, "I hope you will try to meet me in heaven. I shall try to meet you there." Brown continued, "At these auction-stands, bones, muscles, sinews, blood and nerves, of human beings, are sold with as much indifference as a farmer in the north sells a horse or sheep."

The job of picking cotton in the field was rigorous for the unfortunate laborers. Because cotton grew relatively low to the ground, overseers on horses could easily supervise the work.

SEPTEMBER 9–20
Congress adopts the Compromise of 1850, which defers the continuing debate over slavery. The legislation admits California as a free state, allows popular sovereignty over slavery in new territories, sets the boundaries for the state of Texas, enacts a stronger Fugitive Slave Act, and abolishes the slave trade in the District of Columbia.

1851
SEPTEMBER 11
A slaveholder is killed at Christiana, Pennsylvania, while trying to recapture fugitive slaves.

The distribution of labor on a Southern plantation was clear cut. On plantations with 20 or more slaves, the owner often hired white overseers to supervise. These men would direct the activities of slaves in the field by either riding on horses or standing on high objects such as tree stumps. Rules for slave management were often developed on the larger plantations, directing overseers in such tasks as the number of lashes to administer for specific offenses.

This whipping post was a common site in many Delaware communities for more than 200 years. Although whippings were banned in most states by 1800, they continued in Delaware until 1952. This woodcut from Harper's Weekly *depicts the whipping post in New Castle.*

Harriet Tubman

One of the most famous and courageous conductors on the Underground Railroad was Harriet Tubman. Following her own escape from a Maryland plantation in 1849, she returned to the South 19 times to rescue more than 300 slaves, including her own family, from the "jaws of hell."

Often called "Moses," since she led her people to the "Promised Land," Tubman recalled with pride that "my train never ran off the track and I never lost a passenger." During her sojourns south, Tubman carried a gun to protect her group from slave catchers as well as to threaten to kill those slaves who attempted to return to their plantations. She was so infamous throughout the South that rewards for her capture once totaled more than $40,000.

Tubman accompanied the Union Army to South Carolina, where she served as a nurse and scout and lived among refugee blacks, helping them procure clothing, food, and shelter. In June 1863 she went on a federal raid up the Combahee River to destroy railroad bridges and track down enemy troops. During this foray she helped liberate about 750 slaves.

Returning to Auburn, New York, in 1864, Tubman spent her remaining years raising money for black charities.

Tubman said, "There was one or two things I had a right to, liberty or death; if I could not have one, I would have the other; for no man should take me alive; I should fight for my liberty as long as my strength lasted, and when the time came for to go, the Lord would let them take me."

This picture shows children in front of plantation slave cabins. On most estates, Sundays were usually free of field and plantation work, providing slaves with an opportunity to relax or perform household duties that had been on hold during the week.

Minstrel show entertainer Thomas "Daddy" Rice first used charcoal and burnt cork to blacken his face and hands around 1830. His act included an outlandish dance to a song with the chorus, "Weel about and turn about and do jis so, Eb'ry time I weel about, I jump Jim Crow." By 1850, a Jim Crow character was part of most minstrel shows in America. The term Jim Crow later became synonymous with discriminatory laws and practices against blacks.

Author of such standards as "Oh! Susanna," "Old Folks at Home," and "Old Kentucky Home," Stephen Collins Foster was a musical sensation—his songs were known by millions. Although critics accused Foster of making light of slavery, his work often depicted a society where people, regardless of class or race, shared compassion and understanding with each other. "Nelly Was a Lady," written in 1849, and "Angelina Baker," in 1851, described the sorrow felt by slaves on the death or sale of loved ones.

1852
MARCH 20
Uncle Tom's Cabin by Harriet Beecher Stowe is published in book form.

1854
The Knights of the Golden Circle is established to aid in the expansion of slavery.

APRIL
The Emigrant Aid Society is founded in Massachusetts to encourage the emigration of free-soilers to Kansas.

Uncle Tom's Cabin

When Harriet Beecher Stowe was introduced to President Abraham Lincoln, he allegedly said, "So you're the little woman who wrote the book that started this great war." The truth of this anecdote has been questioned, but no one will dispute that few events fueled the flames of hatred across the nation as much as the publication of *Uncle Tom's Cabin*. The story of Tom, a saintly black slave ordered beaten to death by his wicked master, Simon Legree, was lauded by abolitionists across the North and condemned by Southern critics as grossly inaccurate in its portrayal of plantation life.

While researching a series of articles she intended to write, Stowe became aware of an account describing a slave woman who escaped from her masters in Kentucky across a frozen Ohio River. This became one of the primary images of Uncle Tom's Cabin, *as the female protagonist, Eliza, escaped across the ice.*

Stowe was a staunch abolitionist who was more concerned about illustrating the inherent evils of slavery than creating an accurate depiction of plantation life. Although she lived for 18 years in Cincinnati, Ohio, just across the river from the slave state of Kentucky, she had little first-hand knowledge of Southern plantations. Most of the material in the book was drawn from abolitionist literature and her own imagination.

Stowe's work was first serialized in 1851 in the abolitionist newspaper *National Era*. Its popularity led to the book's publication in 1852. An instant success, *Uncle Tom's Cabin* sold 10,000 copies in the first week and more than 300,000 by the end of its first year. The book was even more popular in Britain, where more than one million copies sold within a year. Stowe exposed the general public to an issue of which few had direct knowledge and further provoked heated debates in state and federal legislatures.

MAY 30
The Kansas-Nebraska Act is signed into law, repudiating the Missouri Compromise.

JULY
The Republican party organizes throughout the North.

OCTOBER 18
The Ostend Manifesto embarrasses the administration of Franklin Pierce. It promotes the purchase, or takeover by force if necessary, of Cuba from Spain to become a slave state.

This relaxed depiction of the life of a slave family belies the truth of their existence. Scenes such as in this painting by Eastman Johnson were often used by the proponents of slavery as propaganda against abolitionist attacks. There were three classes of slaves: field hands, craftspeople, and house servants. Those working in the fields often worked from dawn to dusk five-and-a-half or six days per week.

1855
March
The proslavery forces win in Kansas elections with an influx of illegal voters from Missouri.

July
The Kansas legislature enacts strict proslavery laws.

October–December
Free-soilers meet in Topeka and adopt a new constitution prohibiting slavery.

A lawyer from Springfield, Illinois, Abraham Lincoln was elected to Congress as a Whig in 1846. This was not his first foray into politics—he had served four terms in the state house of representatives. During his one term in Congress, Lincoln was outspoken against the Mexican War. He declined to run for a second term but was twice a Whig candidate for U.S. senator, most notably losing to Stephen A. Douglas in 1858.

Elijah P. Lovejoy published The Observer, *a religious, abolitionist newspaper in Alton, Illinois. Although regularly threatened by proslavery factions who destroyed his presses several times, Lovejoy continued publishing. The arrival of a new press on November 7, 1837, caused a riot—a proslavery mob killed Lovejoy, destroyed the press, and burned the building that housed it. Lovejoy's brother Owen continued Elijah's abolitionist path. Becoming successful in state politics, Owen Lovejoy helped found the Republican party and became a close friend and advisor to Abraham Lincoln.*

Born a slave in 1797, Isabella Baumfree escaped from her New York owner in the late 1820s. Following a vision in 1843, she assumed the name Sojourner Truth, believing she had been chosen by God to "travel up an' down the land, showin' the people their sins, an' bein' a sign unto them." Her deep religious beliefs and skill as an orator aided her as she traveled throughout the North speaking against slavery and for women's rights.

Mexican War/Civil War Generals

A number of Civil War figures received military experience during the Mexican War of 1846–48. General Winfield Scott rose to become commander of all U.S. forces. Future generals such as Robert E. Lee, Ulysses S. Grant, Thomas J. "Stonewall" Jackson, George B. McClellan, P.G.T. Beauregard, Joseph E. Johnston, and many others saw battlefield action. Colonel Jefferson Davis would become U.S. secretary of war and president of the Confederacy.

Ulysses S. Grant

Robert E. Lee

Thomas J. "Stonewall" Jackson

NOVEMBER 26–DECEMBER 7
Proslavery and antislavery factions face off against each other around Lawrence, Kansas. The standoff ends peacefully and comes to be known as The Wakarusa War.

1856
MAY 21
Civil war breaks out in Kansas as 800 "Border Ruffians" sack Lawrence, destroying two newspaper presses and burning down the

Free State Hotel. Residents of Lawrence do not resist.

MAY 22
In response to Massachusetts Senator Charles Sumner's "Crime Against Kansas" speech two days

Violence in the Nation

"A man born and educated in Western Missouri had concluded that slavery was an evil and that Kansas ought to be free. Having some of the boldness of the 'Border Ruffians' themselves, he wrote on his wagon cover the words: 'Kansas ought to be a free State.' As he was driving his wagon through the neighborhood to a country town he had not gone far till he heard screams, indicating that biped bloodhounds were about to overtake the object of their pursuit. His ears were next greeted by a volley of oaths and epithets. At the same instant he saw blades of knives gleam through the wagon cover, cutting great dashes in it and coming so close to him as to make holes in his clothes and piercing his hat. By skilful [sic] dodging and by warding off the blows aimed at him he escaped other than mutilated clothes and hat and a few flesh wounds, but 'the wagon sheet,' as the flag of liberty, was mortally mutilated and wounded."

Newspaper editor J. H. Washburne, describing mild violence in Kansas in the 1850s

Nathaniel Currier and James Ives began their lithography business partnership in 1857. To produce a lithograph, a piece of limestone was ground flat and a picture drawn on it with a special grease pencil. The stone was etched, leaving the area covered in grease slightly raised. A special ink was used to print the image on paper, which was then often colored by hand. The partners printed lithographs of many scenes, including this one depicting Southern life.

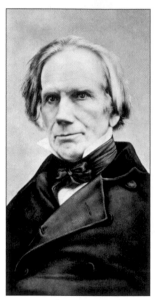

Henry Clay of Kentucky had a long, distinguished career in both houses of Congress. Elected speaker of the House during his first term in that chamber, Clay was particularly adept at bringing opposition parties together, often including the forces for and against slavery. His efforts in crafting the Missouri Compromise and the Compromise of 1850 won him the nicknames "The Great Pacificator" and "The Great Compromiser."

earlier, Representative Preston Brooks of South Carolina enters the Senate chamber and physically attacks Sumner with a cane.

MAY 24–25
John Brown leads his raid on proslavery settlers along Pottawatomie Creek.

JULY 3
The House of Representatives votes in favor of admitting Kansas as a state based on the antislavery constitution, but the Senate rejects the idea five days later.

Bleeding Kansas

The Missouri Compromise, which banned slavery from all territories north of Missouri's southern border, was still in effect when the Kansas and Nebraska territories were established. In 1854, however, Congress passed the Kansas-Nebraska Act and put an end to those restrictions. It negated the Missouri Compromise and left the slavery question up to the citizens of each territory.

The fate of slavery in Kansas would be left to popular vote. Both proslavery and antislavery factions rushed settlers into Kansas to impact that vote. When elections were finally held in 1855, thousands of residents from the slave state Missouri crossed the border to vote illegally, resulting in the election of a proslavery legislature. Later that year, free-soil Kansans held their own convention and adopted a constitution that abolished slavery.

In May 1856, 800 proslavers, many from Missouri, attacked and damaged much of the antislavery stronghold of Lawrence, Kansas, killing one man. A few days later, the fanatic abolitionist John Brown led four of his sons in an attack on a small settlement of proslavers, killing five. It would be another five years, several bloody clashes, and about 200 more deaths before Kansas was admitted to the Union as a free state.

These antislavery militia members were photographed in Topeka in 1856. Ragtag outfits both for and against slavery fought a small but savage war for control of the Kansas Territory during this period. The ambush of the unsuspecting and the slaying of the unarmed and the innocent were common occurrences in a conflict that eventually cost the lives of some 200 men, women, and children.

While most fugitive slaves traveled the treacherous road to freedom alone, on foot, and often at night, Eastman Johnson's 1863 painting A Ride for Liberty—The Fugitive Slaves *shows what appears to be a young family racing toward a new life. Circumstances, such as a potential sale or inflicted punishment, sometimes forced families to make the attempt together.*

Flyers such as this were common throughout the South. A reward of $300 was relatively large even for two runaway slaves. The amount offered often depended on the owner's confidence that the fugitives would be returned. If the owner felt that they would be quickly captured, the reward would be relatively low. On the other hand, if the owner thought there was a good chance the escape would be successful, the reward was high.

300 DOLLARS
REWARD!

RUNAWAY from John S. Doak on the 21st inst., two **NEGRO MEN**; **LOGAN** 45 years of age, bald-headed, one or more crooked fingers; **DAN** 21 years old, six feet high.   Both black. I will pay **ONE HUNDRED DOLLARS** for the apprehension and delivery of **LOGAN**, or to have him confined so that I can get him. I will also pay **TWO HUNDRED DOL- LARS** for the apprehension of **DAN**, or to have him confined so that I can get him.
                    JOHN S. DOAKE,
Springfield, Mo., April 24th, 1857,

John Brown

O n a chilly November night in 1837, a proslavery mob of 200 men shot the Reverend Elijah P. Lovejoy outside the office of his abolitionist newspaper in Alton, Illinois. Reaction to his death across the North was swift and strong. During one protest meeting at a church in Ohio, the minister challenged his congregation, saying, "Are we free, or are we slaves under mob law?" From the back of the church, a grim figure rose, raised his right arm, and cried, "Here, before God, in the presence of these witnesses, I consecrate my life to the destruction of slavery." The man was John Brown.

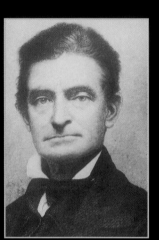

Fanatical abolitionist John Brown is pictured in a daguerreotype made right around the time he and his band slaughtered five proslavers at Pottawatomie Creek, Kansas.

For the next 22 years, Brown attempted to make good on his pledge. Violence flared from his hand at Pottawatomie Creek, Kansas, where he and four of his sons hacked five unarmed proslavery men to death. Three years later in 1859, Brown devised a grandiose scheme to ignite an armed slave uprising and establish a stronghold for escaped slaves in the Appalachian Mountains. His plot failed miserably after he and about 20 followers captured the federal arsenal at Harpers Ferry, Virginia. Ten of Brown's men died in a shoot-out with local militia and federal troops. Brown and six of his followers were tried for treason and sentenced to hang.

From the scaffold, Brown stood as grim and defiant as he had in the church two decades earlier and handed one of his guards a note. It read: "I, John Brown, am now quite certain that the crimes of this guilty land will never be purged away but with Blood."

CAUTION!!
COLORED PEOPLE
OF BOSTON, ONE & ALL,
You are hereby respectfully CAUTIONED and
advised, to avoid conversing with the
Watchmen and Police Officers
of Boston,
For since the recent ORDER OF THE MAYOR &
ALDERMEN, they are empowered to act as
KIDNAPPERS
AND
Slave Catchers,
And they have already been actually employed in
KIDNAPPING, CATCHING, AND KEEPING
SLAVES. Therefore, if you value your LIBERTY,
and the *Welfare of the Fugitives* among you, *Shun*
them in every possible manner, as so many *HOUNDS*
on the track of the most unfortunate of your race.
Keep a Sharp Look Out for
KIDNAPPERS, and have
TOP EYE open.
APRIL 24, 1851.

THEODORE PARKER'S PLACARD
Placard written by Theodore Parker and printed and posted by the Vigilance Committee of Boston after the rendition of Thomas Sims to slavery in April, 1851.

The master in this illustration is training his dogs to catch runaway slaves. Instead of using a real slave, the owner has created a rough model, likely made of wicker, and filled it with raw meat, teaching the dogs to associate runaways with food. Sometimes real slaves were used in the training. They would be sent running, and the dogs would be used to track them down. If they found the slave, they would be rewarded with raw meat. Although not pictured here, bloodhounds were most commonly associated with tracking fugitive slaves. After the war, Ulysses S. Grant noted that as a result of the bloodhound's reputation, Union soldiers were ordered to kill them on sight.

While the Fugitive Slave Act of 1793 made it illegal to protect a runaway slave, the Act of 1850 levied fines and prison terms against anyone harboring a fugitive. Local governments also passed their own laws either supporting or defying these acts. In some jurisdictions, free blacks could be detained by authorities until they could prove that they were not slaves. Posters such as this one in Boston were circulated by abolitionists warning blacks of their peril.

In 1850, Stephen A. Douglas, a 37-year-old senator from Illinois, helped Henry Clay in skillfully crafting a compromise over the disposition of the territory the United States acquired after the Mexican War. He became a primary spokesperson for allowing slavery in the territories on the basis of popular sovereignty. His Senate seat was challenged in 1858 by Abraham Lincoln, setting the stage for the legendary Lincoln-Douglas debates.

1857
MARCH 6
The U.S. Supreme Court issues the Dred Scott decision.

SUMMER
The Impending Crisis of the South: How to Meet It by Southerner Hinton R. Helper is published. Predictably, it results in a storm of criticism from proslavery Southerners.

OCTOBER 19–NOVEMBER 8
A constitutional convention meets in Lecompton, Kansas. Boycotted by free-soilers, the group adopts a proslavery constitution.

Many free blacks in the antebellum South set up their own businesses and became barbers. One of the most successful was Robert Campbell in Augusta County, Virginia. By 1860, his wealth reached $19,000. He was the only black to receive an obituary in the local paper when he died.

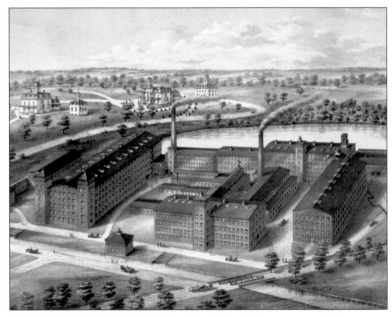

Iron-casting plants like this one produced the thousands of tons of steel needed to supply the Northern war effort with weapons and machinery. While a few large plants like this existed at the beginning of the war in Southern cities such as Chattanooga, Tennessee, and Richmond, Virginia, the resources necessary to produce quality steel were exhausted in the region by 1865.

Industries like the Assabet Manufacturing Company in Massachusetts, pictured here, flourished in the North. Textiles, lumber, shoes, clothing, iron, and machinery were among the leading industries. The burgeoning cities of the North satisfied the need for labor and capital to develop and operate its factories, mills, and mines.

DECEMBER 21
The proslavery constitution is ratified by Kansas voters. This election is tainted, as free-soilers continue to boycott.

1858
FEBRUARY 2
President James Buchanan submits the Lecompton constitution to Congress, recommending its approval and the admission of Kansas as a slave state.

MARCH 23
The Senate approves the Lecompton constitution and Kansas statehood.

1860 Presidential Election

Two men with differing views on slavery confronted each other in the 1858 race for senator of Illinois. Although personally opposed to slavery, incumbent Senator Stephen A. Douglas believed citizens of each territory should have the right to determine their own stance on the issue. His Republican opponent, Abraham Lincoln, took a position more moderate than the abolitionists, tolerating slavery in the South where it was established but opposing its expansion into the territories. Sometimes, however, his rhetoric took a stronger slant. When he accepted the Republican nomination, Lincoln stated, "I believe this government cannot endure half slave and half free."

In a series of seven debates across the state, Lincoln presented compelling arguments against slavery, while Douglas reaffirmed his "popular sovereignty" stance. Lincoln lost the election but drew national attention for his oratorical skills and his firm antislavery views, which catapulted him into contention for the 1860 Republican nomination for president of the United States.

The Republican convention was held in Chicago, where a number of local supporters helped Lincoln secure the nomination on the third ballot. The task of Democrats was not as easy. Some in the party demanded constitutional rights for slaveholders north of the Mason-Dixon line, while others did not want stricter

This 1860 election banner for the Republican party shows Abraham Lincoln and his running mate, Hannibal Hamlin from Maine. Hamlin was a representative, a senator, and a governor prior to becoming vice president. He was not a powerful vice president, and he apparently bore Lincoln no ill will when he was dropped from the ticket in 1864.

fugitive slave laws but advocated popular sovereignty. To avoid tearing their party apart, the Democratic delegates had to choose a compromise candidate.

The Democrats met in Charleston, South Carolina, but the convention ended abruptly when 50 Southern delegates stormed from the hall. The party reconvened in Baltimore in June, attempting once again to reach a compromise. This time 110 members of the Southern delegation walked out. The remaining Democrats nominated Douglas, supporting his popular sovereignty platform.

The Southern delegation nominated their own candidate, Vice President John C. Breckinridge of Kentucky, on a platform protecting the constitutional rights of slaveholders. Breckinridge was supported by President James Buchanan and former Presidents Franklin Pierce and John Tyler. A fourth candidate, former Senator John Bell of Tennessee, was nominated by the Constitutional Union party, which was also dubbed the "Do-Nothing" party for its refusal to take a stand on the slavery issue.

Although hated in the South and distrusted by many in the North, Lincoln won, thanks to the splintering of the Democratic party. He received less than 40 percent of the popular vote, but he easily won in the electoral college after carrying all but one Northern state.

Abraham Lincoln

"This morning, as for some days past," President Abraham Lincoln wrote on August 23, 1864, "it seems exceedingly probable that this Administration will not be reelected. Then it will be my duty to so cooperate with the President elect, as to save the Union between the election and the inauguration; as he will have secured his election on such ground that he can not possibly save it afterwards." At that time, the federal war effort was at perhaps its darkest moment. With the November presidential election well underway, Lincoln felt that the Democratic peace candidate, George McClellan, could possibly defeat him. The capture of Atlanta, however, and victories in Virginia's Shenandoah Valley enabled Lincoln to win the election.

There had been little indication in Lincoln's early years that he would eventually lead the country through its most trying test. Lincoln was born in a log cabin near Hodgenville, Kentucky, on February 12, 1809. Primarily self-educated, he held a number of manual labor jobs before obtaining a license to practice law in 1836. He was elected to the U.S. House of Representatives in 1846 as a member of the Whig party on a platform that opposed the Mexican War and the spread of slavery. Quickly disillusioned with national politics, however, he decided not to run for reelection after only one term.

In the mid 1850s, Lincoln switched to the newly formed Republican party, and his outspoken stance supporting the antislavery issue drew him back into the national spotlight in 1858. That year he lost the Illinois senatorial race to "popular sovereignty" can-

didate Stephen A. Douglas, but he was propelled into the national spotlight as a result of his performance in seven debates with Douglas across the state. That attention helped launch his bid for the presidency in 1860.

Although Lincoln did not enter the Republican convention as the favored candidate, he was nominated on the third ballot. His opponent Stephen Douglas's Democratic party was hopelessly divided over slavery, which ultimately led to Lincoln's victory. Lincoln was hated in the South, and his name was not even on the ballot in many states. His election was the catalyst for legislatures across the Southern states to vote to secede from the Union. Lincoln made several attempts to bring the seceded states back into the fold to no avail. Once Fort Sumter was bombarded, he immediately exerted his executive powers and called for 75,000 volunteers, ordered the blockade of Southern ports, and suspended habeas corpus in all states wavering toward secession.

The strength of Lincoln's character and his resolve to save the Union have often been credited for holding the federal government together throughout this, its most difficult crisis. During four years of war, Lincoln was always affable but was less than an efficient administrator. After several early attempts to influence the prosecution of the war, he turned military control over to the professional soldiers and paid closer attention to public matters. One such issue was whether or not to free slaves.

Even though pressured by Congress and members of his Cabinet to unconditionally emancipate

Thomas Lincoln moved his wife and daughter to a one-room cabin at Sinking Spring Farm near Hodgenville, Kentucky, about two months before his son Abraham was born. Today, a replica of the cabin stands on the original site encased in a neoclassical marble-and-granite structure, a design similar to the Lincoln Memorial in Washington, D.C. There are 56 steps leading up to the entrance, signifying each year of his life.

the war was finally rewarded with the defeat of the Confederacy. In his second inaugural address, delivered a month before Confederate General Robert E. Lee's surrender, Lincoln reaffirmed his desire for a quick reconciliation with the Southern states when he called for "malice toward none" and "charity for all." Lincoln's opportunity to savor the hard-won victory was short-lived. On April 14, 1865, he was shot by John Wilkes Booth. His death the next morning sent shock waves throughout the North and South and marked the beginning of the long, difficult road to national reconciliation.

Modeled after the Parthenon in Athens, Greece, the Lincoln Memorial rests on the western edge of the National Mall in Washington, D.C. The 36 columns surrounding its exterior represent the number of states at the time of Lincoln's death. The text of the Gettysburg Address is inscribed on the south wall and his Second Inaugural Address on the north. The left hand of the 19-foot statue is clenched, representing Lincoln's strength, and the right is open, depicting his compassion.

slaves, he was hesitant to release such an order, preferring instead to compensate slaveholders. Once he realized that freeing slaves would improve public opinion and ensure that European nations would not enter the war on the side of the Confederacy, Lincoln issued the Emancipation Proclamation, effective January 1, 1863. It proclaimed all slaves in the rebellious states were unconditionally freed.

Ten months after the proclamation, on November 19, 1863, Lincoln delivered his most famous speech during a ceremony dedicating a military cemetery near the battlefield in Gettysburg, Pennsylvania. It lasted less than two minutes and was, by the President's own reckoning, a "flat failure."

Although he found it personally painful to support the mounting cost in human lives that the war inflicted on citizens of the North and South, Lincoln's commitment to the vigorous prosecution of

Radical Republicans

Whigs and Democrats were the primary political parties in 1850. Many Whigs abandoned their party, however, upset by the concessions granted to proslavery factions with the passage of the Compromise of 1850 and the Kansas-Nebraska Act of 1854. As the Whigs dissolved, this splintered group became the nucleus for the Republican party.

While the platform of the new party called for the ban of slavery from the United States, three factions formed. Conservatives and moderates argued for a gradual movement toward emancipation, while more radical members demanded the immediate freedom of slaves without compensation to their owners. Although radical Republicans were far from the majority of the party, they were aggressive, uncompromising, and very vocal in their beliefs.

Charles Sumner

One prominent radical was Senator Charles Sumner of Massachusetts. In a speech he delivered in May 1856, he denounced the Kansas-Nebraska Act and charged those in Congress who backed it as selling out to slaveholders. Two days later, Preston Brooks, a representative from South Carolina, beat Sumner with a cane while he sat at his desk on the Senate floor.

The most vocal and influential of the radical wing of the Republican party was Representative Thaddeus Stevens. As chairman of the Ways and Means Committee, he exerted his power in shaping congressional legislation toward slavery.

Lincoln's Emancipation Proclamation did not go far enough for the radicals due to the exclusion of border states where slavery still existed. These radicals exerted their most significant influence during postwar Reconstruction.

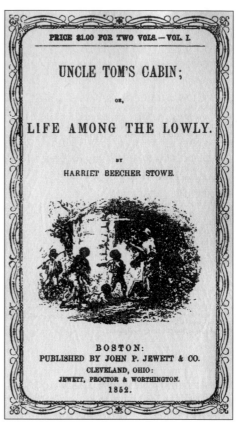

Originally appearing as a serial in The National Era *in 1851,* Uncle Tom's Cabin *was published in book form in 1852. In the 19th century, it outsold all other books except for the Bible in the United States.*

One of the North's most skilled propagandists, artist Thomas Nast drew this cartoon for Harper's Weekly in 1861. Hailed by President Lincoln as "our best recruiting sergeant," Nast here parodies the strength of the South built on the oppression of the black slave.

The appearance of Uncle Tom's Cabin *in 1852 thrust Harriet Beecher Stowe into the spotlight of the slavery debate. Though scholars argue over its literary merit, the novel's graphic portrayal of Southern plantation life appealed to those opposed to slavery and made the book a best seller. Believing they had been unjustly stereotyped, citizens of the South united in their condemnation of the book.*

At the start of the 19th century, technological innovations in the textile industry helped propel America into the Industrial Revolution. Francis Cabot Lowell created the first American power loom and built a factory that, for the first time, housed all the processes that converted cotton into cloth under a single roof. Lowell, Massachusetts, soon became a major textile center.

Joseph Cinque, a captive on the Spanish slave ship Amistad, *led a revolt in June, 1839, which killed the ship's captain and cook, as well as ten blacks. After having taken over the ship, Cinque and his band were tricked by their Spanish captives, and instead of reaching Africa, they sailed into Long Island, New York. The former slaves were found not guilty of piracy and murder by the U.S. Supreme Court in March 1841.*

APRIL 1
The House votes to resubmit the Lecompton constitution to a popular vote in Kansas.

APRIL 30
The House and Senate compromise on the Lecompton constitution, agreeing to admit Kansas to the Union as a slave state if the constitution wins a popular vote.

JUNE 16
Abraham Lincoln delivers his "House Divided" speech in accepting the Republican nomination for the Illinois Senate in Springfield, Illinois.

Abolitionists

Even before the Constitutional Convention of 1787, many Northerners embraced the antislavery movement, banding together to lobby colonial governments to enact laws prohibiting the practice. The Society of Friends, commonly called Quakers, initiated their campaign to ban slavery in the early 18th century. The "peculiar institution" gradually disappeared from the North, but it dramatically expanded throughout the South.

By the turn of the 19th century, a widely accepted belief was that whites and free blacks could not live harmoniously in the new nation. The American Colonization Society, founded by a group of Presbyterian ministers in 1816 and 1817, called for the return of free blacks to Africa. It acquired a tract of land on the western coast of that continent, calling it Liberia. During its existence, the society financed the emigration of as many as 20,000 black settlers. Other organizations were founded for the purpose of black colonization, but by 1830 sentiment turned toward emancipating slaves and giving them the freedom to live wherever they desired.

William Lloyd Garrison, editor of a radical antislavery newspa-

The calm, bespectacled expression of William Lloyd Garrison belied his fanatic abolitionist sentiment. Refusing to compromise on the issue of slavery, Garrison once called the Constitution "a covenant with death and an agreement with hell" and burned a copy as a protest.

per, *The Liberator*, became the national spokesperson for the abolitionist movement. He began his journalistic career by writing for the monthly periodical *The Genius of Universal Emancipation*. His editorials there became increasingly extremist and uncompromising, demanding that slaves receive immediate, unconditional freedom. Garrison began *The Liberator* on January 1, 1831, and used it to express his antislavery beliefs. He also cofounded the New England Anti-Slavery Society. Hundreds of other abolitionist organizations sprang up. The largest was the American Anti-Slavery Society, which at its height boasted 250,000 members.

Even though the numbers of abolitionist organizations were rapidly increasing, most Northerners rejected the call to support the movement. Although the opponents of slavery were firm in their convictions and loud and relentless in their appeal, they managed to attract only a small, though active, following throughout the North. While many citizens opposed slavery, few wanted to have millions of freed slaves mixing with white society and competing for jobs. One New York merchant argued that the business com-

---

AUGUST–OCTOBER
The Lincoln-Douglas debates take place in Illinois.

AUGUST 2
In an open and fair election, Kansas voters reject the Lecompton constitution.

OCTOBER 25
Senator William H. Seward, speaking in Rochester, New York, calls the current political strife "an irrepressible conflict."

munity could not afford to let the abolitionists succeed. "It is not a matter of principle with us," he insisted. "It is a matter of business necessity."

Abolitionist views ranged from Garrison's radical doctrines to the more moderate sentiments of the Reverend Henry Ward Beecher, but the impassioned pleas of both men combined to fix the plight of slaves onto the nation's conscience and helped chart a new course for the country. Too often, the reaction to these views led to violence and bloodshed, spurred on by the belief on both sides of the issue that Congress was unable to take a decisive stand. To most abolitionists, the various fugitive slave laws, the Compromise of 1850, and the Kansas-Nebraska Act were examples of Congress attempting to appease Southern legislatures at the expense of enslaved blacks.

As America expanded westward, the question of admitting territories as free or slave states not only inflamed congressional debates but also caused abolitionist ranks to reassess their nonpolitical stance. Many abolitionists realized that the only way to address this issue was to form a strong political party and exert influence in Washington. Poet John Greenleaf Whittier and politician James Birney formed the Liberty party, which nomi-

Henry Ward Beecher, brother of Harriet Beecher Stowe, was himself an outspoken critic of slavery. An ordained minister, Beecher disapproved of the actions of radical abolitionists. He called John Brown's raid at Harpers Ferry an "act of a crazy old man." He had a knack for oratory and theatrics that helped attract public attention to his antislavery message.

nated Birney for president in 1840. After a poor showing in that and the 1844 election, the party merged with other groups to form the Free-Soil party in 1848. Its primary platform was opposition to the extension of slavery in the territories and the admittance of only antislave states to the Union. While it did not have the numbers to place many of its own candidates in congressional seats—an exception was Liberty party cofounder Salmon P. Chase—the party was influential in the election of abolitionists such as Charles Sumner.

Abolitionist ranks were not limited to white members. A number of blacks, many of whom had once been slaves, were active in the movement. The most famous of the group was Frederick Douglass, the self-educated son of a slave woman and white man. He gained international fame as an orator and writer, publishing an autobiography, *Narrative of the Life of Frederick Douglass, an American Slave,* in 1845. He would release two more memoirs during his lengthy career. One of the first black women to speak out against slavery was Sojourner Truth. Like Douglass, she was born a slave. Her career as an orator began in 1843 when she answered what she later referred to as a call from God to speak out in support of her race.

1859
MARCH 7
The Supreme Court issues its decision in *Ableman* v. *Booth,* which affirms the constitutionality of the Fugitive Slave Law of 1850.

MAY 9–19
The Southern Commercial Convention at Vicksburg, Mississippi, advocates the repeal of laws prohibiting the foreign slave trade.

OCTOBER 4
Voters in Kansas overwhelmingly ratify an antislavery constitution.

The population of New York City was more than 800,000 when the Civil War began. It was a Democratic party stronghold with a rather large contingent of citizens who urged an alliance with the secessionist states during the early months of 1861. Once Fort Sumter was fired upon, however, New Yorkers rallied around the Union flag and raised a number of regiments to meet Abraham Lincoln's call for volunteers.

The spirit of abolitionist John Brown dominates this dramatic depiction of the many symbols of the Civil War. With a Bible in one hand and a gun in the other, Brown towers above the living and dead victims of the war. Some in the North saw Brown as a martyr, but he was a secondary figure in the events that led to war.

In 1856, Massachusetts Senator Charles Sumner delivered a lengthy speech to the Senate entitled "The Crime Against Kansas," specifically attacking Stephen A. Douglas and ailing Senator Andrew P. Butler for supporting the Kansas-Nebraska Act. Two days after Sumner concluded, Butler's cousin, South Carolina Representative Preston Brooks, entered the Senate chamber and attacked Sumner with his cane, reducing it to splinters. Sumner required years of recovery, while Brooks became a hero at home, receiving replacement canes from across the South.

OCTOBER 16
John Brown and his raiders attack Harpers Ferry, Virginia. Roughly 36 hours later, most will have been killed or captured.

DECEMBER 2
John Brown is hanged for treason in Charles Town, Virginia.

1860
APRIL 23–MAY 3
The Democratic national convention in Charleston, South Carolina, fails to nominate a presidential candidate.

This 1865 view of Harpers Ferry, West Virginia, shows the confluence of the Shenandoah and Potomac rivers. In 1859, while still a part of Virginia, the town's federal arsenal was seized by John Brown and his followers. When Brown was executed later that same year for his role in the raid, the antislavery cause had found itself a new martyr.

The Kansas Territory saw some of the earliest skirmishes of what would become the Civil War. Armed conflict over the place of slavery in the future state broke out as proslavery and abolition forces sent their supporters into the territory to influence the vote for statehood. Although small in scale to what would follow, the violence was serious enough to earn the area the nickname "Bleeding Kansas."

Edwin Drake (in top hat) stands in front of the wooden derrick that houses the first oil well. His initial attempts along Oil Creek, near Titusville, Pennsylvania, were ridiculed as "Drake's Folly," but he finally struck oil on August 27, 1859. "The excitement attendant on the discovery of this vast source of oil," a reporter wrote, "was fully equal to what I saw in California." The 69½-foot well produced about 20 barrels per day.

MAY 9
The Constitutional Union party forms in Baltimore and nominates John Bell of Tennessee for president.

MAY 16
The Republican convention meets in Chicago. Two days later, delegates endorse Abraham Lincoln for president.

JUNE 18–23
Democrats reconvene in Baltimore and again fail to nominate a presidential candidate. The party splits—Stephen A. Douglas is nominated by the Northern

Chicago had never hosted a national political convention until 1860. When it was picked as the site of the national Republican convention of that year, a convention center had to be built at a cost of $5,000. Nicknamed the "Wigwam," it was erected on the southeast corner of Market and Lake Streets and provided the setting for Abraham Lincoln's nomination to what would be the first successful Republican national ticket.

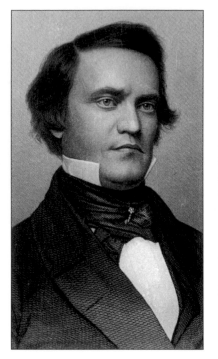

There was little hope of compromise when Democratic party delegates met to choose their candidate for president in 1860. Northern Democrats, led by Stephen A. Douglas, stood by their "Popular Sovereignty" platform, while their Southern counterparts called for passing laws to protect the rights of slaveholders in every corner of the Union. When the party nominated Douglas, unhappy Southern Democrats broke away and nominated President James Buchanan's vice president, John C. Breckinridge, shown here.

By the early 1860s, when this photograph of the New York harbor district was taken, New York was a major world port. It remained busy throughout the war.

wing; John C. Breckinridge is nominated by the more radical proslavery wing.

OCTOBER 15
Grace Bedell, an 11-year-old from Westfield, New York, writes Abraham Lincoln a letter suggesting he would look better if he grew a beard. Lincoln does.

NOVEMBER 6
Lincoln wins the presidential election.

DECEMBER 18
The U.S. Senate appoints a

After Lincoln's election, many Southerners made the case for leaving the Union. This typical argument, by prominent South Carolina clergyperson James C. Furman, appeared in the Greenville Southern Enterprise in November 1860: "By a vote of Congress . . . universal emancipation will be declared.—Then every negro in South Carolina . . . will be the equal of every one of you. If you are tame enough to submit, Abolition preachers will be at hand to consummate the marriage of your daughters to black husbands!"

Refusing to take a stand on either side of the slavery issue, a faction of former Whigs created the Constitutional Union party. Their platform called for preserving the Union at all costs, proclaiming, "The Constitution of the Country, the Union of the States, and the enforcement of the laws." Popularly called the "Do-Nothing" party, it nominated John Bell, a former Tennessee senator, as its presidential candidate in 1860.

In December 1860, Kentucky Senator John Crittenden proposed a compromise to halt the momentum of the secessionist movement. A committee of 13 senators was formed to discuss the proposal. Membership included all political segments of the Senate from radical Republicans to avowed secessionists, including Jefferson Davis and Robert Toombs. Unable to gain committee support, Crittenden's compromise never reached the Senate floor, leading to satirical cartoons such as this one depicting Southern states heading toward a precipice.

13-member committee to investigate the "present condition of the country." Senator John J. Crittenden of Kentucky presents his compromise for dealing with the sectional crisis.

DECEMBER 20
South Carolina secedes from the Union.

DECEMBER 26
Union Major Robert Anderson transfers his garrison from Fort Moultrie to Fort Sumter in Charleston Harbor, South Carolina.

1861

THE WAR BEGINS

HOPES FOR A SHORT CONFLICT ARE DASHED

*T*he clearing skies and mild winter temperatures belied the storm that was about to break over the badly divided country. Tipping his hat to the crowd of 30,000, Abraham Lincoln rode up Pennsylvania Avenue. It was March 4, 1861, and the man who would be the 16th President of the United States was on his way to deliver his inaugural address. Like the anxious audience gathered at the Capitol, an expec-

Abraham Lincoln strode to the end of the wooden platform on the portico of the Capitol, where sharpshooters were stationed in windows of the unfinished dome to guard the new President. "We must not be enemies," Lincoln pleaded in his first official address to the troubled nation. A reporter described the President that day as "pale and composed."

This painting by James Massalon shows the inauguration of Jefferson Davis as president of the Confederacy. The ceremony took place on the portico of the Alabama State House in Montgomery, then the Confederacy's capital.

tant nation waited to hear his message. In a clear and distinct voice, the new leader tried to ease Southern fears that the federal government would move to end slavery. But he also denied that states had the right to secede. "In your hands, my dissatisfied fellow countrymen, and not in mine," Lincoln cautioned, "is the momentous issue of civil war."

By this time, however, North and South had practically reached the point of no return and were on the verge of armed conflict. On December 18, 1860, a last-minute attempt to head off secession was offered by Kentucky Senator John J. Crittenden. Stamped "The Crittenden Compromise," it proposed amendments to the Constitution that would ensure federal protection of slavery in states and territories below the old Missouri Compromise line. The possible extension of slavery into new territories rankled President-elect Lincoln as well as other Republican leaders, and the proposed measure soon died in committee.

OF COURSE, I WAS HIGHLY GRATIFIED BY THE COMPLIMENT, & DELIGHTED TO PERFORM THE SERVICE.

Longtime secessionist Edmund Ruffin, on being asked to fire the first shot against Fort Sumter

On December 20, 1860, South Carolina seceded from the Union, followed in short order by Mississippi, Florida, Alabama, Georgia, Louisiana, and Texas, respectively. A month to the day prior to Lincoln's inauguration, the seceded states had opened a convention in Montgomery, Alabama. Four days later, they had adopted a constitution for a provisional Confederate government. On February 18, 1861, Jefferson Davis, former

1861
JANUARY 3
The Delaware legislature rejects a call to secede from the Union.

Under orders from Governor Joseph E. Brown, Fort Pulaski near Savannah, Georgia, is seized by Georgia state troops.

JANUARY 4
Alabama troops take over the federal arsenal at Mount Vernon.

U.S. secretary of war and senator from Mississippi until that state seceded, was inaugurated as provisional president of the Confederacy.

Standoff at Fort Sumter

Confederate forces had already begun to seize federal property throughout the South, including government arsenals filled with vital caches of small arms, artillery, and ammunition. Fort Sumter had been a flash point for the disputing sides since late December 1860. Following the secession of South Carolina on the 20th of the month, Major Robert Anderson and his command rowed from their onshore post at Fort Moultrie to the haven of Fort Sumter in the middle of Charleston Harbor. What may be considered the first shots of the coming war were taken soon after. On January 9, 1861, secessionist artillery in Charleston Harbor fired on the supply ship *Star of the West*, preventing it from delivering reinforcements and provisions to the besieged federal garrison in Fort Sumter. Farther south, in Florida, a small contingent of federal troops clung to Fort Pickens, at the mouth of Pensacola Bay, against the vehement demands for its surrender by the governors of both Florida and Alabama.

Newly inaugurated President Lincoln had vowed not to fire the first shot at Fort Sumter, but when a necklace of Confederate batteries around the harbor opened fire on the fort on April 12, Union forces defended themselves. After 34 hours of bombardment, Anderson realized he was defeated. On the 14th, "with the flag flying and the drums beating 'Yankee Doodle,'" the federal garrison filed out of the battered fort. The next day, President Lincoln issued a call for 75,000 three-month volunteers to help quell the rebellion.

"Civil war is actually upon us," wrote U.S. Senator John Sherman of Ohio, "and strange to say, it brings feelings of relief." Within days of learning the news from Charleston, 100,000 patriotic spectators assembled at Union Square in New York City to view the tattered flag that had flown over Fort Sumter. The scene was bedlam. The partisan crowd cried for revenge.

This Northern political cartoon shows Jefferson Davis about to be hanged in a secession trap. Supporters of the Confederacy on the right—Senator Robert Toombs, P.G.T. Beauregard, Senator Alexander H. Stephens, and Francis Pickens, governor of South Carolina—all quake in fear as Davis whines on the scaffold. The letter of marque above Davis's head is a reminder to Northerners that the Confederacy granted permission to privateers to seize U.S. merchant ships as prizes of war.

JEFF DAVIS ON THE RIGHT PLATFORM, or the last "act of secession".

JANUARY 5
Alabama troops occupy Forts Morgan and Gaines in Mobile Bay, Alabama.

JANUARY 8
President Buchanan presses for acceptance of the Crittenden Compromise.

JANUARY 9
Mississippi secedes from the Union.

Jefferson Davis and his cabinet with General Robert E. Lee. From left to right: Judah P. Benjamin (attorney general), Stephen R. Mallory (navy), Leroy P. Walker (standing, war), Davis, Lee, John H. Reagan (postmaster general), Christopher G. Memminger (treasury), Alexander H. Stephens (seated, vice president), and Robert A. Toombs (state).

Southerners reacted to the hostilities with equal intensity. "All pent-up hatred of the past months and years is voiced in the thunder of these cannon," a Charleston resident observed, "and the people seem almost beside themselves in the exultation of a freedom they deem already won."

From farms, villages, and cities across the North and South, spirited young men flocked to recruiting offices. "War! and volunteers are the only topics of conversation or thought," wrote an Ohio college student. "I cannot study. I cannot sleep, and I don't know as I can write." Meanwhile, a journalist traveling in the South witnessed "crowds of armed men singing and promenading the streets, the battle blood running through their veins—that hot oxygen which is called 'the flush of victory' on the cheek." These eager but untested armies of young volunteers, naive and unfamiliar with the horrors of the battlefield, hospital, and prison pen, hurriedly prepared to do combat, where their results would be measured in blood.

The USS *Star of the West* is fired upon and turned away while trying to bring supplies to Fort Sumter.

JANUARY 10
Florida secedes from the Union.

The Louisiana militia seizes federal forts and arsenals throughout the state.

JANUARY 11
Alabama secedes from the Union.

JANUARY 12
Florida troops occupy federal forts around Pensacola except for Fort

Initial Enthusiasm

"Business to a great extent was suspended. It was useless to talk of sales and collections. The stores might as well have lowered their shutters. Banks seemed to have gone into bankruptcy. Factories did not hum with any lively sound, and the thoughts and eyes of their workers were in the street. The excitement had found its way into every home, and the populace, moved by a common impulse and alarm, rushed to the main streets and thoroughfares, to get the latest intelligence. . . . Groups of men were on the pavements and at the street corners; loud words were spoken, attended by gestures very emphatic, and above all was heard the reiterated cry of hoarse newsboys selling extras with the latest reports."

Robert W. Patrick,
on the clamor in Philadelphia
over the news of war

Expanding the Confederacy

While the North marshaled its forces to crush the rebellion, leaders of the fledgling South pressed the remaining slaveholding states to join the Confederacy. Within weeks of the spark at Fort Sumter, Arkansas, Tennessee, and North Carolina seceded from the Union. In Virginia—a populous state and an essential source of manufacturing and munitions—legislators passed an ordinance of secession but waited until a public referendum on May 23 to make its entry official. Confident of the loyalties of the "Old Dominion," the Confederate Congress voted to move the capital from the remote reaches of Montgomery, Alabama, to Richmond, Virginia, a few days earlier. The new capital was just 100 miles from Washington, D.C.

Standing along a geographic and sentimental equator between North and South were the states of Delaware, Maryland, Kentucky, and Missouri. Here loyalties wavered. These "border states" shared strong sectional ties with the Confederacy and equally firm economic links with the Union. Though uncommitted, Kentucky and Missouri each added a star to the rebel flag because they had representatives in the Confederate Congress.

Maryland's position was particularly sensitive to the Lincoln administration. The U.S. capital sprawled along the banks of the Potomac River, directly across from enemy Virginia on the opposite shore. The other three sides of Washington, D.C., and its suburbs were enwrapped by Maryland. Only a week after Fort Sumter was fired upon, blood was spilled in the streets of Baltimore.

While moving through Baltimore en route to guard Washington, the 6th Massachusetts Infantry Regiment was attacked by an angry mob of Southern loyalists. Nine civilians and four soldiers died in the confrontation. In the wake of this struggle, some in the Maryland legislature

An attractive, strong-willed, accomplished hostess and mother of six, Davis's second wife, Varina Howell Davis, was 18 years younger than her husband and remained devoted to him during the war. After the war, she used her gifts as a prolific writer to defend his reputation in books and numerous magazine articles. John C. Calhoun described Varina as an "intellectual equal."

Pickens, which remains in Union hands.

JANUARY 17
President-elect Lincoln announces his selection of New York Senator

William H. Seward as secretary of state for his Cabinet.

JANUARY 19
Georgia secedes from the Union.

JANUARY 21
Jefferson Davis of Mississippi, along with senators from Alabama, Florida, and Georgia, resigns from the U.S. Senate.

Born to a prominent Kentucky family, Mary Todd married Abraham Lincoln in 1842. Though standing just 5 feet 2 inches tall, she had a graceful, aristocratic bearing. A friend remembered Mary, mother of three sons, as vivacious and impulsive, though "she now and then could not restrain a . . . sarcastic speech that cut deeper than she intended." But Lincoln loved her dearly and defended her time and again. She never recovered from his assassination.

Construction of a new dome on the Capitol was authorized by Congress in 1855 but had not been completed when the Civil War began. In 1862, President Lincoln ordered the construction to be continued as "a sign we intend the Union shall go on." To echoes of a 35-gun salute (one for each state, both North and South), the dome was completed on December 2, 1863. It is capped by a bronze statue of Freedom.

urged immediate secession. But their action brought a response from Union authorities to prevent the measure. Ultimately, the mayor of Baltimore, the city's chief of police, several state legislators, and numerous other contentious citizens were summarily jailed without writ of habeas corpus. Afterward, federal troops maintained a tight grip on the city and on Maryland state borders, thus securing the Union capital.

JANUARY 26
Louisiana secedes from the Union.

JANUARY 29
Kansas is admitted to the United States as the 34th state. It is a free state.

FEBRUARY 1
Texas secedes from the Union. Governor Sam Houston opposes the decision and will ultimately be deposed from office rather than take a loyalty oath to the Confederacy.

Jefferson Davis

Criticized throughout the Civil War, Jefferson Davis aged greatly from the effect of four years of warfare and two years of postwar imprisonment. Defiant to the end, he never sought to regain the citizenship stripped from him—congressional action in 1978 posthumously restored it.

Born in Kentucky in 1808, Jefferson Davis graduated from West Point and served in the Army for seven years. While in the Army, he met his first wife, Sarah Knox Taylor, the daughter of his commanding officer and future president, Zachary Taylor. Sarah became ill and died only three months into the marriage. Davis remarried ten years later.

Elected to Congress in 1845, Davis became a staunch advocate of states' rights. He returned to the military during the Mexican War, came home a hero, and was selected to fill a vacant Mississippi Senate seat. Following an unsuccessful run for governor of the state in 1851, he was appointed secretary of war under Franklin Pierce. He returned to the Senate in 1857 but left when Mississippi seceded. Appointed to the presidency of the Confederate States of America in February 1861, Davis was popularly elected to office in November.

As the Confederacy's fortunes ebbed, those closest to Davis saw him gradually change from a confident, poised leader to a stubborn chief executive, increasingly withdrawn when leadership and guidance were desperately needed. Before the fall of Richmond, Virginia, Davis and his cabinet fled to escape the Federals. He evaded capture until May 10, when he was seized in Irwinville, Georgia. He was imprisoned for two years in Fort Monroe, Virginia, under the threat of trial for treason. Finally released on bail, Davis spent several years overseas before returning to Mississippi. "He did not know the arts of the politician," Varina Davis confessed of her husband, "and would not practice them if understood."

Davis died on December 6, 1889, without having his U.S. citizenship restored.

FEBRUARY 8
The seceded states adopt a constitution to establish a provisional Confederate government.

FEBRUARY 9
Tennessee voters reject a proposal to call a secession convention.

FEBRUARY 11
Abraham Lincoln leaves Springfield to journey to the nation's capital.

Blockade of the South

The very day military and civilian blood had mingled on the cobblestones in Baltimore, President Lincoln took the first steps to secure the nation's coastal borders. He issued a proclamation blockading all Confederate ports. Any ships caught trying to enter or exit an enemy harbor would first be warned. Failure to heed a warning would subject the ship and its cargo to capture and confiscation.

The blockade was only one facet of a broad Union strategy to defeat the South. Devised by 74-year-old U.S. Army General in Chief Winfield Scott—nicknamed "Old Fuss and Feathers" for his exactness in military procedure dating back to the War of 1812—the strategy was adopted by President Lincoln soon after the war began. The aged

The Confederate Stars and Bars flag waves in the breeze above Fort Sumter. The Union garrison surrendered the fort to Confederate forces on April 13, 1861, after 34 hours of bombardment, and left the fort the next day. It was not until four years later on April 14, 1865, that the U.S. flag once again flew over the fort.

FEBRUARY 18
Jefferson Davis is inaugurated as president of the Confederate States of America.

Union forces in Texas surrender.

FEBRUARY 23
President-elect Lincoln arrives in Washington earlier than planned. His schedule had been changed

in reaction to assassination threats.

FEBRUARY 28
Tennessee voters again reject secession, as does North Carolina.

Scott proposed to strengthen the naval blockade of the 3,500-mile rebel coastline, to cut off the Confederacy from the outside world, and to put a stranglehold on the Southern economy. "In connection with such a blockade," Scott wrote, "we propose a powerful movement down the Mississippi to the ocean." Against the rebel interior, the general would launch the army along the Cumberland and Tennessee rivers. Another thrust overland would be aimed at the Confederate capital, Richmond. Scott summed up his position with the claim, "300,000 men under an able general might carry the business through in two or three years."

An impatient Northern press and public scoffed at the scheme. They dubbed it "The Anaconda Plan" because of the slow and methodical strategy it advocated, and they cried for action now. "Let us make quick work," wrote the editor of *The New York Times*. "A strong active pull together will do our work effectually in thirty days. We have only to send a column of 25,000 to Richmond, and burn out the rats there."

Manassas

"The scene on the road had now assumed an aspect which has not a parallel in any description I have ever read. Infantry soldiers on mules and draft horses with the harness clinging to their heels, as much frightened as their riders; Negro servants on their masters' chargers; ambulances crowded with unwounded soldiers; wagons swarming with men who threw out the contents in the road to make room, grinding through a shouting, screaming mass of men on foot who were literally yelling with rage at every halt and shrieking out: 'Here are the cavalry! Will you get on?' This portion of the force was evidently in discord."

*British journalist **William Howard Russell** describing the beginning of the Union rout at the First Battle of Bull Run, July 21, 1861*

Confederate Planning

Meanwhile, Jefferson Davis and his new government were developing a military strategy of their own. The tremendous resource advantages enjoyed by the North cooled any thought of an offensive policy. Instead, Davis set out to defend his lengthy borders in the hope that either the North would weary of a bloody and costly war and accept the Confederacy as a separate nation or Europe would intervene on behalf of the South to preserve its interests in the cotton markets. Many Southerners were confident that abundant supplies of their cotton would bring in return abundant stocks of European arms and munitions.

A bespectacled but aggressive West Pointer, Lieutenant Adam J. Slemmer took the initiative to occupy Fort Pickens in Pensacola Harbor early in January 1861. This prevented Confederate authorities from seizing the fort and its vital munitions. Slemmer held the fort despite demands for its surrender. Fort Pickens remained in Union control throughout the war. Severely wounded at the Battle of Murfreesboro, Slemmer survived the war only to die of heart failure at the age of 39.

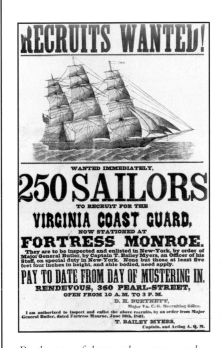

By the tens of thousands, young people across the North responded to recruiting posters like this when the war began. Many states quickly exceeded their quotas for volunteers. At times, the number of recruits even exceeded the number of weapons available to arm them all. "I studied the cost and measured the way before I enlisted," wrote an Illinois recruit, "and I intend to stick it through manfully."

President Buchanan signs into law the organization of the Colorado Territory.

MARCH 2
Congress organizes the Nevada Territory.

MARCH 4
Abraham Lincoln is inaugurated as the 16th President of the United States.

The Confederacy adopts its first flag and raises it over the capitol at Montgomery, Alabama.

The Bombardment of Fort Sumter

On December 26, 1860, Major Robert Anderson and about 70 Federals under his command rowed from their garrison at Fort Moultrie to the safety of Fort Sumter in the middle of Charleston Harbor. Since the secession of South Carolina from the Union six days earlier, Anderson felt that the move from the mainland was necessary to ensure the safety of his soldiers. President James Buchanan had decided to hold Sumter at all costs.

Although newly inaugurated President Abraham Lincoln had sworn to defend all federal property within the boundaries of the seceded states, he also pledged that he would not be the one to fire the first shot. The stalemate continued until the early hours of April 12, 1861, when four Confederate emissaries rowed to Fort Sumter, demanding its surrender. After negotiations failed, Confederates opened fire at 4:30 A.M.

After 34 hours of shelling, Anderson recognized that further resistance was futile. He agreed to evacuate the fort on the 14th only if his troops were permitted to fire a 100-gun salute to the federal flag.

At 2:00 P.M. on the 14th, the salute began. Halfway into the salute, a cartridge bag prematurely ignited, killing one soldier and wounding several more—one mortally. Anderson cut short the salute. By 4:00 P.M., the Federals filed out of the fort carrying the flag that had flown throughout the bombardment. The same flag would once again be triumphantly raised over the fort four years later.

Many Charleston residents reacted quickly to the first sound of cannon fire at Fort Sumter. Mary Chesnut wrote, "I put on my double-gown and a shawl and went, too. It was to the housetop. The shells were bursting.... And who could tell what each volley accomplished of death and destruction?"

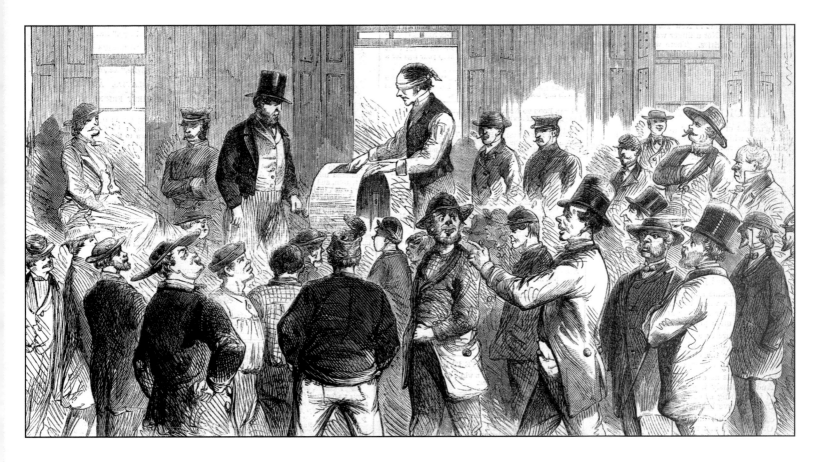

Leaders in each Confederate state were also busy mobilizing their citizens to face invasion. Virginia Governor John Letcher's task was especially urgent. The Potomac River was the sole barrier between his state and the federal capital. He understood that Virginia would be the prime avenue for a Northern invasion. To command and train the growing legion of state volunteers, Letcher chose a native son who had recently resigned from the U.S. Army—54-year-old Colonel Robert E. Lee.

Davis created military departments along geographical lines and parceled out troops among them. "Each was a separate nation for military purposes," wrote a government official, adding grimly, "without . . . cooperation or concert." Though smaller in number and weaker in weapons and equipment, Confederate armies would have the advantage of fighting on defense and on interior lines. Soldiers and supplies could be concentrated more quickly at threatened points.

By May 22, Davis had planted an army of more than 20,000 troops on the doorsteps of Washington, D.C., concentrated astride the banks of Bull Run, a sluggish creek near Manassas, Virginia. The force was commanded by Brigadier General Pierre G. T. (P.G.T.)

Early in the war, potential soldiers rushed to join the Confederate Army. Expecting a short war, many feared they would miss the fighting. "So impatient did I become for starting," recalled a Confederate volunteer, "that I felt like ten thousand pins were pricking me in every part of the body, and started off a week in advance of my brothers."

MARCH 11
The Confederate Congress adopts a constitution.

MARCH 18
The Arkansas convention defeats an ordinance of secession.

APRIL 4
The Virginia state convention rejects a secession ordinance.

Lincoln orders supplies and reinforcements to be sent to Fort Sumter.

The sharp action at Carrick's Ford in rugged western Virginia on July 13, 1861, was small in scale but produced big results. This decisive Union victory helped establish the newborn state of West Virginia for the North and propelled the victorious Union general, George B. McClellan, toward command of the Army of the Potomac, which he assumed on July 27, 1861. The Confederate commander, General Robert S. Garnett, became the first Civil War general to die in combat.

Beauregard. Washington politicians, the Northern press, and the Northern public alike urged their army to act. They demanded to see the rebel forces driven from a position so close to the Union capital. Since assuming command of the Union Army on May 28, Brigadier General Irvin McDowell had been pressured to attack and end the rebellion as soon as possible. Both he and General in Chief Scott were reluctant to commit their raw, undisciplined troops to battle. President Lincoln was especially anxious for his generals to act since the terms of service for many of the volunteers, who had enlisted in April for 90 days, were about to expire. The President reminded his commanders, "You are green, it is true, but they are green, also; you are all green alike."

The First Battle of Bull Run

Though the forces gathered in sizable numbers, the majority of soldiers in both the Union and the Confederate armies were ill trained, poorly equipped, and led by inex-

APRIL 12
Confederates open fire on Fort Sumter. Union forces there surrender on the 13th.

APRIL 15
Lincoln asks for 75,000 three-month militia soldiers to suppress the rebellion.

APRIL 17
Virginia secedes from the Union.

APRIL 18
Five companies of Pennsylvania troops reach Washington, the

Naval Service

"Several shots came on board of us, causing the vessel to leak badly, and beside other injuries crippling the port wheel, the wrought-iron shaft being gouged by a shot which would have shattered it if of cast iron, a point considered by me in selecting this vessel for purchase. Fortunately, I have again neither killed nor wounded to report, though the shot at times fell thick among us, testing the gallantry and steadiness of my people, which I consider of standard proof for any emergency....

"More than 100 shots have fallen aboard and around us, any one of which would have struck a frigate. We have had more than 1,000 shots discharged at us within range, and have ourselves fired upward of 300 shots and shells, with 1,700 pounds of powder. What damage we have inflicted remains to be seen. That we have received none not easily repaired is truly remarkable."

Commander James H. Ward, USS Thomas Freeborn, *describing the bombardment of Confederate batteries on the Chesapeake Bay at Aquia Creek, Virginia, on June 1, 1863, less than a month before becoming the first naval officer to be killed in action during the war*

The tumult and chaos of the Union flight from the First Battle of Bull Run battlefield are evident in this watercolor by historical artist William Trego. Union troops and the civilians who came to observe them had prepared themselves for an easy afternoon's struggle against a fairly tame enemy. No one expected the ferocious response the Confederates provided. Soldiers made no allowances for civilians who were also caught in the retreat. "Hacks containing unlucky spectators . . . were smashed like glass."

perienced officers. There was no lack of enthusiasm, however. A Massachusetts soldier summed up the feeling common in all ranks, that "the rebellion would be over before our chance would come." With the cry "On to Richmond" echoing from the home front, McDowell advanced against the rebel forces near Manassas. The armies of amateurs collided on July 21, 1861.

Throngs of sightseers from Washington had braved the sweltering heat and dust-choked roads to crowd hilltops above the rolling meadows and wood lots where the armies battled. They had come to cheer their troops and witness the spectacle. What they witnessed instead was a seesaw struggle that ended in bloody repulse and utter rout for the Union Army. Utterly demoralized, the routed, beaten, bloodied Union soldiers straggled back to Washington.

The next day, as he watched the confusion in the streets of the Union capital, a British journalist wrote, "Why Beauregard does not come I know not, nor can I well guess." Beauregard's rebel troops, as well as those under Joseph E. Johnston, had been too exhausted and disorganized to follow up

first Union soldiers to appear in the capital.

Union troops abandon the arsenal at Harpers Ferry, Virginia, after burning many of its buildings.

APRIL 19
Lincoln calls for a blockade of Southern seaports.

The 6th Massachusetts Infantry Regiment is attacked by a mob in Baltimore, which results in deaths on both sides.

The First Battle of Bull Run

On Sunday morning, July 21, 1861, Brigadier General Irvin McDowell's federal army was preparing for battle. More than 30,000 strong, they were mostly young 90-day recruits who had answered the President's first call for volunteers after Fort Sumter fell. In their innocence they were eager for a fight. Many had feared they would miss the first and only battle of the war. Surely that would be all that was necessary to defeat the rebels...or so they thought.

Four miles ahead, along the steep banks of Bull Run Creek, Brigadier General P.G.T. Beauregard and an equally raw, eager, and determined army of 22,000 stood squarely in McDowell's path. Confederate forces had been building and fortifying around Manassas, a sleepy railroad junction 30 miles outside Washington, D.C., since early May. "Here, overlooking an extensive plain," wrote a journalist from the New Orleans press, "divided into verdant fields of wheat and oats and corn, pasture and meadows,

are the headquarters of the advance forces of the army.... General Beauregard is very popular here. I don't doubt if Napoleon himself had more the undivided confidence of his army."

Another 12,000 Confederate troops under General Joseph E. Johnston were stationed at Harpers Ferry, Virginia, protecting the approaches into the strategic Shenandoah Valley from General Robert Patterson's federal forces. Although each Confederate army was outnumbered by the Federals facing them, they were linked by the Manassas Gap Railroad. This gave both Confederate generals the ability to quickly reinforce each other if necessary.

Beginning July 16, McDowell led his army out of Washington amid the cheers of excited onlookers. A West Pointer and veteran of the Mexican War, he could trace his elevation to the command of the army back to friendships he maintained with members of the new Republican administration, friends

This chromolithograph by Kurz and Allison depicts the First Battle of Bull Run. Victorious Southern troops inflicted 2,900 Union casualties at the cost of 2,000 Confederates. Artists Louis Kurz and Alexander Allison were at the height of their skills when they created this and many other stylized battle scenes during the latter 19th century. Their fanciful art shows a romantic vision of the Civil War still commonplace at the time.

who now were among the loud chorus demanding "On to Richmond." Reluctant to commit his ill-trained regiments to battle, McDowell realized he had no choice. "This is not an army," he cautioned a friend. "It will take a long time to make an army."

There was almost a picnic air to the Union army's advance toward Manassas. "They stopped every moment to pick blackberries or get water," McDowell lamented. "They would not keep in the ranks." Another witness recalled "the waving banners, the inspiring strains of the numerous bands, the shouts and songs of the men." At the army's heels, on horseback or in buggies, toting fine wines and other delicacies, came throngs of curious civilians to witness the clash of armies. "I noticed about twenty barouches and carriages," recalled a Massachusetts soldier, "that contained members of Congress and their friends."

McDowell sighted Beauregard's troops along Bull Run on July 18 and tested the strength of the rebel position at Blackburn's Ford. The sharp encounter produced information about enemy positions and several dozen killed, wounded, and missing on each side. A Boston news reporter recorded his most vivid recollections: "Louder, wilder, and more startling than the volley which they had fired was the rebel yell. A thousand Confederates were howling like wolves." Later this reporter observed the ambulance corps come to collect the wounded. "I recall the first man brought back on a stretcher, his thigh torn to pieces by a cannon shot.... The reflection came that this was war. All its glamour was gone in an instant."

McDowell opened the main battle with a two-pronged assault early on July 21. He advanced about half his army against the rebel center near a stone bridge spanning Bull Run, a feint to hold Beauregard in place. McDowell himself, meanwhile, led the balance of his force in a wide sweep around the weak Confederate left flank and rear, planning to crush the rebel flank and collapse the enemy line upon itself. At the right moment, the Union decoy force in the center would charge over the stone bridge to seal Beauregard's doom. All, however, did not go as planned. Confederates observed the Union flanking maneuver, and Southern troops were rushed to delay the enemy's progress. McDowell pressed his assault. When the rebel defense finally gave way, Beauregard, reinforced by Johnston's troops, formed a stout defense on Henry House Hill. Johnston's force, via railroad and on foot, had begun to slip away from the Shenandoah Valley days earlier.

A Virginia brigade commanded by Brigadier General Thomas J. Jackson anchored the Confederate line on the heights. "There is Jackson standing like a stone wall," cried Confederate General Bernard Bee, whose own troops were faltering. "Rally behind the Virginians." Each novice army put up a stiff fight as combat swirled across Henry House Hill throughout the afternoon. "The air is full of fearful noises," wrote a witness. "Trees are splintered.... There is smoke, dust, wild talking, shouting, hissings, howlings, explosions. It is a new, strange, unanticipated experience to the soldiers of both armies, far different from what they thought it would be."

Neither side gained an advantage until late in the afternoon when another of Johnston's fresh brigades arrived by rail and marched from the train directly to the battlefield. These troops, joined by another of Beauregard's brigades, delivered a fierce attack. "They... opened a fire of musketry on our men, which caused them to break and retire down the hillside," McDowell reported later. "This soon degenerated into disorder, for which there was no remedy."

Startled civilian sightseers forced their way onto the sole avenue of retreat. Chaos ensued. "What a scene," wrote the *New York World* correspondent. "For three miles, hosts of Federal troops... all mingled in one disorderly rout—were fleeing.... Army wagons, sutler's teams, and private carriages choked the passage, tumbling against each other amid clouds of dust and sickening sights and sounds." The panicked retreat did not end until the last of the survivors straggled back to Washington in a rainstorm the next day. Disorganized and fatigued, Confederate forces did not follow up their victory.

Union losses amounted to 2,900 killed, wounded, and missing; Confederate totals approached 2,000. The first major battle of the war began with an air of pageantry and fun and ended in terror and death, a fitting prelude to the four years of war that followed.

Promoted to brigadier general in May 1861, Irvin McDowell was thrust from his desk job in the adjutant general's office into command of the ill-trained Union army around Washington, D.C. "In the full flush of mature manhood, fully six feet tall, deep-chested," a fellow officer wrote of McDowell, the 42-year-old West Pointer appeared "in every respect a fine and impressive soldier." After his disastrous defeat at the First Battle of Bull Run, McDowell reported, "The retreat soon became a rout, and this soon degenerated . . . into a panic."

Shortly after the war began, Hugh Henry wrote a letter to his sister, who nursed their invalid mother in a house near Manassas, Virginia. "Should troops be passing about the neighborhood you and mother need not fear them," he tried to reassure her, "as your entire helplessness . . . would make you safe." The mother, 85-year-old Judith Carter Henry, was the only civilian killed during the First Battle of Bull Run when Union artillery targeted rebel sharpshooters who occupied her home.

their victory. Their forces only managed to pursue the enemy for several miles before halting.

Defeat stalked Northern forces elsewhere. In August, youthful and fiery Brigadier General Nathaniel Lyon led a small Union army into Missouri to drive rebel forces from

SAVE IN DEFENSE OF MY NATIVE STATE, I NEVER DESIRE AGAIN TO DRAW MY SWORD.

Robert E. Lee

the border state. Lyon's army was beaten, and he was killed at the Battle of Wilson's Creek—often called "The Bull Run of the West"—near Springfield. On October 21, Union forces suffered another disastrous rout at Ball's Bluff, along the Potomac River near Leesburg, Virginia. Among the Federals killed was Colonel Edward Baker, a sena-

Robert E. Lee resigns his commission in the U.S. Army.

The Gosport Navy Yard at Norfolk, Virginia, is abandoned and burned by Union troops.

APRIL 27
President Lincoln suspends the writ of habeas corpus in parts of Maryland and Pennsylvania, allowing for arrests to be made without specific charges.

On August 10, 1861, General Nathaniel Lyon and 5,500 federal troops were defeated at Wilson's Creek, Missouri, by 11,000 Confederates commanded by General Sterling Price. Among the more than 2,300 casualties suffered by both sides in this battle was Lyon himself, who was killed when a bullet pierced his heart.

APRIL 29
The Maryland legislature votes against secession.

MAY 3
Lincoln calls for another 42,000

three-year volunteers and 18,000 sailors.

MAY 6
Arkansas secedes from the Union.

MAY 7
The Tennessee legislature votes to secede from the Union. This decision is validated by popular vote on June 8.

Naval Blockade

Within one week of the firing on Fort Sumter, President Lincoln declared a blockade of Southern ports. With more than 3,500 miles of coastline containing nearly 200 harbors and inlets, the blockade stretched from South Carolina to the border of Mexico. After Virginia and North Carolina joined the Confederacy, the blockade was extended to Chesapeake Bay.

In the beginning the blockade was ineffective. The U.S. Navy had fewer than 60 ships to cover the entire coast—and not all of them were even up to the task. "Old Abe blockaded our port," wrote a Charleston resident. "A nice blockade indeed! On the second day a British ship...ran the gauntlet with a snug freight of $30,000." In the months ahead, the Union Navy steadily increased the size and strength of its forces. Although vast amounts of arms, food, and clothing continued to slip through the federal ring aboard sleek, fast "blockade runners," the volume of goods was never enough to bolster the sagging Confederate economy.

Built for speed and endurance, sleek vessels like the ones pictured here were used to penetrate the Union naval blockade of the Southern coastline.

This sleek, dual-stack sidewheeler served the Confederacy as a blockade runner under the name CSS Robert E. Lee. *The game of cat and mouse on the high seas could be very profitable for the blockade runners who managed to elude their guards. A successful captain could make as much as $5,000 on a single trip.*

To assist in financing the war, Congress passed an act on August 5, 1861, authorizing the issue of millions of dollars in three-year treasury notes with an interest rate of 7.3 percent. The interest rate of 7.3 percent was chosen out of convenience, since it amounted to an even 2 cents per day on a $100 note. The U.S. government accrued a total debt of more than $2.5 billion during the course of the war.

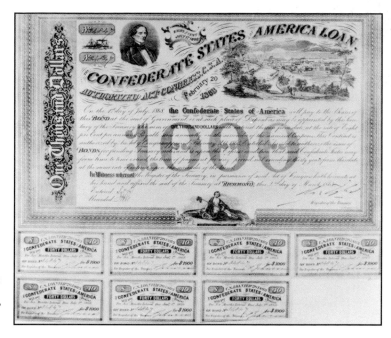

tor and close friend of the President. This fiasco spurred the creation of Congress's Committee on the Conduct of the War, which scrutinized all Union military operations thereafter.

Not all dispatches from Union battlefronts were filled with grim news, however. In mountainous northwestern Virginia, a pro-Union stronghold, federal forces under overall control of Major General George B. McClellan won battles at Philippi, Rich Mountain, Carrick's Ford, and Cheat Mountain. Though small in scale, the string of victories secured control of the region for the North. They also propelled McClellan into the national spotlight.

Clearly, this conflict would not be the casual skirmish each side had expected. Lincoln was serious about keeping the Union together, and the Confederate states were equally serious about leaving. The Civil War would not be over until one side had triumphed and the other had been vanquished.

This $1,000 bond was issued by the Confederate government in 1863. The sale of bonds was brisk at the start of the war and amounted to about $15 million by the end of 1861. As money became tighter throughout the South, bond sales drastically decreased.

A portrait of President Lincoln's first secretary of the treasury, Salmon P. Chase, adorns the first one-dollar paper bill issued.

Unsupported by gold and with few printing restrictions, paper money flowed from national, state, and local presses. Banks, railroads, and private businesses often issued their own currency.

MAY 10
Union militia in St. Louis surround and capture Camp Jackson, the headquarters of pro-Southern militia. Mob violence also strikes the city.

MAY 13
Great Britain declares its neutrality but recognizes the Confederacy as a belligerent.

The U.S. Naval Academy reopens classes in Newport, Rhode Island, after being moved from Annapolis, Maryland.

The balloon Intrepid, pictured here being inflated, was one of seven military observation balloons approved by the U.S. government in August 1861. Aeronaut Thaddeus Lowe commanded the fledgling balloon corps until May 1863, when Lowe resigned due to lack of support from military leaders.

The 11 seceding states that joined together as the Confederate States of America are shown here in gray. The border states of Delaware, Maryland, Kentucky, and Missouri, shown in yellow, were all slave states that remained in the Union, partially as a result of occupying U.S. forces. The western territories remained under Union control. It would not be long before the northwestern section of Virginia would secede from the state to rejoin the Union.

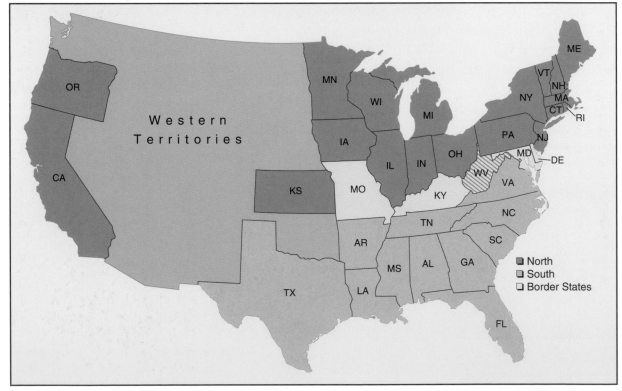

Union General Benjamin Butler and his troops arrive in Baltimore to begin federal occupation of the city.

MAY 20
North Carolina secedes from the Union.

Kentucky proclaims its neutrality in the Civil War.

Federal marshals raid telegraph offices across the North in an attempt to weed out spies, confiscating files of messages sent.

This cartoon shows Jefferson Davis attempting to sneak out of the Union carrying the armaments of Fort Sumter with him. Uncle Sam is in the doorway asking Davis where he is going with federal property. As this cartoon illustrates, the South relied heavily on weapons and equipment seized from the United States to supply its own armed forces.

Below: *Dubbed "Little Aleck" because of his physical stature, Alexander H. Stephens advocated states' rights and slavery, but he was opposed to secession. He predicted an American civil war would be "the bloodiest in history." As vice president of the Confederacy, he clashed with President Davis over many issues. Stephens spent most of his time away from Richmond. Arrested and imprisoned at war's end, Stephens was soon released and later served Georgia in Congress and as governor.*

President and Mrs. Jefferson Davis greet guests at a reception in Richmond. This engraving centers on Varina Howell Davis, the lovely and charming wife who was Davis's best friend and confidant.

Above: *Born in the West Indies of English and Jewish parents, Judah P. Benjamin shook off anti-Semitic brands to serve the Confederacy as attorney general, secretary of war, and secretary of state. Affable, with an affection for good living, this wealthy lawyer and former U.S. senator from Louisiana was referred to as the brains of Davis's cabinet. The Confederate president called Benjamin "a master of law, and the most accomplished statesman I have ever known."*

Arlington, Virginia, across the Potomac River from Washington, D.C., was the family home of Martha Washington's grandson, George Washington Parke Custis. Custis's daughter, Mary Anna, married Robert E. Lee. Mary inherited the estate after the death of her parents, and the Lees made it their home. With the outbreak of war, Union General Irvin McDowell crossed the river and occupied the area, using the mansion as his headquarters. The Lees relocated to Richmond.

The Confederate Congress votes to move the capital to Richmond, Virginia.

MAY 24
Union troops occupy Alexandria, Virginia. Colonel Elmer Ellsworth of the 11th New York Infantry is killed and is quickly regarded as the North's first martyr.

Union General Benjamin Butler declares that escaped slaves would be treated as "contraband of war."

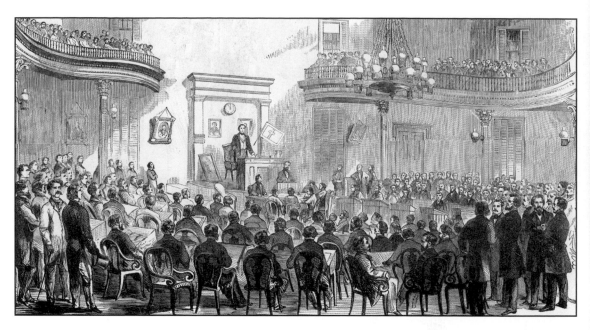

This woodcut shows delegates from the seceded states in open session in Montgomery, Alabama. Howell Cobb was elected president of the convention, but he soon left politics to serve as colonel of the 16th Georgia Infantry. He was later promoted to brigadier and then major general and commanded the District of Georgia and Florida.

The "White House of the Confederacy" was President Davis's residence. The Confederate Congress leased the Brockenbrough House at the corner of Clay and 12th streets in Richmond, Virginia, for an executive mansion. Although Davis, a tireless worker, had an office in the Virginia State Capitol, he also had a small private office on the second floor of this house.

Benjamin Harvey Hill was a Georgia lawyer who changed his political affiliations as the situation warranted. He was a member of both sessions of the Confederate Congress, serving as a senator and chairperson of the Judiciary Committee. Generally, he was one of President Davis's strongest supporters.

MAY 29
Secretary of War Simon Cameron authorizes Dorothea Dix to establish military hospitals.

MAY 31
The U.S. Postal Service ceases service to the South.

JUNE 3
The Battle of Philippi is fought in western Virginia.

Senator Stephen A. Douglas of Illinois dies in Chicago.

Napoleonic Tactics

In the summer of 1856, Major Thomas J. Jackson fulfilled a longtime dream. The man who would later earn fame as "Stonewall" in the Confederate Army toured Britain and much of Europe. He took special interest in the great battleground of Waterloo. "His study of Napoleon and Wellington had been so thorough," one historian wrote, "that French officers with whom he conversed were often astonished."

Jackson, like many other ranking officers in the Union and Confederate Armies, had been well versed in the tactics and feats of Napoleon Bonaparte. Napoleonic principles of rapid marches and maneuvers and the value of exploiting geography dominated military education of the era. Union General in Chief Winfield Scott's strategy

Napoleon Bonaparte

to defeat the South, nicknamed "The Anaconda Plan," adopted a classic Napoleonic concept: to surround, divide, and conquer an enemy. Some officers, such as Confederate General P.G.T. Beauregard and Union Major General George B. McClellan, even emulated Napoleon in posture and style, if not always on the battlefield.

The end of the Civil War foreshadowed an end to Napoleonic tactics that called for bold frontal attacks by massed formations. Development of modern weapons such as long-range rifled muskets and artillery made such practices obsolete. Wrote one Confederate officer after witnessing a particularly deadly assault late in the war, "This is not war but murder."

William L. Yancey was an Alabama politician who advocated extreme Southern nationalism. His faction of the Democratic party nominated John C. Breckinridge as a presidential candidate in 1860. As a member of the Confederate Congress, Yancey fought against Davis, calling him a "conceited, wrong-headed, wranglesome, and obstinate" traitor.

A secret organization formed in 1854, the Knights of the Golden Circle supported pro-Southern interests and promoted conquest of Mexico, the Caribbean, and parts of Central America to extend slavery. Founded by Virginia-born Cincinnati doctor George Bickley, the "Circle" peaked in 1860 with members scattered from New York to California, though never in large numbers. With mounting Union victories during the Civil War, the organization lost appeal and ceased to exist after the conflict.

Confederate Vice President Alexander Stephens bluntly explained the conflict on March 21. Slavery "was the immediate cause of the late rupture and present revolution." He claimed the Founders' expectation that slavery would be short-lived "rested upon the assumption of the equality of races. This was an error. . . . Our new government is founded upon exactly the opposite idea; its foundations are laid, its cornerstone rests upon the great truth, that the negro is not equal to the white man; that slavery—subordination to the superior race—is his natural and normal condition."

Above: *German-born Christopher Memminger faced daunting odds when Davis appointed him secretary of the treasury in February 1861. He struggled the next three years to finance the Confederacy, confronting stiff opposition from inside and outside the government whenever he attempted to establish credit, enact taxes, and control the currency. Unable to stabilize the Southern economy, Memminger resigned "under a cloud of hot shot poured in from every point of the compass," a journalist wrote.*

Below: *Political necessity trumped personal integrity when Simon Cameron was appointed secretary of war by Lincoln. A powerful party boss in Pennsylvania politics, Cameron garnered his Cabinet post by swinging the Keystone State to Lincoln in the 1860 presidential election. Cameron's lack of expertise and notorious corruption embarrassed Lincoln. "An honest politician," Cameron is quoted, "is one who, when . . . bought, will stay bought." In January 1862, Lincoln accepted Cameron's resignation and named him minister to Russia.*

Above: *Salmon Portland Chase, a stately, refined man, served as U.S. senator and then governor of Ohio before being selected secretary of the treasury by President Lincoln. Chase's ambition to be president often led him into conflict with Lincoln and others in the administration. In 1864, Chase resigned as treasury secretary. Lincoln, however, valued Chase's abilities and soon appointed him Chief Justice, of the U.S. Supreme Court, a post he held until his death in 1873.*

Below: *Suffering from dropsy, vertigo, and obesity, Winfield Scott was not up to the task of crushing the rebellion. However, the plan he devised before his retirement in November 1861, calling for the blockade of Confederate ports and the control of the Mississippi River, contributed to the federal success.*

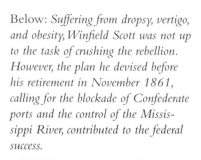

Cadets of the West Point class of 1862 relax for the camera. The young man standing to the left is Ranald Mackenzie, who would rise to the rank of general within three years of graduation and go on to greater fame fighting American Indians. Ulysses Grant stated in his memoirs, "I regarded Mackenzie as the most promising young officer in the army."

JUNE 8
The U.S. Sanitary Commission is established.

JUNE 10
Troops engage in the Battle of Big Bethel in Virginia.

Napoleon III declares French neutrality.

JUNE 11
A pro-Union government is organized in western Virginia.

Marcellus N. Moorman's resplendent uniform as a member of the Virginia Military Institute (VMI) class of 1856 is quite different from the more practical garb he would wear later as a member of a Virginia artillery unit.

Irish and German immigrants enlist on the Battery in New York. More than 500,000 foreign-born soldiers served during the Civil War, mostly for the Union. The majority of them welcomed the chance to show patriotism for their adopted nation. But prejudice against immigrants often obscured their performance in battle.

A grandnephew of Patrick Henry, General Joseph E. Johnston was the highest-ranking staff officer when he resigned from the U.S. Army to cast his lot with the Confederacy. Though he was a stern disciplinarian, his soldiers affectionately called him "Uncle Joe." Wounded at the Battle of Fair Oaks, he relinquished his command to Robert E. Lee. After his recovery, Johnston went on to command several armies in the Western Theater before surrendering on April 26, 1865.

Fife and drums appeal for Confederate recruits in this 1861 woodcut. Scenes like this were common early in the war. As military losses increased, furor to join dramatically dropped. The Davis government was forced to enact several unpopular draft laws. "From one end of the Confederacy to the other," complained Superintendent of Conscription John S. Preston, "every constituted authority, every officer, every man and woman is engaged in opposing the enrolling officer."

JUNE 15
Union troops occupy Jefferson City, Missouri.

JUNE 17
Troops fight at Boonville, Missouri, leading to a Union victory.

JUNE 20
Francis H. Pierpont is named the provisional governor of western Virginia.

Weapons of War

Soon after the war began, a Wisconsin infantry regiment was armed with "Dresden rifles," cumbersome weapons that were nearly obsolete in 1861. Federal government agents had purchased nearly 30,000 of the antiques from the Dresden Arsenal in Saxony. They were "miserable old things," lamented a Union recruit, "that . . . do about as much execution to the shooter as the shootee."

This was a common reaction from soldiers in both armies to the abundant supply of foreign-made guns issued during the first half of the war. When the conflict erupted, demand for weapons of all kinds exceeded supplies then available in federal arsenals, many of which were located below the Mason-Dixon Line and captured by Confederate forces.

Many of the more than half a million weapons acquired overseas by Union buyers were outmoded castoffs from European armies. Soldiers equipped with these imported arms derisively labeled them "mules" and "pumpkin slingers." A young soldier

These men of the 7th Illinois Infantry are photographed with Henry repeating rifles, one of the most advanced weapons of their time. Soldiers would have had to obtain these rifles at their own expense.

The Springfield rifle was the most widely used firearm during the war. Its rifled bore, interchangeable parts, and conical ammunition set it apart from guns used in earlier conflicts.

from Illinois called his Belgian rifle the "poorest excuse for a gun I ever saw."

Out of similar necessity, many Confederate soldiers were forced to rely on old smoothbore and flintlock muskets from an earlier era as well as shotguns and other types of sporting weapons. As war drew near, a Southern orator boasted, "We can whip the Yankees with popguns." The South would have to work feverishly to keep more than "popguns" in the hands of its soldiers.

Brigadier General Josiah Gorgas, an innovator who provided superior leadership, guided Southern munitions industries to overcome many shortcomings by early 1864. "Where three years ago we were not making a gun, pistol nor a saber, no shot nor shell," he claimed, "we now make all these in quantities to meet the demands of our large armies."

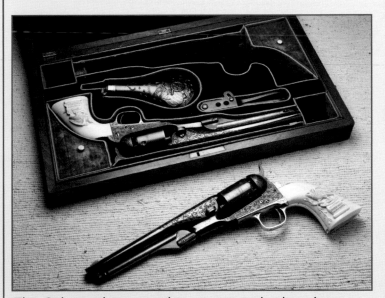

The Colt revolver was the most popular handgun used by Federals during the war. This is the army .44-caliber model. A six-shot percussion revolver, it weighed more than two pounds and was usually carried in a holster.

Civil War officers, no matter what branch of service, still carried swords for both formal affairs and field use. These blades are typical of those carried during the conflict by foot officers. Their blades are generally straight; those used by mounted troops had more of a curve.

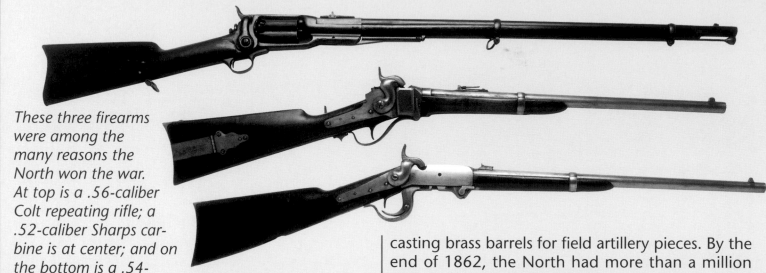

These three firearms were among the many reasons the North won the war. At top is a .56-caliber Colt repeating rifle; a .52-caliber Sharps carbine is at center; and on the bottom is a .54-caliber Burnside carbine, invented before the war by future General Ambrose Burnside. Weapons such as these provided their users with more firepower than opponents, who fired the standard single-shot rifled muskets of the day.

Northern industry began to convert to weapons production early in the war. The Grover and Baker Company in Roxbury, Massachusetts, for example, turned from producing sewing machines to making rifles. And the Revere Copper Company was soon casting brass barrels for field artillery pieces. By the end of 1862, the North had more than a million rifles and pistols in production.

Northern munitions industries grew in size and output as the war progressed but were guided by more conservative military leaders. The most vocal among them was Brigadier General James W. Ripley, the Army's chief of ordnance throughout most of the war. In his late 60s, a relic of service under Andrew Jackson, Ripley was a stickler for red tape and "old army" regulations. He abhorred innovation and characterized new weapons such as the Sharps breech-loading carbine and the 15-shot Henry and 7-shot Spencer repeating rifles as "newfangled gimracks." Consequently, such technologically advanced arms were not purchased in quantities sufficient enough to impact the outcome of the war.

The basic small arm in both Northern and Southern armies was the single-shot rifled musket. These muzzle-loaded shoulder arms fired a conical-shape slug called a "minié ball." Accurate at 500 yards and still deadly at 1,000, rifles were responsible for inflicting 90 percent of all battle wounds. The two most popular rifled muskets were the .57-caliber Enfield, manufactured in Britain, and the .58-caliber American-made Springfield. "We have not got the

Foot soldiers carried cartridge boxes and percussion cap pouches in order to fire their weapons. The cartridge box in this photograph is typical of the period. Each could hold 40 rounds of ammunition, even more if the soldier discarded the two tin inserts and crammed additional rounds into the box. The percussion pouch at top right held the caps needed to spark the black powder in each weapon.

Soldiers carried a wide array of revolvers, pistols, and derringers during the war. Shown here are just a few of the myriad of such weapons available. Derringers were often bought by private soldiers for added fire-power early in the war. However, owing to accidents in camp, the high command quickly prohibited them.

The revolver at top right is the .44-caliber Colt, widely used by both sides. Revolvers of the period had to be loaded by hand, using either wrapped cartridges or loose powder and lead bullets. After firing all six shots, the user either had to reload or pop in an extra preloaded cylinder. Also seen here are two smaller pistols, a powder flask, a box of cartridges, and a few other period artifacts.

enfield rifles," a New Hampshire recruit wrote home in 1861, "but the spring field they are just as good."

About 20 types of handguns were manufactured during the war. They were a principal weapon of officers and regular cavalry in both armies. Over 40 percent of the revolvers supplied to the federal government came from a single manufacturer—Samuel Colt's factory in Hartford, Connecticut, the world's largest privately owned armory.

Artillery backed up small arms on the battlefield and played a pivotal role in many engagements. Like the smaller weapons, cannons came in a wide variety of types and sizes and were usually named for their inventor or maker. Their presence on a battleground was dictated by their use. Against infantry formations the two most popular field guns were the 12-pounder "Napoleon" smooth-bore and the rifled 10-pounder Parrott. With ranges up to 1,500 and 2,000 yards, respectively, they were capable of firing solid or scattershot with deadly effect. "A battery of artillery," wrote Union General William T. Sherman, "is worth a thousand muskets."

For sheer spectacle, edged weapons attracted attention. Contrary to popular belief, they were little used in combat and inflicted few casualties. Union records show out of about 250,000 wounds treated in military hospitals during the war, only 922 were inflicted by bayonets or sabers.

Shown here are three more styles of swords carried by foot officers during the war. The blade in the center is a staff officer's sword, easily identified by its thin blade, which was not designed for combat. After the war, the formal Grand Army of the Republic sword was modeled after this variety.

Jay Cooke

Jay Cooke bought himself an island in 1864. It was a tranquil place named Gibraltar, surrounded by the waters of Lake Erie and not far from his boyhood home in Sandusky, Ohio. A devoted family man, Cooke visited the island with his wife and children as often as he could to escape the stresses and strains of the outside world. "Our days here are indeed days of pleasantness," he wrote, "& all our paths are peaceful." An avid freshwater fisher, Cooke had a talent for hooking Lake Erie black bass. This man of peace also had a talent for finances and was largely responsible for the Union's ability to make war.

Cooke was born on August 10, 1821. His father, a lawyer and politician, had moved his family to the Ohio frontier. An ambitious youth, Cooke quit school at age 14 to clerk at a store in Sandusky. After some time in St. Louis, he eventually moved to Philadelphia, where he found his niche in the banking business. By 1861 he had formed a partnership, Jay Cooke & Company, that ultimately emerged as one of the most respected banking houses in the country.

Through his father and his brother, Henry David Cooke, Jay Cooke associated with Salmon P.

Financier Jay Cooke (1821–1905) worked with Secretary of the Treasury Salmon Chase in 1861, when the federal government had an $80 million deficit, on a plan to sell government bonds on commission. His agency sold more than $1 billion in bonds. Some consider his company's bond sales to have contributed as much to the Union's success in the war as any victory in battle.

Chase, Lincoln's treasury secretary and the former governor of Ohio. Staggered by the Union defeat at the First Battle of Bull Run in July 1861, Chase struggled with ways to pay for a long and costly war. His relationship with Cooke provided the answer.

The financier opened an office in Washington early in 1862 and became a treasury agent, conducting an aggressive campaign to sell bonds throughout the nation and across all levels of society. Within a few months, using extensive advertising and establishing a network of agents throughout the country, Cooke and his organization sold $850 million worth of bonds. By the end of the war, that number rose to more than a billion dollars' worth. These generous funds paid for the Union armies to remain in the field.

But success eluded Cooke in the years after the war. His company continued to market treasury bonds, but bad investments connected to the construction of the Northern Pacific Railroad collapsed his banking firm and helped trigger the Panic of 1873. Cooke lost his fortune in the process, but shrewd investment in the silver-mining industry allowed him to regain it before his death in 1905.

JUNE 23
Confederates begin construction of the ironclad CSS *Virginia*.

JUNE 30
The commerce raider CSS *Sumter* passes through the Union blockade at the mouth of the Mississippi and escapes to sea.

JULY 4
President Lincoln, speaking to Congress on Independence Day, reiterates his intention to keep the Union together. He calls for another 400,000 volunteers.

Titled "The Awkward Squad," this woodcut illustrates problems Civil War drill instructors faced turning raw recruits into soldiers. The task was frequently made more difficult from challenges posed by the high percentage of illiterate and immigrant volunteers. "With all their awkwardness and slowness at becoming acquainted with a soldier's duties," one veteran observed, "the recruits of the earlier years in time of need behaved manfully." More than three million men served North and South.

Noted Southern artist A. J. Volck penned this scene of Southern women at a home industry making clothing for the soldiers. Since the South had comparatively few manufacturing establishments, it had to rely on the generosity and patriotism of its women to help feed and clothe its armies.

In February 1861, two months before the war started, Charleston photographer George S. Cook took his camera to Fort Sumter and persuaded the officers of the garrison to pose for him. Shown here is Kentucky-born Major Robert Anderson, commander of the fort.

The CSS Sumter ran the Union blockade into the Gulf of Mexico. Commanded by Raphael Semmes, who was instructed "to do the enemy's commerce the greatest injury in the shortest time," the Sumter captured or destroyed 18 Union vessels in six months. Mechanical trouble forced its sale to a British buyer in December 1862.

JULY 11
The Battle of Rich Mountain is fought in western Virginia.

JULY 13
Troops meet at the Battle of Carrick's Ford in western Virginia.

JULY 21
The First Battle of Bull Run is fought near Manassas, Virginia. Union forces are surprised by the resistance they meet.

The locomotive General Haupt, *pictured here, was named in honor of Briga-dier General Herman Haupt. In 1864 and 1865, the Union's 365 engines and more than 4,000 cars transported more than five million tons of military supplies.*

Sprawling on the banks of the James River in Richmond, Virginia, the Tredegar Iron Works was a marvel of its time. Directed by West Point graduate Joseph R. Anderson, it was the largest factory in the South, producing cannons, armor plating, railroad equipment, and munitions of all kinds. "The capacity of the establishment is almost without limit," a Southern editor boasted. "It seems like a special providence that it exists."

Garbed in overcoats, these three Confederate privates of the 3rd Georgia Infantry appear ready for cold weather. Winter conditions generally limited active campaigning. Both Union and Confederate armies used the time to rest, regroup, and reequip themselves. The lucky soldier might also be granted a furlough to visit home during this season.

This Northern volunteer of 1861 displays a spit-and-polish militia uniform that was soon replaced with standard Union blue. For most recruits, the novelty of military life soon wore off, too.

JULY 25
The Crittenden Resolution, which defines the purpose of the war as the preservation of the Union rather than the abolition of slavery, passes Congress.

JULY 27
Major General George B. McClellan assumes command of the Union troops in Washington, D.C. These soldiers will later be called the Army of the Potomac.

JULY 31
Hamilton R. Gamble, a pro-Unionist, is elected governor of Missouri by state convention.

New Military Technology

On an evening in mid-August 1863, President Lincoln took time from his busy schedule managing the war to test fire a new weapon. He stepped eagerly from his office in the White House to the grounds of the Treasury building nearby. John Hay, his personal secretary, and Christopher Spencer, the weapon's inventor, accompanied the anxious President. For an hour, the three men put the gun to the test, shooting at a small wooden target. "My shooting was the most lamentably bad," Hay admitted. "The president made some pretty good shots."

The weapon was Spencer's repeating rifle. "A wonderful gun," Hay judged, "loading with absolute simplicity and ease with seven balls & firing the whole...in less than half a minute." The President liked the firearm and advocated its use.

By 1864, the Spencer carbine was the standard arm of the federal cavalry. It was only one link in a chain of military innovations fostered by new technology during the Civil War. And Lincoln, himself an inventor holding the patent for a device that refloated boats that had run aground, was always receptive to any gadgetry that might help shorten the war. The President encouraged the use of observation balloons, approved the purchase of experimental machine guns, and delighted in observing the test firing of improved artillery. Newly developed artillery used against fortifications and other fixed positions included larger Parrott guns, such as the 24-pounder and 32-pounder. Among the most powerful artillery pieces of the war was a Union heavy mortar capable of firing a 200-pound ball more than two miles.

The Civil War was the staging ground for many other firsts in military technology. Among the more significant were the military use of railroads and portable telegraphs, the development of ironclad warships and submarines, and the wide-scale systematic and organized medical care and treatment provided for battlefield casualties. Many of these military innovations were carried over into the postwar years and even continue to this day. "I hold that while man exists," Lincoln declared in a speech he delivered on the eve of the Civil War, "it is his duty to improve."

This mighty cannon, called "Whistling Dick" because of the distinctive sound of its missiles, was mounted in Confederate batteries at Vicksburg. It was a product of the Tredegar Iron Works.

Below: *To Abraham Lincoln, Elmer Ellsworth was "the greatest little man I ever met." This former apprentice in Lincoln's law office gained fame before the war by leading a championship military drill team, the U.S. Zouave Cadets. When hostilities erupted, Ellsworth raised a regiment largely composed of tough New York City firefighters. "I want men who can go into a fight now," he declared on April 17. Ellsworth led his regiment toward Washington 12 days later.*

This Confederate soldier is well equipped for the photographer, but as the war dragged on, Southern armies suffered many shortages. Johnny Rebs like him endured the hardships of camp and the horrors of battle for $11 per month. Of the one million men who served in the Confederate military, roughly two out of every ten would never return home. Late in life one Confederate veteran observed, "Some good to the world must come from such sacrifice."

Above: *A young victim of the war, Confederate Private Edwin Francis Jemison of Louisiana was only 17 years old when he was killed at the Battle of Malvern Hill in July 1862.*

To some the Marshall House in Alexandria, Virginia, was considered a second-class hotel, but to proprietor James Jackson it was home. A staunch Southerner, Jackson defiantly hoisted a huge Confederate flag to the roof of the building, which led to his deadly encounter with Union Colonel Elmer Ellsworth. Following the tragic incident, the Marshall House attracted thousands of souvenir hunters. Within weeks, "The stairs on which Ellsworth was shot had been taken away piecemeal. . . . Walls broken . . . carpets carried off. . . flag staf [sic] . . . demolished."

AUGUST 1
Brazil recognizes the Confederacy as a belligerent nation.

AUGUST 5
Lincoln signs the first national income tax to aid the war effort.

AUGUST 10
Confederates win the Battle of Wilson's Creek in Missouri.

Nestled in a gap of South Mountain where the Shenandoah and Potomac rivers meet, Harpers Ferry was home to a thriving federal arsenal and armory for more than 60 years before civil war struck. Made famous by John Brown's raid, the federal installation was hit by violence again when it was torched to keep it from falling into Confederate hands. It was "too late to extinguish the flames," a rebel officer wrote. "Nearly twenty thousand rifles and pistols were destroyed."

Death stalked the halls of the Marshall House in Alexandria, Virginia, early on May 24, 1861. After tearing down a Confederate flag from the rooftop, Union Colonel Elmer Ellsworth was shotgunned by irate innkeeper James Jackson. Jackson in turn was shot and bayoneted by Private Francis Brownell. The North was grief stricken by the popular Ellsworth's death and considered him "the first martyr of the war." Likewise, Jackson became a martyr to the South. Brownell received the Medal of Honor for his actions.

Pierre Gustave Toutant Beauregard earned renown early in the war by directing Confederate victories at Fort Sumter and the First Battle of Bull Run. His reputation faded soon after his defeat at the Battle of Shiloh in April 1862. He went on to direct the defense of Charleston, South Carolina, and finished the war in command of the Department of North Carolina and Southeastern Virginia.

AUGUST 16
Several Northern newspapers, such as *The Brooklyn Eagle* and the *New York Daily News,* are taken to court because of perceived Southern sympathies.

AUGUST 29
Union troops capture Hatteras Inlet, North Carolina.

AUGUST 30
General John C. Fremont, in command of the military's Western Department, proclaims martial law and issues an unauthorized emancipation proclamation.

Photography

By the time of the Battle of Antietam in September 1862, more than 2,000 photographers were listed in the United States. Most of them worked throughout the North, photographing local scenes and soldier portraits. Southern photographers, like George S. Cook, who photographed Fort Sumter after its surrender, and Charles Rees, who took wartime photos around the Confederate capital of Richmond, were most active early in the war. Later, supplies necessary for Confederate photographers to ply their trade were cut off by the blockade. A select few photographers followed in the wake of the armies to make a close-up record of the war.

Photographers of that era could not record battle action because of the long exposure times—5 to 15 seconds—needed to capture scenes on a chemically treated glass plate. Instead, they photographed the results of battles and the people and places touched by the conflict. Their photographs were as different as the people who took them.

Mathew Brady, whose name is synonymous with Civil War photography, was already a famous photographer when the war started. He had successful studios in New York City and Washington, D.C. Because his eyesight was failing during the war, Brady relied on his assistants to take photographs.

Captain Andrew J. Russell was the Union Army's only official photographer. He followed the U.S. Military Railroad Construction Corps and photographed scenes of fortifications, bridges, and battle-damaged buildings. George Barnard won fame for his panoramic vistas of war-scarred landscapes and cities that he took during General Sherman's campaign through Georgia and the Carolinas.

Brady sent Alexander Gardner and James Gibson to Sharpsburg. The photographs they made there were among the first ever taken of war dead—and the first ever viewed by the American public. A month after the battle, Brady displayed these images in his New York gallery, under the title "The Dead of Antietam." The public flocked to view

them. "There is a terrible fascination...that draws one near these pictures," a reporter for *The New York Times* wrote, "and makes him loth to leave them."

Oliver Wendell Holmes, whose son was wounded in the battle, wrote about the Antietam photographs. "It was so nearly like visiting the battlefield," he wrote, "that all the emotions excited by the actual sight of the...sordid scene...came back....What a repulsive, brutal, sickening, hideous thing it is, this dashing together of two frantic mobs to which we give the name of armies."

Mathew B. Brady was a well-known photographer before the war, but his genius for the new art form made his the first name in Civil War photography. As the war progressed, however, Brady passed more and more of the details to assistants, and after 1862, he himself did not take many images.

Hampton, Virginia, a den of pirates during the Colonial era, was home to a nearby seaport and fort. The town became home to many free blacks before the Civil War. Massive Fort Monroe grew nearby to protect the Hampton Roads harbor. Held by the Union throughout the war, Fort Monroe became a staging area for federal troops to advance against Richmond. Outnumbered Confederate forces torched Hampton the night of August 7, 1861, before retreating inland.

Union troops under Colonel Louis Blenker brought up the rear in the retreat from Bull Run, collecting what had been abandoned earlier in the rout. The Confederates were not advancing, so Blenker's rear guard had the luxury of taking their time. Previously, in a case of mistaken identity, Confederates in blue were taken for friendly troops and allowed to approach federal batteries from behind and open fire. One witness recalled, "I never saw. . . destruction so complete."

SEPTEMBER 3
Confederate troops encroach upon Kentucky soil, ending the state's neutrality.

SEPTEMBER 6
General Ulysses S. Grant moves his troops in to occupy Paducah, Kentucky.

SEPTEMBER 10
The Battle of Carnifex Ferry takes place in western Virginia.

Joining scores of curious civilians, New York Representative Alfred Ely followed the Union Army into Virginia on July 21, 1861. Like the others, he expected to see a Northern victory near Manassas. Instead, Ely witnessed the stunning defeat and utter rout of McDowell's federal army. And all the hapless member of Congress saw for the next six months was the inside of a rebel prison after being captured by jubilant Confederate troops near the battlefield.

Poet Walt Whitman wrote of this bridge Monday, July 22, 1861, after the Union disaster at the First Battle of Bull Run: "regiments, swarming wagons, artillery... now recoiling back, pouring over the Long Bridge." Nearly a mile in length and the width of three carriages, Long Bridge spanned the Potomac River between Washington, D.C., and Confederate Virginia. Lincoln kept his eye on it from a White House window. The Army guarded it with cannons. But the enemy never came.

These are the ruins of the Stone Bridge over Bull Run, where the federal retreat became a rout. Beauregard failed to follow up on this great victory of the South.

General Albert S. Johnston is named to command the Confederate forces in Tennessee, Kentucky, Arkansas, and Missouri.

SEPTEMBER 11
President Lincoln orders General Fremont to rescind his order of emancipation in Missouri.

SEPTEMBER 12
The federal government orders alleged disloyal members of the Maryland legislature to be arrested.

Newspaper Suppression

On the night of March 5, 1863, soldiers from the 2nd Ohio Cavalry, camped outside of Columbus, Ohio, attacked the office of a local newspaper. The *Crisis* had printed antiarmy stories denigrating Ohio soldiers. Local police were "persuaded" to remain aloof from the fray until the angry troopers exacted their revenge.

In June of that year, Union General Ambrose Burnside shut down the *Chicago Times* for "repeated expression of disloyal and incendiary sentiments." This paper had become anti-Lincoln, antiblack, and antiwar. In fact, newspaper editors across the North could be targeted if the content of their papers contained content unpopular with the military or civilian leaders or with the public at large. It was not uncommon for editors to be tarred and feathered or run out of town.

President Lincoln, although an advocate of free speech, at times allowed the suppression of newspapers when a paper either willingly misrepresented government policy or became rabidly antigovernment. The President also had the power to arrest editors after the writ of habeas corpus was suspended.

Newspaper editors anywhere in the country were targets of mob action if their papers printed material contrary to local opinion. This illustration from Frank Leslie's Illustrated Newspaper *depicts a Northern editor being tarred and feathered for printing pro-Southern sentiments. Several times during the war, newspaper offices were ransacked and editors thrown out of town.*

Washington, D.C., was all but defenseless in the wake of the Union debacle at the First Battle of Bull Run. Closely supervised by its new commander in chief, Major General George B. McClellan, the Union Army constructed a "girdle of forts, earthworks, and camps" completely around the beleaguered city. Fort Richardson, shown here crowded with heavy cannons, stood atop the highest point in the chain of fortifications. Its barracks were noted for "beauty and comfort."

A "dingy, crumbling structure" with a bewildering maze of dust-choked rooms, this derelict building in Washington, D.C., was nearly 50 years old when the Civil War gave it new life as Old Capitol Prison. Erected during the War of 1812 to provide Congress with a place to meet after the British burned the existing Capitol, the structure was revitalized in 1861. It hosted "captured rebel soldiers, military offenders, and prisoners of the state." Very few managed to escape.

Virginia-born Sterling Price opposed secession as congressperson and governor of Missouri before civil war broke out. Offended by Unionist strong-arm tactics in Missouri, Price sided with the South. As a Confederate general, he led victories at Wilson's Creek and Lexington in 1861. This success earned him a promotion and the esteem of his soldiers, who called Price "Pap." It also drew attention from Union leaders who would make life difficult for Price as the war continued.

Heartened by Confederate victories at Wilson's Creek and Lexington, rebel sympathizers launched a terror campaign to rid Missouri of pro-Northern factions. Union men across the state were killed or driven beyond the borders in a brutal guerrilla war. Afterward, rebel leaders decided to force the men's families away. "The suffering that followed the women and children is indescribable," a historian of the period wrote. The refugees reached federal lines "almost destitute of food . . . and scantily clothed."

SEPTEMBER 12–14
Confederates mount an unsuccessful expedition against Union forces at Cheat Mountain in western Virginia.

SEPTEMBER 12–20
The Siege of Lexington, Missouri, ends in Union surrender.

SEPTEMBER 17
Judah P. Benjamin shifts from Confederate attorney general to secretary of war.

The carefree attitude of these Confederate cannoneers of the famed Washington Artillery of New Orleans belies the heavy action they saw. Fighting under General Bragg in the Army of Tennessee, the company saw 42 of their own killed and 100 wounded during 40 battles and engagements.

Simple chores of everyday life occupied much of a soldier's time in camp. Here a member of the 31st Pennsylvania Volunteers is seen with his family at Camp Slocum near Washington, D.C., late in 1861. Wives and children sometimes joined soldiers, particularly officers, during their winter encampments. However, one infantryman without a wife claimed he mended his trousers "as good as a heap of women would do."

Confederate soldiers of the 9th Mississippi Infantry strike a pose for the camera in their camp at Warrington Navy Yard in Pensacola, Florida, in early 1861. Their ragged outfits and scruffy appearance attracted the pen of a British journalist who called them "great long bearded fellows in flannel shirts and slouch hats, uniformless in all save brightly burnished arms and resolute purpose." They erected brush-covered arbors for shade against the hot Florida sun.

These brightly uniformed Union Zouaves took their fashion inspiration from Zouave regiments in the French military. They are pitching quoits, a game similar to horseshoes. Billy Yank and Johnny Reb found many ways to relieve the boredom and routine of soldiering. Other diversions included playing baseball, checkers, and dominoes, and gambling of all kinds. Minstrel shows were also popular. Writing and receiving mail were among their favorite pastimes. And as one historian noted, "Rebs and Yanks . . . were the 'singing-est' soldiers in American history."

OCTOBER 9
A Confederate attack on Fort Pickens in Pensacola Harbor, Florida, is repelled.

OCTOBER 12
The first Union ironclad, the USS *St. Louis*, is launched at Carondelet, Missouri.

OCTOBER 21
The Battle of Ball's Bluff in Virginia is a disaster for Union troops.

The Soldiers

Like thousands of other young men, 17-year-old Texan Robert Campbell was anxious to join the action when war broke out. "I was in Louisiana at school," he recalled. "The students raised a company and I was honored with the office of Capt." But learning their pupils intended to volunteer, "the faculty...broke the company up."

Campbell finally realized his desire in the spring of 1862. "Perceiving that Lincoln and the Yankee Govt. were determined on coercion—my father cheerfully gave his son to this country's cause." When first clad in his uniform of "rebel grey," Campbell "went around biding friends adieu. It was the proudest day of my life."

From North and South tens of thousands of volunteers like Campbell filled the ranks of the Union and Confederate armies. With only 16,327 officers and enlisted soldiers in the Regular Army when the first shots were fired at Fort Sumter, the conflict was destined to be a true "citizens' war."

Many had belonged to militia units back home. With names like the Cleveland Grays and the Washington Artillery of New Orleans, these local defense units had provided the rudiments of soldiering to some of the volunteers. More often than not, however, these units were an excuse to parade about the village square in gaudy uniforms.

The would-be soldiers were first recruited by each state, while the opposing governments geared themselves to handle the large-scale influx of troops. Early on, civic leaders and other prominent, wealthy citizens often raised and equipped compa-

Turning the thousands of raw recruits into soldiers and fusing them into an efficient army was the first task facing the Union. These smartly marching troops from the 26th New York Regiment had a chance to see intense action during the war.

Items from a typical mess kit include a small pot with lid (left), the top of a canteen with its cork stopper (bottom), eating utensils, a collapsible cup, and the haversack, or ration bag.

nies. Many times these same leaders commanded the units, as well. Other officers were frequently elected by the ranks, where popularity usually counted for more than experience. "Oh! that I could but once have gone to school . . . as a diligent student of the company and battalions drills," wrote a newly elected lieutenant from North Carolina, "learning to give and superintend the execution of commands."

Recruits came from all walks of life, and whole cities of tents and barracks sprouted across the North and South to shelter and train them. "Here was the broad shouldered 'six footer from the backwoods,'" a recruit from Indiana wrote, "swearing he was . . . ready to chaw up any amounts of rebels. Here we found the lawyer, the doctor, the mechanic from his shop, the ploughman from his field, the clerk from the dry goods store who, tired of measuring tape, was anxious to measure his strength with the foeman of his country. All these scattered fragments had to be consolidated . . . and brought to act as one man."

The excitement and enthusiasm for soldiering wore off quickly in camp. Many soon tired of drills to master the use of weapons and the complexities of maneuvers conducted for hours at least twice daily. Uniforms and accoutrements were ill fitting and uncomfortable. Army food varied widely in quality and quantity. Salted pork or beef, hardtack, and coffee or some substitute were common rations. The hard bread was often stale or moldy, and the meat could be even worse. "Yesterday morning was the first time we had to carry our meat," a Union soldier jested, "for the maggots always carried it till then."

Life in camp or on the march was difficult at best. Personal hygiene and sanitation were lax, body lice rampant, and diseases such as malaria, typhoid, and dysentery could reach epidemic proportions. Infectious diseases like mumps and measles proved deadly when soldiers were gathered in great numbers for the first time. "Though we enlisted to fight, bleed and die," a Maine soldier claimed, "nothing happened to us so serious as the measles."

By war's end, twice as many soldiers had died from disease as were killed in action. Many who had survived the war had also paid a stiff price. After serving for three years in the 5th Texas Infantry Regiment, Robert Campbell wrote: "At 2nd Battle of Manassas, I was shot [twice] through the leg—at Chickamauga, through the arm—at Darbytown Va. through the lungs."

Despite its many hardships, life for soldiers in blue and gray was not all bad. When not on the march or performing some other camp duty, they had time for leisure. "Went round mornings and evenings among the men," a journalist wrote, "heard their conversations etc.—the bivouac fires at night, the singing and story telling among the crowded crouching groups." Dice and card games, baseball, roughhousing of all kinds, staging theatrics, or simply writing letters to the folks back home were among favorite pastimes. Receiving mail in return was a great boost to morale. "You can hardly have any idea," a member of the Pennsylvania infantry wrote, "how anxious we poor devils in camp are to hear from those we love."

Female Spies

A slap on his rump awakened Union Brigadier General Edwin H. Stoughton. Startled, he rose to stare into the face of his captor. John Singleton Mosby had led rebel raiders deep behind enemy lines to snatch Stoughton and dozens of his troops from Union headquarters in Fairfax, Virginia. The daring exploit on March 8, 1863, earned Mosby a promotion and launched his career as the Civil War's outstanding partisan leader. The raid also revealed the outstanding contribution of one of the South's heroic female spies.

Antonia Ford, only 25 at the time, had carefully studied Union positions around her Fairfax home and passed this information to Mosby and other Confederate leaders. Later arrested and imprisoned for her activities, Antonia's health suffered during her confinement—she died a few years after the war.

Just 17 when she began to spy for the Confederacy around her home in Martinsburg, Virginia (now West Virginia), Belle Boyd often took great risks to provide intelligence useful to Stonewall Jackson, among others. She was imprisoned several times during the war and afterward enjoyed a lusty career in theater, where she extolled her wartime deeds.

Pauline Cushman was already an actress when she began her clandestine affairs. Her role as a

Celebrated by admirers as "La Belle Rebelle," Isabella "Belle" Boyd was a renowned Confederate spy who began to coax military secrets from Union officers when only a teenager.

Union counterespionage agent in Tennessee won her fame as "the spy of the Cumberland." When her career as an agent was over, she returned to acting and then lectured widely on her exploits.

Another spy for the North was a Southerner in the Confederate capital of Richmond, Virginia. Elizabeth Van Lew despised slavery and did all she could to help the Union. Under the guise of an eccentric known as "Crazy Bet," she assisted Union prisoners and gleaned important intelligence from Confederate authorities who considered her harmless. Union General Ulysses S. Grant found Van Lew particularly useful, claiming she had given him "the most valuable information received from Richmond during the war."

Van Lew's counterpart in the Union capital was Rose O'Neal Greenhow. Well known in Washington society, Greenhow obtained confidential information that helped Confederate leaders prepare for the Union advance against Manassas in July 1861.

Rose O'Neal Greenhow and her daughter appear in a Brady photograph taken after the famous spy was captured.

Sarah Emma Edmonds used both male and female impersonations as a spy. Some of her comrades never knew she was a woman until a reunion in the 1880s.

Union spy Pauline Cushman was caught by Confederates, sentenced to hang, and rescued by advancing Union troops.

Soldiers of both sides whiled away long hours of boredom in a variety of ways. One popular pastime was carving trinkets out of pieces of bone. Shown here are a bone lapel pin and two tie clasps. Private William A. Failor, Company G, 202nd Pennsylvania, produced the clasp on the left.

Federal eagle drums and infantry bugles were the two mainstays of what was termed "field music." Each infantry regiment had fifers and drummers expected to master all 148 calls and tunes of the standard military music text. Before rapid communication by radio and walkie-talkie, these instruments were essential for camp and battlefield contact. A unit's youngest members were often detailed as musicians—127 Union enlistees were only 13, despite the legal age limit of 18.

Whether they beat the morning call to duty or tapped the signal for lights-out at night, the army drum corps played a key role in the daily life of the soldier. Between times the young musicians performed common chores about camp. In battle they put their drums aside to assist with removal and care of the wounded. Nearly 40,000 boys enlisted as musicians in the Union Army during the Civil War.

Soldiers in the Civil War were perhaps the most literate generation of warriors the world had yet seen. To most, the war was the most significant experience of their lives, and many took time to record their observations. Thousands kept pocket diaries, while thousands more sent letters home by the score. Much of their literature has survived, providing a valuable source for reconstructing the daily lives of troops in blue and gray.

OCTOBER 24
The transcontinental telegraph is completed.

People in western Virginia vote to form a new state.

OCTOBER 26
The Pony Express across the western plains is officially discontinued after being in business for 18 months.

NOVEMBER 1
George B. McClellan is named general in chief of Union troops after General Winfield Scott resigns because of his old age.

*"A private soldier's world,"
wrote Edwin Forbes, who
penned this sketch, "does not
extend far beyond . . . his
immediate vicinity of action.
Imagine . . . then how eagerly
he longed for the arrival of the
newspapers." Forbes, who was
a prolific artist/correspondent
for* Frank Leslie's Illustrated
Newspaper, *also noted, "The
sale of popular newspapers in
the army was immense, and
the men who furnished them
made a fortune."*

If the adage is true that an army travels on its
stomach, then the armies of the blue and the
gray covered a good bit of the distance on
hardtack. Otherwise called crackers, army bread,
or hard bread, hardtack was a staple food of
soldiers during the Civil War. A simple flour-
and-water biscuit, hardtack measured approximately three inches by three inches and was a
half inch thick. It was often eaten plain—or
crumbled, boiled, or fried. "Hardtack was not so
bad an article of food, even when traversed by
insects," recalled one veteran. "Eaten in the
dark, no one could tell the difference between it
and hardtack that was untenanted."

*Soldiers often craved religion when faced with death in battle or from
disease. Camp life spawned many religious revivals, but other soldiers
tended to deal with religion more privately. The American Tract Society and
the United States Christian Commission handed out tens of thousands of
Bibles, such as the one shown here, and religious tracts.*

*Soldiers whiled away the off-duty hours when they were stuck in camp by
trying to keep busy. Some of the troops created intriguing works of art. One
soldier painted this spoon to show a man standing guard over the camp. Others
would whittle on whatever pieces of wood and bone they could find.*

NOVEMBER 2
Major General John C. Fremont is
relieved from command in Missouri and replaced by General
David Hunter.

NOVEMBER 6
Jefferson Davis is elected to a
six-year term as Confederate
president.

NOVEMBER 7
A Union expedition captures Port
Royal Sound, South Carolina.

Union troops under General
Ulysses S. Grant attack a Confed-

The James River Terminal was home to the U.S. Military Railroad at City Point, Virginia. An engine house, water tanks, and three locomotives are pictured here. City Point was the site of a huge supply depot to support the Union siege of Petersburg. Each day, 18 trains ran from City Point to the battlefront over a 21-mile-long railroad built especially for that purpose.

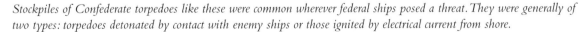

Stockpiles of Confederate torpedoes like these were common wherever federal ships posed a threat. They were generally of two types: torpedoes detonated by contact with enemy ships or those ignited by electrical current from shore.

To care for Confederate wounded in the wake of the First Battle of Bull Run, diminutive Sally Tompkins of Richmond, Virginia, used her personal wealth and family connections to operate a private hospital. To allow her to maintain an official status, President Davis commissioned her a captain in the Army. "But I would not allow my name to be placed upon the pay roll," wrote Tompkins. By war's end she and her staff had treated 1,333 casualties.

erate camp at Belmont, Missouri, but are forced to retreat.

NOVEMBER 8
Confederate commissioners James M. Mason and John Slidell

are seized by the U.S. Navy from the British mail steamer *Trent*.

NOVEMBER 9
Major General Henry W. Halleck is placed in command of Union

troops in Missouri, Arkansas, Illinois, and western Kentucky.

General Don Carlos Buell replaces William T. Sherman in command of federal troops in central and eastern Kentucky.

Soldier Uniforms

Although the North and South have come to be known as blue and gray, respectively, this was not always the case on the battlefield. A wide variety of uniforms characterized the early stages of the war. Union recruits were as likely to wear gray as Confederates were to don blue. Unprepared for a long conflict, the Union Quartermaster Department, responsible for clothing the armies, simply did not have enough uniforms to go around. The United States Regular Army had standardized uniforms, but the vast majority of new recruits wore outfits provided by their individual state or militia organizations.

The cut and color of Confederate uniforms varied widely, which remained the case throughout the war. The Confederacy simply did not have the resources and means to manufacture uniforms in abundance. Although each state was relied upon to clothe its own regiments at first, much of what Southern troops wore was homespun, or outfits of simple design based upon whatever material was handy. As needs demanded, Confederate soldiers stripped the dead of their clothes or concocted uniforms from civilian garb. Coats and pants, dyed with the juice from walnut hulls, gave a distinctive light-brown or butternut color to the homemade outfits.

While in command of the Kentucky State Guard in 1860, General Simon B. Buckner tried to standardize its uniforms. The advent of civil war interfered with his plan, and the general never got further than providing uniforms for the ranking officers. This is a surviving example of the general's unique design, which was copied by other states.

Many federal units clothed themselves in the French-inspired Zouave uniforms, which varied according to the colonel's whims. This image shows three different jackets worn by Zouave regiments. Trousers and headgear also varied from one pattern to another. Many Zouave regiments changed to regulation blue after it became readily apparent that their fancy uniforms attracted hostile fire.

Shown here is a federal cavalry bugler's shell jacket, identified as such by its yellow piping. More often than not, though, musicians wore uniforms just like their comrades rather than purchasing or requisitioning these fancier duds. Mounted troops relied on their buglers for calls rather than on the drums and fifes of foot soldiers.

In the 1850s, William J. Hardee designed this black felt hat as the Army's regulation dress hat. Named after its founder, the Hardee Hat was worn by Union Army regulars and volunteers alike. Some units, such as the famed Iron Brigade, adopted it as their daily cap instead of the usual forage cap.

Captain Alexander Stern of the Rifle Regiment, New York State Militia, wore this dress uniform in the decade before the Civil War. The color gray, based on the West Point cadet uniform, was standard for militia units throughout the United States. When uniformed militia units went to war, they sometimes disconcerted both friend and foe because of the variety of colors worn on each side.

Leather shoes were a staple of army wear. Depending on the contractor and terrain, a pair of shoes could last only a few days or could survive an entire campaign. Shoes were required by the Union Army to be blacked with polish. The pair on the right has heel plates added for better traction.

This Union winter greatcoat was a heavy, woolen overcoat designed to be worn over the regular uniform. Stretching from the neck to below the knees, this garment provided an extra layer of protection from winter chills. When units began to move out of winter camps as the weather warmed and the roads dried off, such winter gear was gathered and sent back to a government warehouse, where it was stored for future use.

For his success at Fort Sumter and the First Battle of Bull Run, General Beauregard was lionized throughout the South early in the war. The uniform coat attributed to Beauregard pictured here would befit his grade as the fifth-ranking general in the Confederacy at the time. Ambitious and vain though he was, one biographer noted that Beauregard was "not disposed to flashing uniform or to caparisoned steed."

The 79th New York Infantry Regiment was nicknamed the "Highlanders" because of the large number of troops of Scottish origin in its ranks. The regiment's early war dress uniform, shown here, included a plaid kilt and a Scottish bonnet.

Soldiers stand in front of a federal kitchen during a winter encampment. Complaints about the quality of the food were common. "I'll bet when I get home I shall have an appetite to eat most anything," observed a volunteer from Vermont. "I have seen the time when I would have been glad to picked the crusts of bread that mother gives to the hogs."

At the height of the bombardment depicted in this 1862 lithograph, the Union fleet pumped up to 24 shells per minute into Confederate defenses at Port Royal, South Carolina. The rebels abandoned their stronghold within five hours. A soldier with the federal landing party noted the effects of the barrage: "Many of the dead were half buried where they fell; guns were dismounted, army wagons smashed. Knapsacks, blankets, and rifles lay in confusion all around."

NOVEMBER 30
Great Britain officially protests the seizure of Mason and Slidell and demands an apology.

DECEMBER 2
The first Union prisoners arrive at Salisbury Prison in North Carolina.

DECEMBER 4
John Breckinridge of Kentucky, former vice president and presidential candidate, is expelled from the U.S. Senate after having joined the Confederate Army.

A Confederate soldier himself, seriously wounded at the Battle of Shiloh, Conrad Wise Chapman captured the drama and poignancy of the Civil War in his art, as seen in this camp scene. Born in Washington, D.C., and schooled in Europe by his artist father, Chapman returned to enlist. Recovered from his wound, Chapman served in Virginia and South Carolina. In Charleston, Chapman often worked under fire to sketch the city's defenses for General Beauregard.

A heavy camp stove such as this iron one was used only in forts, permanent installations, and winter camps. It contains one grate and an attachment for the venting pipe that could be poked through a tent or wooden roof.

Confederate commissioners James M. Mason and John Slidell, on a diplomatic mission to Europe aboard the British mail ship Trent, were seized by the Union warship San Jacinto on November 8 and taken to jail in Boston. The British, furious their ship had been boarded, demanded the diplomats' release. On the brink of war with Great Britain, Secretary of State William Seward disavowed any guilt but stated the Union was willing to free Mason and Slidell, who were released in January 1862.

DECEMBER 9–10
Congress creates the Joint Congressional Committee on the Conduct of the War to investigate the war effort, especially the debacle at Ball's Bluff.

DECEMBER 20
Fighting at Dranesville, Virginia, results in the first Union land victory east of the Alleghenies.

DECEMBER 27
The U.S. government agrees to release Mason and Slidell and issues an unapologetic statement to the British government.

1862

THE YEAR OF BATTLES

UNION AND CONFEDERATE LEADERS REALIZE THERE IS NO END IN SIGHT

The winter of 1862 slowed the conflict considerably. There were some skirmishes, but nothing that threatened to shift the balance of power. President Lincoln's new general in chief of Union troops, George B. McClellan, seemed no more eager to engage the enemy than Winfield Scott had been. He argued with Lincoln over the best way to take the war to the Confederates. Lincoln was under fire from a Congress that wanted to see conclusive action, and he supported an

Though they were the most famous ships in the Civil War, no photographs have ever been found showing the complete profiles of either the CSS Virginia or the USS Monitor. This postwar lithograph accurately depicts the two pounding at each other from a distance of only yards.

overland campaign south from the Potomac to Richmond. McClellan, on the other hand, promoted a sea landing on the Virginia coast and a march up the peninsula between the James and York rivers toward the Confederate capital. Lincoln was getting frustrated. Tired of being ignored, he issued the remarkable General War Order No. 1. This gave all his generals on all fronts one month to advance their armies and navies. With this order, Lincoln effectively bypassed McClellan and Henry W. Halleck, his main generals in both theaters, and spoke directly to their subordinates.

By the beginning of the year, General Ambrose Burnside had already sailed from Annapolis, Maryland, down the eastern seaboard, and he was soon successfully making inroads along the North Carolina coast. In February, he and his troops took Roanoke Island, forcing a surrender of roughly 2,500 Confederates. Beyond establishing a Union position in the area, Burnside's victory also helped the Union reinforce and tighten its Southern blockade.

The War in the West

After the prodding from Lincoln, Union forces in the West began to advance effectively into enemy territory, as well. The architect of much of this success was a quiet, unassuming man who, at the outbreak of the war, had been a clerk in his family's leather goods store in Galena, Illinois. Ulysses Simpson "Sam" Grant graduated in the West Point class of 1843. He served with distinction in Mexico, receiving two citations for bravery. Following the war, he was assigned to the Pacific Northwest where boredom and loneliness drove him to the bottle. He resigned his commission in 1854 to avoid a court-martial.

Union troops wade ashore from the Neuse River as they prepare to march toward New Bern, North Carolina, on March 13. Modern styles of landing craft had not yet been invented, so shallow-draft vessels came as close to shore as possible, and the troops jumped overboard and waded to dry land. In some instances, rowboats and lifeboats were collected, tied together in rows, and towed by steamers close to shore. The task of rowing to the beach would then be completed manually.

Back at home he was unsuccessful in a number of business undertakings. At the outbreak of war, his offers of service to a number of politicians and military officers were spurned until he was finally appointed colonel of the 21st Illinois Volunteer Infantry on June 17, 1861. Elihu Washburne, a member of Congress and family friend, helped him secure an appointment as brigadier general of Illinois volunteers on August 7, 1861.

The targets of Grant's first major military operation were two forts on the western end of the Kentucky-Tennessee border. Fort Henry overlooked the Tennessee River, while Fort Donelson, about ten miles to the

---

1862

JANUARY 1–FEBRUARY 20
Stonewall Jackson wages his Romney Campaign in western Virginia.

JANUARY 11
Secretary of War Simon Cameron resigns to become ambassador to Russia.

JANUARY 15
Edwin M. Stanton replaces Cameron as Lincoln's secretary of war.

The U.S. Navy purchased a number of New York City ferryboats in 1861 and converted them to gunboats. Seen here is the USS Commodore Perry, a 512-ton sidewheel steamer built in 1859. The Perry carried five naval cannons and was used in shallow rivers in North Carolina, easily able to traverse them because its engines could be reversed to move forward or backward as needed.

east, guarded the Cumberland. A somewhat uncoordinated attack of Union navy and infantry forced Fort Henry to surrender in early February. Grant then marched his 15,000 troops to a position outside of Fort Donelson, which had become the last stronghold standing in the way of federal control of Kentucky and western Tennessee.

IF I COULD SAVE THE UNION WITHOUT FREEING ANY SLAVE, I WOULD DO IT; AND IF I COULD SAVE IT BY FREEING ALL THE SLAVES, I WOULD DO IT; IF I COULD DO IT BY FREEING SOME AND LEAVING OTHERS ALONE, I WOULD ALSO DO THAT.

Abraham Lincoln

Another coordinated effort between the navy and Grant's infantry was launched against the fort. After a three-day siege, the Confederate soldiers surrendered. Within just ten days, Grant had captured the two strategic rebel citadels guarding the western gate to the Confederacy, inflicted more than 2,000 casualties, captured some 15,000 prisoners with a loss of less than 3,000 soldiers himself, and gained the nickname "Unconditional Surrender" Grant.

JANUARY 16
Seven ironclad river gunboats are commissioned at St. Louis for the Union river fleet.

JANUARY 19
The Battle of Mill Springs, Kentucky, is fought. Union forces gained the victory.

JANUARY 30
The USS *Monitor* is launched at Greenpoint, Long Island, New York.

The Capture of Forts Henry and Donelson

Fort Henry on the Tennessee River and Fort Donelson on the Cumberland were separated by ten miles. Built to protect western Tennessee, the two dirt forts were isolated from Confederate reinforcement but key to protecting the western rivers.

Fort Henry itself was situated on low ground, with higher ground on either side. Confederates intended to fortify their position, but before substantial supporting works could be constructed, Union Captain A. H. Foote and his gunboats came around the river bend. Confederate General Lloyd Tilghman, commander of both forts, begged for reinforcements, but none were sent.

Foote, who had been instructed to wait for Ulysses Grant to launch a simultaneous ground assault, went ahead without him and began shelling the fort on February 6. Tilghman's gunners returned fire until most of their guns were dismounted. By the time Grant's land troops arrived, fighting was over. After the fort surrendered, the Federals discovered their entire fleet had been fighting only 100 rebels. Tilghman had ordered the bulk of his forces to Fort Donelson but had stayed behind to share the fate of his gunners.

Grant's attention quickly focused on Fort Donelson. In command were Generals John B. Floyd, a former U.S. secretary of war and Virginia governor, and Gideon J. Pillow, a lifelong politician whose previous military experience as a major general during the Mexican War had been contentious. Grant attacked Donelson and, over two days of fighting, the Confederates twice tried to break out of the slowly suffocating Union noose. Both times, the commanding generals lost their nerve and retreated back into the fort.

During the night of February 16, Generals Floyd and Pillow passed command of the fort to a third general, Simon Boliver Buckner, an old friend of Grant. Buckner, the only professional general among the three, had earlier tried in vain to get the two amateurs to follow his suggestions. Now it was too late to evacuate the fort.

Floyd and Pillow fled in the night, with Floyd taking his Virginia brigade with him. A junior officer, Colonel Nathan Bedford Forrest, was dismayed at the planned surrender and escaped with his troops, as well. The two generals left the rest of the 15,000 Confederate soldiers and a few dozen cannons to capture, for which they were later stripped of their military commands.

The following morning, Buckner requested terms of surrender. Grant responded, "No terms except unconditional and immediate surrender can be accepted." This earned him a nickname he would carry through the rest of the war, as his initials were said to stand for "Unconditional Surrender."

This engraving portrays the charge of General Charles F. Smith's division at Fort Donelson, which provided the push needed for a Union triumph. In his report on the battle, Grant wrote that this charge "was most brilliantly executed, and gave to our arms full assurance of victory."

Confederate Fort Donelson was perched atop a bluff on the west bank of the Cumberland River. The earthen fort guarded the approach to Nashville and helped to hold western Kentucky and Tennessee for the Confederacy. In mid-February 1862, the combined Union army and navy force under General Grant battered the fort. Its capture helped the Union control the Cumberland River.

FEBRUARY
Julia Ward Howe's "The Battle Hymn of the Republic" is first published in the February issue of *The Atlantic Monthly*.

FEBRUARY 3
The CSS *Nashville* sails from England.

FEBRUARY 5
Indiana Senator Jesse D. Bright

is expelled from the Senate for alleged complicity with enemies of the country.

FEBRUARY 6
Union troops capture Fort Henry, Tennessee.

Inventor Norman Wiard designed 6- and 12-pounder boat howitzers for use on both land and sea. The guns he designed were intended to be lighter and more maneuverable than standard cannons of the period. The carriages of Wiard guns were wider to allow greater elevation of the barrel. This photo also clearly shows the studs on the wheels that allowed quicker repair and compensated for wood shrinkages when wet.

Following the fall of Forts Henry and Donelson, Confederate General Albert Sidney Johnston withdrew his army of 44,000 from Tennessee to Corinth, Mississippi. Grant's force, increased to 40,000, slowly advanced down the Tennessee River, stopping at Pittsburg Landing to await the arrival of Major General Don Carlos Buell's Army of the Ohio. Failing to secure his position, Grant was caught by surprise when Johnston attacked on the morning of April 6 near Shiloh Church. The unsuspecting Union troops raced wildly between their tents. Trails of uniform coats, knapsacks, bedding, rifles, and equipment of all kinds littered the ground as they were driven from their camp in the wake of the rout.

After their initial surprise, federal officers were able to rally several thousand soldiers to form ragged firing lines to slow the Confederate advance, but each of these lines was ultimately overrun. Union Brigadier General Benjamin Prentiss organized his command along a sunken road and drove back more than ten charges before the effects of Confederate artillery forced him to surrender his 2,000 troops.

FEBRUARY 7–8
Ambrose Burnside invades North Carolina in the Battle of Roanoke Island.

FEBRUARY 10
Union naval vessels destroy a Confederate squadron at Elizabeth City, North Carolina.

FEBRUARY 13–16
Union troops under Ulysses S. Grant compel surrender of 15,000 Confederates at Fort Donelson, Tennessee.

Frenzied confusion overwhelmed the rear of the federal line at the Battle of Shiloh when 44,000 Confederates came bursting from the woods to interrupt what had been a quiet morning breakfast for Union soldiers.

Johnston was mortally wounded during the attack and replaced by General P.G.T. Beauregard, one of the heroes of the First Battle of Bull Run. The Confederates advanced to the fringe of a defensive line Grant had hastily constructed along the Tennessee River. Discovering the federal infantry was protected by numerous artillery pieces and two gunboats, Beauregard decided to suspend fighting for the day.

This engraving of the Battle of Shiloh is based upon a painting by Alonzo Chappel. It portrays some of the savagery involved as the armies went back and forth, losing and regaining ground. These Union soldiers are recapturing artillery that had been lost to the rebels earlier in the day.

This decision may have ruined any advantage Beauregard had. Grant's army was reinforced during the night and ready to counterattack the next morning. The rebels stubbornly resisted the federal assaults until the sheer number of enemy troops drove them from the field. Grant won the victory, but at a heavy price. His army suffered 13,000 casualties, a number that includes all those killed, wounded, missing in action, or captured, while the Confederates lost over 10,000.

FEBRUARY 18
The first session of the First Confederate Congress convenes in Richmond.

FEBRUARY 19
The town of Winton, North Carolina, is burned by Union soldiers.

FEBRUARY 20
William "Willie" Lincoln dies of typhoid fever in the White House at age 11.

FEBRUARY 21
Confederates defeat Union troops in the Battle of Valverde, New Mexico Territory.

FEBRUARY 22
Jefferson Davis is inaugurated as President of the Confederacy.

FEBRUARY 25
Union troops occupy Nashville,

Tennessee, the first Confederate state capital to be captured.

The Legal Tender Act, providing for paper currency in the United States, is signed by Lincoln.

After the fall of Forts Henry and Donelson, Confederate General Earl Van Dorn thought he might turn the tables on Grant by driving on St. Louis. He was prevented from doing so during the Battle of Pea Ridge, Arkansas, when his 14,000 troops were routed by a small but determined federal army commanded by General Samuel R. Curtis.

MARCH 3
General John Pope's Union troops begin to move against New Madrid, Missouri.

MARCH 4
The Senate approves Lincoln's appointment of Andrew Johnson as military governor of Tennessee.

MARCH 7–8
Troops clash at the Battle of Pea Ridge, Arkansas, resulting in Union victory.

The Battle of Shiloh

A large battle in the spring of 1862 seemed inevitable as Union forces took aim at the converging rail lines at Corinth, Mississippi. The Federals were rolling almost unopposed, with U. S. Grant's army moving south after the capture of Fort Donelson and Don Carlos Buell's army moving southwest after taking Nashville. If Corinth were captured, the Union would be closer to completing Lincoln's grand plan to split the Confederacy by controlling the western rivers. Memphis, on the Mississippi River, would be the next logical Union target.

Grant advanced to Pittsburg Landing, north of Corinth on the Tennessee River's west bank, to await Buell. Their backs to the unfordable river, Grant and subordinate General William Tecumseh Sherman carelessly set up their camp. Confederate General Albert Sidney Johnston moved 44,000 troops out of their defenses in Corinth to smash Grant's army.

Johnston's force attacked at dawn on April 6, pushing most of Grant's totally surprised army to the banks of the river. But the attack lost the momentum necessary to bring Union forces to disaster when hungry Confederates stopped to eat the Union breakfasts and hundreds of Federals made a determined stand in a sunken road known as "The Hornets' Nest." During the melee, Johnston himself was mortally wounded when a stray Confederate bullet tore through an artery in his leg.

That night, when forced to admit he had been beaten that day, a calm Grant replied: "Whip 'em tomorrow, though." Not long after that conversation, Buell arrived. On April 7, the combined Union armies retook the ground lost the previous day. In two days of fighting, Shiloh had become the bloodiest battle of the war so far, with 23,000 casualties on both sides.

Federal troops under Grant's overall command drove back a furious Confederate assault at Pittsburg Landing, where most of the April 6 fighting occurred. Killed in this battle was commanding Confederate General Albert Sidney Johnston; General William T. Sherman was slightly wounded. As a consequence of this federal victory, Confederate forces were compelled to evacuate much of Tennessee.

Civil War fighting stretched to the edges of the country's western frontier. Forts that had been built to monitor American Indians came under attack by Confederates, particularly in New Mexico. This western outpost in Wyoming was photographed in 1866 to commemorate the visit of such dignitaries as General Philip Sheridan (third from left), General Ulysses Grant (eighth from left), and General William T. Sherman (center).

Union General Samuel R. Curtis served most of his career in the obscure "Trans-Mississippi," the region west of the river that rarely got much attention from either Washington or Richmond. Despite being outnumbered by more than 6,000, Curtis still won the one major battle he commanded at Pea Ridge, Arkansas (also known as Elkhorn Tavern), which kept Missouri in the Union.

This made Shiloh the deadliest battle of the war so far. The Union army pressed southward, and less than two months later, Corinth, Mississippi, a major rail center to both Memphis, Tennessee, and Mobile, Alabama, fell into Union hands.

Across the Mississippi, the battle for control of Missouri was fought near Elkhorn Tavern, Arkansas, along Pea Ridge, just south of the Missouri border. The Confederate army of General Earl Van Dorn attacked Union General Samuel Curtis's troops on March 7. Achieving some success by the end of the day's fighting, the rebels were low

WHO COULD NOT CONQUER, WITH SUCH TROOPS AS THESE?

attributed to Thomas J. "Stonewall" Jackson

on ammunition when the battle continued the next morning. Federal artillery and infantry charges drove Van Dorn's army from the field, securing Missouri for the Union.

Even action in far-flung New Mexico made Lincoln's emphasis on the West look like a stroke of genius. Rumored to be rich in gold to fill Confederate coffers, the New

MARCH 8
The CSS *Virginia* sinks two Union warships, the USS *Cumberland* and the USS *Congress*, near Hampton Roads, Virginia.

MARCH 9
Ironclad ships clash in the first such naval engagement when the USS *Monitor* and CSS *Virginia* fight to a draw.

MARCH 11
General George McClellan is removed from his position as Union general in chief.

The *Monitor* vs. the *Virginia*

Confederate Secretary of the Navy Stephen Mallory had a major challenge from the first day of his appointment. His navy had no ships. What Mallory did have, however, was a shipyard: the Gosport Navy Yard at Norfolk, saved from fires set by the Union when Virginia seceded. Within that shipyard was the best and largest dry dock on American soil.

Recognizing that the Confederacy had no hope of matching the North in its capacity to build standard wooden war ships, Mallory decided to build better ships. He was fascinated with drawings of an ironclad ship presented to him by a young former U.S. Naval officer named John Mercer Brooke. Brooke assured Mallory that iron plating mounted at an angle over a wooden backing would cause any shells fired at it to glance off.

Mallory now realized he did have a ship—the recovered hull of the USS *Merrimack*, a steam frigate that had been burned to the waterline by retreating Union sailors. He ordered Brooke and a local shipbuilder named John Luke Porter to build

The flat deck of the Monitor *made an odd sight taking on the heavier, more obviously dangerous ironclad* Virginia. *When Confederates first spotted it floating in the water on March 9, they did not know what to make of it. One officer called it "such a craft as the eyes of a seaman never looked upon before—an immense shingle floating on the water, with a gigantic cheese box rising from its center; no sails, no wheels, no smokestack, no guns. What could it be?. . . A few visionary characters feebly intimated that it might be the* Monitor.*"*

Brooke's ironclad on the hulk of the *Merrimack*. The ironclad would be armed with six large smooth-bore cannons and four rifled cannons. This powerful floating artillery battery would be christened the *Virginia*.

Porter reluctantly agreed to help. He was convinced Brooke had somehow stolen his ironclad idea, which Porter had personally presented to the U.S. Navy several years earlier. The Navy at that time considered ironclad ships a folly and rejected the bitter Porter. Now Porter's idea was enthusiastically being championed, but he was getting no credit for it.

When Union spies got word to Washington of the planned Confederate ironclad, officials created a committee to develop their own ironclad design. After having been rejected by a naval review board, a radical design for an ironclad ship that would ride low in the water finally won the approval of President Lincoln. It would be armed with just two 11-inch cannons mounted in a revolving turret. The "cheese box on a raft," as it was derisively called, was designed by cantankerous Swedish-born inventor John Ericsson.

Lieutenant William Flye of the Monitor, *wearing a straw hat, inspects the ironclad's turret. Effects of cannon fire from the* Virginia *are clearly visible on the* Monitor's *iron plates.*

Both sides raced to finish their ironclads. The *Monitor* was finished first in late January 1862, but it took several weeks before the ship was ready for combat. It headed south from Brooklyn, New York, on March 6 in search of the *Virginia*. The *Virginia* moved out on March 8 on its shakedown cruise, which Captain Franklin Buchanan quickly turned into an attack on the federal wooden fleet blockading Chesapeake Bay.

There was virtually no contest. The *Virginia* smashed the wooden Union ships to pieces, sinking one by ramming, setting another afire, and causing three more to run aground. It would return the next day to finish the job.

Later that evening, however, the *Monitor* arrived on the scene, too late to stop the first attack, but just in time to lay in wait for the return of the *Virginia* on March 9. The appearance of the *Monitor* surprised the Confederates. They had heard that it was under construction, but their spies had failed to keep them informed when it started making its way south. Shortly before 9:00 the next morning, the two ships clumsily began circling each other, continuing for four hours. Shot after shot was fired, sometimes at a range of just a few yards. Both ships dented the other, with the *Monitor* succeeding in jamming some of the *Virginia*'s gun ports and cracking its armor plate in spots, but neither could land a conclusive blow. Eventually, leery of running aground himself, Buchanan pulled the *Virginia* away. Neither ship had sunk the other—the battle was a draw. Nevertheless, this battle of the ironclads revolutionized naval ship design.

The *Monitor-Virginia* Battle

"Several times the *Monitor* ceased firing, and we were in hopes she was disabled, but the revolution again of her turret and the heavy blows of her 11-inch shot on our sides soon undeceived us.

"Coming down from the spar-deck, and observing a division standing 'at ease,' Lieutenant Jones inquired:

"'Why are you not firing, Mr. Eggleston?'

"'Why, our powder is very precious,' replied the lieutenant; 'and after two hours' incessant firing I find that I can do her about as much damage by snapping my thumb at her every two minutes and a half.'"

Lieutenant John T. Wood, CSS Virginia, *describing the effect of firing on the USS* Monitor

Mexico Territory was briefly in Confederate hands after the February Battle of Valverde. In March, Union forces won the Battle of Glorieta Pass, wresting final control of the Southwest, stretching all the way to California. Any Southern dreams of gold mines and vast western lands for cotton production were now dashed.

The Peninsula Campaign

Back in Washington, McClellan was finally ready to begin his Peninsula Campaign toward Richmond. His hesitancy had already caused Lincoln to relieve him as general in chief of Union forces, but he held on to his command of the Army of the Potomac. Before he could set out for Virginia, however, McClellan had to make a few last-minute adjustments. After an indecisive battle at Hampton Roads, Virginia, between two ironclad vessels, the USS *Monitor* and the CSS *Virginia,* the mouth of the James River remained protected against a Union landing. Instead of advancing up two rivers, McClellan was left with one—the York, which ran north of Richmond. After the campaign was under way, the Army of the Potomac advanced more slowly than expected but was generally successful. Unconvinced by his own success, however, McClellan remained overly cautious.

Contributing to McClellan's caution was a very successful campaign being waged by Confederate General Thomas J. "Stonewall" Jackson in the Shenandoah Valley, which is considered one of the most brilliant campaigns in military history. With a force that never exceeded 17,000 troops, Jackson defeated three federal armies in five battles between May 8 and June 9, inflicted about 5,000 casualties while suffering less than half that number, and prevented valuable reinforcements from reaching McClellan.

The Fall of New Orleans

Over in the West, Union forces continued their success along the Mississippi. It had been considered the lifeblood of the rebel armies in the West—as long as it remained in Confederate control, rapid transportation of troops and supplies could stymie federal campaigns west of the Appalachian Mountains. In the spring of 1862, the Union had finally begun to implement Winfield Scott's "Anaconda Plan" to cut the secessionist states in half by gaining control of the Mississippi from Cairo, Illinois, to New Orleans, Louisiana. Union forces were moving down from the north, capturing New Madrid, Missouri, and Island Number 10 at the Missouri–Tennessee border. Their next stop would be Fort Pillow and Memphis, Tennessee.

MARCH 13
General Henry W. Halleck is named to the command of the new Department of the Mississippi.

MARCH 14
In the Battle of New Bern, Union forces capture North Carolina's second-largest town, New Bern.

MARCH 18
Judah P. Benjamin, the Confederate secretary of war, is transferred to the post of secretary of state by Jefferson Davis. George Randolph is appointed the new secretary of war.

At the other end of the river, two heavily armed masonry forts, Jackson and St. Philip, guarded the approach to New Orleans from the Gulf of Mexico. Iron chains were strung across the river within easy range of the forts' guns to trap any enemy ships foolish enough to challenge the defenses. A series of fortifications and natural obstructions blocked land access to these fortresses. "Nothing afloat could pass the forts," one New Orleans citizen proclaimed. "Nothing that walked could get through our swamps."

The dubious task of tackling these forts fell to Union Captain David Glasgow Farragut, a 60-year-old career naval officer. Commanding 24 wooden vessels and 19 mortar schooners, his fleet approached the two forts and fired its first shots on April 18. After shelling the forts for five days and cutting the chains across the river, Farragut advanced his ships up the Mississippi at 3:30 A.M. on April 24. His flotilla faced heavy fire from the forts and the Confederate fleet stationed near them, but by daylight his ships had passed the forts' guns and sunk or captured all but one of the rebel vessels at a minimal loss to their own. New Orleans surrendered four days later. The largest city in the Confederacy was now in Union hands.

Following the fall of New Orleans, the federal navy pressed up the Mississippi River. By the end of the year, only Vicksburg remained as a Confederate stronghold on the river. Several attempts by Grant to take the city failed, causing him to regroup his force and plan a spring 1863 campaign against the rebel citadel.

The blandly named Island Number 10, located in the middle of the Mississippi River on the Kentucky, Tennessee, and Missouri borders, was the site of a battle fought on April 7, 1862, the same day as the second day of Shiloh. When the 4,500-troop Confederate garrison surrendered, it was the culmination of a three-week siege, which included the use of mortar boats lobbing shells, as depicted in this lithograph.

MARCH 22
The CSS *Florida*, built in the shipyards of Liverpool, England, sets out from that port.

MARCH 23
Stonewall Jackson loses the Battle of Kernstown in northern Virginia, but his presence worries leaders in Washington. Instead of accompanying General McClellan on his Peninsula Campaign, some troops are held back to protect the capital.

MARCH 26
Union troops push Confederates

Retreating Confederate soldiers burned bales of cotton to keep the crop from falling into Union hands as the Federals occupied Memphis in June 1862. Frank Vizetelly drew this sketch and instructed the printer to finish the scene—note the directions on the building.

Robert E. Lee

All this success in the West did little to raise spirits in the Northern states, as McClellan was still doing little or nothing in Virginia. The Army of the Potomac had approached Richmond toward the end of May, but incorrectly convinced that the Confederates had him outnumbered, McClellan failed to press his advantage. He split his army across the Chickahominy River, a situation Confederate General Joseph E. Johnston saw as an opportunity to strike. Attacking the southern flank of the Union forces at Fair Oaks, Johnston was wounded in the fight and taken from the front. Confederate President Davis appointed General Robert E. Lee to replace Johnston as head of the army protecting the capital.

Lee was not a popular choice. Having been offered command of the Union Army after the fall of Fort Sumter, Lee elected to join his native Virginia in secession. One of only five men to be named to the rank of general in the Confederate Army, Lee had been unsuccessful in his first attempt at command—he failed in July 1861 to recover the western counties of Virginia that had fallen into Union hands. Upon learning that Lee was given the ominous task of defending the Confederate capital from an enemy whose numbers were almost twice their own, several of his subordinates expressed concern that they were being led by a career staff officer who had failed to demonstrate the "power and skill for field service."

The Battle of Memphis on June 6, 1862, turned out to be one of the most satisfying victories of the war for the U.S. Navy. What makes it even more interesting is that the battle consisted mostly of specially modified Union ships ramming Confederate ships into submission. When the battle was over, seven Confederate ships had been destroyed compared to only one damaged Union ram. The prize was the South's fifth-largest city.

back at the Battle of Apache Canyon, New Mexico Territory.

MARCH 28
Confederate forces face off against U.S. troops at the Battle of Glo-

rieta Pass, New Mexico Territory. Although the rebels appear to win the fighting, Union soldiers capture and effectively destroy Confederate supplies in the rear. This ends rebel incursions into New

Mexico Territory for the remainder of the war.

MARCH 29
General Albert S. Johnston is placed in command of reorga-

The Union Takes New Orleans

The CSS Manassas was the first Civil War ironclad and the ugliest, resembling a waterlogged cigar. Its armor was 1½ inches of iron, and it was equipped with a ram and a single 32-pounder cannon on its deck. In two battles on the Mississippi, the Manassas was found to be slow, unmanageable, and ineffective. Run aground during the Union capture of New Orleans, the Manassas was abandoned and allowed to drift downriver, where it exploded and sank.

There was no Battle of New Orleans to lead up to the capture of the South's largest city on April 28, 1862. With a population of 200,000, it was five times the size of Richmond. When 60-year-old Union Navy Captain David G. Farragut stepped on the city docks to accept the mayor's surrender of the city, there was not a soldier in sight on either side. The victors were all sailors.

The easy surrender of the Confederacy's busiest port shocked the Confederate government in Richmond. The entire strategy of defending the city had depended upon two forts 70 miles south of New Orleans, Fort Jackson and Fort St. Philip, sinking any Union invasion fleet.

When Union ships swept past both forts and steamed toward the city, a surprised Confederate land commander, General Mansfield Lovell, evacuated rather than fought. Lovell was vilified for refusing to fight, but he later successfully proved in a Confederate congressional inquiry that Richmond had sent him few troops and equipment. Any fight he might have mounted against the heavy naval guns would have been futile and possibly suicidal.

Coming on the heels of the Union land victory at Shiloh less than three weeks earlier, the capture of New Orleans dealt a major blow against Confederate claims to European countries that it could withstand attacks from the United States.

An Account of Battle

"During one of the stormy scenes, when both sides were falling at every heart beat, a tall, able young man of the eleventh Alabama rushed upon me, with his bayonet at a charge, thinking to kill the d——d Yankee officer. But I parried his thrust with my sword, which in the encounter was broken off about ten inches from the hilt, when Bennie Small, of my company, seeing the disadvantage I was at, promptly came up on my left, and bayoneted the Confederate, then clubbing his musket struck him across the forehead, killing him within three feet of where I stood."

Lieutenant L. G. McCauley, 7th Pennsylvania Reserves, describing hand-to-hand combat at Glendale, Virginia, June 30, 1862

Even his opponent, McClellan, had little respect for Lee's ability for field command. "I prefer Lee to Johnston," he stated. "The former is too cautious and weak under grave responsibility—personally brave and energetic to a fault, he yet is wanting in moral firmness when pressed by heavy responsibility and is likely to be timid and irresolute in action." McClellan was soon to discover how wrong he was.

Lee quickly reorganized his army and developed a masterful plan to drive the Federals from the gates of Richmond. When the general, based on intelligence he received from his cavalry commander, Major General James Ewell Brown "Jeb" Stuart, learned that McClellan's right flank was lightly defended, he chose it as the target for his first strike.

McClellan, still cautious to a fault, spent the weeks following the Battle of Fair Oaks preparing for a siege of the Confederate capital. Before Lee could execute his plan, the Federals struck the rebel position near Oak Grove on June 25. However, they were unsuccessful in their attempt to gain command of heights where they could place their siege guns.

Lee attacked the Union right flank at Mechanicsville, northeast of Richmond, on June 26. Although repulsed, the Confederate commander did not relinquish the initia-

On the morning of May 30, 1862, more than 50,000 Confederates were able to evacuate the city of Corinth, Mississippi, in the face of an approaching federal army of more than 120,000. The retreating rebels burned strategic points of the town behind them. Though forced to give up Corinth's railhead, Confederate General P.G.T. Beauregard was able to save his forces to fight another day.

nized Confederate forces at Corinth, Mississippi.

APRIL 5
Union siege operations begin at Yorktown, Virginia, as part of

General McClellan's Peninsula Campaign.

APRIL 6–7
The Union Army triumphs in the Battle of Shiloh, Tennessee.

APRIL 7
Island Number 10 on the Mississippi River surrenders to Union troops.

General Benjamin Franklin Butler was a powerful Massachusetts criminal lawyer and political kingmaker when the war began. Lincoln, trying to win favors from the Democrats, named him a general even though Butler had no military experience. Butler was neither a good nor a popular general, but he did champion the use of black troops in combat. New Orleans residents called him "Spoons Butler" for stealing silverware from occupied houses.

Captain David G. Farragut was 60 when he was given a chance at commanding the West Gulf Blockading Squadron in January 1862. In just five months, he captured the city of New Orleans with minimal losses among his own ships. Capturing Mobile Bay, Alabama, in August 1864, he became truly famous when he ordered the sailor at the helm to ignore floating mines with the shout, "Damn the torpedoes! Full speed ahead!" He was the first U.S. sailor to rise to the rank of full admiral.

tive. In a series of strategic assaults over the next five days, the Federals were driven from the outskirts of Richmond to the northern bank of the James River almost 15 miles away. It took only six days for Lee to prove to McClellan that he was far from "timid and irresolute in action."

With the Army of the Potomac bottled up along the James, Lee turned his attention to the 50,000-strong Army of Virginia, commanded by Major General John Pope, advancing on Richmond from the north. He sent half that number of troops under the command of his most trusted subordinate, Stonewall Jackson, recently arrived from the Shenandoah Valley, to stop Pope. Jackson kept Pope occupied in Northern Virginia in a campaign that culminated in a victory for the Confederates at the Second Battle of Bull Run. Both Pope's and McClellan's armies retreated toward Washington.

In little more than two months, Lee had driven a much larger army from the outskirts of Richmond and defeated another enemy command. He was now deployed close to the same line the Confederates had occupied a year earlier after their victory at the First Battle of Bull Run. Realizing an attack on the federal capital would fail, Lee developed another strategy to keep the initiative in his favor. His army forded the Potomac River on September 4 to carry the war into Union territory for the first time, giving war-weary Virginia an opportunity to catch its breath. Lee hoped he could extend his string of successes north of the Mason-

These 13-inch seacoast mortars were set up by General George McClellan to lob shells weighing more than a ton each into Confederate defenses at Yorktown, Virginia. Confederate General Joseph Johnston abandoned the original colonial fortifications before the siege guns could even be used.

APRIL 11
Confederates surrender Fort Pulaski, located near Savannah, Georgia, to Union troops after a two-day bombardment.

Union troops occupy Huntsville, Alabama.

APRIL 12
In what became known as Andrews's Raid, Union raiders led

by James J. Andrews steal a locomotive but are unsuccessful in disrupting Confederate rail communications in Georgia.

George B. McClellan

"**L**ittle Mac," as General George B. McClellan was known, was the toast of the soldiers composing the Army of the Potomac. He had trained them from a mob of civilians into an efficient fighting force. More importantly, they knew he would not waste their lives in military adventures ordered by politicians in Washington.

But "Little Mac" was the bane of the Lincoln Administration, and in particular, of Lincoln himself. The President once called the Army "McClellan's bodyguard." Another time he asked McClellan if he could "borrow" the Army since McClellan was not using it to fight the Confederates.

The general's Civil War career took off early when he won a few skirmishes in western Virginia. Occurring at virtually the same time the Union was losing its first major battle at Bull Run, these victories may have seemed more impressive than they should have. They were enough for Lincoln to hand over complete control of all the Union armies to McClellan, a move the President would later regret.

McClellan proved to be overly cautious and easily fooled as to the strength of his opponents. During the Peninsula Campaign, the Seven Days' Battles, and Antietam, he believed his forces were outnumbered two to one when in reality, he outnumbered Lee by that margin. Lee used McClellan's careful nature against him to win all three of those battles and eventually end the general's military career.

McClellan never grasped that generals are always subordinate to the Commander in Chief. Lincoln fired him in November 1862. Two years later, McClellan was rejected on an even larger scale when the nation voted to reelect Lincoln rather than support the former general for president.

Fond of comparing himself to Napoleon, General George B. McClellan strikes a pose reminiscent of the French leader. McClellan's tenure as commander of the Army of the Potomac did not recall Napoleon. It was marked by repeated incidents of uncertainty and overcaution on the battlefield.

APRIL 16
Slavery is abolished in the District of Columbia. Slaveholders are compensated up to $300 for each emancipated slave.

President Davis approves an act calling for the conscription of every white male between the ages of 18 and 35 for three years of military service. This is the first national military draft to be instituted in the United States.

APRIL 18
Union mortar schooners begin the bombardment of Confederate Forts Jackson and St. Philip below New Orleans.

When General McClellan decided to change his supply base from the York to the James River as the Seven Days' Battles opened in front of Richmond, he abandoned the large hospital at Savage's Station. The overcrowded hospital, filled with sick and wounded Yankees, ran out of space, and troops were forced to remain outdoors, as shown in this view. Note the number of straw hats worn in the heat of summer.

Cedar Mountain, just south of Culpeper, Virginia, was the scene of a close call, but still a victory, for Confederate General Stonewall Jackson on August 9, 1862. During the battle, Jackson's left flank faltered. He grabbed a battle flag in one hand and his sword in the other and rallied his troops. The sword had rusted in the scabbard, indicating how little attention Jackson paid to his personal appearance and equipment.

Dixon line. "The present," Lee wrote to Davis prior to the invasion of the North, "seems to be the most propitious time since the commencement of the war for the Confederate Army to enter Maryland."

The First Confederate Invasion of the North

As Lee's 50,000 troops of the Army of Northern Virginia crossed into Maryland, regimental bands played "Maryland, My Maryland." Realizing it was against McClellan's nature to act decisively, Lee split his force into four units and sent them on separate missions. Lee's contempt for his federal counterpart was justified. McClellan, even after accidentally coming into possession of Lee's orders, hesitated in his pursuit of the Confederate army.

Discovering that his orders had fallen into enemy hands, Lee quickly worked to reunite his command. By September 16, both armies faced off across Antietam Creek, outside of Sharpsburg, Maryland. The next day, in

APRIL 19
In an engagement at Sawyer's Lane near South Mills, North Carolina, Confederates turn back Union forces.

Wisconsin Governor Louis P. Harvey drowns in the Tennessee River near Savannah, Tennessee, after visiting sick and wounded soldiers from his state in hospitals at Shiloh.

APRIL 24
Captain David G. Farragut's Union fleet successfully engages and passes the Confederate batteries and gunboats guarding New Orleans.

Union General John Pope had seen success in the West, particularly in his tactics against Island Number 10. Unfortunately, he had a tendency to talk up his accomplishments more than they deserved, and many Northern journalists were happy to take him at his word. The somewhat overrated general was brought east to fight Robert E. Lee, who publicly called Pope a "miscreant" for his attacks on civilians. Pope's army was soundly defeated at the Second Battle of Bull Run. Lincoln soon fired Pope from his command.

Union General Ambrose Burnside's 9th Corps spent hours on the morning of September 17 trying to take this stone bridge over Antietam Creek on the right flank of the federal line. A few hundred Georgia sharpshooters kept more than 10,000 Federals from crossing either the bridge or the creek, which could have been waded, until one angry regiment, promised a liquor ration, finally charged across. Burnside's delay in crossing helped Lee save his army.

the bloodiest single day in America's military history, the two forces clashed in a series of three disjointed Union attacks. By day's end, over 26,000 men had been killed or wounded. Although he failed to drive the Confederate army from the field, McClellan claimed victory after Lee withdrew his force back across the Potomac.

Despite this "victory," the North had been invaded, and the grumbling from Northern citizens to let the wayward South go in peace was growing louder. But Lincoln had something that would perhaps turn around the war protesters and bring them back into his corner as war supporters. He had been looking for a firm Union victory to release it, but this would have to be close enough. The Emancipation Proclamation freed slaves

This photograph by Alexander Gardner of Confederate dead lying on the Hagerstown Pike after the Battle of Antietam on September 17 was one of a series of photographs displayed in a special exhibition in New York City. It marked one of the first times Northern civilians had seen what was happening on the battlefields in the South.

APRIL 26
Fort Macon, protecting Beaufort Harbor in North Carolina, surrenders to Union troops after a single day of bombardment.

APRIL 28
New Orleans surrenders to Union sailors.

MAY 2
Colonel John B. Turchin's Union troops sack Athens, Alabama.

MAY 3
Confederate troops evacuate their Yorktown defenses in Virginia, leaving the town for McClellan's Army of the Potomac.

The Battle of Perryville, Kentucky, on October 8 was a federal victory in which Union troops commanded by General Don Carlos Buell defeated General Braxton Bragg's Confederate army. At Perryville, the North repulsed one of two Southern invasions of the Union that year, the other being Lee's Antietam Campaign. Afterward, Bragg retreated to the southeast, and no more major battles were fought on Kentucky's soil.

in the secessionist states. Lincoln believed that without a change of tactics, the Union faced total loss. He decided it was necessary to take this action for three reasons: to heal the rift that existed between the moderate and radical wings of the Republican party, to practically eliminate the risk that European nations might enter the war in favor of the Confederacy, and to encourage slaves in the South to abandon their owners and therefore impact the region's ability to supply its troops. The proclamation was to take effect on January 1, 1863.

An important, though inconclusive, battle was fought for Kentucky in the fall of 1862. From the beginning of the war, Lincoln viewed Union possession of Kentucky as extremely important to the Northern war effort. "I think to lose Kentucky," he said, "is nearly the same as to lose the whole game." The state's fate rested on the result of an action fought outside the town of Perryville, about 44 miles southeast of Louisville. On October 8, the Confederate army of General Braxton Bragg met Union troops under Buell. Although the battle was technically a draw, Bragg withdrew his army to Tennessee. Kentucky remained in Union hands throughout the balance of the war.

Burnside's Command

McClellan's failure to follow up his success at Antietam once again and for the last time cost him his command. He was replaced as leader of the Army of the Potomac by Ambrose Burnside on November 7. Burnside had declined the command twice before finally bowing to pressure from Washington. It was not until the loss of many good soldiers that Lincoln realized the choice of Burnside was a grave mistake.

Burnside started off well, surprising Lee and even Lincoln with a fast march that took him to the banks of the Rappahannock River at Fredericksburg in an attempt to take

MAY 5
U.S. forces engage retreating Confederates at the Battle of Williamsburg, Virginia. The fight is inconclusive, and despite suffering almost 4,000 total casualties,

each side declares victory as the rebels continue to retreat toward Richmond.

MAY 8
Confederates defeat U.S. troops at the Battle of McDowell, Virginia, as Stonewall Jackson continues his Shenandoah Valley Campaign.

The Seven Days' Battles

Tactically, the Seven Days' Battles fought east and southeast of Richmond, Virginia, from June 25 through July 1 demonstrated Robert E. Lee's brilliance at slicing up a superior force so it could be fought and defeated in pieces. Strategically and realistically, this string of battles saved the Confederacy for three more years.

The Seven Days' Battles began as a tactical initiative when Confederate General J.E.B. "Jeb" Stuart reported to Lee that Union General Fitz John Porter's 5th Corps was north of the Chickahominy River and separated from McClellan's main body of 70,000. Lee left a nominal force in front of McClellan and shifted his 60,000 troops north to attack Porter's 30,000.

But Lee's plan was even bolder than this. He had secretly ordered Stonewall Jackson's small 17,000-strong army away from the Shenandoah Valley to open the attack against Porter at Mechanicsville. Jackson's exhausted force was late in arriving, but Porter was eventually forced to begin a series of retreating battles at Gaines' Mill, Glendale, and finally Malvern Hill on July 1.

In reality, Porter's troops fought well, and the Union actually won most of the Seven Days' Battles. But the unexpected appearance of Jackson panicked McClellan, and he ordered a general retreat that ended with his milling on the banks of the James River. Lee's army was too battered itself to move in to finish the job of wrecking the Federals.

Federal troops skirmish with Confederates in the forests of Virginia's James River Peninsula during the Seven Days' Campaign. Lee's inability to destroy McClellan's Army of the Potomac in the six battles of this campaign was matched by the federal commander's failure to take Richmond.

the fighting back to the Confederate capital. He had intended for the bulk of his command to cross the river before Lee could mount any type of defense. But instead of fording the river immediately, Burnside waited for pontoon boats, a delay that allowed Lee to dig in on the heights behind Fredericksburg. One artillery commander said the army's cannons were placed so "that a chicken could not live on that field." By the time Burnside was ready to attack, Lee was ready to defend. Not a single Union soldier reached the Confederate wall. On December 13, more than 12,600 Federals fell to only about 5,000 Confederates.

It is appropriate that the last battle in this year of bloody conflicts rivaled few others in its ferocity and resulting casualties. Braxton Bragg's Army of Tennessee attacked Major General William S. Rosecrans's Army of the Cumberland on December 31 along Stones River near Murfreesboro, Tennessee. Two days of savage fighting left the Union in control of a battlefield littered with more than 23,000 dead and wounded. As the war entered its third year, central Tennessee was securely in federal hands.

This Kurz and Allison print portrays Confederate General Earl Van Dorn's attack on the federal works at Corinth, Mississippi, on October 3 and 4. The Confederates had to march across more than 400 yards of felled timber before they even reached the Union trenches shown here. The rebels briefly took Battery Robinett, a portion of the works, but the overall assault failed. An earthquake just before the battle began startled both sides.

MAY 9
Union General David Hunter, in command of the Department of the South, authorizes the emancipation of slaves within his district, also allowing them to be enrolled as soldiers. Lincoln disavowed this act on May 19.

MAY 10
A Confederate naval squadron engages Union ironclads in the Battle of Plum Run Bend on the Mississippi north of Memphis, Tennessee. After taking heavy losses but damaging two Union vessels, the rebels retreated downriver.

This view from Stafford Heights on the north side of the Rappahannock River shows the easy range the Union artillery batteries had to fire on Fredericksburg, Virginia, seen in the distance. These heavy siege guns are part of a Connecticut battery photographed in February 1963. Although they are in position behind earthworks, the guns are limbered and ready to move.

This lithograph portrays Union troops building the pontoon bridge and crossing in boats to the south shore of the Rappahannock River at Fredericksburg on December 11. Lee had ordered his soldiers to vigorously resist construction of the bridge, but then he allowed the Federals to cross. He wanted the Army of the Potomac on the south side of the river and moving into open ground while he held Marye's Heights above the town.

MAY 11
The CSS *Virginia* is blown up by retreating Confederates off Norfolk, Virginia.

MAY 13
Robert Smalls, a slave, pilots the CSS *Planter* to the Union blockading fleet off Charleston, South Carolina.

MAY 15
Union ships in Virginia's James River are unable to pass the Confederate batteries at Drewry's Bluff.

Union General William S. Rosecrans was a brilliant cadet at West Point, graduating fifth in the Class of 1842. When the war began, Rosecrans's actions at Rich Mountain in July 1861 brought about a Union victory that is usually credited to Rosecrans's commanding officer, George McClellan. Rosecrans steadily built his reputation in the West over several campaigns and battlefield victories. He held his position at the Battle of Stones Creek to turn a potential defeat into a Union victory.

Confederate recruiters marching through the streets of Woodstock, Virginia, attract young men to the military. Scenes like this were common during the early years of the war. As the fighting dragged on and the number of eligible men diminished throughout the South, however, the furor to join the Army greatly diminished.

This patriotic print shows the 42nd Pennsylvania Regiment, known as "The Bucktails," using a brass band to recruit new members. The Bucktails, first organized as the 13th Pennsylvania Reserve Corps, were recruited from rural counties where every man considered himself a crack shot able to hit a running deer at 400 yards. When colorful recruiting failed, both governments resorted to drafting young and middle-age men.

General Benjamin F. Butler issues his infamous General Order Number 28 in New Orleans, directing any woman who shows contempt toward Union troops "to be treated as a woman of the town plying her avocation." Insults to federal forces decreased immediately.

MAY 20
Lincoln signs the Homestead Act into law.

MAY 23
Stonewall Jackson delivers another victory over Union troops at the Battle of Front Royal, Virginia.

Confederates spent the winter in quarters such as these near Centreville, Virginia, photographed in March 1862. More soldiers died from the diseases spread throughout such camps than on the battlefield.

In order to instill nationalism throughout the new Confederate States of America, the Confederate Congress adopted a national flag and tried hard to ensure that everyone would know what it looked like. These are three examples of patches that were worn by both soldiers and civilians to show their pride in their new nation.

Edwin M. Stanton was one of the wealthiest trial lawyers in the nation when he traded money for something he liked even better—power. Early in the year, Lincoln appointed Stanton secretary of war, a post he held throughout the war years. Stanton ran an honest department, but he ruthlessly wielded power, even imprisoning critics of the administration. He rewarded generals who punished Southerners and demoted those who did not.

MAY 25
In the First Battle of Winchester, Virginia, Jackson defeats federal forces and retakes the town. The Union retreats across the Potomac River.

MAY 26
Edward Stanly, appointed military governor of North Carolina by Lincoln, takes office.

MAY 30
Union troops occupy Corinth, Mississippi.

MAY 31–JUNE 1
During the inconclusive Battle of

Robert E. Lee

No other Civil War general enjoyed a more dramatic turnaround in the public opinion of his abilities than Robert Edward Lee. In one week in June 1862, his image changed from "Granny" Lee, a man who would not fight, to the noblest and ablest general the South has ever produced.

Lee had spent 30 years in the U.S. Army as an engineering and cavalry officer when the war opened. Though just a colonel behind several ranking generals, Lee's inherent abilities to command were recognized by his old boss, U.S. Army General in Chief Winfield Scott. Scott convinced President Lincoln to offer Lee command of any Union army that would be formed to put down the rebelling Southern states. But Lee refused, saying he would never draw his sword against his home state of Virginia. He left his home overlooking Washington and took a job in Richmond as commander of all Virginia forces.

For the first year of the war, Lee acted as a military advisor. He failed to engage the enemy in the fall of 1861 at Cheat Mountain and Sewell Mountain in western Virginia—he could not even convince his subordinate generals to cooperate with him. A disappointed President Davis shipped Lee off to South Carolina to advise on its defense.

When General Joseph Johnston fell wounded at Fair Oaks, Lee stepped in and immediately planned the Seven Days' Campaign that saved Richmond from capture. That success was followed by the Second Battle of Bull Run in August, Antietam in September, Fredericksburg in December, and then Chancellorsville in May 1863. Lee was stunned by his defeat at Gettysburg in July 1863. For nearly a year his Army of Northern Virginia had given him nothing but victories against overwhelming odds.

Informed that Robert E. Lee had assumed command of the forces defending Richmond, Virginia, George McClellan wasted no time in expressing his pleasure. He preferred facing Lee over facing Johnston, believing that Lee would prove overly cautious, even timid, as a commander. Never had an assessment been so wrong on all counts. While confronting a larger, better-supplied force throughout his tenure as commander of the Army of Northern Virginia, Lee's ability both to discover his enemy's weakness and to seize the initiative brought him success in many fields of battle.

He would run up against U. S. Grant in May 1864, holding off the general who had been winning battle after battle in the West. But Grant was not like the Eastern generals Lee had faced, who had retreated each time they were beaten. Grant just kept coming, throwing more Union soldiers forward into battle. It took nearly a year, but Grant's superior numbers finally wore Lee's exhausted army down until it was a shadow of its former self at Appomattox Court House in April 1865.

Lee's last orders rejected guerrilla warfare. Instead, he urged his troops to become good citizens of the reforming nation. His last five years were spent inspiring young students as president of Washington College. He died in 1870.

Fair Oaks in Virginia, Confederate General Joseph Johnston is wounded, forcing him to give up his command of the army protecting Richmond.

JUNE 1
Robert E. Lee, replacing Johnston, is appointed by Jefferson Davis to the command of the army he will soon name the Army of Northern Virginia.

JUNE 6
Union vessels triumph over Confederates in the Battle of Memphis, Tennessee, which mostly consisted of each side ramming the other.

Gideon Welles was playfully called "Father Neptune" for his white beard and his job as secretary of the U.S. Navy. Welles was one of Lincoln's best Cabinet members, successfully buying and leasing enough ships to begin blockading Southern ports and building a massive fleet of fighting vessels. Under his watch, the U.S. fleet grew from about 90 to nearly 700 ships. Long before the Army recruited black soldiers, Welles welcomed black sailors as equals to whites.

A private of Company F, 4th Michigan Infantry Regiment, strikes a martial pose for the photographer. Organized at Adrian, Michigan, in May 1861, the regiment participated in every major campaign of the Army of the Potomac until it was mustered out of service in June 1864. Many of its members continued to serve in other units.

Dorothea Dix

The woman most responsible for arguing the case for female nurses was Dorothea Dix. This 59-year-old woman was already famous as an activist for the humane treatment of the insane. Recognizing that the Army was ill prepared to handle medical problems, Dix visited the surgeon general with her proposal and was turned down. Undaunted, she called on every member of Congress she knew until, on May 28, 1861, the War Department accepted her offer to select nurses for the Union Army.

On June 10, Dix was commissioned superintendent of women nurses. To dissuade the "wrong" kinds of ladies from rushing to her cause, Dix issued an order that "no woman under 30 need apply to serve in government hospitals. All nurses are required to be plain-looking women. Their dresses must be brown or black, with no bows, no frills, no jewelry, and no hoopskirts."

Reformer Dorothea Dix's practice of recruiting only plain-looking women over 30 years of age led to much amusement in the hospitals and the press.

Appeals to ladies' aid societies collected 5,000 shirts within a month of a government request for 500. Responses for other materials were so overwhelming that Dix had to appoint a woman to collect and store supplies until they could be sent to the proper distribution points.

Dix ran into personality problems with officers and used her authority to visit hospitals on inspection tours, a practice resented by male medical personnel. Nevertheless, she continued in her position as Union superintendent of nurses without pay throughout the war.

Abraham Lincoln named Henry W. Halleck general in chief of all Union armies as much for his reputation as a military genius as for his successes in the Western Theater. While he was a good administrator, he was not up to the task of designing and implementing a successful military strategy. In March 1864 he was displaced by one-time subordinate Ulysses S. Grant.

This early Civil War portrait of an unusually well-attired Ulysses S. Grant was made while he was still a brigadier general. After the fall of Fort Donelson to the troops under his command, Grant's first two initials came to stand for "unconditional surrender," the only terms by which he would allow the Confederate garrison to capitulate. For his masterly conduct of the battle, Grant was promoted to the rank of major general.

John Ericsson defiantly poses for the camera. Always angry, and always suspecting that someone was stealing his designs, Ericsson had been pointedly ignored by his enemies in the U.S. Navy until President Lincoln himself saw and endorsed the model he had of what would become the USS Monitor. Ironically, the Monitor was in only one real battle, which was a draw. It proved ineffective against elevated shore batteries. On the last day of the year, the Monitor sank in a heavy sea.

The USS St. Louis, one of seven ironclads called Pook Turtles, was hit 59 times by Confederate artillery and disabled during the attack on Fort Donelson on February 14. Renamed Baron de Kalb in September 1862, the ironclad continued to battle Confederate forces until it was sunk by two torpedoes near Yazoo City, Mississippi, on July 13, 1863.

JUNE 8
The Battle of Cross Keys, Virginia, ends in Confederate victory.

JUNE 9
Stonewall Jackson's Shenandoah Valley Campaign comes to

an end with the Battle of Port Republic, Virginia. After the Union loss, Lincoln ordered troops to withdraw. Jackson turned his forces to help Lee near Richmond.

JUNE 12–15
Jeb Stuart's Confederate cavalry rides completely around the Union Army of the Potomac on the Virginia Peninsula.

A Colt navy revolver and other associated artifacts lay atop a sailor's dress blue jumper and hat. Union sailors were also armed with traditional cutlasses and a variety of black powder weapons to assist in repelling anyone attempting to board their ship. In warm weather, sailors would switch to white uniforms.

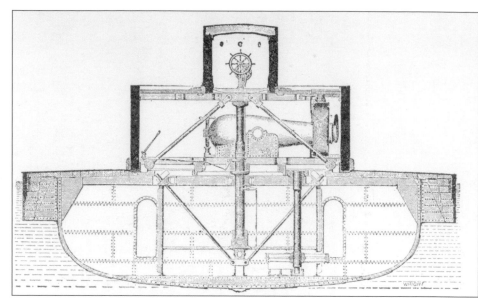

This sectional view of the USS Monitor shows the mechanism for the revolving turret, which housed two 11-inch smoothbore guns. This ship had a wooden frame covered by a thick armored hull. More than nine months after its fight with the CSS Virginia, the Monitor sank in a storm off Cape Hatteras, killing four officers and twelve sailors.

Launched on February 14, 1862, the USS Galena was one of the first Union ironclad ships. Because it was protected by only three inches of iron plating, many doubted it would be able to withstand heavy enemy fire. In its first action, at Drewry's Bluff, Virginia, in May, it suffered heavy damage. After this, its armor plates were removed, and it was placed on blockade duty for the rest of the war.

The act depicted in this stirring print by Eastman Johnson would not have been likely to happen on a real battlefield. No drummer boy would have wanted to be elevated six or seven feet in the air to where he would be a clear target! Enlistment records show boys as young as 9 did serve in both armies, sometimes as musicians or camp helpers. Most would have been orphans or runaways.

JUNE 16
Union forces take heavy losses at the Battle of Secessionville, South Carolina. Within days, Brigadier General Henry W. Benham sees his commission revoked as a result of his reckless assault on the Confederate site.

JUNE 17
General Braxton Bragg takes over command of the main Confederate army in Mississippi.

JUNE 19
Slavery is abolished in all U.S. territories. No states, either Union or Confederate, are included in this act.

More than 2,300 chaplains served in the federal Army throughout the war. Sixty-six died in service, and three were awarded the Medal of Honor. In this photo, Father Thomas Mooney is celebrating Catholic mass for members of the 69th New York Infantry. The regiment's commander, Colonel Michael Corcoran, stands to the left of the priest.

To help supplement drab army rations, the government appointed civilian vendors, or sutlers, to sell a wide variety of goods in camp. Unscrupulous sutlers often jacked up prices and took unfair advantage of troops. Many of these profiteers became the target of pranks and vandalism from disgruntled soldiers.

This collection of artifacts illustrates what Union soldiers could buy from their sutler. The harmonica at top was a popular musical instrument, while the opened tin of food provided a change from the bland army diet. Two different patterns of heel plates could be nailed to the bottom of leather soles to provide traction in slippery terrain. The empty bottle may have held anything from ginger beer to a medicinal liquid.

Many soldiers loved tobacco in all its forms—whether bitten off and chewed, smoked in a pipe, or rolled into a cigar. Troops could purchase tobacco from civilians or sutlers, or they could ask loved ones at home to send it in a care package. Shown here is a clay pipe, a cigar, matches, lighters, and a wrapped tobacco plug.

JUNE 25
The Battle of Oak Grove, Virginia, marks the beginning of the Seven Days' Battles, as McClellan continues his attempt to reach Richmond.

JUNE 26
General Robert E. Lee begins his first offensive as Confederate commander at the Battle of Mechanicsville, Virginia. Despite a Confederate loss, this battle turns the tide against McClellan,

who begins to withdraw from his failed Peninsula Campaign.

General John Pope is placed in command of the new Union Army of Virginia.

Antietam

Robert E. Lee never envisioned fighting on Maryland soil when he crossed the Potomac River with his army on September 4. His real target was Pennsylvania—he believed that bringing the war to the North would demoralize its populace and that a Confederate victory there would convince European governments to recognize the Confederacy as its own nation. To that end, Lee intended to capture wealthy Northern cities like Harrisburg or Pittsburgh and then find some defensible ground. After recent victories around Richmond and at the Second Battle of Bull Run against forces more than twice his size, Lee believed his Army of Northern Virginia to be invincible.

Lee did not count on three things that happened. First, upward of 10,000 of his 50,000 troops refused to cross the Potomac. They had signed on to protect their homes in the South, not to invade the North. Second, the 12,500 soldiers of the federal garrison at Harpers Ferry did not retreat from the Confederate advance. Lee would have to split his army into pieces to deal with them. And third, McClellan obtained a lost copy of Lee's Order 191, which detailed how and where Lee split his forces.

Luckily for him, Lee learned from a civilian that McClellan knew the Confederate strategy, so he made contingency plans. Instead of pushing ahead into Pennsylvania, Lee now had to deal with a knowledgeable foe. He counted on McClellan's caution once again turning into slowness, giving the Southerners time to concentrate their army in a wide arc around Sharpsburg, along Antietam Creek, just a few miles from the Potomac. The Harpers Ferry garrison surrendered on September 15, so Lee was rejoined by much of the army that had detoured there. The only troops missing were A. P. Hill's Light Division, which had stayed behind to mop up. Lee was ready to make a stand, his back to the wide river. If the Confederates did not win, their army would be pushed into the Potomac.

McClellan attacked on the Confederate left flank at dawn on September 17. The Union assault from

Clara Barton arrived on the battlefield of Antietam with medical supplies and gained national prominence for her work there. In this engraving, she tends to a fallen soldier after the heaviest day of fighting ever on American soil.

the East Woods through Miller's cornfield toward the Dunker Church and the Confederate-held West Woods featured some of the most violent fighting of the war. Regiments crashed into each other, firing at a range of yards. No one was safe. A Union corps commander was killed. Union General John Sedgwick was wounded three times from three different directions.

By mid-morning, the fighting shifted to the Confederate center at the Sunken Road, a farm lane worn down by wagon traffic. Confederates held the natural trench though advancing Federals could fire down into the road. Finally, a mistaken order for retreat on the Confederate left opened a breach that allowed Federals into the road. Now they poured fire down the Confederate line, assuring that it would hit anyone now trapped in the depressed lane. As the battle dwindled in the center, Union troops remarked how they could walk on top of dead Confederates in the road without ever touching the ground.

By midday, the fighting moved to the far right as Federals stubbornly tried to take a stone bridge over Antietam Creek. Remarkably, several thousand Union soldiers had been held at bay by several hundred Georgians dug into a hillside. After being promised a liquor ration if they took the bridge, one Union regiment finally stormed across. The Georgians, out of ammunition, retreated.

With growing numbers of Federals on his now weak right flank, Lee was in danger of being cut off from the Potomac fords. At 3:30 P.M., Union forces began moving in to finish off Lee's battle-weary army. They paid scant attention to a blue-clad column moving toward their flank. When a 3,000-musket volley erupted into their ranks, the Federals learned that the unfamiliar column was Hill's Light Division, many of its members now wearing federal overcoats they coveted for the coming winter.

Shocked by this attack, the Union troops rushed for the safety of their rear lines. An always-nervous McClellan believed Hill's attack was just the opening salvo from a huge reserve Lee had kept hidden. In reality, Lee had committed every soldier in his 40,000-strong army, while McClellan had held back the entire 5th Corps, at least 20,000 soldiers, in anticipation of fighting a Confederate reserve force that never existed.

McClellan never attacked, and Lee escaped back across the Potomac. The combined casualty list of this one-day battle was 23,000, virtually identical to the April two-day battle in Shiloh, Tennessee.

Despite insistent pleas from Washington, McClellan chose not to follow Lee across the river into Virginia. This was the last straw for Lincoln. In November the President relieved McClellan of his command once and for all.

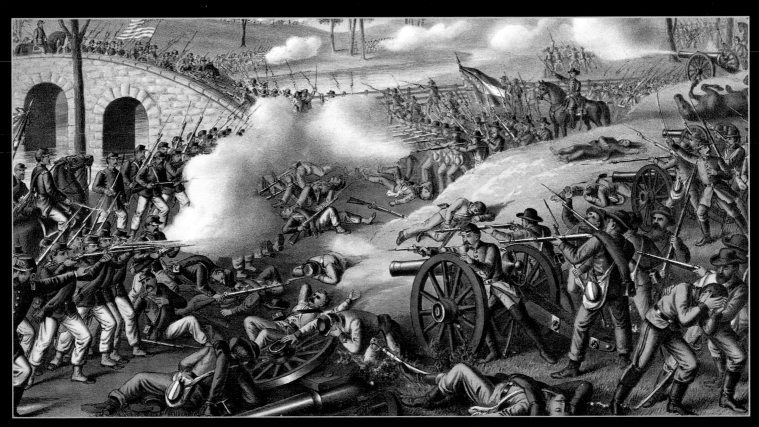

In this Kurz & Allison print, Union soldiers have stormed across Burnside's Bridge at Antietam into a battle with defending Confederates, an action that never happened. The end of the bridge defended by the Confederates ran into a steep hillside rather than the tiny hill depicted in this print. Compare this to the photograph of Burnside's Bridge on page 134.

Published in the 1880s, this Louis Prang lithograph shows "The Hornets' Nest" at Shiloh being defended by Union General Benjamin Prentiss, mounted on the horse at the right. Prentiss's division held this small section of the Sunken Road running through the woods for nearly six hours, enough time for U.S. Grant to form a final defensive line near the banks of the Tennessee River.

Colorado's volunteer soldiers never made it to the eastern battlefields, but one column did assist in defeating a Confederate column that had invaded New Mexico in 1862. The troops, under Colonel John Chivington, also participated in one of the worst massacres in American history when they attacked the Cheyenne camp at Sand Creek on November 29, 1864. Flying the American flag, Chivington's force killed some 150 Cheyenne—only 60 of them men.

Poet, newspaper editor, lawyer in the Indian Territories—Confederate General Albert Pike led an interesting life before the war. He successfully recruited more than 2,000 Cherokee to fight for the Confederacy, including one, Stand Watie, who would also become a general. Pike's career high point was leading a successful charge of his war-painted Cherokee troops at Pea Ridge, Arkansas, on March 7. After the war, the U.S. government persecuted the Cherokee for taking the Confederate side.

JUNE 27
After fierce, bloody fighting, Lee's Confederates take the upper hand at the Battle of Gaines' Mill, Virginia. McClellan retreats to the James River.

JUNE 28
David G. Farragut's Union fleet passes the Confederate batteries at Vicksburg, Mississippi.

JUNE 29
In the Battle of Savage's Station, Virginia, the Union rear guard safeguards the retreating U.S. forces from Confederate attack.

Artist Conrad Chapman
gave an idyllic depiction of
life in a Confederate camp
near Corinth, Mississippi,
in May 1862. In fact, more
soldiers died from disease in
seven weeks at this location
than died during the Battle of
Shiloh the month before.

This woodcut shows
General John Pope's
army clearing trees
through the swamp
surrounding Island
Number 10 to create a
canal for transportation.
Pope was west of the
island, while the Union
fleet had approached
from the east. The area
was too swampy to
march his troops toward
the island, but when
Union gunboats, afraid
of shelling, would not
sail past the island to
pick up his army, Pope
had little choice but to
innovate.

Confederate General Albert
Sidney Johnston was rallying
his troops at Shiloh when he
was shot in the back of the leg.
The bullet severed an artery,
and without a tourniquet to
staunch the bleeding, Johnston
quickly bled to death. At the
time of his death, he was the
Confederacy's highest-ranking
officer.

JUNE 30
McClellan's Army of the Potomac escapes disaster at the Battle of Glendale, Virginia, when disorganized Confederate officers fail to coordinate their attack. The Union continues to retreat.

JULY 1
The Battle of Malvern Hill, Virginia, ends the Seven Days' Battles. Federal forces repel Confederate attacks, but the army completes its retreat. Lee has driven McClellan away from the Confederate capital.

Lincoln issues a call for 300,000 volunteers to the Union cause.

Chimborazo Hospital

Planned by Confederate Surgeon General Samuel P. Moore, Chimborazo Hospital was the first general hospital constructed in Richmond that utilized the pavilion system. Chimborazo was constructed on a high plateau just east of the city. The James River lay immediately to the south, and a creek bordered the site on the west. These water bodies, when combined with the hill's eastern slope, gave the site excellent drainage and a good supply of water. Sweating slaves constructed about 120 buildings in the 40-acre complex. Most were ward buildings, whitewashed wooden structures 75 feet long with room for 30 to 40 cots. Altogether, the hospital could handle 3,000 patients at a time. The Seven Days' Battles led to overcrowding, with more than 3,500 admitted.

The hospital opened in October 1861, with Dr. James B. McCaw in charge. Using a hospital fund provided by the Army to ensure each patient received a balanced diet to speed recovery, McCaw proved an able administrator.

Chimborazo was a typical army hospital. The hot climate meant that the smell of sick men and gangrene permeated the pine boards. Hordes of flies constantly tormented staff and patients alike. So overworked was the medical staff that visitors sometimes claimed wounded men went four or five days without care.

To alleviate these problems, the Confederate Congress passed a law in September 1862 that authorized the hiring of matrons to assist the medical staff. Laudable as this legislation was, though, it did not help. Full-time nursing was not regarded as an accept-able occupation for women, and most men refused to work with members of the opposite sex. Chimborazo, however, by some stroke of luck, managed to hire a number of women for most wards. Patients later recalled that the mere presence of women in the wards raised morale and helped their recovery.

Chimborazo faced the usual shortages throughout the war—food, silverware, dishes, soap, bedding, clothing, bandages, and more. McCaw battled with the quartermaster and commissary departments over jurisdiction in order to acquire badly needed supplies.

The hospital remained open until Richmond fell and the federal Army occupied the grounds. Shortly thereafter, the facility was closed. More than 77,000 patients had been admitted to Chimborazo; more than 20 percent of them died, with 16,000 buried in nearby Oakwood Cemetery.

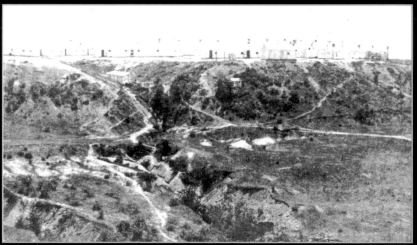

This view of Richmond's Chimborazo Hospital illustrates the fine geographical location of the facility—on a hill, which provided better drainage for the site.

The Pacific Railway Act is signed into law.

JULY 2
Lincoln signs the Morrill Land Grant Act.

JULY 4–28
Colonel John Hunt Morgan, the "Thunderbolt of the Confederacy," conducts his first raid into Kentucky.

JULY 11
Henry W. Halleck is named Union general in chief.

JULY 12
Lincoln signs the bill creating the Congressional Medal of Honor.

Medal of Honor Winner

"As the smoke was lifted by the gentle May breeze, one lone soldier advanced, bravely bearing the flag toward the breast works. At least a hundred men took deliberate aim at him, and fired at point-blank range, but he never faltered. Stumbling over the bodies of his fallen comrades, he continued to advance. Suddenly, as if with one impulse, every Confederate soldier within sight of the Union color bearer seemed to be seized with the idea that the man ought not to be shot down like a dog. . . . As soon as they all understood one another, a hundred old hats and caps went up into the air, their wearers yelling at the top of their voices: 'Come on, you brave Yank, come on!' He did come, and was taken by the hand and pulled over the breast works, and when it was discovered that he was not even scratched, a hundred Texans wrung his hands and congratulated him upon his miraculous escape from death."

Captain A. C. Matthews, 99th Illinois Volunteer Infantry, describing the bravery of color bearer Thomas H. Higgins on May 22, 1863, during the failed assault on Vicksburg, Mississippi, for which Higgins was later awarded a Medal of Honor

Andrews's Raid was an April 12 train-stealing and railroad-wrecking expedition in north Georgia by a band of Union soldiers dressed in civilian clothes. The raiders stole an engine called The General *and started driving north, wrecking rails as they went. Pursued by* The General's *persistent conductor, who gathered reinforcements as he went, the raiders eventually ran out of wood and water. Many of them were captured and hanged, but some escaped to the North.*

JULY 14
Congress votes to abolish the rum ration on U.S. ships.

JULY 15
The ironclad CSS *Arkansas* steams through Farragut's Union fleet north of Vicksburg on the Mississippi River.

JULY 16
Congress authorizes the rank of rear admiral. David Farragut is promoted to this rank.

JULY 17
Congress passes an act to free the slaves of slaveholders who support rebellion.

Medal of Honor

The Congressional Medal of Honor, the most coveted decoration soldiers, sailors, or aviators can receive for gallantry in combat service to their country, started more humbly during the Civil War.

Until the war began, most military leaders ignored the concept of singling out brave soldiers in the belief that recognition of individuality harmed unit solidarity. The only recognition given officers was brevet promotions, a confusing type of honorary promotion entitling the receiving officer to a higher ranking title but not the actual higher rank, nor the higher pay that went with the higher rank.

In late 1861, several U.S. representatives created the Medal of Honor for the Navy and Marines. A second bill approved the same medal for the Army. It was a five-pointed star hanging from a red, white, and blue ribbon resembling the American flag.

Created to honor the bravest, the medal curiously got off to a low-key start. Its first recipients were not combat soldiers but the six surviving spies of Andrews's Raid who had accomplished little more than steal a train engine in northern Georgia.

As the war dragged on, Congress and the Lincoln Administration began issuing Medals of Honor to curry favor back home. One entire unit, the 27th Maine Infantry Regiment, with 864 members, was awarded individual medals for doing nothing more valorous than reenlisting in the Army and continuing their dull, safe duty of living in the forts surrounding Washington.

A common form of "gallantry" cited in the 1,527 medals awarded during the Civil War was for saving the Union colors—its battle flags—from capture or for capturing Confederate colors.

During the war, flags were used to mark the center of the regiment and to provide soldiers a large visual aid on which to line up in the right direction. In theory, taking a Confederate flag would mean braving heavy fire to snatch the flag and return to one's own lines. But in practice, battle flags were often dropped by wounded or killed color bearers. The Union soldier may have done nothing more than snatch the flag up from the ground and run back to his own lines, but the mere possession of the flag was proof enough that the soldier deserved the medal.

Protecting or advancing one's own colors often did involve a brave act. At Fredericksburg in December 1862, Lieutenant John Adams of the 19th Massachusetts snatched both the U.S. flag and the Massachusetts state flag from their dying bearers and marched forward with one in each hand so his regiment could see where to re-form during the futile assault on Marye's Heights.

Some of the medal citations are odd. Seaman Thomas Lyons was lashed to the rigging of his ship while it ran past forts on the Mississippi. Lyons's citation says he "never flinched" while under heavy fire. Some citations are vague. The citation for Private Gotlieb Luty says he "bravely advanced to the enemy's lines under heavy fire and brought back valuable information." Other citations cite dubious bravery. The citation for Sergeant George Lovering reports he "rendered efficient aid in preventing a panic" in his regiment when other Union troops ran through his unit at Port Hudson, Louisiana.

Persistent people could often convince others they deserved a Medal of Honor. The earliest act

Dr. Mary Walker was a 28-year-old pioneering doctor when the war began. Signing up as a nurse, she eventually worked her way up to assistant surgeon for an Ohio regiment, insisting that her skills matched any male doctor. Though never in combat, she successfully lobbied for a Medal of Honor.

Private Francis Brownell of the 11th New York Fire Zouaves won his Medal of Honor for actions in a hotel stairwell in Alexandria, Virginia. Brownell bayoneted the civilian who had killed his commander, Colonel Elmer Ellsworth, in May 1861 before any battle had been fought. Brownell nominated himself twice and had to wait until 1877 to get his medal.

of the war to be awarded a medal occurred in May 1861 when Private Francis Brownell bayoneted to death a civilian who had killed Brownell's colonel, Elmer Ellsworth. Brownell nominated himself twice for the medal but had to wait until 1877 to actually get it with the help of his persistent representative in Congress.

Another persistent person was Dr. Mary Walker, who hounded the Congress to award her the medal

for treating wounded soldiers. The award was finally given, but it was revoked in 1917, as she did not meet the criteria of actually having been in combat. Dr. Walker, who lived until 1919, refused to give the medal back. President Jimmy Carter later reinstated it in 1977. She remains the only woman to have won the medal.

After World War I, when warfare became more brutal, Congress decided that the Medal of Honor's significance had been watered down by so many casual awards in the past. It tightened the rules for winning the medal and revoked more than 900 citations, including those of the 864 men of the 27th Maine who dutifully sat in their forts around Washington for the nine months of their enlistment.

Christian A. Fleetwood (left) and John H. Lawson were each awarded a Medal of Honor for displaying courage under fire. Fleetwood defended the flag at the Battle of Chapin's Farm, Virginia, in 1864. Lawson served in the Navy and won the medal for remaining at his battle station after being wounded at the Battle of Mobile Bay, Alabama, in 1864.

Graphically demonstrating the punching power of rifled artillery, this interior view of Confederate-held Fort Pulaski, Georgia, east of Savannah, was taken in April 1862. The federal rifled cannons fired explosive rounds that burrowed into the brick walls of the fort before exploding and shattering those walls. The centuries-old design of the masonry fort was instantly obsolete.

The gaping holes at Fort Pulaski, Georgia, demonstrate why masonry forts were rendered obsolete—rifled cannon shells could dig their way deep inside them before exploding. Robert E. Lee had inspected the fort a few months earlier and declared it defensible. He had not yet seen what the newly designed rifled cannon could do.

This Prang lithograph shows Captain David Farragut's flagship Hartford *engaging the unfinished ironclad CSS* Louisiana *during the night of April 24. On the right, the ironclad ram CSS* Manassas *races into battle. The* Hartford *momentarily ran aground, and while stuck, was accosted by a rebel steamer that pushed a fire raft against her side. The crew of the* Hartford *prevailed, sank the steamer, doused the fires, and continued upstream.*

JULY 19
Lincoln appoints John S. Phelps as military governor of Arkansas.

JULY 22
Union naval vessels attack the

CSS *Arkansas* at Vicksburg, Mississippi, but fail to sink it.

Union and Confederate representatives sign a prisoner of war cartel.

JULY 29
Confederate spy Belle Boyd is captured near Warrenton, Virginia.

Captain David Farragut ran his fleet of steamships and gunboats past a heavy gauntlet of fire thrown into the Mississippi by Forts Jackson and St. Philip about 70 miles south of New Orleans. The audacious run surprised Confederates, who were convinced that no ship captain would dare try to sail past two heavily armed forts. Farragut never doubted his ships would survive. His navy captured New Orleans.

Naval officers and those ranks who worked on the positions of their ships often used these types of instruments, which include a boxed compass, a spyglass, and other calibrating devices used to measure distance.

Shown here is just one style of a wide variety of field glasses used by both sides during the war. Officers, signalers, and scouts used these early binoculars to see at longer distances than they possibly could with the naked eye. Each set came with its own carrying case and strap.

AUGUST 2
Surgeon Jonathan Letterman of the Army of the Potomac establishes the Army's first ambulance corps.

AUGUST 5
Confederates attack occupying Union troops at the Battle of Baton Rouge, Louisiana.

AUGUST 6
The CSS *Arkansas* is destroyed by its crew near Baton Rouge.

AUGUST 9
Union General Nathaniel Banks is

Though in service only 22 days, the CSS Arkansas *was one of the South's most successful ironclads. Armored with bolted-on railroad rails and armed with ten cannons, the ship looked formidable. On July 15, the* Arkansas *attacked David Farragut's fleet of Union warships on the Mississippi. Smashing its way through, it made for Vicksburg. The* Arkansas's *captain blew the ship up when it broke a propeller shaft. The* Arkansas *was undefeated in combat.*

General David Hunter was an early friend of President-elect Lincoln. Lincoln appointed him general, but Hunter soon spoiled the friendship by arbitrarily freeing all the slaves in his conquered district in South Carolina, Georgia, and Florida on May 9. Lincoln revoked the edict and rebuked his former friend. Hunter earned the lasting hatred of Southerners when he burned the Virginia Military Institute in Lexington in 1864. After his defeat at the Battle of Lynchburg, Virginia, Hunter was pulled from line duty.

As early as the spring of 1862, the Confederates saw the economic strength of the Union when General McClellan was able to establish huge stockpiles of war supplies along small rivers, such as this scene at Cumberland Landing on the Pamunkey River southeast of Richmond.

One of only two wartime photographs taken of Stonewall Jackson, this was taken in 1862 at Winchester, Virginia, when he was visiting the home of his doctor, Hunter Holmes McGuire. One of McGuire's sisters suggested that Jackson have his image taken, so he went to a local photographer and sat for this portrait. Jackson's wife considered this the best ever taken of her husband.

defeated by Stonewall Jackson at the Battle of Cedar Mountain, Virginia.

Farragut burns the Louisiana village of Donaldsonville in retali-

ation for continued artillery fire against his fleet.

AUGUST 16
A Confederate invasion of Kentucky begins under Generals

Braxton Bragg and E. Kirby Smith.

AUGUST 17
An uprising by the Dakota Sioux begins in Minnesota.

The Battle of Stones River

No soldier is lonelier at any time than around the holidays. That would explain why, on the night of December 30 near Stones River in Tennessee, hundreds of military band members and tens of thousands of soldiers on both sides joined together to play and sing "Home Sweet Home." The next day they would start killing each other again.

The Battle of Stones River (called Murfreesboro by the South) opened strangely on the last morning of the year. Both Confederate General Braxton Bragg and Union General William Rosecrans intended to attack each other's right flank. Bragg beat Rosecrans to the punch by two hours. The Union general initially refused to believe a major attack was even underway until he saw his troops streaming to the rear. The Federals finally stabilized their V-shape defense in a four-acre forest dubbed "Hell's Half Acre." The Federals in the tiny forest acted much like those who had defended "The Hornets' Nest" at Shiloh in April. They fiercely beat back every Confederate attack.

On January 1, both sides rested. On January 2, the Confederates launched an infantry assault on an extended Union position, but massed Union artillery cut up the advancing gray columns. That night lower-ranking Confederate generals suggested to Bragg that the battle was at a standstill and they should retreat. Bragg reluctantly agreed and pulled back on January 3.

Judged by its roughly 24,000 casualties, the three-day Stones River was as bad or worse than the two-day Shiloh or the one-day Antietam, but it gave a boost to Union morale coming just two weeks after the devastating loss at Fredericksburg.

The end of one year and the beginning of another found federal Major General William Rosecrans's Army of the Cumberland engaging Braxton Bragg's Army of Tennessee in a bloody but inconclusive battle at Stones River. Having lost nearly a third of his 35,000 troops, Bragg had to evacuate Murfreesboro.

This woodcut shows the March 23, 1862, Battle of Kernstown, Virginia. The Confederate loss turned into a psychological victory, as the Federals would not believe Jackson attacked their force of 9,000 with only 4,000 of his own. Officials in Washington convinced themselves Jackson had more troops in the Shenandoah, so they sent reinforcements. Redeployment of these troops lessened General McClellan's strength as he began his Peninsula Campaign.

This woodcut shows the rear of the federal lines at the Battle of Cross Keys on June 8, with a number of ambulances waiting behind several ammunition caissons. In the middle is cavalry, and in the middle distance is federal artillery. This battle, directed by Confederate General Richard Ewell with very little input from Stonewall Jackson, became mostly an artillery duel and ended in a Confederate victory.

This fanciful lithograph shows a handsomely dressed Stonewall Jackson mounted on a beautiful, prancing horse entering Winchester, Virginia. He had successfully rid the area of Union forces during his Shenandoah Valley Campaign. The pious Presbyterian would likely have been embarrassed by this picture. Jackson was instead known to favor his seedy, decades-old blue uniform left over from his U.S. Army days.

Federal General Winfield Scott Hancock leads the charge against General James Longstreet's Confederates at the Battle of Williamsburg, Virginia, on May 5. In what was essentially a rearguard action, the Southerners succeeded in delaying the advance of McClellan's army up the James River Peninsula for several hours.

AUGUST 21
Jefferson Davis proclaims Union Generals David Hunter and John W. Phelps are to be treated as criminals for arming slaves by recruiting black soldiers.

AUGUST 24
The CSS *Alabama* is commissioned off the Azores Islands.

AUGUST 28
Confederates battle Federals to a stalemate at the Battle of Groveton, Virginia.

This 100-pounder Parrott rifle was placed in Fort Totten, one of the ring of forts protecting Washington from Confederate attack. It might have been better used in a seaside fort, as those offensives never materialized. The only fort that was ever attacked in the area was Fort Stevens, north of the White House, in the summer of 1864. The range on this gun was long enough to aid in the defense of Fort Stevens at that time.

When the war began, most of the capable cavalry officers in the U.S. Army joined the Confederacy. It took more than two years before the Union cavalry could acquire enough quality horses and train enough soldiers to rival the Confederate cavalry. In this print, Union cavalry is charging, waving their old-fashioned sabers rather than firing their modern carbines.

AUGUST 29–30
Miscalculations by General Pope at the Second Battle of Bull Run bring about a major defeat for the U.S. Army. Pope takes his troops back toward Washington.

General E. Kirby Smith routs Union forces at the Battle of Richmond, Kentucky. Thousands of federal soldiers—substantially more than half the fighting force—are taken prisoner.

SEPTEMBER 1
Union troops retreating from Bull Run are attacked during a driving rainstorm at the Battle of Chantilly, Virginia.

Frank Vizetelly's sketch of Southern cavalry leader Jeb Stuart appeared in the Illustrated London News of October 4, 1862. Vizetelly's surviving sketches are some of the best contemporary records of the Southern war effort.

The USS Commodore Barney *started its life as a New York City ferry. Bought by the U.S. Navy in 1861, the ship served in the blockade of the Atlantic Coast and in the 1863 expedition up the James River in Virginia.*

Artist Winslow Homer's first assignment related to the Civil War was to sketch Abraham Lincoln's inauguration. Homer later joined George McClellan's army as a sketch artist. While sketching the army at Yorktown, he noted a sniper perched in a tree going about his grim business of killing Confederates who exposed themselves. Homer converted that sketch into his first famous painting. His postwar career endured until his death in 1910.

Observation balloons were used by both sides to keep track of military movements early in the war, particularly during the beginning of the Seven Days' Campaign. Though the federal Army had access to several "aeronauts" who could supply them with instant intelligence from unobstructed heights of several hundred feet, the old-fashioned generals on the ground did not trust their observations.

SEPTEMBER 2
George McClellan is restored to the command of the troops in and around Washington.

SEPTEMBER 3
Confederate troops occupy Frankfort, the capital of Kentucky.

SEPTEMBER 4
Lee's Army of Northern Virginia

crosses the Potomac River to begin its invasion of Maryland.

SEPTEMBER 7
Bowling Green, Kentucky, is occupied by Union troops.

General Braxton Bragg

Confederate General Braxton Bragg's list of victories stands at one. That was Chickamauga, Georgia, which was won thanks to the lucky assault of General James Longstreet's corps. Bragg even failed to follow up that victory by crushing the retreating Federals.

Bragg's list of battlefield defeats or strategic failures under his command is longer: Pensacola, Corinth, Perryville, Stones River, Chattanooga, Dalton, and finally Wilmington in 1865.

The only reason Bragg was not sacked earlier in that four-year string of defeats is that he had made a good friend named Jefferson Davis during the Mexican War. President Davis always stood by his friends, no matter what level of incompetence they might have displayed.

In contrast to the unconditional respect most troops gave to Robert E. Lee, Bragg was universally despised by his subordinate generals and soldiers. The general's personality was abrasive, and

Braxton Bragg assumed command of the battered Confederate Army of Tennessee in June 1862. Following a brilliant flanking movement around the federal army in Chattanooga, Bragg's troops passed through Tennessee and entered Kentucky in September. His army was driven from the border state after the Battle of Perryville on October 8. One subordinate summed up Bragg's performance by stating, "General Bragg is either stark mad or utterly incompetent."

Confederate General Braxton Bragg's frock coat, shown here, is a traditional general's coat with two rows of eight brass buttons each, gold braid on the sleeves, and the appropriate number of stars within a wreath on the collar.

he ignored everyone's constructive advice. Refusing to admit his own blunders, he chose to blame his defeats on the lack of courage among his soldiers and their officers.

Bragg spent the last year of the war advising Davis, perhaps his only friend, on how to keep fighting. As demonstrated by his battlefield experiences, nothing Bragg suggested to Davis worked. Put back into the field to stop Union General William T. Sherman's army, Bragg drew vital reinforcements away from where they were desperately needed at the Battle of Bentonville, North Carolina. Fittingly, Bragg ended his involvement in the war by losing the last battle the South had a chance to win.

Republican Legislation

When the Southern states started to secede at the end of 1860, Southern legislators likewise left the U.S. Congress. Most of these members of Congress were Democrats, and once they were gone, Republicans had an overwhelming majority. Many of their pet projects and bills could now proceed virtually without opposition. At the end of the line, they would be met by Republican President Lincoln, who presumably would sign the bills, rather than Democratic President James Buchanan, who had had a habit of vetoing them. Republicans quickly got to work and in 1862 passed a number of far-reaching pieces of legislation.

The Homestead Act, vetoed by Buchanan in 1859, opened up U.S. territory in the West to pioneers, offering 160 acres to anyone who would remain on the land and improve it for five years. Thousands went into the territories looking to build on this opportunity. Between January 1863 and June 1864, more than 1.2 million acres were claimed.

The Morrill Land Grant Act likewise set aside public lands to build colleges for agricultural and mechanical arts. Each state was given 30,000 acres for each senator or congressional representative it had to pay for the schools. Even Confederate states were included in the bill: They would receive the same deal when they returned to the Union. Schools such as Penn State, Cornell, the University of Wisconsin, Texas A&M, MIT, and many others benefited from this act.

The Pacific Railway Act used land grants to encourage the building of a transcontinental railroad. Railroad companies would be given a certain amount of public land for each mile of track they laid in an effort to bring California, Oregon, and the West Coast into closer contact with the rest of the country. The Department of Agriculture was also brought into being by this Congress, although it did not originally enjoy Cabinet status.

To help finance the war, Republican legislators instituted the first income tax in 1861 and the following year passed the Legal Tender Act, which established paper currency based on government credit rather than reserves of gold. These bills came to be called "greenbacks." As the Republicans themselves began to disagree and splinter into factions, they also came into more conflict with the President. Congress's efficiency in passing such groundbreaking legislation began to diminish.

Passed on May 20, 1862, the Homestead Act provided for the free distribution of public lands for settlement. Despite some abuse by speculators, the plan enhanced the population and development of the West. It also increased popular support for President Lincoln and the Republican party. Before the Civil War, Southern members of Congress had blocked such legislation to prevent the spread of antislavery sentiment to the West.

SEPTEMBER 13
Union troops find three cigars wrapped in a copy of General Lee's plans to divide his forces. These plans are passed along to McClellan.

SEPTEMBER 14
Union forces push Confederates back at the Battle of South Mountain, Maryland.

SEPTEMBER 15
The Union garrison of Harpers Ferry, Virginia, surrenders to Stonewall Jackson's forces.

As the Federals advanced up the Virginia Peninsula toward Richmond, they encountered many small streams and rivers that had to be bridged. Here is the Grapevine Bridge over the Chickahominy south of Richmond. The Federals would destroy this bridge during the Seven Days' Battles, and Stonewall Jackson's men would rebuild it to continue their pursuit of the Army of the Potomac.

On May 27, 1862, a month before going into the Seven Days' Battles, these Federals proudly posed behind a captured Confederate 12-pound Napoleon howitzer. This gun was very popular with Confederate artillery soldiers as it was light enough to be pulled easily by horses but heavy enough to pound fortifications. It was particularly deadly when firing canisters at close range.

Perhaps the most infamous intelligence network used by federal troops during the war was that of Allan Pinkerton. Having won Lincoln's confidence, Pinkerton joined the staff of an old friend, General George McClellan, to coordinate intelligence-gathering activities. Pinkerton's agents grossly overestimated Confederate strength at each stage of McClellan's Peninsula Campaign, contributing to its dismal failure. When McClellan was replaced as commander of the Army of the Potomac in November 1862, Pinkerton's influence also faded.

SEPTEMBER 17
In what has come to be known as the bloodiest day of the war, Union and Confederate armies fight to a draw at the Battle of Antietam, Maryland.

Confederates capture the Union garrison of Munfordville, Kentucky.

An explosion at the Allegheny Arsenal in Pittsburgh, Pennsylva-

nia, kills dozens of women and boys working there.

SEPTEMBER 19
Union forces hold off a Confederate attack at the Battle of Iuka, Mississippi.

These apparently calm Union howitzer gunners posing on the ground they won at the Battle of Fair Oaks on June 1, 1862, have no idea that they will meet a new general by the name of Robert E. Lee by the end of the month. Note the mud on the wheels of the cannon carriage.

This photograph of Battery M of the 2nd U.S. Artillery shows six three-inch ordnance rifles, with their gun crews and supporting ammunition caissons in the rear. The guns and limbers are pulled by six-horse teams. The Confederates had to make do with much less equipment and support.

Artillery projectiles used during the war were a varied lot. Seven are on display here, together with a ring gauge, a round instrument used by inspectors to check the size of a round ball. On the top row, from left to right, are a Parrott shell, a Read shell, and a British-made Whitworth shell. On the bottom, left to right, are a Blakely shell, a Schenkl shell, a round shot, and a Hotchkiss shell.

Louis Philippe d'Orleans Paris and Robert d'Orleans Chartres, dressed in captain uniforms of the Union Army, were two of an undetermined number of Europeans who rode with both armies to observe the war. Each side treated the foreign observers with respect in hopes they would report favorably to their home governments. Britain, France, Germany, and Russia were among the countries watching to see how the war's outcome would affect their own governments.

SEPTEMBER 22
Lincoln issues his preliminary Emancipation Proclamation.

SEPTEMBER 24
Lincoln suspends the writ of habeas corpus for anyone who helps the enemy.

Fourteen Northern governors meet in Altoona, Pennsylvania, to pledge their support for the war effort and for the emancipation of slaves.

SEPTEMBER 27
The first black regiment is mustered into service in New Orleans.

On June 27 at Gaines'
Mill during the Seven
Days' Battles, the 5th
U.S. Cavalry charged an
infantry division led by
a former member of the
5th, Confederate General
John Bell Hood. In overall
command of the Confeder-
ates was Robert E. Lee, a
former commander of the
2nd U.S. Cavalry, from
which the 5th had sprung.
This deadly charge saved
some federal cannons from
being captured.

The New York Herald *was the only Northern newspaper to organize its
correspondents covering military operations. While other reporters eked out an
existence dependent upon the goodwill of officers, the* Herald *provided tents,
supplies, and food for its employees. Timothy O'Sullivan captured this image of
the* Herald's *staff at Bealton, Virginia, in August 1863.*

*This tintype of a Union soldier posed with a banjo is housed in a gutta-percha,
a hard plastic, hinged case lined with velvet. Such keepsakes survived by the
thousands and today grace both public and private collections.*

SEPTEMBER 29
Union General Jefferson C. Davis
shoots and kills General William
Nelson, his commanding officer,
during an argument in a Louisville hotel.

OCTOBER 1
Lincoln visits General McClellan
at his headquarters near Antietam, Maryland.

The Union Mississippi River gunboat fleet is transferred to the

U.S. Navy, with David D. Porter
placed in command.

OCTOBER 3–4
Union troops rebuff Confederate
forces at the Battle of Corinth,
Mississippi.

Some estimates claim that hundreds of women served in the Union Army disguised as men. Frances Clalin is shown here in the uniform of a cavalry trooper in the Missouri militia.

Loreta Velazquez was a woman who either successfully posed as a man long enough to win a Confederate officer's commission or was a complete fraud. Historians are unsure, as even her birth and death dates are unknown. Velazquez's postwar memoir, The Woman in Battle, featured her claim that she fought in the war posing as Harry Buford.

The patriotism of Southern women is illustrated in this 1862 woodcut. The women on the left are working to produce uniforms for soldiers; on the right, other women exhort their men to enlist in order to protect the South from Yankee invaders.

With men away at war, women joined the workforce in increasing numbers. Working in arsenals and other government facilities, women performed the dangerous task of making ammunition for the Army. The slightest spark could set off unstable black powder and cause a catastrophe.

These refugees are from the town of New Ulm, Minnesota. Dakota warriors, beaten back in a previous attack they had made on a U.S. Army fort, overran and set fire to the town on August 23. Nearly 200 buildings burned, leaving 2,000 residents no choice but to walk to Mankato, 30 miles away. The Dakota did not attack the column, which included women and children.

OCTOBER 5
Union soldiers engage retreating Confederates at the Hatchie River in Tennessee.

OCTOBER 8
Troops under Union General Don Carlos Buell defeat Braxton Bragg's army at the Battle of Perryville, Kentucky, effectively ending Confederate action in the state.

OCTOBER 11
The Confederate Congress exempts from the draft slaveholders who own at least 20 slaves.

This image, one of a series made for the Quartermaster Department in 1862, shows a model in the dress uniform of a hospital steward. Unlike surgeons and assistant surgeons, hospital stewards did not operate on wounded soldiers but performed the useful tasks of compounding and administering medicines and looking after patients.

In August 1862, the Dakota Sioux in Minnesota revolted after years of broken promises from the U.S. government with a series of raids. The Army responded by capturing 2,000 men, women, and children and selecting 300 warriors for execution in retaliation for over 500 white deaths. President Lincoln approved only 38 hangings. On December 26, the largest mass execution in American history took place in Mankato, Minnesota. The remaining Dakota Sioux were shipped away from their ancestral homes.

During the Battle of Cedar Mountain in August, the Confederate field hospital shown here treated the wounded. The Confederate medical corps had not yet developed the shortage in medical supplies it suffered later in the war.

Samuel P. Moore, shown here in postwar civilian dress, was the Confederacy's only surgeon general. When faced with a blockade that kept some medicines in short supply, he commissioned scientists to experiment with plants to find substitute medicines. He was the first surgeon general to recognize the importance of dentistry when he commissioned several dentists into his medical corps. He helped develop some of the South's most efficient hospitals, such as Chimborazo Hospital.

Confederate cavalry led by Jeb Stuart occupy Chambersburg, Pennsylvania.

OCTOBER 18
John Hunt Morgan and his Con-

federate raiders take Lexington, Kentucky.

OCTOBER 24
Union General Buell is removed from command of his troops in Kentucky and Tennessee. General

William S. Rosecrans is placed in command of the new Department of the Cumberland.

In this scene from a now-lost cyclorama of the Second Battle of Bull Run, troops from Fitz John Porter's 5th Corps attack Stonewall Jackson's line on August 30. Lieutenant Colonel William Chapman, mounted with his sword raised, leads his brigade of Army regulars forward.

Another scene from the Second Battle of Bull Run cyclorama depicts General Robert E. Lee, riding a light-colored horse and looking over his shoulder, and his staff. Lee is speaking with General James Longstreet, whose troops are moving into position to flank the Union troops assailing Jackson's line.

This Currier & Ives print of a Union charge at the Second Battle of Bull Run leaves a mistaken impression of the conflict. General John Pope made strategic errors in assuming fewer Confederates were on the field than were actually present. Although Pope ordered his troops to attack, rebels under the command of James Longstreet counterattacked and provided the Union Army with its second loss on this field in just over a year.

OCTOBER 26
More than a month after Lee's retreat from Antietam, McClellan takes his army back across the Potomac into Virginia.

NOVEMBER 4
In congressional elections, Democrats make some gains, but Republicans maintain a majority in the House of Representatives.

NOVEMBER 7
After moving slowly for too long, McClellan is replaced by Ambrose Burnside as commander of the Army of the Potomac.

When observed from a distance, these logs made phony cannons that looked just as deadly as the real things. Johnny Reb and Billy Yank referred to them as "Quaker guns." In March 1862, Confederate forces left these "guns" in place when they abandoned their camps at Manassas. Union troops discovered the ruse when they occupied the site. "The rebels had mounted painted logs," observed a surprised bluecoat. Elsewhere he found an old locomotive smokestack.

This postbattle view of the battlefield at the Second Battle of Bull Run shows the wide expanse of open land the Federals had to cross in order to attack Stonewall Jackson's troops, who were protected by the Unfinished Railroad Cut. The idea of marching across open fields into dark woods worried Union General Fitz John Porter and caused him to ignore orders from General Pope, an action for which he was later court-martialed.

These soldiers inspect all that is left of a federal railroad car after Stonewall Jackson's troops were done with it. Jackson had found the car, filled with supplies, on his way through Manassas Junction in August 1862 to fight the Second Battle of Bull Run. Note these soldiers' use of blanket rolls rather than knapsacks.

NOVEMBER 21
James A. Seddon is appointed Confederate secretary of war.

NOVEMBER 24
General Joseph E. Johnston is

placed in command of the Confederate troops between the Mississippi River and the Allegheny Mountains.

NOVEMBER 28
Union forces are victorious in an engagement at Cane Hill, Arkansas.

This Prang lithograph from the 1880s shows federal troops advancing on the West Woods, the strongest Confederate position at Antietam. The Dunker Church can be seen at right. Within minutes, the Confederates would launch a counterattack that would drive back the farthest forward advance the Union army made on the Confederate left flank.

Legends about real people die hard when poems are written about them. Such is the case of "Barbara Fritchie," written by John Greenleaf Whittier in 1863. The poem describes how the elderly Fritchie (sometimes spelled Frietchie) defiantly flew an American flag out her Frederick, Maryland, window as Stonewall Jackson passed on his way to capture Harpers Ferry in September. The poem portrays Jackson as gentlemanly in his confrontation, but in actuality, he never saw Fritchie.

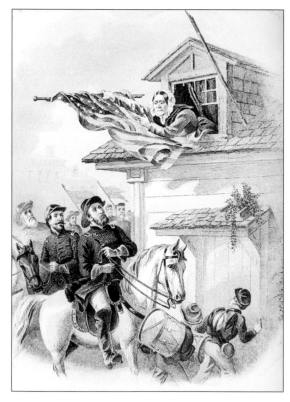

The setting of this photo of Confederate dead after the Battle of Antietam on September 17 was called "Artillery Hell" after the number of shells that were launched from—and into—this small area across from the Dunker Church, which is seen in the background. Alexander Gardner displayed this image to shocked New Yorkers in his gruesome collection of battlefield photographs.

DECEMBER 7
Confederates attack in the Battle of Prairie Grove, Arkansas, but are unable to force Union troops to withdraw.

John Hunt Morgan's troops capture the Union garrison of Hartsville, Tennessee.

DECEMBER 11
Union General Burnside crosses

the Rappahannock to take Fredericksburg, Virginia. Lee holds his defensive position, and Confederates give only token opposition to the crossing.

When Lee retreated after the Battle of Antietam, he was forced to leave some of his wounded, who are gathered here in makeshift "shebangs" outside of a barn east of Sharpsburg, Maryland. Note the random-length pieces of wood holding up the tent canvas and the posts resting on a fence in the rear so that more tents can be erected. Lee's army had nearly 8,000 soldiers wounded.

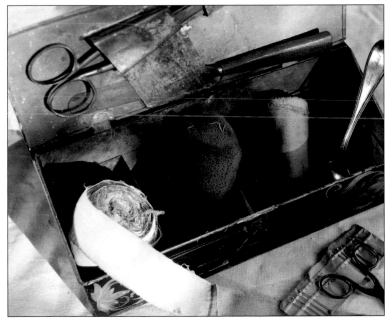

This small nurse's kit contains needles, scissors, and a variety of bandages to close small wounds. More serious wounds required the presence of a surgeon, who brought expertise and instruments.

Although she had no formal nursing training, Clara Barton volunteered to aid wounded federal soldiers after the First Battle of Bull Run, arranging for the collection and distribution of badly needed medical supplies. Her successful efforts earned her a special pass that allowed her to travel with army ambulances, as well as the nickname "the angel of the battlefield." Barton later founded the American Red Cross in 1881.

DECEMBER 11–20
Union troops led by General John G. Foster advance from New Bern to Goldsboro, North Carolina, to interdict railroads.

DECEMBER 11–JANUARY 1, 1863
Nathan Bedford Forrest raids Union-held western Tennessee intending to disrupt General Grant's army.

DECEMBER 12
The USS *Cairo* is sunk by a Confederate mine in the Yazoo River in Mississippi.

This is a view of the notorious Sunken Road at Antietam as it appears today. Here, on September 17, defending Confederate soldiers held off attack after attack until they were outflanked by Union troops and finally driven back. The roadway became known as "Bloody Lane" because of all the dead bodies that littered it after the battle.

Rappahannock Station was a railroad stop near the Rappahannock River north of Warrenton, Virginia. During the Second Manassas Campaign of August 1862, Lee fought a series of skirmishes in the area that allowed Jackson's troops to slip out of their camps to make a fast march on Bristoe Station and Manassas Junction.

Two weeks after the federal victory at the Battle of Antietam, President Lincoln visited McClellan at his headquarters to discuss the Army's next move. Lincoln wanted McClellan to vigorously pursue Lee's beaten army; McClellan was reluctant to do so. He paid for his reluctance with his job when Lincoln relieved him of command on November 7.

Even taking into account that people had to stand perfectly still in a photograph of this time to avoid blur, this Alexander Gardner photo of President Lincoln meeting with General McClellan (sixth from left) seems particularly stiff and uncomfortable. It would have been. Lincoln had come to McClellan's camp south of Sharpsburg in October to urge him to pursue the battered Confederate army. When McClellan did not move fast enough, Lincoln fired him in November. Captain George A. Custer, who in 1876 would be killed at Little Bighorn by Sioux, is at the far right.

DECEMBER 13
Burnside leads his troops in the ill-fated Battle of Fredericksburg, Virginia. Fighting against dug-in Confederate troops, Union forces lose more than 12,000 soldiers.

DECEMBER 15
General Nathaniel P. Banks replaces Benjamin Butler in New Orleans as commander of the Department of the Gulf.

DECEMBER 17
General Grant issues controversial General Order Number 11, which expels all Jews from his department. The order is rescinded on January 4, 1863.

Union General Fitz John Porter became a victim of vicious Washington politics. During the Seven Days' Battles, Porter's 5th Corps defeated Lee's army in most battles, only to be ordered to fall back by McClellan. Moving to support John Pope at the Second Battle of Bull Run, Porter ignored Pope's possibly unrealistic orders to attack immediately. When Pope lost that battle, he blamed Porter, who was fired and then court-martialed. An Army review board reversed the guilty verdict in 1879.

Europeans desperately wanted Southern cotton for their mills and were quite upset that the Union blockade made it impossible for them get it. The Confederacy hoped this would be enough to convince European governments to enter the war on their behalf, but the issue of slavery was a barrier. The Europeans did not want to appear to support the institution, which they had banned decades earlier.

The federal blockade of the Confederacy's coastline grew ever tighter as the war dragged on. The increasing effectiveness of the blockade had its greatest impact on the Confederate inflation rate. A one-dollar gold piece in Richmond in May 1861 was worth just over a dollar in Confederate currency; but by war's end, the same dollar of gold was worth more than $60. The drawing shows the auction of a five-dollar gold piece in Virginia at the height of the money crisis.

Secretary of State Seward tries to resign, but Lincoln refuses to accept the proffer.

December 20
A Confederate cavalry raid destroys Grant's supply base at Holly Springs, Mississippi, halting his advance toward Vicksburg.

Secretary of the Treasury Salmon Chase tries to resign but is rebuffed by Lincoln.

December 21
John Hunt Morgan's command begins another raid into Kentucky.

The Battle of Perryville, Kentucky, on October 8 ended all Confederate hopes that large numbers of sympathetic Kentuckians would join the South and finished Braxton Bragg's invasion of the state. Because of what is known as an acoustical shadow, an oddity of nature that hides the sounds of battle, Union commander Don Carlos Buell did not even know his army was under attack until midway through the battle. Bragg retreated when he realized how large the federal force was.

DECEMBER 26
In retaliation for a recent Dakota Sioux uprising, 38 Sioux are hanged at Mankato, Minnesota.

Samuel P. Carter's Union cavalry departs from Manchester, Kentucky, on a raid into the upper Tennessee River valley.

DECEMBER 29
General Sherman's troops are rebuffed by Confederates at the Battle of Chickasaw Bayou, Mississippi.

Federal troops build pontoon bridges by which the Army of the Potomac, now under the command of General Ambrose E. Burnside, will cross the Rappahannock River. The Federals are being harried by Confederate snipers in dug-in positions on the opposite bank and in the town of Fredericksburg, which federal artillery has set afire. After these bridges were completed, General Lee allowed the Union army to cross the river with little resistance, setting it up for disaster when the soldiers reached his shore at the Battle of Fredericksburg, Virginia, on December 13.

The Commonwealth of Pennsylvania erected this statue to honor General Andrew A. Humphreys. His division of eight Keystone State regiments vainly but gallantly charged the stone wall on Marye's Heights at Fredericksburg, Virginia.

The tenure of Ambrose E. Burnside as commander of the Army of the Potomac lasted less than three months, primarily due to his devastating defeat at Fredericksburg, Virginia. "It was plain, that he felt he had led us to a great disaster," one subordinate later wrote, "and one knowing him . . . could see he wished his body was also lying in front of Marye's Heights."

South Carolina Sergeant Richard Kirkland, moved by the pleas of suffering wounded Union soldiers lying near the stone wall on Marye's Heights, decided to help. He collected canteens of water from his comrades, cautiously stood up, and slowly climbed over the wall. As he began to aid the wounded nearest him, gunfire on both sides stopped as the combatants allowed him to minister to the suffering troops in blue. The "Angel of Marye's Heights" was honored with this statue.

DECEMBER 31
The USS *Monitor* sinks in a storm off Cape Hatteras.

Union troops engage Forrest's retreating Confederate horse

soldiers at Parker's Store, near Lexington, Tennessee. With a Union force on either side of him, Forrest attacks both and escapes through the middle with his troops.

DECEMBER 31–JANUARY 2, 1863
The Union army defeats Confederate forces at the Battle of Stones River, Tennessee.

1863

THE TURNING POINT

DECISIVE VICTORIES IN EAST AND WEST SHIFT THE MOMENTUM NORTH

*A*fter almost two years of civil war, 1863 opened with President Lincoln's formal issuance of the Emancipation Proclamation. This gave the war for the preservation of the Union an added meaning. Although the proclamation did not actually free any slaves—freedom was restricted to areas under control of the Southern Confederacy—its meaning resounded throughout the divided nation and into Europe. In one

This engraving, from a drawing by A. R. Waud, depicts Pickett's Charge, the July 3 climax to the three-day Battle of Gettysburg in Pennsylvania. Even though General George Pickett shared command of the charging troops with two others, it is forever his name that has become associated with the event. The rebels advanced across a mile of open territory up Cemetery Ridge into the waiting guns of the Union army. Although some broke through the federal lines, when the battle was over, the Confederates had been decimated.

Vicksburg, called the Gibraltar of the Confederacy, was the South's major bastion on the Mississippi River. Beginning in November 1862, Union General Ulysses S. Grant launched a series of maneuvers and assaults to take the Confederate stronghold. The city and its garrison, near starvation, finally surrendered on July 4, 1863, after a 47-day siege.

bold stroke, Lincoln removed any possible European intervention and rallied disparate elements in the North behind him. Now the freedom of blacks became enmeshed with the preservation of the Union. But Lincoln still had a rebellion to end, and he needed military victories to win the war. In Virginia, affairs continued badly. General Burnside, aching to avenge his defeat at Fredericksburg, ordered an advance upriver to outflank Lee's strong position at the city. But when the weather turned foul, the four-day march that was supposed to find a northern ford of the Rappahannock River ended in abject failure. In what came to be known as the "Mud March," Union troops barely covered

1863
JANUARY 1
Lincoln issues the Emancipation Proclamation.

In naval fighting at Galveston, Texas, Confederates retake the city from the light Union force occupying it. For the duration of the war, the island provides refuge for Confederate blockade runners.

JANUARY 8–14
Confederate cavalry led by General Joseph Wheeler raids into middle Tennessee.

ten miles in the waist–deep mud. Two days later, after Burnside had met with the President, Lincoln accepted his resignation and replaced him with Major General Joseph Hooker. The new general spent the winter and early spring rebuilding the Army of the Potomac's shattered morale—instituting a furlough system, consolidating the cavalry into a corps, adopting corps badges, and asking deserters to come back without penalty.

In the West, there was little movement until spring brought dry roads. General William S. Rosecrans remained in the vicinity of Murfreesboro, Tennessee, waiting for reinforcements and fending off Southern cavalry raids against his supply lines. Ulysses S. Grant, upriver from Vicksburg, Mississippi, after William T. Sherman's failed attack at Chickasaw Bayou, was still determined to capture that city, the major Confederate stronghold on the Mississippi River. Grant hoped that General Nathaniel P. Banks, in command of Union troops at New Orleans, would move upriver and threaten Port Hudson, Louisiana, the South's other major fortified town on the Mississippi.

The Vicksburg Campaign

In March, Grant sent some of Sherman's troops, accompanied by a portion of Admiral David D. Porter's river fleet, up the Yazoo River to see if Vicksburg's defenders could be flanked and the town approached from the north. But the channel of the twisting river, infested with rebel troops, proved impossible to conquer. Stymied in his effort, Grant decided to move his army down the river below Vicksburg and attack from the south. On the night of April 16, Porter's ships successfully steamed past the formidable Vicksburg batteries even as Grant's troops moved south through swampy terrain just west of the Mississippi.

JACKSON STOOD HEAD AND SHOULDERS ABOVE HIS CONFRERES, AND . . . LEE COULD NOT REPLACE HIM.

Union General Oliver O. Howard

To further confuse the enemy as to his intentions, Grant had Colonel Benjamin H. Grierson lead a force of three cavalry regiments south from Tennessee into central Mississippi in mid-April. Grierson's job was to distract attention from Grant's planned move against Vicksburg, and in this Grierson was quite successful. His troops severed railroads temporarily, cut telegraph lines, forced General John C. Pemberton at Vicksburg to send his cavalry chasing after the Yankees, and generally ran roughshod over central Mississippi. Grierson's troops eventually rode into Baton Rouge at the beginning of May after one of the most celebrated cavalry forays of the war.

JANUARY 10
General Fitz John Porter is sentenced by court-martial to be cashiered from the Army for his actions at the Second Battle of Bull Run.

JANUARY 11
Union forces capture Fort Hindman, Arkansas, sometimes called Arkansas Post, and almost 5,000 Confederates.

The CSS *Alabama* defeats the USS *Hatteras* off Galveston, Texas.

JANUARY 12
The third session of the First Confederate Congress convenes in Richmond.

The Emancipation Proclamation

Five days after the bloody Battle of Antietam in September 1862, President Abraham Lincoln issued a preliminary Emancipation Proclamation to his Cabinet. Scheduled to go into effect on January 1, 1863, the document called for all slaves living in any state still in rebellion at that time to be forever free. Lincoln's plan caught everyone's attention, but it was not greeted with universal approval. Because the proclamation referred only to states in rebellion, radicals believed he had not gone far enough. Editorials in foreign and antigovernment domestic presses lambasted the President, pointing out that Lincoln had only freed slaves in areas where the federal government was not recognized.

But Lincoln was acting within his constitutional powers to seize enemy resources, in this case, the enemy's slaves. He also remained within his powers by not acting against slavery in loyal areas. The President knew he had to wait for legislation to end slavery in the Union itself. But with his proclamation, he turned the war into one of liberation for the slaves, and he helped doom Confederate hopes for foreign recognition. The final January 1863 Emancipation Proclamation also authorized the government to enlist black soldiers and sailors. "In giving freedom to the slave, we assure freedom to the free," Lincoln averred. "We must disenthrall ourselves, and then we shall save our country."

Lincoln presents his preliminary Emancipation Proclamation to his Cabinet.

On the last day of April, Grant's troops began crossing the Mississippi south of Vicksburg, near Grand Gulf. On May 1, lead elements of the Union army encountered part of the Grand Gulf garrison at Port Gibson, Mississippi. Driving the rebels back, the Federals forced their retreat to Grand Gulf. With the way open, Grant decided to move inland rather than turn north to go against Pemberton directly at Vicksburg. Union intelligence knew that General Joseph E. Johnston was collecting a new Confederate army at Jackson, Mississippi, to reinforce Pemberton in the coming struggle with Grant's troops. By driving inland, Grant placed his army between the two Confederate forces before they could unite against him. Troops of James B. McPherson's corps drove off a Confederate brigade at Raymond on May 12. Two days later, troops under Sherman and McPherson pushed Johnston's outnumbered Confederates out of Jackson.

This midnight scene depicts the March 14 attempt by seven Union ships to run past the earthwork forts at Port Hudson, about 25 miles upriver from Baton Rouge, Louisiana. By the time the USS Mississippi *was sunk, the other ship captains were losing their will. They saw the work done by Confederate gunners on the heavy British-imported Armstrong cannon (foreground), which could throw 135-pound shells. The naval repulse resulted in a retreat by the Union army.*

JANUARY 20
General Burnside sends his army upriver from Fredericksburg in search of a place to cross the Rappahannock. Falling rain ensures this action will soon be known as the "Mud March."

JANUARY 23
The exhausted Army of the Potomac climbs out of the mud and returns to its original position.

JANUARY 25
General Joseph Hooker replaces Burnside in command of the Army of the Potomac.

JANUARY 31
Two Confederate ironclads, the

As Sherman's force paused to destroy the military usefulness of the state capital, Grant had McPherson's and John A. McClernand's corps turn toward Vicksburg. On their way, they met Pemberton's army at Champion's Hill on May 16, which proved to be the most significant battle of the Vicksburg Campaign. Union troops bested Pemberton's in a day of fierce fighting. After his defeat, rather than head north to join Johnston, Pemberton elected to retreat toward Vicksburg's strong defenses, relying on them to hold the Yankees while Johnston approached their rear. But the Southern rear guard of Pemberton's army was savaged at the Big Black River on May 17. In addition, one of Pemberton's divisions was largely cut off during the retreat and forced to join Johnston.

Now nothing stood between Grant and Vicksburg. Unwilling to begin siege operations, Grant launched an attack on Vicksburg's defenses on May 19, but his forces were repulsed. Grant tried again on May 22 with more troops, but the result remained the same. The general then extended his lines as his soldiers dug trenches and surrounded

On May 4, photographer Andrew J. Russell captured this image of dead soldiers of the 18th Mississippi who had attempted to defend Marye's Heights at Fredericksburg from attacking Union troops of the 6th Army Corps.

Chicora and the *Palmetto State,* lead an attack against Union vessels off Charleston, South Carolina. Although they inflict damage, they cannot break the blockade.

FEBRUARY 14
Confederates capture the Union ram *Queen of the West* in the Mississippi River.

FEBRUARY 24
Congress establishes the Arizona Territory, separating it from the New Mexico Territory.

Vicksburg. General in Chief Henry Halleck, acting under administration orders, sent reinforcements to Grant from other posts farther north—by mid-June more than 70,000 Yankees were besieging Vicksburg. Grant ordered part of his army under Sherman to move east to watch Johnston, who was building up his troop strength behind the siege army in Mississippi.

Aided by naval gunfire from Admiral Porter's ships, Grant's troops edged their siege lines closer to the rebels. In two instances, they dug mines under the enemy entrenchments and blew holes in the defenses, but they failed to breach the enemy lines.

Meanwhile, Grant's hopes for a squeeze of the Mississippi came to fruition as General Banks's troops from New Orleans and vicinity moved upriver and assailed the Confederate earthworks surrounding Port Hudson on May 27. They were repelled, suffering heavy casualties, so Banks likewise started his own siege operations.

Both soldiers and civilians in Vicksburg suffered as food ran short. After a month and a half under siege, Pemberton consulted with his subordinates and determined that his army was too physically weak to endure the rigors of an attempted breakout—he opened negotiations with Grant for a resolution. On July 4, Pemberton's 30,000 soldiers surrendered and were paroled. After hearing of the surrender, General Franklin Gardner gave up the Port Hudson garrison as well, ending organized Confederate resistance along the Mississippi. Farther inland, Sherman moved against Johnston. After brief operations around Jackson, Mississippi, Sherman's force again marched into the city as Johnston evacuated under pressure on July 16.

Loss and Victory for New Union Leadership

Even as Grant's forces were moving down the Mississippi toward Vicksburg in the spring, Joseph Hooker's 120,000-strong Army of the Potomac stirred in Virginia. Sending his cavalry to distract Lee's attention and raid his supply lines, Hooker divided his army in two, sending three corps up the Rappahannock to cross far above Freder-

Joseph Hooker, whose nickname was "Fighting Joe," replaced Burnside in command of the Army of the Potomac in January. The 48-year-old federal commander designed a brilliant campaign to defeat Lee west of Fredericksburg, Virginia, but his moral courage failed him when Lee stood and fought instead of retreating. Hooker's failure caused Lincoln to reflect, "My God! My God! What will the country say?"

FEBRUARY 25
The National Banking Act, which moves to centralize banking functions across the country, is passed by Congress.

FEBRUARY 26
The Cherokee National Council repeals its ordinance of secession and abolishes slavery.

Admiral Porter sends a dummy ironclad down the Mississippi River to scare the Confederates trying to salvage the recently beached USS *Indianola*.

A Black Soldier

"On Wednesday evening we reached that historic village named Fairfax Court House. The inhabitants, what few there were, looked at us with astonishment, as if we were some great monsters risen up out of the ground. They looked bewildered, yet it seemed to be too true and apparent to them that they really beheld nearly 10,000 colored soldiers filing by, armed to the teeth, with bayonets bristling in the sun—and I tell you our boys seemed to fully appreciate the importance of marching through a secesh town. On, on we came, regiment after regiment, pouring in, as it seemed to their bewildered optics, by countless thousands—with colors flying and the bands playing; and, without intending any disparagement to other regiments, I must say that the 43d looked truly grand, with the soldierly and imposing forms of our noble and generous Colonel and Adjutant C. Bryan riding at the head."

Sergeant John C. Broke, 43rd U.S. Colored Troops, describing the regiment's march through Fairfax Court House en route to join the Army of the Potomac, May 1864

icksburg. This wing then moved across the Rapidan River and into the Wilderness to a crossroads mansion called Chancellorsville. However, in spite of remonstrances from his corps leaders, Hooker suddenly called off his offensive and took a defensive position around Chancellorsville. Lee, meanwhile, discovered that Hooker's right flank was exposed. He once again split his army, sending Stonewall Jackson on a march against Hooker's right. Jackson's late-afternoon attack on May 2 smashed the Yankees and drove them from their camps, but disorganization and nightfall brought his attack to a halt. That night, while reconnoitering in front of his troops, Jackson was wounded by friendly fire. And even though the rebels continued the Battle of Chancellorsville to a successful conclusion, Jackson, whose wounded arm was successfully amputated, contracted pneumonia and died on May 10. The three-day Chancellorsville battle cost Lee over 12,000 soldiers and Hooker 17,000.

One of the most famous Civil War photographs by Alexander Gardner shows a dead Confederate sharpshooter behind a rock barricade in Devil's Den at Gettysburg. Sleuthing by photo expert William Frassanito revealed that the body originally lay some 75 yards away from the wall and was moved into position for this classic shot.

Ulysses S. Grant

It did not take long in the war for Ulysses S. Grant's greatest trait as a military leader to surface. He would fight. Most other Union generals, particularly those in the East, considered themselves grand strategists, deep thinkers who sat at desks studying maps of cities they wanted to capture. Grant cared little about geographical goals. He believed the purpose of his Union forces was to destroy Confederate forces. If that meant ordering thousands of soldiers to their deaths in frontal assaults, he did it. If such charges earned him the label of "butcher" from his critics, he did it anyway.

After graduating from West Point as part of the class of 1843, Grant fought in the Mexican War. Some of the years after that war were difficult for him. Away from his wife and family in California, Grant left the army in 1854. Historians continue to speculate over how large a part alcohol may have played in his resignation. It is widely believed that Grant resigned to avoid court-martial, but the circumstances were kept private, and firm evidence that he was asked to leave over drinking is meager.

Grant was eking out a living as a leather goods clerk at his father's store in 1861 when the war started. The federal government did not respond to his offers to serve, so he started as a colonel of Illinois volunteers. He was named a brigadier general at the end of July. After proving his boldness by occupying Paducah, Kentucky, in September and then attacking Belmont, Missouri, in November, Grant began attracting attention. But it was not until February 1862, when he captured Fort Donelson, Tennessee, that his skills were fully recognized. Reluctant superiors, still suspicious of his character, made him a major general. He did not disappoint.

Ulysses S. Grant was named general in chief of Union armies with the rank of lieutenant general on March 9, 1864. In this portrait, Grant stands in front of his tent at Cold Harbor, Virginia, in June 1864.

In April, he recovered from his early blunders on the first day of Shiloh and, after confidently predicting to depressed subordinates that he would "whip" the Confederates the next day, he did just that. Even after this triumph, however, he was removed from direct command by his superior, Henry Halleck. Grant considered leaving the field entirely, but he stayed and was given orders to capture Vicksburg, which he did by siege on July 4, 1863.

Grant's subsequent capture of Chattanooga brought him a promotion to general of all armies and a trip east to fight Robert E. Lee. When Lee beat Grant in the two-day Battle of the Wilderness in May 1864, Grant did something no other Eastern general had ever done. Instead of retreating, he planned another attack on Lee's army. For the next year, Grant attacked Lee at Spotsylvania Court House, North Anna River, Cold Harbor, and Petersburg in bloody battles. He built a huge supply base while cutting the Confederates off from their own supplies. He wore Lee down, knowing the Confederates could not recruit any more troops.

Grant's brutal, unrelenting methods were just what Lincoln and the Union had been waiting for. They may not have been pretty, but they were necessary to finish the war.

This unassuming, small white-frame house served as General George Meade's headquarters during the Battle of Gettysburg. It was here that he held a meeting of his officers, who reassured him that they wanted to fight the battle out to a conclusion. The house, on the reverse side of Cemetery Ridge, was damaged during the Confederate artillery bombardment on July 3.

Having regained the advantage over the Army of the Potomac, Lee again decided to carry the war into the North. In early June, his troops sidled west into the Shenandoah Valley and north across the Potomac River into Maryland and Pennsylvania. The campaign began successfully when Lee's 2nd Corps, led by Richard S. Ewell, smashed the Union garrison at Winchester, inflicting some 4,500 casualties, a great many of them captured. By late June, the Confederate army was in southern Pennsylvania, approaching the defenses of Harrisburg, which was protected only by Pennsylvania and New York militia. Hooker moved his army north across the Potomac to protect Washington and Baltimore. However, after arguing with Halleck over strategy, Hooker asked to be relieved. Lincoln had already intended to fire Hooker, so he granted the general's request, replacing him with corps commander George G. Meade.

Lee, acting with scanty intelligence, finally learned of Meade's approach and recalled his troops to concentrate in the mountains east of Chambersburg. Elements of both armies collided at nearby Gettysburg in Adams County on July 1. By day's end, the rebels had driven part of Meade's army from their positions north and west of Gettysburg to higher ground south of town. Both Lee and Meade brought up their troops and formed for renewed battle. On July 2, Lee attacked both of Meade's flanks and

Van Dorn—General Nathan Bedford Forrest among them—rout a Union force at the Battle of Thompson's Station, Tennessee.

MARCH 9
John S. Mosby's Confederate

irregulars capture Union General Edwin H. Stoughton in his bed at Fairfax Court House, Virginia.

MARCH 10
President Lincoln issues an amnesty proclamation to all

deserters from military service, allowing them until April 1 to report back to their units without penalty.

MARCH 11–16
Union attempts to open an attack

failed, and on July 3, a grand Confederate attack on the Union center was bloodily repelled. Lee began to retreat to Virginia on July 4, pulling back from the northernmost point he would reach during the war. His army lost at least 28,000 in the three-day battle, while Meade lost 23,000.

Even as the Union army pushed back the Confederate invasion of the North, the war remained unpopular in many quarters. Labor shortages forced the administration to follow the Confederate example and institute a draft. However, the law allowed a number of ways draftees could avoid conscription. Those in a position to do so could buy their way out with $300 or, as in the South, hire a substitute to fight in their place. Combined with other factors, this situation led to widespread riots in New York City on July 13. Sparked in reaction to the draft, the riots quickly turned anti-black as crowds lynched blacks, burned their properties, and chased police. General Meade, so recently triumphant at Gettysburg, had to send some of his troops north to counter the riots. The arrival of veterans from the Army of the Potomac helped quiet the city.

Action in the Mid-South

While Lee and Meade had been moving north and Grant had besieged Vicksburg, the remaining major armies of the North and South campaigned in central Tennessee. General William S. Rosecrans had stayed in the Murfreesboro area after the Battle of Stones River, building up his troop strength and fending off Southern mounted raids against his supply lines. Goaded by Lincoln to act, Rosecrans finally began moving against Braxton Bragg's Army of Tennessee on June 23. In a campaign of maneuver rather than battle, Rosecrans completely outfoxed Bragg and forced him out of Tennessee without any major fighting. Known as the Tullahoma Campaign, this was Rosecrans's masterpiece. His soldiers occupied Chattanooga on September 9 as Bragg's outnumbered army withdrew into northern Georgia.

Worried over Rosecrans' advance, the Davis administration reached wide to bring reinforcements to Bragg. Much of Joseph E. Johnston's army was dispatched from Mississippi to Georgia, and two divisions from Lee's army in Virginia were sent by rail.

Protests in New York City against the newly instituted draft erupted into a four-day riot in July. Buildings where the draft was conducted and where newspapers were published were attacked. Blacks, whose freedom from Southern slavery had recently been proclaimed by Lincoln to be the new objective of the war, were also targeted. At least five buildings, including a black orphanage, were burned. As many as 1,000 people may have been killed or hurt.

route to Vicksburg are frustrated as Confederates at recently built Fort Pemberton thwart federal gunboat operations on the Yalobusha River in Mississippi.

MARCH 13
An accidental explosion occurs at the Confederate States Laboratory, an ammunition factory on Brown's Island in the James River at Richmond, Virginia, killing

about 50 workers, most of them young girls.

MARCH 14
Although Farragut is able to send two ships past Confederate batteries at Port Hudson, Louisiana,

Chickamauga Creek, an Indian term meaning River of Death, lived up to its name in September. During a two-day battle in the Georgia woodlands between the Union Army of the Cumberland and the Confederate Army of Tennessee, one out of every four soldiers became a casualty. Only the last-ditch stand by troops under General George H. Thomas prevented the complete rout of the Union army.

the majority of his boats do not advance, causing Union land and naval forces to retreat.

MARCH 17
Union and Confederate cavalry

meet at the inconclusive Battle of Kelly's Ford, Virginia.

MARCH 22–APRIL 1
John Pegram's Confederate cavalry raids into Kentucky.

MARCH 25
General Burnside assumes his new command of the Department of the Ohio.

Secretary of War Stanton awards the first Medals of Honor to the

Bragg turned about and gave battle to the Union forces dogging his trail, and Rosecrans narrowly avoided disaster as he recalled his scattered divisions. The two-day Battle of Chickamauga in September was a hard-won Confederate victory. Rosecrans was defeated and withdrew to Chattanooga, but Bragg suffered more casualties. The Southern general put the city under siege as Yankee reinforcements were sent to Rosecrans, first from Meade's army in Virginia and then from Grant's at Vicksburg.

Grant himself, now the ranking Union general west of the Alleghenies, went to Chattanooga. He replaced Rosecrans with George Thomas and called upon reinforcements. Ambrose Burnside, commander of the Department of the Ohio, marched into eastern Tennessee and occupied Knoxville. Bragg sent James Longstreet and part of his army to counter the federal force. But even as Bragg's strength waned, Grant's grew. The culmination of the standoff was the Battle of Chattanooga at the end of November. Although losses were not heavy on either side, the result of this battle was that Bragg's army fell back into northern Georgia, never again to threaten Chattanooga. Longstreet's subsequent three-week siege of Knoxville in late November was broken as Union reinforcements from Chattanooga forced him to withdraw into southwestern Virginia for the winter.

Confederate cavalry attack a federal supply train near Jasper, Tennessee, at the end of October. In nearby Chattanooga, besieged federal troops eagerly awaited the foodstuffs that the wagons would bring them. They had been on half rations for several weeks following their defeat at the Battle of Chickamauga.

THE WORLD WILL LITTLE NOTE, NOR LONG REMEMBER WHAT WE SAY HERE.

Abraham Lincoln, the Gettysburg Address

Since both Lee and Meade had sent reinforcements westward in September, military affairs in Virginia remained quiet until October. Early in the month, Lee tried to outflank Meade's army, but Meade withdrew from the Rappahannock River line and retreated all the way to Centreville. En route, Union forces were able to maul A. P. Hill's pursuing Confederates at Bristoe Station on October 14. Lee himself retreated to the Rappahannock.

six members of Andrews's Raiders who were not killed or captured.

APRIL 2
A bread riot breaks out in Richmond, Virginia.

APRIL 4
President Lincoln, with a group including his wife and his son Tad, leave Washington to meet with General Hooker and his army at Falmouth, Virginia, near Fredericksburg.

APRIL 7
Union naval forces stage an unsuccessful attack on Charleston, South Carolina.

The Siege of Vicksburg

Vicksburg, Mississippi, was a major trading center on the Mississippi River before the war. During the conflict, it earned the name of "Gibraltar of the Confederacy"—at least up until the middle of 1863.

The bluffs above the river on which the city was built provided coveted high ground that gave Confederate cannon crews the ability to fire down on Union ships. North of the city was the snag-filled Yazoo River, which fed into impenetrable swamps that soldiers could not cross on foot or horseback. To the east was Confederate-held territory, and to the west was the river. The only direction that was open to attack was from the south—and no one expected enemy troops to be there.

U. S. Grant was in a position to change that. In March 1863, he began marching his army down the west bank of the Mississippi, intending to transport it across the river south of the city. This would be the largest amphibious operation the continent had ever seen, a massive use of force that Grant alone had mastered against the Confederates. Here on the Mississippi, the future commander of all Union armies perfected his ability to move huge numbers of soldiers, which became the key to the eventual defeat of the South.

At the same time Grant's troops were moving by land, Admiral David Porter was able to move his gunboats successfully up and down the river past the once-feared heavy batteries.

Vicksburg's Pennsylvania-born Confederate commander, John C. Pemberton, was in an untenable position, a fact he had known months before his situation become critical. He had limited resources, of course, as resupply had been restricted since New Orleans had been captured the previous year. Another Confederate army was nearby under Joseph E. Johnston, who wanted to combine his forces with Pemberton's. Back in Richmond, however, President Davis demanded that Pemberton stay put inside his extensive trench line.

This division of Confederate forces played into Grant's plans. Slowly but surely, he defeated smaller Confederate forces as he moved his way northeast. He sent William Sherman east toward Johnston's army at the state capital of Jackson, which fell on May 14. The rest of his force turned west toward Vicksburg.

Pemberton did his best to repel the Federals, but he was outnumbered and had never been known as a strong leader. He lost a holding action at Champion's Hill on May 16 and then another at Big Black River on May 17. At that point, he ordered a

This woodcut shows a typical Union trench, which was not too far from similarly entrenched Confederates. The large woven baskets were called gabions. They were made in advance, rolled into place, and then filled with dirt to make portable—and bulletproof—walls from which soldiers could fire. Soldiers on both sides were often so close to each other that they could chat and toss traded goods back and forth. Sometimes they would toss hand grenades, as well.

wholesale flight back to the trenches of Vicksburg.

Pemberton, still believing the city to be strategically important, ignored one final plea from Johnston to evacuate. He refused to face the reality that Porter already controlled the river so that Confederate supplies no longer came through Vicksburg as they once had. The city had instead become a symbol of Southern resistance.

Although the Confederate garrison was trapped and could have been waited out, Grant initially refused to do that. In late May, he launched two old-style frontal assaults on the Confederate dirt forts and trenches. Just as Burnside learned at Fredericksburg six months earlier, the Confederates knew how to fight from trenches. The Union forces were beaten off with heavy losses. This exacerbated some tensions that already existed in the ranks. Corps commander General John McClernand wrote a congratulatory order to his troops asserting that, had the other corps only done their duty to support his valiant soldiers, Vicksburg would have

This remarkable photograph shows how the civilian population of Vicksburg survived their daily bombing by Union cannons: They carved caves out of the bluffs and moved their furniture inside. Once inside the cave mouth, the entrance turned at right angles so shrapnel from shells exploding outside would not fly into the living quarters. Cut off from food supplies, families here were reduced to eating mules, rats, and even family pets before the city was finally surrendered.

fallen. Not only was this defiant, it was not true. After McClernand's order found its way into the Northern press, Grant relieved him of his command.

Grant gave up on frontal assaults and dug his own trenches and gun pits, bringing the Federals ever closer to the defenders. He ordered his guns trained on the city, which continued to house civilians as well as soldiers. For 46 days, the city and trenches were shelled on a regular basis. Much of the civilian population moved underground, digging out multiroom caves in the hills. Food became even more scarce, and once-horrible thoughts such as catching and roasting rats became the norm.

Troops on both sides stuck to their grim business of shooting at each other while under the eye of their officers. But when the officers were out of sight, the same troops often traded—Confederates handing over their prized tobacco in exchange for coffee and food.

Finally, on July 4, day 47 of the siege and the day after Lee was defeated at Gettysburg, Pemberton and his officers surrendered nearly 30,000 soldiers, about twice that many new rifled muskets, and 172 cannons. Grant's victory cost him more than 10,000 casualties, but with patience he had captured the city and the admiration of Lincoln.

Today, the battlefield on Lookout Mountain is filled with monuments like this one to honor the troops who took part in the "Battle Above the Clouds" in November 1863.

This Kurz & Allison print of the Battle of Missionary Ridge, Tennessee, on November 25, is surprisingly accurate, a trait not always shared by many such prints depicting battles. The Confederate cannons were unable to depress their barrels enough to sweep the slopes with canister fire to stop the Federals from crawling up the steep heights. The loss of this ridge led to the resignation of Braxton Bragg as Confederate commander in Tennessee.

Before they were officially accepted into the military, many blacks served the Army as laborers. Called contrabands, *these fugitive slaves performed as teamsters and cooks as well as other behind-the-line workers. In March 1865, Congress created the Freedmen's Bureau to assist former slaves.*

These soldiers are pictured at Camp William Penn in Pennsylvania. The great majority of officers over black regiments were white. "The officers and men are both carefully picked," wrote Governor John Andrews concerning the formation of the 54th Massachusetts. "We have arrived at getting officers of high character, making careful selections out of many candidates."

Clement L. Vallandigham

The most famous thorn in the side of the Lincoln administration, Clement L. Vallandigham was an Ohio Democrat in the House of Representatives. He consistently opposed Lincoln and the war against the South. In 1862, he went as far as to demand peace at any cost, which may have led to his defeat in his bid for reelection that fall. After giving an especially antiwar speech the next year, he was arrested for treason by General Ambrose Burnside, then commander of the Department of the Ohio, and confined in a Cincinnati prison. Lincoln and his Cabinet, embarrassed by Burnside's action, decided to banish Vallandigham to the Confederacy.

Unwanted in the South, Vallandigham made his way to Canada, where he conducted an Ohio gubernatorial campaign from exile. After losing this office, as well, Vallandigham returned to Ohio in mid-1864. He was officially ignored by Lincoln, who nevertheless had the Democrat watched closely. Vallandigham took part in the 1864 Democratic party convention in Chicago and then returned to the practice of law after the war.

Clement L. Vallandigham was a prominent Democratic member of Congress from Ohio when the war started. A strict constructionist on Constitutional questions, Vallandigham was extremely outspoken against the war, a position that brought him a great deal of trouble from the Lincoln administration.

Meade, again moving forward and rebuilding the rail lines as he went, attacked Lee's advanced outposts on November 7, whereupon Lee withdrew behind the Rapidan. Meade tried to outflank his opponent in December, but cold weather and strong rebel defenses brought the Mine Run Campaign to a quick close. Both armies retired to winter quarters.

Black Troops Enter Combat

One of the most important facets of Union operations during the year was the introduction of black soldiers into the Union army. Although individual commanders had enrolled such troops in 1862, the administration did not officially give permission to start raising black troops until 1863. Eventually numbering almost 200,000 soldiers, most regiments of U.S. Colored Troops were composed of freed slaves, but a number of Northern states contributed regiments of free blacks. Although black soldiers had fought at previous battles, such as on June 7 at Milliken's Bend, Louisiana, when Confederates attacked this outpost during Grant's Vicksburg operations, the first high-profile black regiment was the 54th Massachusetts.

The 54th took part in Union siege operations against Charleston, South Carolina. The scene of the beginning of the war, Charleston was high on the list of Lincoln administration objectives. Admiral Samuel F. DuPont launched a naval attack on April 7, but the Southern forts defending the harbor pummeled DuPont's ironclads and

Union Admiral John Dahlgren invented and gave his name to a naval gun popular with sailors, who called it the "soda bottle" gun. The most popular model was a 9-inch smoothbore, but the same design was adopted up to 15-inch bores. Although Dahlgren's sense of self-promotion made him unpopular in a humble navy, he was finally given command of the South Atlantic Blockading Squadron in 1863. But his greater accomplishments were his guns, which helped those officers with whom he was competing rule the waves.

This painting of the Confederate submarine H. L. Hunley was made by Conrad Wise Chapman. The Hunley recorded the first sinking of an enemy vessel by a submarine. When its victim, the USS Housatonic, sank, the Hunley and its crew went down with it.

APRIL 7–11
General Joseph Wheeler's Confederate cavalry raid Union railroads in Tennessee.

APRIL 11–MAY 4
General James Longstreet's Confederate troops conduct operations around Suffolk, Virginia. Although they never cut the city off from the outside world, this

engagement has come to be known as the Siege of Suffolk.

APRIL 12–13
Union forces engage and take Fort Bisland on the Bayou Teche, Louisiana.

Fort Sumter, shown here at the end of the fighting in April 1865, was the target of shelling throughout much of the war. It survived attacks by Union ironclads and heavy land batteries set up on nearby captured islands. As evidenced by the shapeless walls in this photograph, the fort's top two stories of bricks were shelled into dust. The Confederates simply piled up the debris into walls and continued fighting.

The short speech President Lincoln made at the dedication of a national cemetery at Gettysburg is one of the most famous he ever uttered. Direct and to the point, the Gettysburg Address provides the best summation of why the Civil War was fought.

repelled the attack. Soon after, Union troops from Hilton Head began landing south of Charleston to start operations against Battery Wagner and other Confederate strongpoints on Morris Island. From July 10 through September 6, Union soldiers inched their way through the sand toward the enemy as heavy cannon from both sides filled the air with lead projectiles. During these operations, Fort Sumter was pounded into a shapeless mass of broken brick walls reinforced with sandbags.

On July 18, the 54th Massachusetts spearheaded a massive Union charge against Battery Wagner. The attackers were repelled, and the 54th suffered heavy losses, including Colonel Robert G. Shaw. But the reb-

els knew the end was near, and on September 6 they evacuated Morris Island under cover of darkness. Unfortunately, the Yankees were unable to capitalize on their hard-won sandy island, and operations against Charleston continued at a much lower level.

Throughout the year, operations also continued in places as widely spaced as Galveston, Texas, and Portland, Maine, which was the object of a small seaborne Confederate raiding party. Lawrence, Kansas, was sacked by Confederate irregulars even as civilians were forcibly removed from three Missouri counties by order of the local Union commander. The Confederacy adopted a new flag, and West Virginia was admitted to the Union as the 35th state. A Union warship engaged Japanese soldiers far across the world, while Confederate commerce raiders continued to wreak havoc on American shipping. President Lincoln

APRIL 14
An engagement at Irish Bend, Louisiana, results in a Union victory over Confederates retreating from Fort Bisland.

APRIL 16
Admiral Porter's ships successfully steam south past the Confederate batteries at Vicksburg, Mississippi.

APRIL 17
Colonel John S. Marmaduke's

Confederate cavalry begins a two-week raid from Arkansas into Missouri.

APRIL 17–MAY 2
Colonel Benjamin H. Grierson

*President Lincoln was invited to the November 19 dedication of a national cemetery on 17 acres of the Gettysburg battlefield to contribute a few observations follow-
ing the featured speaker, Edward Everett. Despite this painting's depiction of a dramatic presentation, his delivery was probably quite subdued. The audience's surprised reaction when Lincoln concluded after just two minutes gave rise to the idea, sometimes repeated today, that the crowd was indifferent to the President's words.*

signed the National Banking Act into law, creating a truly national banking system for
the nation.

But it was Lincoln's speech at Gettysburg on November 19 that ranks as perhaps the
most important event of the year 1863. In a brief address lasting perhaps two minutes and
containing just 272 words, Lincoln, who followed a two-hour oration by the popular
speaker Edward Everett, embodied the patriotic ideals for which the nation was then struggling in time of war. The President himself feared that his remarks had fallen flat, but over
the years, his Gettysburg Address has come to be considered one of his finest speeches.

leads a Union cavalry raid covering 600 miles through Mississippi to Baton Rouge, Louisiana,
distracting Confederate attention
from Grant's movements toward
Vicksburg.

APRIL 19
Lincoln again visits the Army of
the Potomac in Virginia, this time
with Secretary of War Stanton
and General in Chief Halleck.

APRIL 20
General John D. Imboden's Confederate cavalry initiates a three-
week raid into western Virginia.

Here is the camp of the 18th Pennsylvania Cavalry at Brandy Station in Virginia. The soldiers have spent the winter in cabins that were roofed by canvas. Note the barrels used as chimneys for each tent's fireplace.

Shown here is the winter camp of the 150th Pennsylvania Volunteer Infantry in March 1863. The regiment is lined up for a march in the midst of its tented camp, which is shrouded in the smoke from its campfires.

When Hiram Ulysses Grant registered as a cadet at West Point, he did not correct the clerk who erroneously recorded his name as Ulysses Simpson Grant (although sources differ as to the strength of the effort he made). He fell in love with and married his classmate's sister, Julia Dent. When apart from his family, Grant drank whiskey, but when they were near, he did not. Grant's admirers recognized this quirk in his nature and maneuvered to have Julia near him during his Civil War service.

APRIL 21
Colonel Abel D. Streight, his Union cavalry riding mules, launches a raid into Alabama and Georgia.

General William E. Jones takes his Confederate cavalry into western Virginia. Jones coordinates his maneuvers with Imboden to disrupt the Baltimore & Ohio Railroad.

APRIL 24
Desperate for revenue, the Confederate Congress establishes a variety of taxes on income, property, and various business transactions.

The Confederate ironclad Atlanta plied the river near Savannah, Georgia. In June, it steamed downriver to attack Union blockade vessels. During the attempt, the Atlanta ran aground and was forced to surrender. The Atlanta is shown here serving in the U.S. Navy on the James River in Virginia.

Professional politician and Union General John McClernand ignored the chain of command throughout his career, preferring to write directly to the Army's commanding general or even President Lincoln rather than to his superiors. McClernand irritated Grant early on by warning that Confederates were nearby at Shiloh. His superiors ignored him, and the surprise attack on April 6, 1862, vindicated him. Grant later fired McClernand over a congratulatory report inappropriately praising his corps' performance.

In the summer of 1862, when the batteries of Vicksburg appeared invulnerable, an engineer sold U. S. Grant on a grand scheme to dig a canal at a bend in the Mississippi to divert the river away from Vicksburg. That would have left the city high, dry, and unimportant in controlling the river. At first white Union soldiers were put to work, but slaves were later impressed. The canal was never finished.

These old 32-pounders at Vicksburg kept the Federals at bay for months in the spring and summer until Grant finally starved the Confederates into submission. Note the cannonballs stacked to one side near the muzzle and the explosive shells stacked to the rear of the piece.

APRIL 28
The federal War Department establishes the Invalid Corps, later renamed the Veteran Reserve Corps.

Hooker's Army of the Potomac crosses the Rappahannock River in an attempt to circle behind Lee's Army of Northern Virginia.

APRIL 30
Grant's troops begin crossing the Mississippi River south of Grand Gulf, Mississippi.

The Battle of Chancellorsville

When Joseph Hooker took over the Army of the Potomac from Ambrose Burnside in January 1863, the morale of the Federals was broken. Rainy weather had turned Burnside's plausible plan to cross the Rappahannock River into the farcical, deadly "Mud March."

Hooker liked Burnside's plan but not its midwinter timing. He waited until spring, using the time to nurse his army back to health. Once it was warm, he broke his plan into three parts. First, he would send his cavalry deep behind Confederate lines to draw off rebel horse soldiers who might detect the infantry movement. Second, he would leave a sizable force at Fredericksburg to appear as though the entire army remained in place. Third, he would rapidly move the rest of his army on the drying roads to cross the river and confront Lee's left flank. Hooker believed Lee's troops would still be in the trenches on Marye's Heights.

The plan started well, even though the federal cavalry failed to draw off its Confederate counterpart. Hooker moved across the river virtually unmolested and was positioned to attack Lee's flank as planned.

But on April 30, Hooker hesitated. He may have been slowed because his troops were having a hard time hacking their way through underbrush so thick locals called it the Wilderness. But reports also surfaced that Hooker, a notorious drinker claiming to be on the wagon for this campaign, had returned to the bottle.

Hooker's hesitation was all Lee needed. The Union general was only the latest to learn that he

After replacing Ambrose Burnside in January, Joseph Hooker devised a brilliant plan to steal a march on Robert E. Lee. He was at the brink of success when his courage failed him. Turning the initiative over to Lee, Hooker's army was decisively defeated. "To tell the truth," Hooker later wrote, "I just lost confidence in Joe Hooker."

who hesitates in front of Lee lives to regret it. Leaving a token force of 10,000 on Marye's Heights, Lee rushed the remaining 50,000 west toward a brick tavern called Chancellorsville. First on the scene was Stonewall Jackson, who slammed hard into Hooker's tentative advance. Though the Federals greatly outnumbered the Confederates, Hooker lost whatever courage he had left. He ordered his soldiers to dig in until he could figure out why his surprise plan had failed.

That night, Lee's army was in the open while Hooker's troops had entrenched. The Confederates knew federal forces were far stronger—scouts had told them the Union left and center were heavily defended and any attack on those parts of the line would be disastrous. J.E.B. Stuart arrived later that night, however, with interesting news. Fitzhugh Lee, the general's nephew, had discovered that the far right of the Union flank was "in the air," not entrenched at all. A push on that flank might start a headlong panic that could roll up the rest of the Union army.

Early the next morning, Jackson and his 28,000 troops began a 12-mile march out of sight of the Union lines. Lee, reflecting Hooker's own strategy at the beginning of the campaign, stayed behind with a force of 15,000 demonstrating in front of Hooker's 70,000 directly on the scene. This was a tremendous risk. Had Hooker pushed out of his trenches with a frontal assault, Lee's army—as well as the general himself—would almost certainly have been killed or captured.

Jackson spent most of the day maneuvering around Hooker. The Union commander had re-

At the Battle of Chancellorsville on May 1–3, Major General Joseph Hooker, commander of the Army of the Potomac, amassed as many as 130,000 troops in and around this battlefield against less than half that many Confederates commanded by Robert E. Lee. But these superior numbers were of no avail when pitted against the genius and fighting skills of Lee and his army, who inflicted on the hapless federal force one of its worst defeats of the war.

ceived some intelligence of troop movements, but he misread them as retreat. Late that afternoon, Jackson opened an attack perpendicular to the federal line. The Union 11th Corps was eating when Confederates rushed from the woods. As the 11th broke, it spilled into the next corps, and then the next.

Anxious to keep that panic up, Jackson made a mistake. Rather than ordering a scout to determine the strength of the Federals he faced, the commander rode out in front of his own lines to see for himself. Finally persuaded by nervous aides that the middle ground between armies was no place for a lieutenant general, he turned back. Jackson had not warned any regimental commanders that he would be scouting in front of their positions, and as his party crashed through the woods to safety, a rebel regiment mistook them for federal cavalry and opened fire. Jackson was wounded in three

places. His left arm was so shattered that it had to be amputated.

The next day Stuart took over command of Jackson's corps and captured Hazel Grove, high ground looking down over Hooker's headquarters. One well-placed cannon shell took out a column at Hooker's headquarters as he leaned against it, nearly obliterating the general himself. That scare was enough. He ordered a retreat across the Rappahannock.

At almost the same time, the force left at Fredericksburg broke through the rebel line at Marye's Heights. Lee had to detach another of his divisions to counter the attack on his flank at Salem Church. That action was also successful. Lee had driven the entire Union force back across the Rappahannock.

Within a week of the battle, however, Jackson was dead of pneumonia. Lee was forced to restructure his army.

On May 16, Confederate General John C. Pemberton left the safety of Vicksburg's trenches in an attempt to hit Union General Grant's approaching army in the open areas east of the city. His plan was discovered, and Grant's troops beat Pemberton's to Champion's Hill, a high elevation that commanded the surrounding ground. In what would be the only major attempt to strike Grant's army before it could besiege Vicksburg, the Confederates were soundly defeated.

MAY 1
Union forces initiate their march toward Vicksburg by defeating the Confederates at the Battle of Port Gibson, Mississippi.

The Confederacy adopts the Stainless Banner as its official flag.

MAY 1–3
Lee decisively defeats Hooker's army at the Battle of Chancellorsville, Virginia.

MAY 3
Colonel Streight's Union raiders surrender to Nathan B. Forrest near Cedar Bluff, Alabama.

If U. S. Grant had a single mind about tactics, it was to try the frontal assault first. On June 25, he tried opening a breach in Confederate lines by exploding a mine under a redan, or small fort. Federals poured into the crater but were beaten back. More than a year later, he would allow another engineer to plant an even larger mine under Confederate trenches at Petersburg. That too would fail.

This is an artillery officer's kepi. A kepi, with its stiffer back, differed from the floppy forage cap worn by most soldiers. The color of the artillery branch was red, and its insignia was the crossed cannon, visible on the front of this kepi.

Attack after attack by the Federals failed to carry the Confederate works at Port Hudson, Louisiana, from May 27 through July 9, as each time the Federals were beaten back. The rebels were forced to surrender when Vicksburg fell, however. Until the Confederates raised the white flag, their total losses had been less than 1,000. Federal losses had been 5,000. A total of about 7,000 Confederates inside earthworks had held off a force of almost 40,000 Federals.

Franklin Gardner, born in New York, was an officer in the U.S. Army who married a Louisiana woman and joined the Confederate forces in 1861. He rose through the ranks and commanded the garrison of Port Hudson, Louisiana, in 1863. This is his general officer's kepi.

The Roman Catholic bishop of Iowa warns parishioners to leave the pro-Southern Knights of the Golden Circle or face excommunication.

MAY 5
Clement L. Vallandigham is arrested by Union troops in Dayton, Ohio.

MAY 7
Confederate General Earl

Van Dorn is killed by a jealous husband.

MAY 10
Stonewall Jackson, wounded by friendly fire at Chancellorsville, dies of pneumonia.

This unusual straw hat for summer contains three stars, the symbol of a Confederate lieutenant general. The heat of summer in the South led to improvisations such as this for comfort.

Disease, starvation, and poor shelter and clothing took a frightful toll on Union and Confederate prisoners of war. At Andersonville, 13,000 Union prisoners died during its 14 months of operation. Confederate prisoners fared a little bit better in Northern camps. Prisons, like the one at Camp Morton in Indianapolis, pictured here, were notorious. Prisoner exchanges eased conditions until General Grant ended the practice in April 1864.

Several hundred women in Richmond, primarily motivated by hunger, marched to Capitol Square on April 2, demanding concessions from the governor. Failing to have their needs met, they surged into the shopping districts, smashing windows and stealing clothes and food.

While it was sometimes popular to imagine that all Southerners were slaveholders living in large houses, the truth is that most Southerners lived as most Northerners did—in modest homes and without slaves. Women left at home, such as those seen here, learned to make do with little.

MAY 12
Federals defeat Confederates in the hard-fought Battle of Raymond, Mississippi.

MAY 14
Union troops occupy Jackson, Mississippi.

MAY 16
Grant's force moves toward Vicksburg after winning the Battle of Champion's Hill, Mississippi.

The New State of West Virginia

The state of Virginia was as divided over the issues of the Civil War as was the nation itself. Citizens of the mountainous counties in western Virginia were more pro-Union than pro-Confederate. For some time they had viewed the state government as filled with Tidewater-area plantation owners who had no interest in them. The Allegheny and Blue Ridge mountains ran through Virginia, cutting westerners off from most of their fellow Virginians. At the same time, rivers such as the Monongahela, the Kanawha, and the Ohio put them in close contact with Northerners in Pennsylvania and Ohio.

After voting against Virginia secession in 1861, it was only a matter of time before the western counties organized themselves to leave the state. Early Union victories in the area provided them with military backing.

The U.S. Constitution declares, "No new states shall be formed or erected within the jurisdiction of any other state...without the consent of the legislatures of the states concerned." But Virginia's secession from the Union left a vacuum western Virginians were only too happy to fill. In Wheeling, delegates from the western counties declared themselves the Restored Government of Virginia and voted themselves out of the state. Congress agreed to admit the new state, and in June 1863 West Virginia was welcomed into the Union.

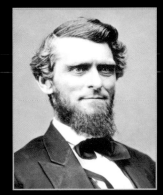

Arthur I. Boreman was the first governor of West Virginia. He remained in office until 1869 and followed that with one term as U.S. senator. During the war, Boreman organized militia units to track and fight Confederate sympathizers.

Copperhead, *comparing Democrats to poisonous snakes, was a derogatory term Republicans used to label Democrats who dared question Lincoln's policies or bills sponsored by radical Republicans. Some antiwar Democrats adopted the label and identified themselves by wearing heads taken from copper pennies on their lapels. In this cartoon, a number of recognizable Copperhead politicians attempt to visit Jefferson Davis but are stopped at his front door when he refuses to see them. Many accused Copperheads were imprisoned without trial during the war.*

Around 164,000 civilians, including paid substitutes, entered the Union Army as a result of the 1863 draft. This is a small number compared to the more than 2 million who actually served. This sketch shows the draft lottery, which decided who would be drafted and who would not.

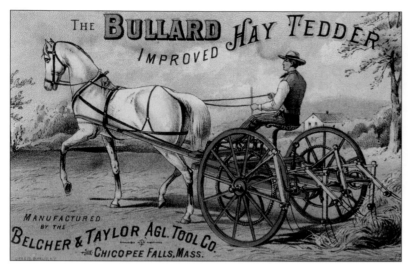

Before the war, labor for farming was available and cheap, and new machines progressed slowly. As labor was diverted to the fighting, however, all kinds of improved farm machinery—mowers, reapers, cultivators, and threshers—became widespread.

War always forces armies to invent new devices. This canvas pontoon boat displayed at Fredericksburg by the 50th New York Engineers could be put together in a matter of minutes. The photo is dated March 1864, 15 months after the federal army had been forced to wait days for traditional wooden pontoon boats to arrive at Fredericksburg. While they waited, Lee's army had arrived and begun its defense of the town.

Before paving roads, there was "corduroying," which meant cutting down trees and placing them across a road so the wagons could get the traction they needed without sinking into the mud that often came with spring rains.

MAY 17
A Confederate loss at the Battle of Big Black River, Mississippi, convinces General Pemberton to retreat all the way to Vicksburg.

MAY 19
Grant stages his first assault on Vicksburg's defenses. It is unsuccessful.

MAY 22
Grant makes his second assault at

Vicksburg. When it is also unsuccessful, Union troops begin siege operations.

MAY 25
Clement L. Vallandigham is banished to the Confederacy.

This painting shows an extremely exaggerated last meeting between Robert E. Lee and Stonewall Jackson. In reality, their final conference took place in a clearing near Chancellorsville at 4:00 in the morning of May 2. Lee's nephew, General Fitzhugh Lee, discovered during a cavalry scout that the Union 11th Corps on the Union's far right had not dug any entrenchments. That was the opportunity Lee needed. They agreed that Jackson would attack on the evening of May 2. Later that night, he was accidentally struck down by his own troops.

MAY 26
Confederate Secretary of the Navy Stephen R. Mallory issues regulations concerning new flags for the Confederate States Navy.

Gold is discovered at Alder Gulch (which later changes its name to Virginia City) in the future Montana Territory, setting off a minor gold rush despite the war.

MAY 27
Union General Banks launches a series of unsuccessful assaults on the defenses of Port Hudson, Louisiana. His troops dig in for a siege.

General George G. Meade

Prior to the war, George G. Meade's military experience was in engineering. Although he served during the Second Seminole War of the 1830s and during the Mexican War, Meade spent much of his military career building lighthouses along the Atlantic Coast.

After the Civil War broke out, Meade quickly proved he remembered his West Point education with a brave and competent performance during the Seven Days' Battles. By Chancellorsville, he

General Meade wore this frock coat on dress occasions. Meade's two pieces of headgear included a general's kepi (left) and his more familiar slouch hat (top right). Also shown here are two presentation swords, his epaulets, and his field glasses.

was leading the 5th Corps. Meade was shocked when Lincoln promoted him to Army command, replacing the fired Joseph Hooker. He was not the President's first choice—General John F. Reynolds refused the Army command when he could not be assured of total independence.

Meade handled Gettysburg's troop disposition admirably. He even sent reinforcements when one of his subordinates, Daniel Sickles, moved his 3rd Corps into an open position that invited attack. On the second night of the battle, Meade held a meeting of his generals. They decided to stay on the field and force Lee to continue as the aggressor.

Though he angered Lincoln by not pursuing Lee sufficiently after Gettysburg, Meade remained in command of the Army of the Potomac through the end of the war. His contributions were overshadowed by Grant, who came east in 1864 to take over command of all Union armies. Meade's adroit handling of troops at Gettysburg turned the tide for the Union, but the general ended the war as a historical footnote to Grant.

Within days of assuming command, George Gordon Meade defeated Robert E. Lee at Gettysburg, Pennsylvania. He was later criticized for his less-than-aggressive pursuit of Lee's defeated army after the battle.

General officers such as Robert E. Lee had larger tents than the enlisted soldiers. Lee's tent included his folding cot, dining equipment, a makeshift desk for writing orders, a mount to keep his saddle off the ground, and other necessary items used while on campaign.

The Chancellor House, Joseph Hooker's headquarters during the Battle of Chancellorsville, was hit by artillery fire during the battle and burned to the ground. As it was still smoldering, Robert E. Lee rode past to the cheers of his troops. Ironically, the house itself was not the scene of much ground fighting. Hooker narrowly escaped death when a Confederate cannonball hit a column against which he was leaning.

These Yankees were shot during the successful Union attack on Marye's Heights in May. They have already been to the hospital and are awaiting evacuation to the rear. The man on the left has had his right arm amputated, and the soldier lying in the stretcher has lost his lower right leg.

Confederate batteries at Vicksburg sink the ironclad USS *Cincinnati*.

JUNE 1
General Burnside shuts down the *Chicago Times* for publishing disloyal statements.

JUNE 3
Lee's Army of Northern Virginia begins moving away from Fredericksburg to invade the North.

JUNE 4
Lincoln rescinds Burnside's order, allowing the *Chicago Times* to renew publication.

The Battle of Gettysburg

When Lee invaded Pennsylvania at the end of June 1863, his target was the state capital, Harrisburg. Lee believed once his troops feasted on the bounty of the rich Pennsylvania farmland, they would be strong enough to give him another great victory—perhaps one that would finally convince England and France to recognize the existence of the Confederate States of America.

But as his previous Northern invasion in September 1862 had been discovered, so was this Potomac crossing. With no word from Stuart's cavalry on the Federals' position in relation to his, Lee took his army, which was widely spread out, and concentrated it at a town 35 miles southwest of Harrisburg, where five roads met. He could not begin to guess the significance his stop in Gettysburg would have.

Lee wanted to wait until he was ready before engaging the enemy, but the situation was too fluid for that luxury. Neither side was quite sure of the location of their opponent. Forward guards from both sides found each other near Gettysburg on July 1, and a mutual test of strength led to a full-fledged battle. Lee had not planned to fight at this time and place, and he did not arrive on the scene until the fighting was well under way. His army was still spread out and trying to come together, but forced into battle, Lee threw brigades into action as they arrived on the field.

This 1880s Prang & Company lithograph of Pickett's Charge shows Union General Winfield Scott Hancock directing reinforcements toward the stone wall, obscured here by gun smoke. In the left background is the clump of trees that was the aiming point for the attack.

The Federals were overcome on the first day and forced backward into a strong position on a ridge and some hills east of the town. That night, as more Union forces arrived on that ridge, they formed a fishhook—the barb encircled the hills behind the town, and the long shank ran to the south.

On the second day of the engagement, Lee sent his 1st Corps commander, a reluctant James Longstreet, on a mission to pound the southernmost part of the line. Longstreet had lobbied in vain for Lee to find some defensible ground of his own. He wanted to let the Federals attack them rather than, as the weaker of the two, be forced into the position of aggressor. Lee refused, insisting they had to use the advantage they had gained the day before.

Longstreet slowly, somberly followed his orders. Just before his attack, the Union forces discovered an undefended piece of high ground called Little Round Top. If it fell into rebel hands, it could provide the Confederates with key ground. A few hundred soldiers, including the 20th Maine Regiment, rushed to the ridge and constructed breastworks before Longstreet arrived. The Union troops held their ground and kept the key position.

At the northern, barbed end of the Union line, Confederates attacked up Culp's Hill, which had been lightly defended on the previous evening. However, when Stonewall Jackson's replacement, Richard Ewell, declined to attack in the growing twilight, he ensured that, as at the southern end of the hook, the Confederates would fail to gain ground.

On the battle's third day, Lee made the assumption that the center of the Union's line would be weak after reinforcing both ends, which had been under attack the previous day. Early in the morning, Lee decided to focus his attack on that center. To a force of about 12,000 under Generals Pickett, Johnston Pettigrew, and Isaac Trimble, Lee issued broad instructions to punch a hole through the federal line.

Before the attack, the federal line was subjected to a tremendous artillery barrage, but due to poor placement of the cannons, the artillery did little actual damage. The federal line remained nearly as strong as it had been. Once the smoke cleared in mid-afternoon, the Confederates stepped off from

These slain Georgians of Brigadier General Paul J. Semmes's brigade were killed in the field just west of the Rose Woods at Gettysburg. Photographer Alexander Gardner's photographic wagon appears on the horizon to the left of the trees.

rebel-held Seminary Ridge to attack. Although this offensive could accurately be called the Pettigrew-Pickett-Trimble Assault after the commanders of the three divisions that took part, Richmond newspapers honored their native son and labeled it Pickett's Charge, a name that has stuck ever since.

The mile-wide Confederate line marched more than a mile across open fields under unyielding artillery fire. As the infantry neared Emmitsburg Road, it was slowed by heavy rail fences that could not be knocked down. Hundreds of Confederates were shot down as they tried to climb the fences. Only a few hundred North Carolinians and Virginians ever reached the stone wall that was their objective. In half an hour, 50 percent of the troops who started the march were casualties.

In three days of fighting, both sides lost a combined 50,000 killed, wounded, and missing. A Union counterattack never came, which gave Lee yet another opportunity to retreat for Virginia. Lee never had another chance to invade the North. Gettysburg marked the northernmost point a Confederate army would reach.

Pickett's Charge

"None on that crest now need be told that *the enemy is advancing.* Every eye could see his legions, an overwhelming resistless tide of an ocean of armed men sweeping upon us! Regiment after regiment and brigade after brigade move from the woods and rapidly take their places in the lines forming the assault.... More than half a mile their front extends; more than a thousand yards the dull gray masses deploy, man touching man, rank pressing rank, and line supporting line. The red flags wave, their horsemen gallop up and down; the arms of eighteen thousand men, barrel and bayonet, gleam in the sun, a sloping forest of flashing steel. Right on they move, as with one soul, in perfect order, without impediment of ditch, or wall or stream, over ridge and slope through orchard and meadow, and cornfield, magnificent, grim, irresistible."

*Union **Lieutenant Frank A. Haskell**, Brigadier General John Gibbon's staff, at Gettysburg, July 3, 1863*

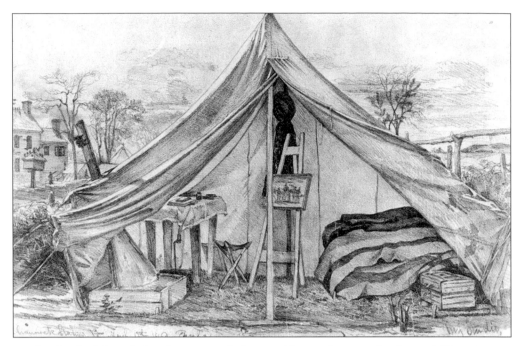

My Studio, *by Edwin Forbes, shows a snug little tent with space for an easel and a stool. The artist enjoyed the luxury of a tent in winter quarters or when the army was not marching, but during battle he took shelter wherever he could find it.*

Philippe Regis Denis de Keredern de Trobriand emigrated to America from France and in 1861 became colonel of a New York regiment. By war's end, de Trobriand became the only French citizen besides Lafayette to attain the rank of major general in the U.S. Army. These are his dress epaulets, worn over each shoulder on formal occasions.

The U.S. Christian Commission *was an offshoot of the recently formed Young Men's Christian Association. Though formed in the North, it tried to minister to both sides during the war by providing food, medicine, and religious tracts. While the Sanitary Commission attracted high-level political support, the Christian Commission concentrated on attracting support from local churches. Sanitary Commission leaders often grumbled that the Christians were stealing their donors.*

JUNE 7
Union forces fend off a Confederate attack at the Battle of Milliken's Bend, Louisiana.

JUNE 9
Confederates hold off Union horse soldiers at the Battle of Brandy Station, Virginia, the largest cavalry engagement of the war.

JUNE 13–15
Lee's army begins another invasion of the North with a victory at the Second Battle of Winchester, Virginia.

Thousands of civilians eventually found work with the Sanitary Commission. While the pay might have been small, this job had the benefit that no one was shooting at you. As the commission grew in political power and funding, its services expanded beyond providing medical help to include helping wounded soldiers write letters and even telegraphing the parents of troops to alert them on how their sons were doing.

This hinged case contains two images of soldiers posed for the camera. The slow shutter speed of period cameras meant that any slight movement would become blurred as the men posed. Such poses were often taken against backdrops in studios and sold to each subject in quantity for sending home to loved ones.

These wagons haul supplies for the U.S. Sanitary Commission, an organization founded in June 1861 by civilians to help wounded and sick soldiers. The Sanitary Commission would hold sanitary fairs around the country, selling food and merchandise to raise money so it could provide still more services. Organizations affiliated with the commission could be found in most Northern cities, so virtually every civilian could participate in the war effort in some manner.

JUNE 14
Banks stages his second assault on Port Hudson, which is rebuffed.

JUNE 16
General Henry H. Sibley sets out from Minnesota on an almost three-month campaign against hostile Dakota Sioux in Dakota Territory.

JUNE 17
The ironclad CSS *Atlanta* is captured by two Union monitors—*Weehawken* and *Nahant*—in Warsaw Sound, Georgia.

"Contrabands of war" was the name Union General Benjamin Butler gave to escaped slaves who began drifting into Fort Monroe, Virginia, early in the war. While the term implied the slaves were thought of more as property than humans, it did fit the way escaped slaves were treated by the Union early in the war. These contrabands were put to work digging—rather than fighting— near Culpeper, Virginia.

Sutlers were civilian shopkeepers who set up and traveled with both armies to provide the soldiers with goods that were not issued by the government, such as razors, soap, stamps, and tobacco. High prices angered the soldiers, and providing liquor to the troops angered their commanders. Both sides assumed sutlers were swindlers, and their shops were sometimes raided by unhappy customers. This federal sutler is at Brandy Station, Virginia, in 1864.

Songs about home, sweethearts, dying, fighting, and winning and losing battles were popular diversions for the soldiers of both sides. Songs such as "God Save the South," which this sheet music claims as the national anthem of the Confederacy, demonstrate that the South could claim divine blessing and protection as readily as the North did in its own "Battle Hymn of the Republic."

JUNE 18
Grant relieves McClernand of his command.

JUNE 20
West Virginia is admitted to the Union as the 35th state.

JUNE 23
Rosecrans opens the Tullahoma Campaign in Tennessee.

Confederates capture the Union garrison of Brashear City, Louisiana.

JUNE 27
The CSS *Archer* unsuccessfully raids Portland, Maine.

JUNE 28
General Hooker is superseded by General George G. Meade as

The New York City Draft Riots

In a matter of hours, an angry mob had "swollen to a frightful size," according to one witness. "[A] vast crowd of those who lived by preying upon others, thieves, pimps, professional ruffians, the scum of the city, jail birds, or those who were running with swift feet to enter the prison doors, began to gather on the corners, and in streets and alleys where they lived." Many armed themselves with clubs, crowbars, and paving stones. In time, the devilish masses spilled from the dark reaches of New York City and swarmed to the 9th District draft office with blood in their eyes.

It was Monday, July 13, 1863, and the angry New Yorkers were reacting to the beginning of a nationwide military draft brought on by a shortage of volunteers. By the middle of 1862, the gruesome stories from the battlefields, the long lists of soldiers killed in action, and the scores of overcrowded military hospitals had soured public enthusiasm for the war. The rioters were angry that the rich could buy their way out of the draft. The Irish, many of whom were recent immigrants, felt particularly targeted by the conscription.

Over the next few days, the rioters brought a reign of terror to the city. Government offices, political officials, military personnel, and black residents of any age became the targets of the mob's wrath. It took several regiments of troops with artillery newly arrived from Gettysburg to force an end to the savage street battles. When it was all over, more than 70 people were killed, hundreds more were injured, and property damage exceeded $1.5 million. Similar uprisings on a smaller scale erupted in Boston and other Northern cities. The "nation is at this time," wrote the editor of a Washington, D.C., newspaper, "in a state of revolution."

Mobs of protesters roamed the streets of New York City for four days, fighting pitched battles with police. Provost guards brought in to subdue the rioting New Yorkers had to use artillery force.

The 54th Massachusetts Infantry

The 54th Massachusetts Infantry, perhaps the best-known black regiment participating in the Civil War, is often mistakenly assumed to be the first. Former slaves in South Carolina, Louisiana, and Kansas had been enlisted several months earlier.

The 54th began recruiting early in 1863, drawing from a large, educated black population that had previously been rejected for service. The regiment was clearly seen as an idealistic venture by its supporters in Boston, who included Frederick Douglass and Sojourner Truth. By May, it had its full complement of 1,000 troops and was sent to its first posting in Beaufort, South Carolina.

In its first action, the 54th was ordered to join a pioneering black regiment, the 2nd South Carolina Volunteers, led by a radical abolitionist, in burning a coastal Georgia town. Colonel Robert Gould Shaw, the 54th's commander, was extremely angry to see reinforced the Southern stereotype of armed blacks as a ransacking force. On July 18, the 54th got its first chance to fight in an assault on Battery Wagner, a stoutly built and defended sand fort at the mouth of Charleston Harbor. The attack, ordered by white generals, sent the black troops running down a narrow causeway of sand right into the teeth of the Confederate guns. The ill-advised offensive was a

The 54th Massachusetts Infantry was the most famous of the many black regiments that served in the war. Led by Colonel Shaw, who died in the assault, the 54th attacked Battery Wagner near Charleston, South Carolina, on July 18. Before being forced to retreat, the 54th lost 272 of its 650 soldiers engaged in the attack.

dismal failure with more than a third of the regiment cut down in its tracks. Still, the reputation of the 54th bravely following orders was established.

The 54th went on to play a major role at the Battle of Olustee, Florida, in 1864 when it covered the retreating Federals. Had the 54th broken, the entire Union force would likely have been wiped out.

On July 18, the 54th Massachusetts Regiment, made up of free blacks and runaway slaves, was put in the forward position in a futile attack against Battery Wagner, a sand fort that protected the entrance to Charleston Harbor. The poorly planned and executed assault by Union generals, easily repulsed by the Confederates, doomed the 54th to losing more than a third of its strength. This print shows Colonel Robert Gould Shaw, commander of the 54th, at the moment of his death.

Railroad bridges were always important military targets. Their destruction was the cavalry's job, and their rebuilding was the job of military engineers. This bridge is on the Orange & Alexandria railroad over Cedar Run, about 15 miles south of the Bull Run battlefield in Virginia. J.E.B. Stuart's cavalry destroyed this bridge, and Federals are rebuilding it.

The 114th Pennsylvania, a Zouave unit, gets ready to stand guard at Brandy Station. Note the white gloves and the regimental band standing to the left. Zouaves were regular soldiers whose officers got permission for them to wear colorful red, white, and blue uniforms patterned after French troops who served in Morocco. The 114th wore white turbans that wound around a red fez atop their heads.

Two Union cavalry brigades coming from two different directions surprised J.E.B. Stuart's resting cavalry at Brandy Station, Virginia, north of Culpeper, on June 9. For most of the day, some 22,000 cavalry soldiers clashed sabers and crashed horses into each other, making this the largest cavalry engagement ever fought. The Confederates barely won the battle, but the federal cavalry proved to be their equals for the first time in the war.

Cavalry troopers wore a short shell jacket rather than the longer sack coat of the foot soldiers. Contractors supplied a variety of styles such as this one, worn by a Pennsylvania sergeant. It is trimmed in yellow, the color of the mounted arm of service. The single row of nine brass buttons is traditional, as well.

commander of the Army of the Potomac.

JULY 1–3
The invasion of the North by Lee's Army of Northern Virginia is stopped at the Battle of Get-

tysburg, Pennsylvania, by Meade and the Army of the Potomac.

JULY 2
Confederate Colonel John Hunt Morgan sets out on what will be

an unsuccessful raid through Kentucky, Indiana, and Ohio.

JULY 3
In order to overwhelm the Union line at Gettysburg, Confederates

The Army of the Potomac generals shown here left to right are Gouverneur K. Warren, William French, George Meade, Henry Hunt, Andrew Humphreys, and George Sykes. Warren, the man who recognized the value of Little Round Top at Gettysburg, would be relieved of command late in the war in a dispute with Philip Sheridan. Hunt's artillery decimated Lee's force at Malvern Hill and Gettysburg. Sykes would have a falling out with Meade, who relieved him of his command less than a year later.

Confederate General James Longstreet, shown here in postwar civilian clothes, was nicknamed "My Old War Horse" by Lee after fighting at Sharpsburg. He also won Lee's praise for an outstanding defense at Fredericksburg. Longstreet did not support Lee's aggression at Gettysburg, however, and was later accused of intentionally slowing the battle, perhaps hoping Lee would change tactics. Lee supporters later blamed the Gettysburg loss on Longstreet's reluctance to fight. He became a Republican after the war.

These Confederates were killed on the second day of Gettysburg near Rose's Woods and have been gathered for burial. Photographers arrived within a few days of the battle and photographed the dead. Note that the soldiers' muskets, leather goods, and even hats have already been taken from the bodies. After the war, philanthropists paid for the Confederate dead to be dug up and moved back to Southern states.

launch a direct assault that has come to be known as Pickett's Charge. The Federals repulse the attack.

JULY 4
Attempting to relieve some of the

pressure on General Pemberton at Vicksburg, Confederates attack a Union garrison in the Battle of Helena, Arkansas.

Vicksburg, Mississippi, surrenders to General Grant.

Robert E. Lee begins the process of withdrawing his forces from the Gettysburg battlefield. He will never advance his troops this far north again.

Regimental surgeons often set up their temporary field hospitals as close to the battle area as possible to expedite medical care. In this scene from the famous Gettysburg Cyclorama painted by French artist Paul Philippoteaux, a surgeon works on his patients under cover of a farm outbuilding.

Timothy O'Sullivan photographed this group of dead Union and Confederate soldiers somewhere on the Gettysburg battlefield. Unfortunately, the hazy background precludes modern identification of the specific site. Note that the dead soldiers are missing their shoes—it was common for Confederate soldiers to take shoes from those who would never need them again.

JULY 6
Admiral John Dahlgren replaces Samuel F. DuPont as commander of the South Atlantic Blockading Squadron.

JULY 9
Port Hudson, Mississippi, surrenders to General Banks.

JULY 10
General Sherman digs in to begin a siege against Jackson, Mississippi.

Union siege operations begin against Battery Wagner, Charleston, South Carolina.

Alfred Waud, a native of England, was assigned to sketch the war by Harper's Weekly *because the relatively new medium of photography was too slow to capture live action. Waud's pencil sketches captured the live action much better than any photograph at the time could and told the realistic story of combat.*

New York Congressman Dan Sickles got his general's commission and then won a place in history for exposing his 3rd Corps to attack by moving forward from Gettysburg's Cemetery Ridge without orders on July 2. His movement resulted in savage fights in the Wheat Field and the Peach Orchard and exposed the federal left flank. Only heavy fighting by his soldiers saved the Union army. Sickles never admitted his mistake of moving without orders.

This artist's rendering of Little Round Top at Gettysburg shows Confederate forces beginning their assault on the hill. This painting depicts the steep, rocky grade that made attacking the Union-held ground so difficult and deadly for the rebels.

JULY 11
Union forces unsuccessfully assault Battery Wagner.

JULY 13–16
Violent draft riots break out in New York City.

JULY 16
General Johnston abandons Jackson, Mississippi, to Union forces.

The USS *Wyoming* engages Japanese ships and shore batteries in the Straits of Shimonoseki, Japan.

JULY 17
Federal troops defeat their Confederate counterparts at the Battle of Honey Springs, Indian Territory.

The U.S. Sanitary Commission

Throughout the North, local groups raised money and obtained donations of clothing, food, and other items for the soldiers. Pennsylvania had its own state agency, while the Michigan Soldiers' Relief Association aided its own soldiers. The single largest Union relief agency was the U.S. Sanitary Commission, formed in June 1861 to impose order on the unorganized benevolence. The agency's board of directors chose Frederick Law Olmsted, the landscape architect who had laid out New York's Central Park, to direct the commission.

Initially opposed by President Abraham Lincoln and his Cabinet, the Sanitary Commission eventually converted doubters into believers. Their sanitation reports embarrassed the Army. To help hard-pressed surgeons, the commission's medical experts compiled booklets on a wide range of topics—scurvy, dysentery, and amputation, to name a few. As a result of commission pressure, the Army replaced aged Surgeon General Clement A. Finley and grudgingly accepted commission suggestions on reform of the medical department.

From offices across the North, women volunteers funneled donations to commission warehouses for distribution to soldiers. Throughout the war, the Sanitary Commission distributed more than $25 million in aid. Commission wagon trains followed the armies and arrived on battlefields as soon as possible, bringing medical supplies and food to wounded soldiers and their surgeons. Volunteers staffed hospital boats, railroad cars, and wagons to transport the wounded to safety when the Army was unable to provide adequate transportation.

The commission also established "soldiers' homes" as lodging for troops in transit. One of the best known was the Cooper Shop Volunteer Refreshment Saloon in Philadelphia. Until it closed in July 1865, the Cooper Shop facility dispensed more than 800,000 meals to passing regiments. It also provided medical service, washrooms, paper and stamps, and a laundry room.

Beginning in the fall of 1863, the Sanitary Commission sponsored a series of fairs to raise money for its activities. The first was held in Chicago and included exhibition halls filled with captured battle flags, farm machinery, and art. Such fairs alone raised more than $4 million for the commission.

All in all, the relief drive led by the commission aroused patriotism, kept up soldier morale, and in general helped unify the Northern populace behind the war effort.

Officers and nurses of the Sanitary Commission are gathered at Fredericksburg, Virginia, in 1864.

General William S. Rosecrans

Few Civil War careers started so well and ended so miserably as that of William S. Rosecrans. A brilliant man, he graduated fifth in West Point's class of 1842. He was also apparently a kindly older cadet, having once saved a newer student named U. S. Grant from hazing. Following in the footsteps of another brilliant cadet named Robert E. Lee, Rosecrans spent most of his prewar career on engineering projects.

When the war opened, Rosecrans won a minor victory at Rich Mountain in western Virginia that helped burnish the reputation of his commander, George McClellan. McClellan parlayed that notice into overall command of the Union armies, while Rosecrans was transferred to the West, where his methodical engineer's mind was criticized by Grant.

Still, Rosecrans performed well in several campaigns, including winning Stones River, but he angered Lincoln by taking almost six months out after that victory to refit his army. In the Tullahoma Campaign that finally followed, Rosecrans successfully maneuvered Bragg out of Tennessee with very few Union losses. This feat pleased the engineer in Rosecrans, but as it did not result in the demolition of Bragg's forces, the Tullahoma Campaign, particularly in light of the overwhelming Gettysburg and Vicksburg victories at about the same time, was seen in Washington as only partially successful.

Rosecrans's failure to destroy Bragg came back to haunt him three months later at Chickamauga when he almost lost his own army. This overwhelming defeat caused Grant to abandon his long-ago friend, who was relieved of his command and transferred to a faraway post in Missouri to finish out the war.

Placed in the command of the federal Army of the Cumberland in October 1862, William S. Rosecrans executed a brilliant campaign the next summer that resulted in the capture of Chattanooga, Tennessee, in September. Within days, however, his army suffered bitter defeat at the Battle of Chickamauga, Georgia, and retreated back to Chattanooga. Besieged there by rebels, he was relieved of command on October 18. An excellent organizer and strategist, Rosecrans was markedly less successful on the battlefield.

JULY 18
Federals mount another unsuccessful attack on Battery Wagner. The 54th Massachusetts loses more than a third of its troops.

JULY 19
General Morgan loses more than 800 raiders at an engagement at Buffington Island, Ohio.

JULY 26
Morgan and the remnants of his

raiders surrender near Salineville, Ohio.

Former Texas Governor Sam Houston and former Kentucky Senator John J. Crittenden each die at their homes.

A Northern Wife Left Behind

"It seems as if it could not be that I have to spend this day her[e] & Mr C in the army—& the good man only knows where he is. My God protect him & bring him safely back. In honor of the day we had as good a dinner as circumstances would permit....O! It seems so dreadful to be thus separated. If he only be spared to come home again that we may yet long live together I will not murmur at this cruel separation. The great sin of slavery has brought all this calamity on us—God grant us grace & strength for our day & trial."

Rachel Cormany, writing in her diary on the third anniversary of her marriage to Samuel Cormany, who served in the 16th Pennsylvania Cavalry, November 25, 1863

General Joshua Lawrence Chamberlain was a college professor when he took leave from his school to join the Army. He gained fame at Gettysburg while commanding the 20th Maine and stopping repeated Confederate assaults against his position on Little Round Top. Over the next year and a half he worked his way up to major general while surviving several wounds. He was later elected governor of Maine and presented with the Congressional Medal of Honor.

One of the most decisive battles in human history, the Battle of Gettysburg was started almost by accident when Union and Confederate cavalry blundered into each other on the outskirts of the town on July 1. On that day and the two that followed, Federals and Confederates fought with tremendous valor and violence over places with names like Culp's Hill, Cemetery Ridge, the Peach Orchard, the Wheat Field, and Little Round Top.

AUGUST 1
In an attempt to strengthen Confederate armies, Jefferson Davis offers amnesty to deserters.

AUGUST 5
Union cavalry led by General

William W. Averell leave Winchester, Virginia, on a raid into West Virginia.

AUGUST 8
Lee offers to resign his commission, an offer Davis refuses.

AUGUST 16
Rosecrans's Army of the Cumberland begins moving south from Tullahoma, Tennessee, beginning the Chickamauga Campaign.

Taking part in the attack that would forever bear the general's name, George Pickett's division of Virginians was all but destroyed in the last major action of the Battle of Gettysburg. He was later described by a fellow Confederate officer as "a singular figure indeed [whose] . . . long ringlets flowed loosely over his shoulders, . . . his beard likewise was curling and giving out the scents of Araby." The 38-year-old general would be forever tormented by his failed role in the "High Water Mark of the Confederacy."

General Winfield Scott Hancock, commander of the 2nd Corps at Gettysburg, bore the brunt of the Confederate attack on the third day. He survived a wound and stayed in the field directing his corps' defense of the stone wall. Hancock's service was so valued during the war his fellow generals nicknamed him "Hancock the Superb." He was a close friend of Confederate General Lewis Armistead, who fell mortally wounded not far from Hancock during Gettysburg.

Photographer Peter S. Weaver captured this posed scene at Camp Letterman, Gettysburg's largest hospital, in October. A surgeon prepares to operate on a patient's foot while other soldiers look on. The man with the white beard and hands on his hips is the Reverend Gordon Winslow, who at the time was acting as sanitary inspector of the Army of the Potomac.

AUGUST 21
Confederate guerrillas led by William Quantrill sack Lawrence, Kansas.

AUGUST 25
In response to Quantrill's raid,

General Thomas Ewing in Missouri orders all civilians to leave the counties of Bates, Jackson, Cass, and part of Vernon.

AUGUST 29
Rosecrans and his army begin to

cross the Tennessee River on their way toward Chattanooga, Tennessee.

SEPTEMBER 2
Union troops under Burnside occupy Knoxville, Tennessee.

Captain Harvey Fisher poses with the remnant of Company A, 150th Pennsylvania Volunteer Infantry. These men wear bucktails in their caps, emblematic of their shooting ability. The man at the right of the company poses with his ax—he is on detached duty as a pioneer, a period term for the soldiers who cleared fences, chopped trees, and performed other such duties.

This 1866 painting by Lilly Martin Spencer, titled War Spirit at Home, *captures what life must have been like on the home front. Although the children celebrate the news of Grant's victory at Vicksburg, the women in the painting carry much more of the weight of the times. The missing husband and father, presumably fighting in the war himself, has left a void in the home, and his family strives to carry on without him.*

SEPTEMBER 4
A bread riot erupts in Mobile, Alabama.

SEPTEMBER 5
Britain detains two unfinished ironclads being built for the Confederacy in Liverpool.

SEPTEMBER 6
Confederate troops evacuate Batteries Gregg and Wagner on Morris Island, South Carolina.

General Bragg pulls out of Chattanooga before the Union army arrives.

SEPTEMBER 7
Union soldiers assault the bat-

Sister M. M. Joseph of the Sisters of Mercy, along with other members of her order, served in a military hospital in Beaufort, North Carolina.

An ironclad, 50-foot-long, cigar-shaped torpedo boat, the CSS David guarded the waters off Charleston, South Carolina. Several craft of similar design were constructed to defend the inland and coastal waters of the Confederacy. The semisubmersible vessels were such a threat to Union ships that Rear Admiral John A. Dahlgren offered a cash reward for their capture or destruction.

Anxious to fight, the U.S. Colored Troops often found themselves relegated to guarding forts, camps, and prisoners. When they were allowed into battle, the black troops were often thrown into wasted combat by incompetent white generals at engagements such as those at Battery Wagner and Olustee. The ultimate insult to the U.S. Colored Troops was being barred from marching in the Grand Review, the two-day end-of-war celebration in Washington when only white combat units paraded down Pennsylvania Avenue.

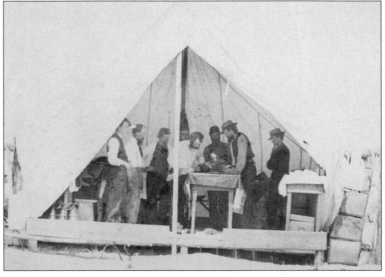

Photographer Hass S. Peale captured this image of a tent hospital at the Union base on Hilton Head Island, South Carolina. Surgeons posed for the camera's lens, an agonizingly slow process that must have seemed even slower for the poor man lying on the operating table.

teries on Morris Island only to find them abandoned.

SEPTEMBER 8
Confederates rout attacking Union forces in the Second Battle of the Sabine Pass, Texas.

SEPTEMBER 9
Federal troops occupy Chattanooga.

An early morning Union boat attack on Fort Sumter fails.

James Longstreet's troops are detached from Lee's army and sent by rail to reinforce Bragg's Army of Tennessee.

The Battle of Chickamauga

The two-day Battle of Chickamauga on September 19 and 20 featured one Union general who stubbornly followed an order to move his division from the battle line when he knew he should not have and one lucky Confederate general who attacked through the subsequent hole that move caused. The battle was one of the more unusual engagements of the war.

By mid-September, Braxton Bragg's subordinate generals were so angry their commander had abandoned Tennessee without a fight that they were ignoring his direct orders. On September 9 and on September 13, several of Bragg's generals refused to follow through on attacking isolated Union columns of William Rosecrans's army. But on the morning of September 19, Bragg's generals were forced to fight when the Union and Confederate armies began leapfrogging units on the north end of the battlefield in an attempt to outflank the other side. Both Bragg and Rosecrans ignored their crafted battle plans and threw in units as they were needed. The day ended with both armies drifting to the north but with no advantage over the other.

Scattered fighting opened the next day. Then Rosecrans, believing his line had a hole when, in fact, none existed, ordered Thomas Wood's division from its spot in line to close the nonexistent gap. A peevish Wood knew he would create a real gap by moving his division, but he followed his orders to the letter. At that moment, two divisions of James Longstreet's 1st Corps, which had just arrived after a nine-day train trip from Virginia, struck in the hole created by Wood.

Longstreet's troops first smashed the smaller part of the Union army to their left and then turned right to roll up the remaining force. Rosecrans's army panicked, with most fleeing for Chattanooga. Only the corps of Virginia-born Union General George H. Thomas and a brigade of mounted infantry armed with repeating rifles stayed behind.

Thomas's troops and a force of stragglers and reserves built their defense atop Snodgrass Hill. They held off the Confederates for the rest of the day, a renowned defense that earned Thomas the nickname "The Rock of Chickamauga."

Chickamauga resulted in 35,000 casualties on both sides, second only to Gettysburg in bloodshed in 1863. Bragg could have pursued Rosecrans and crushed him before he had time to set up a defense in Chattanooga, but he did not. This caused one of Bragg's subordinates to call Chickamauga a "barren victory."

The failed September 13 Confederate attack at Lee and Gordon's Mill at Chickamauga Creek, where federal General Thomas Crittenden was stationed, was an indication of the general disagreement between Bragg and his subordinates.

The Siege of Chattanooga

Chattanooga, Tennessee, at a point on the Tennessee River where four railroads converged, was a plum waiting to be picked by the Union for much of the war. When Bragg allowed Rosecrans to retreat into the town after the devastating Union defeat at Chickamauga, U. S. Grant may have smiled. All he would need to do was lift the weak Confederate siege, and the plum would be harvested.

Jefferson Davis helped Grant's cause when he visited Bragg in October and reiterated his full support for the general's command abilities. Far more talented Confederate generals than Bragg were reassigned away from him to get them out of his sight. This dilution of forces and talent doomed the possibility of ever regaining Chattanooga by force.

After a curiously underperforming William T. Sherman failed to lift the siege, Grant found unexpected success on November 25. Under orders only to capture Confederate rifle pits at the base of Missionary Ridge, Union soldiers stormed all the way to the top of the high ground, almost capturing Bragg himself. The rebels not only had to abandon the siege, they had to retreat into northern Georgia.

Though it was too late to do any good, a disheartened Bragg finally asked his friend Davis to replace him. Joseph E. Johnston was given the job. Within four months Grant was promoted to the Army's top job and sent east to deal with Lee. Sherman, who took Grant's place in the mid-South, started strategizing how he would use Chattanooga as a supply base from which to attack Atlanta.

U. S. Grant and his officers watch in disbelief as his troops scamper up Missionary Ridge east of Chattanooga, Tennessee, on November 25. Ordered to take the rifle pits at the base of the ridge, the soldiers accomplished that goal and then continued to crawl up the mountain. Unsure of the ultimate success of the unplanned attack, Grant at first demanded to know who gave the order to climb the heights. No one had.

SEPTEMBER 10
Union troops occupy Little Rock, Arkansas.

SEPTEMBER 13
General Leonidas Polk ignores a direct order from General Bragg

to attack disorganized Union forces at Lee and Gordon's Mill. This allows troops under Union General Thomas L. Crittenden to consolidate.

SEPTEMBER 19–20
Bragg defeats Rosecrans and his army at the Battle of Chickamauga, Georgia. Rosecrans retreats back to Chattanooga.

On the evening of July 18, a federal storming column attacked Battery Wagner, which defended Charleston Harbor. Colonel Robert G. Shaw and his 54th Massachusetts Infantry led the attack. Southern defenders repelled the attackers and inflicted more than 1,500 casualties. Frank Vizetelly penned this view of the morning after, as Southern troops inspected the grisly scene.

Colonel William Quantrill and his band of about 450 raiders left Lawrence, Kansas, in ruins on August 21, 1863. They killed more than 150 men and older boys during their reign of destruction on this pro-Union town. His raiders pillaged and burned, inflicting more than $1.5 million dollars in damages. Six weeks later, Quantrill's band sacked Baxter Springs, Kansas, killing about 100 Union soldiers without mercy before withdrawing to the safety of Texas's border.

By the end of the war, Fort Sumter was reduced to rubble, but it still proudly held out. The Confederacy's Stainless Banner, its second national flag, continued to fly tattered in the wind. In the distance of this painting by Conrad Wise Chapman are Union blockading ships.

SEPTEMBER 22
Confederate General Joseph O. Shelby's horse soldiers begin a raid from Arkansas into Missouri.

SEPTEMBER 24
Two Union corps under General Hooker from the Army of the Potomac are sent roughly 1,200 miles by rail to Bridgeport, Alabama, as reinforcements bound for Chattanooga. They begin to arrive six days later.

SEPTEMBER 30
Confederate General Joseph Wheeler's cavalry sets out for

At 125 pounds, John Singleton Mosby was far from an imposing figure. His actions during the war, however, made him a legend feared by many Union commanders. In early 1863, he organized a fighting force of partisan rangers, seen here, that raided various targets, such as supply trains and railroads, behind enemy lines. Mosby and his troops launched lightning strikes before dispersing into the countryside. Although thousands of Union soldiers were dispatched to stop them, Mosby's rangers were active until the war's end.

"It is heart sickening to see what I have seen since I have been back here," wrote Union Colonel Bazel Lazear after witnessing the forced evacuation of four Missouri counties. "A desolated country and men & women and children, some of them all most [sic] naked. . . . Oh God." Union General Thomas Ewing issued General Order Number 11, giving citizens 15 days to leave their homes in retaliation for Quantrill's raid on Lawrence, Kansas, in August 1863.

In September, another Confederate capital, Little Rock, Arkansas, fell. This painting depicts the 3rd Minnesota Regiment entering the city. While Federals were preparing their invasion, the rebels were distracted. Two Confederate generals charged with the city's defense, John Marmaduke and Lucius Walker, fought a duel. The nature of their disagreement likely related to Walker's failure to protect Marmaduke's flank in battle two months earlier. Marmaduke killed Walker, and Little Rock fell a few days later.

more than two weeks to strike into Tennessee and disrupt Union supply lines.

OCTOBER 3
Lincoln issues a proclamation of

thanksgiving, to be observed on the last Thursday in November.

OCTOBER 4
James R. Chalmers's Confederate horse soldiers launch a raid into Union-held territory in

northern Mississippi and western Tennessee.

OCTOBER 9
Union soldiers win an engagement at Vermillion Bayou, Louisiana.

These federal Parrott rifles threw 100-pound shells into both Charleston and Fort Sumter in 1864, but the rain of artillery at all hours of day and night never broke the will of either the civilians or Confederate soldiers inside the fort. Parrott rifles were manufactured as small as 10-pounders and were among the most dependable, safest cannons manufactured by the United States. The ring around the breech made them less likely to burst from heavy use.

On April 7, a fleet of nine Union ironclads attacked Fort Sumter, but sharp-shooting from the Confederate gunners hit every ship multiple times. One ironclad, the USS Keokuk, was sunk. Samuel DuPont, the reluctant federal commander of the ships, had not believed the monitors could fight properly. He was forced to resign after his spectacular failure to demolish the fort.

Generals on both sides were uncomfortable with newspaper reporters, but that did not stop reporters from covering the war and delivering newspapers right to the soldiers in the field. Newspaper vendors were very popular with soldiers of both armies. Here a supplier of New York, Philadelphia, and Baltimore papers plies his trade.

Large-scale field kitchens were never developed during the war. Instead, small groups would gather around individual fires as mess mates shared their food among themselves. Here a handful of soldiers are cooking a stew or perhaps a huge pot of coffee, which most troops swore they needed each morning before they would agree to fight the enemy.

OCTOBER 14
Confederates unsuccessfully attack Meade's retreating army at the Battle of Bristoe Station, Virginia.

OCTOBER 18
Grant assumes command of the new Military Division of the Mississippi. He replaces Rosecrans with General George Thomas as commander of the Army of the Cumberland.

OCTOBER 23
Grant arrives at Chattanooga.

OCTOBER 27
Union troops seize Brown's Ferry over the Tennessee River, open-

Sanitary Fairs

By October 1862, the U.S. Sanitary Commission was in dire need of money to continue its relief efforts on the battlefield and in army camps and hospitals. Without new support, this privately funded civilian aid society would have had to consider disbanding.

In response, Commission members Mary Livermore and Jane Hoge of Chicago conceived the idea of a sanitary fair. Through newspaper ads and church bulletins, the two women solicited goods and "battle relics and mementoes of the war" to be sold or displayed for charity. They offered a gold watch for the largest contribution. In return, they hoped to raise $25,000.

The 1863 fair opened after a tumultuous parade in downtown Chicago. Schools, businesses, and courts shut down for the event. It was a huge suc-cess, averaging more than 5,000 spectators a day for 20 days at 75 cents admission. In came a flood of donations, from a steam engine to a "curious tooth pick." By the end of the spectacle, organizers had netted close to $100,000. President Abraham Lincoln won the gold watch for donating his copy of the Emancipation Proclamation, sold at auction for $3,000. "I had some desire to retain the paper," Lincoln admitted, "but if it shall contribute to the relief and comfort of the soldiers, that will be better."

Due to its success, the sanitary fair in Chicago became a model for similar fund-raisers held in cities and small towns throughout the North. The largest fair, held in New York City in the spring of 1864, raised over $1 million. By the end of the Civil War, sanitary fairs had generated nearly $5 million in donations.

This is the main building at the 1865 Great North Western Sanitary Fair in Chicago. For a small admission, visitors were treated to elaborate exhibits of military relics and other goods for display or sale. The money raised here and at other sanitary fairs was used by the U.S. Sanitary Commission to aid sick and wounded soldiers and their families.

ing up a new supply line to Chattanooga.

OCTOBER 28
Confederates attack Union forces after dark at Wauhatchie, Tennessee, but are repulsed.

NOVEMBER 1
Union cavalry under William W. Averell's command leaves Beverly, West Virginia, toward Lewisburg, West Virginia, on a raid.

NOVEMBER 2–6
Union troops occupy Brazos Santiago and Brownsville, Texas.

This selection of cooking gear includes a coffee pot, a saltshaker, ladles, silver-ware, cups, and tin plates. The cups on the plate at right were a nonstandard collapsible style that proved popular early in the war but were not used much in the field. In a more permanent camp, each company detailed cooks to keep the troops fed, but on the march, soldiers were generally on their own.

Virginia-born George H. Thomas paid the price for his loyalty to the Union by being disowned by his Southern family and often being passed over for promotion in favor of less-skilled Northern-born generals. He served admirably in every campaign, finally winning the nation's recognition with his spirited defense of Snodgrass Hill at Chicka-mauga in September. After the battle, he won the nickname "The Rock of Chickamauga."

This federal blockhouse guarding a railroad bridge over the Tennessee River is typical of the small forts the Union built to defend bridges. Note the holes through which rifles could be placed to fire on the enemy while giving the attackers little at which to shoot. This is a particularly stout example of a block-house, its construction demonstrating the hand of a trained engineer.

Confederate General Joseph "Fighting Joe" Wheeler won his nickname fighting American Indians before the war. He built on his reputa-tion during the war with spectacular service in the West, where even Braxton Bragg expressed admiration for his skills at using cavalry to confuse opposing federal forces. Wheeler was particularly effective in slowing Sherman's advance into Georgia and all the way into the Carolinas. He later helped North-South reconciliation by serving with the U.S. Army during the Spanish-American War.

NOVEMBER 3
Confederates are victorious in an engagement at Bayou Bourbeau, Louisiana.

NOVEMBER 6
Averell's raiders engage the enemy at Droop Mountain, West Virginia. Triumphant, they con-tinue on and off to raid Virginia and West Virginia.

NOVEMBER 7
Meade's troops attack the Con-federates at Kelly's Ford and Rappahannock Station, Virginia, pushing Lee's army back across the Rapidan River.

The Battle of Chickamauga as depicted here is a little inaccurate, as much of the fighting took place in dense woods. A Union messenger failed to see a Union division in the woods, which caused a mistaken order to be given that moved another division out of line. That relocated division created its own hole in the line through which James Longstreet's Confederates poured.

These soldiers of Company A of the 9th Indiana Infantry fought with General Thomas on Snodgrass Hill at the Battle of Chickamauga. The brave stand of these and other troops under Thomas's command saved Rosecrans's army from complete destruction.

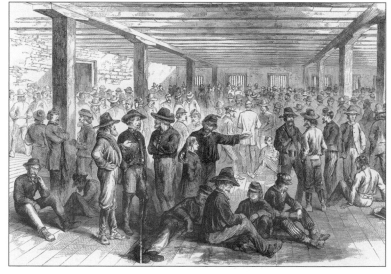

Libby Prison in downtown Richmond started its service as a tobacco warehouse, but it became infamous for housing captured Union officers. At its peak, it held more than 1,000 prisoners at one time. Conditions were crowded, and food was short during the later part of the war because Union war planners refused to exchange prisoners with the South, believing the practice only put soldiers back into the dwindling Confederate ranks.

NOVEMBER 9
Lincoln sees John Wilkes Booth perform in *The Marble Heart* at Ford's Theatre.

NOVEMBER 16
Burnside successfully retreats into Knoxville, Tennessee, after an engagement with Longstreet's troops at Campbell's Station, Tennessee.

NOVEMBER 17–DECEMBER 4
Longstreet conducts a siege of Knoxville, Tennessee.

Lincoln's Gettysburg Address

In early November 1863, President Abraham Lincoln received an invitation to make "a few appropriate remarks" at the November 19 dedication of a national cemetery at Gettysburg, Pennsylvania. Lincoln accepted the invitation and arrived at the town by train the night before.

After a long, slow procession to the cemetery south of town, Edward Everett, a famous orator of the time, delivered an eloquent two-hour speech describing the Battle of Gettysburg and drawing lessons from European military history. After thundering applause from thousands in attendance, President Lincoln rose, stepped to the front of the platform, and delivered his brief tribute to those who fought and died during those first three days of July 1863.

"Fourscore and seven years ago our fathers brought forth on this continent a new nation, conceived in liberty and dedicated to the proposition that all men are created equal. Now we are engaged in a great civil war, testing whether that nation or any nation so conceived and dedicated can long endure. We are met on a great battlefield of that war. We have come to dedicate a portion of that field as a final resting-place for those who gave their lives that that nation might live. It is altogether fitting and proper that we should do this. But, in a larger sense, we cannot dedicate, we cannot consecrate, we can not hallow this ground. The brave men, living and dead who struggled here have consecrated it far above our poor power to add or detract. The world will little note nor long remember what we say here, but it can never forget what they did here.

"It is for us the living rather to be dedicated here to the unfinished work which they who fought here have thus far so nobly advanced. It is rather for us to be here dedicated to the great task remaining before us—that from these honored dead we take increased devotion to that cause for which they gave the last full measure of devotion—that we here highly resolve that these dead shall not have died in vain, that this nation under God shall have a new birth of freedom, and that government of the people, by the people, for the people shall not perish from the earth."

Applause interrupted the speech five times, and a tremendous ovation and three cheers followed its completion. While Lincoln confided later that he felt the speech a "flat failure," Everett summed up the impact of the President's "few remarks" when he wrote him the next day, "I should be glad, if I could flatter myself that I came as near to the central idea of the occasion, in two hours, as you did in two minutes."

Taken on November 19, this is the only known photograph to show Lincoln at the dedication ceremony. The President can be seen slightly left of the center of the picture looking down. The blur of the moving crowd is also a good example of the difficulty photographers had in taking action shots.

Worried that Bragg's army was preparing to retreat from Chattanooga, Grant ordered an attack on November 23. The first day of fighting took place over Orchard Knob. The rebels had not established a strong defense of the hill, and Union forces were able to take it with less effort than they had expected. Two more days of battle lay ahead in Chattanooga, and those would not be so easy.

This post-battle photograph of Missionary Ridge, east of Chattanooga, shows the low ridge almost denuded of trees after the fighting that took place on November 25. The ridge was not as high as a mountain, but its steep slopes made slow going for climbing Union soldiers. The slopes were steep enough that Confederate gunners were unable to depress their cannons to fire on the advancing Federals. Bragg was criticized for not preparing an adequate defense.

Taken near Knoxville, Tennessee, this view shows a military bridge with Union Fort Stanley atop the hill in the distance. Confederate General James Longstreet attacked nearby Fort Sanders on November 29. After the attack, he would learn Missionary Ridge had fallen and his army was now isolated, unable to return to Chattanooga.

NOVEMBER 19
Lincoln attends the dedication of a national cemetery at Gettysburg, Pennsylvania, and delivers his Gettysburg Address.

NOVEMBER 23–25
The Battle of Chattanooga, Tennessee, results in Grant's army pushing Bragg's forces out of the area.

NOVEMBER 26
Meade's army opens the Mine Run Campaign against Lee in Virginia.

On November 24, federal troops stormed the summit of Lookout Mountain, Tennessee, in an engagement that was part of the Battle of Chattanooga. In years to come, it would be popularized as the "Battle Above the Clouds" because of the patches of fog that shrouded areas of Lookout Mountain's slopes.

Another photograph of the crowd awaiting the dedication ceremony for the cemetery at Gettysburg, this picture is remarkable for how still hundreds of people stood to avoid blurring of the image. In the left distance is the Evergreen Cemetery gatehouse; in the middle ground are armed soldiers; and in the foreground is a man who appears to be wearing a Confederate shell jacket.

NOVEMBER 27
Hooker's soldiers fight retreating Confederates at the Battle of Ringgold Gap, Georgia, ultimately allowing them to get away.

John Hunt Morgan and others escape from the Ohio State Penitentiary in Columbus.

NOVEMBER 29
A Confederate attack on Fort Sanders in Knoxville, Tennessee, is repelled.

238

The gatehouse to Evergreen Cemetery would become one of the most recognizable landmark buildings in Gettysburg. It was the scene of some heavy fighting in the evening of July 2, when Confederates were beaten back from Cemetery Hill.

When Confederate General James Longstreet's force attacked Fort Sanders outside of Knoxville on November 29, they were really attacking their own Fort Loudon, renamed by the Union forces who had captured it. Positioned on a knoll that fell away sharply, attackers had only one direction from which to assault. The Federals had improved on the fort's defense by stringing telegraph wires among the stumps to trip attackers. The Confederates failed to retake their cleverly positioned fort.

NOVEMBER 30
Braxton Bragg resigns from command of the Army of Tennessee.

DECEMBER 1
Meade's campaign in Virginia is unsuccessful. He calls it off, and his army establishes winter quarters.

DECEMBER 3
Although still unfinished, a Union prison camp at Rock Island, Illinois, accepts its first Confederate prisoners.

DECEMBER 3–4
Longstreet ends his siege of Knoxville, withdrawing his troops to winter quarters. Only very light Union forces follow him.

DECEMBER 8
Lincoln issues his Proclamation of Amnesty and Reconstruction.

DECEMBER 14
Longstreet lashes back and

defeats his pursuers at Bean's Station, Tennessee.

DECEMBER 27
Joseph E. Johnston assumes command of the Army of Tennessee.

1864

The Year of Bloodletting

The Body Count Rises as the North Cannot Muster a Decisive Blow

*F*ew noticed the unkempt man in the major general's uniform on March 8, 1864, as he walked with a young boy across the lobby of the Willard Hotel in Washington, D.C. The officer was, as one bystander observed, an "ordinary, scrubby-looking man with a slightly seedy look, as if he was out of office on half pay; he had no gait, no station, no manner." Once he signed the register "U. S. Grant and Son, Galena, Illinois," however, he

Confederate troops commanded by Nathan Bedford Forrest massacre captured black troops and their white officers at Fort Pillow, Tennessee, on April 12. This incident occurred during Forrest's raids on federal operations in Kentucky and Tennessee. In a report of the attack a few days later, Forrest wrote, "It is hoped that these facts will demonstrate to the Northern people that negro soldiers cannot cope with Southerners."

was immediately the focus of everyone's attention. President Lincoln had brought this man to Washington to save the nation. Under his direction, the war would take a successful, albeit costly, turn.

The lack of coordination among Union armies by an ever-changing cast of general officers had been the hallmark of the conflict through its first three years. Ulysses Grant shifted the focus from one of capturing cities, forts, and territory to the extermination of the enemy's armies, primarily the Army of Northern Virginia in the East and the Army of Tennessee in the West. His strategy would be to apply constant pressure on Confederate forces by calling for an attack along all fronts, thus reducing the enemy's numbers and exhausting its resources.

Failure in the West

While the new federal commander planned his spring campaign, two events in the West marked a poor beginning to the year for Union fortunes. Four days after Grant arrived in Washington, federal Major General Nathaniel Banks launched a combined army and naval campaign up the Red River of Louisiana toward Shreveport. Although his siege at Port Hudson had seen success, Banks was essentially a political officer who had had no military experience prior to 1861. His force slowly advanced along the river for almost a month until, on April 8, it was soundly defeated by a much smaller rebel com-

When Major General Nathaniel Banks began his retreat from the Red River Campaign, he was not prepared for a river significantly lower than when he had advanced up the waterway more than a month earlier. The gunboats of Admiral David D. Porter, which supported him in the campaign, were without enough water to move, leaving them effectively trapped. Fortunately, Lieutenant Colonel Joseph Bailey, an engineer, had a plan for a dam. The common wisdom was very much against this idea. Porter himself later wrote, "This proposition looked like madness, and the best engineers ridiculed it, but Colonel Bailey was . . . sanguine of success." Bailey built his dam in 10 days, raising the water level high enough to allow Porter's boats to escape downriver.

1864

JANUARY 16–17
A Union flanking maneuver in eastern Tennessee is repelled near Dandridge.

FEBRUARY 3
Union troops led by General William T. Sherman move out from Vicksburg across Mississippi toward Meridian. On their way, they will tear up railroads and

cause other damage to the state's economy.

FEBRUARY 9
Using a tunnel, 109 Union officers escape from Libby Prison in Rich-

mand near Mansfield, Louisiana. Banks abandoned the campaign the next day and retreated back down the river. Only the ingenuity of one of his officers saved his accompanying ships from being stranded in the river's shallow waters.

At the same time Banks advanced up the Red River, Confederate Major General Nathan Bedford Forrest led about 3,000 cavalry troops on an expedition into Kentucky to enlist recruits and gather much-needed supplies. The rebels captured Paducah, Kentucky, on March 25. After gathering up supplies and horses, Forrest withdrew into Tennessee, where he attacked the federal garrison at Fort Pillow on April 12. When the fort fell, witnesses later stated, the rebels cried, "No quarter! No quarter!" as they killed black and white defenders in cold blood after the soldiers had thrown down their arms and attempted to surrender. Forrest's troops left more than 250 Federals dead and about 75 wounded. Although Confederates denied that a

massacre had taken place, Forrest himself reported, "The river was dyed with the blood of the slaughtered for 200 yards." The Confederate cavalry commander would remain a serious threat to federal operations in the West throughout the remainder of the war.

Instead of advancing up the James River to Petersburg as planned, General Benjamin Butler allowed his Union army to become trapped in Bermuda Hundred, a small peninsula where the Appomattox River meets the James. Troops expecting to take the offensive against the Confederate forces were instead reduced to building earthworks like those shown here to protect themselves from attack.

Action in Virginia

Back in Washington, Grant made final plans for his spring campaign. In the Western Theater, he ordered Major General William T. Sherman to cut through Georgia, destroying the Confederate Army of Tennessee on the way to Atlanta. In the Eastern Theater, Grant had a three-part plan. Major General Benjamin Butler would take his army up the James River to capture Petersburg and attack Richmond from the south. Major General Franz Sigel was to advance up the Shenandoah Valley to take Lynchburg and attack the Confederate capital from the west. Major General George Meade's Army of the Potomac was assigned to maneuver around the Confederate Army of Northern Virginia in central Virginia, crush it, and then attack Richmond from the north. Even though he considered the operation in Georgia important, Grant later wrote, "Lee, with the capital of the Confederacy, was the main end to which all were working." But Grant would soon be sorely disappointed with the performance of his supporting cast.

mond, Virginia—59 reach Union lines, 48 are recaptured, and 2 drown.

FEBRUARY 14
Sherman's army arrives at Meridian, Mississippi.

FEBRUARY 17
The submarine CSS *H. L. Hunley* sinks the USS *Housatonic* off Charleston, South Carolina, the first time in history a submarine sinks a warship.

FEBRUARY 20
A Union expedition in Florida is defeated at the Battle of Olustee. Union casualties number 1,860, compared to 946 Confederates, in Florida's only major engagement of the war.

Union General Winfield Hancock's 2nd Corps clashed with General A. P. Hill's 3rd Corps along the Orange Plank Road in a fierce struggle during the Battle of the Wilderness, Virginia, on May 5 and 6. The Confederates were driven back on the morning of May 6, but a counterattack, briefly led by Robert E. Lee, stymied the federal advance. Fearing for the safety of their leader, the rebels are said to have shouted, "Lee to the rear."

The tattered condition of the regimental colors of the 56th and 36th Massachusetts indicates the brutality of the fight along the Orange Plank Road during the Battle of the Wilderness. The 56th's commander, Colonel Charles Griswold, was killed during the fighting when an enemy bullet passed through his neck.

On May 5, Butler, another political officer of questionable military skill, transported his force of 39,000 to Bermuda Hundred, a neck of land between the Appomattox and James rivers. After Butler's force achieved initial success, rebel General P.G.T. Beauregard's patchwork army of 18,000 troops staged a series of attacks and, less than two weeks after the federal campaign began, succeeded in bottling the Union army up on Bermuda Hundred. Grant used this bottle image in his official report and later stated, "On the 16th [Beauregard] attacked Butler with great vigor, and with such success as to limit very materially the further usefulness of the Army of the James as a distinct factor in the campaign."

Four days before Butler's troops landed at Bermuda Hundred, Sigel's army of 10,000 marched up the valley. On May 15, it was soundly defeated at New Market by a Confederate force half its size that included 225 cadets from the Virginia Military Institute. "Just when I was hoping to hear of good work being done in the valley," Grant wrote, "I received instead the following announcement from [General in Chief Henry] Halleck: 'Sigel is in full retreat on Strasburg. He will do nothing but run; never did anything else.'"

Sigel was replaced by Major General David Hunter, whose performance proved just as disappointing. Hunter's force advanced to the outskirts of Lynchburg on June 17, looting and burning everything, including the Virginia Military Institute, on the way. After two days of fighting at Lynchburg, Hunter was driven back into West Virginia by Lieutenant General Jubal Early's 2nd Corps. His withdrawal left the Shenandoah Valley undefended and opened an unimpeded highway north to Maryland. Early would soon make use of it.

The Wilderness and Spotsylvania

In central Virginia, Meade's 120,000-troop Army of the Potomac began crossing the Rapidan River early on the morning of May 4. Meade's orders from Grant were simple: "Lee's army will be your objective point. Wherever Lee goes, there you will go also." Meade planned to maneu-

FEBRUARY 27
Andersonville Prison opens for business near Americus, Georgia.

FEBRUARY 28–MARCH 4
A Union cavalry raid on Richmond, Virginia, is launched

by General Judson Kilpatrick only to fail a few days later. The raid turns controversial with the death of Colonel Ulric Dahlgren, when papers found on his body indicate a Union plot to assassinate President Davis.

MARCH 9
President Lincoln commissions Ulysses S. Grant as lieutenant general, the first American to achieve that rank since George Washington. The next day he is

Timothy O'Sullivan took this photograph near the Alsop farm outside Spotsylvania Court House on May 20, 1864, the day after 6,000 Confederate troops were attacked by Federals while on a reconnaissance mission to find the Union's right flank. This action marked the end of fighting at this strategic crossroads. The rifle lying on the rebel's dead body was most likely a prop placed there by the photographer.

ver between the enemy and Richmond by executing a quick march around the rebels' right flank. Standing in the way, however, was an area south of the Rapidan called the Wilderness, a stretch of dense undergrowth 12 miles wide and 6 miles deep. The Federals hoped to pass through this treacherous expanse of land before crushing the enemy with its superior numbers.

You MIGHT AS WELL APPEAL AGAINST THE THUNDERSTORM AS AGAINST THESE TERRIBLE HARDSHIPS OF WAR.

General William T. Sherman

Three corps crossed the river west of the Wilderness and one corps, the cavalry, and the supply train crossed on the eastern end of the Rapidan. Before these units could unite outside of this perilous terrain, however, Lee struck the separated columns. The battleground was as inhospitable as possible. Essentially a thick forest dense with trees and tangled growth, the Wilderness did not allow easy maneuverability. A Confederate officer wrote, "It was a desperate struggle between the infantry of the two armies, on a field

given command of all Union troops.

MARCH 12
Union General Nathaniel Banks begins the Red River Campaign in Louisiana.

MARCH 16
Nathan Bedford Forrest's Confederate cavalry begins a month-long raid into west Tennessee and Kentucky.

MARCH 28
In an antiwar outbreak in Charleston, Illinois, Southern sympathizers attack Union soldiers home on furlough.

Prison Life

"There were in this prison 1,800 Yankees. Each man's ration consisted of one quart of corn meal and a piece of bacon one inch square, which constituted his allowance for five days. It is needless to say that many of the men ate their full allowance at one time. It was white meal, with the cob and corn ground up together. There were no cooking utensils of any kind and no salt. I finally found a flat stone about one foot square and an inch or so thick, on which I succeeded in baking a corn-cake in the sun. I kept a portion of my ration, which I was obliged to hide under my head at night, in order to know where it was in the morning."

Captain Mahlon S. Ludwig, 53rd Pennsylvania Volunteer Infantry, captured on June 22, 1864, and sent to Camp Oglethorpe Prison, near Columbia, South Carolina

whose physical aspects were as grim and forbidding as the struggle itself. . . . Officers could not see the whole length of their commands."

Two days of fighting blindly through this unyielding wilderness resulted in heavy casualties on both sides. Grant, however, refused to fall back to heal his wounds, a practice that up to now had been common for the Army of the Potomac after a major battle. Instead, he pushed his forces around Lee's right flank on May 7 and advanced in the direction of Spotsylvania Court House. Discovering Grant's intention, Lee raced the 12 miles to Spotsylvania, arriving before the Federals.

For almost two weeks the armies slugged it out along this line. The fiercest fighting was around an area appropriately called the Bloody Angle. The struggle for that part of the rebel line, which sometimes consisted of hand-to-hand combat amid piles of dead bodies, lasted for almost 20 hours between May 12 and 13.

This was not the only trouble Lee faced while at Spotsylvania. He also received the devastating news that his flamboyant cavalry commander, Major General Jeb Stuart, had been mortally wounded at Yellow Tavern, Virginia, on May 11. Lee lamented that Stuart "never brought me a piece of false information."

On May 21, Grant once again turned past Lee's right flank and headed south toward Richmond. In a report to Halleck, Grant wrote that he was prepared to "fight it out on this line if it takes all summer." It would take much longer than that.

Grant and Lee each raced south over the next two weeks, fighting at North Anna and Totopotomoy Creek before settling in at Cold Harbor, about eight miles east of Richmond. On June 3, Grant sent three corps against strong rebel entrenchments. Lee had enough lead time to reinforce his lines, however, and the Federals attacked into withering fire. Union losses from this single assault were in the thousands.

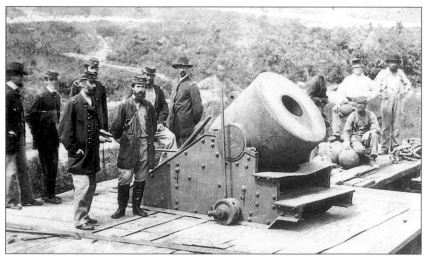

The "Dictator" was a 13-inch mortar that weighed more than 17,000 pounds and could hurl a 220-pound ball more than two miles. This iron monster was transported via railroad to Union siege lines around Petersburg, Virginia, to bombard the Confederate defenses.

Staging a Siege on Petersburg

A door of opportunity for the Federals to seize lightly defended Petersburg, Virginia, opened briefly, but Gen-

APRIL 4
The U.S. Sanitary Commission opens the Metropolitan Fair in New York City to raise money for needs of the soldiers. The fair will bring in more than $1.2 million.

APRIL 8
General Banks's Union troops are defeated at the Battle of Mansfield, Louisiana, ending the Yankee advance up the Red River.

The U.S. Senate passes a joint resolution approving the 13th Amendment, which abolishes slavery.

Andersonville Prison

This is a portion of the notorious prison camp at Andersonville. Located in southwestern Georgia, this stockade was in operation for just a little more than a year. Almost 13,000 prisoners died here by war's end, due primarily to malnutrition and disease.

"It is hardly possible to conceive of greater accumulation of woes...than fell to the prisoners of Andersonville," wrote a survivor of that infamous Confederate prison, also known as Camp Sumter, built in southwestern Georgia. The 16-acre stockade received its first federal prisoners in February 1864.

Originally designed to hold no more than 10,000 prisoners, Union commander Ulysses Grant's suspension of prisoner exchange in spring 1864 filled all Confederate prisons beyond capacity. To hold the growing number of soldiers captured during the fighting in Virginia and Georgia, the stockade was expanded to 26 acres.

By August 1864, 33,000 prisoners were packed into the enclosure with more than 100 deaths each day. No shelter was provided—prisoners had to build makeshift tents and lean-tos out of whatever material they could find or scavenge. A single stream flowed through the camp, but it served as an upstream garbage dump for the guards and a hospital.

"Rations [were] very small and very poor," wrote one of the Union captives. "The meal that the bread is made out of is ground, seemingly cob and all, and it scourges the men fearfully.... Hundreds of cases of dropsy. Men puff out of shape and are perfectly horrible to look at." Lack of adequate medical care increased the mortality rate at the camp. While the exact number of deaths at the prison is unknown, 12,912 soldiers were buried in the cemetery outside the stockade.

Located about 23 miles south of Richmond, Petersburg was a supply and transportation center for the Confederacy. In June 1864, Petersburg became the focus of a ten-month siege for control of the Confederate capital. The city fell to General Ulysses Grant's Union forces on April 2, 1865. Richmond fell the next day.

eral Beauregard once again rallied a much smaller force to stop General Butler's advance. It had only been six weeks since the Army of the Potomac had crossed the Rapidan to begin the Overland Campaign, but in that brief period of time, it had suffered almost 55,000 casualties, compared to more than 31,000 for the rebels. Grant realized he could make little headway against the defenses of Richmond without similar loss, so he decided to send his full army across the James River on June 14 and 15 to capture Petersburg and cut the southern supply line to the Confederate capital. By the time the Army of the Potomac was in a position to launch a coordinated assault on the rebel defenses, however, Lee had filled those defenses with much of his army, and the attack was repelled. Instead of further sacrificing his troops against heavily reinforced entrenchments, Grant decided to place the city under siege.

Establishing that siege was no easy matter. Several federal attempts to tear up sections of the Weldon Railroad, a major supply line into Petersburg, were thrown back by Confederate forces. In an effort to capture a critical position overlooking the city, Union

IF THE REBELLION COULD FORCE US TO FOREGO OR POST-PONE A NATIONAL ELECTION, IT MIGHT FAIRLY CLAIM TO HAVE ALREADY CONQUERED AND RUINED US.

Abraham Lincoln

coal miners dug a tunnel under the Confederate line and blasted a 200-foot-wide crater in their entrenchments on July 30. But poor planning caused black troops storming the breach to be helplessly slaughtered by rebel defenders, costing Grant almost 4,000 casualties. From the middle of June 1864 to April 1865, the Union strategy would become one of gradually extending its line to the west to cut off all roads and railroad lines connecting Lee to the rest of the Confederacy.

APRIL 9
Pursuing Confederate troops are defeated at the Battle of Pleasant Hill, Louisiana, as Banks's forces make a stand during their retreat.

APRIL 11
Isaac Murphy is sworn in as the pro-Union governor of Arkansas.

APRIL 12
Nathan Bedford Forrest's troops

attack and capture Fort Pillow, near Memphis, Tennessee. Controversy still remains as to how many black soldiers were slain as they tried to surrender after the shooting stopped.

The Northern Advance on Atlanta

As the Army of the Potomac fought its way across Virginia, General William Sherman, Grant's replacement in the West as well as a close personal friend, was maneuvering his 110,000-strong army across Georgia. His opposition was General Joseph E. Johnston's Army of Tennessee.

Johnston had assumed command in December 1863, restoring order and confidence to an army that had been soundly defeated at the Battle of Chattanooga. Although President Davis pressed Johnston to attack Sherman's superior force immediately, the general preferred a strategy of defense, provoking Sherman to attack him on terrain of Johnston's choosing.

It took Sherman about a month and a half and a series of maneuvers around Johnston's flank to drive the rebels 100 miles to the outskirts of Atlanta. During the push through Georgia, the armies fought numerous skirmishes and two major battles at Resaca and Kennesaw Mountain.

Upset that Johnston had allowed the Federals to advance to the gates of Atlanta with little fighting and relatively few Union casualties, Davis replaced the commander with General John Bell Hood, an officer with a reputation for being "bold even to rashness." He had lost the use of his left arm at Gettysburg and had his right leg amputated after Chickamauga, but he consistently proved to be an extremely competent subordinate. On July 17, he was given his chance to lead an army.

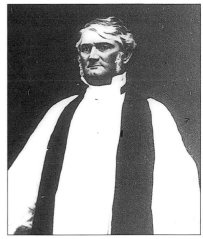

A graduate of West Point in 1827, Leonidas Polk resigned his commission to enter seminary. He was named Episcopal bishop of Louisiana in 1841. An advocate of secession, Polk entered military service after the outbreak of the war and commanded a corps in the Army of Tennessee. He failed to distinguish himself as a corps and army commander before a federal shell killed him as he surveyed the enemy position at Pine Mountain, Georgia, on June 14, 1864.

On July 30, 1864, 8,000 pounds of black powder placed at the end of a 510-foot tunnel exploded, creating a 170-foot gap in the Confederate fortifications outside of Petersburg. A total of 15,000 Federals, many of them black, crowded in and around the 30-foot-deep crater. Rebel artillery and infantry cut the helpless enemy troops down. When the fighting ended, the Union had suffered more than 4,000 casualties.

APRIL 17
Grant halts all prisoner of war exchanges to further exacerbate the Confederacy's shortage of personnel.

APRIL 18
General Beauregard is placed in command of the Confederate Department of North Carolina and Virginia.

APRIL 22
Congress authorizes the phrase "In God We Trust" to be stamped upon coins.

Three days after assuming command, Hood struck the Federals along Peachtree Creek. His troops came close to breaking the Union line, but after two hours of heavy fighting, Hood retreated to the fortifications around Atlanta. He again attacked Sherman's army on July 22, July 28, and August 31, but each time his forces failed to stop the federal sweep of vital supply lines around the city. Realizing his army was close to being trapped, Hood destroyed all the supplies he could not carry and abandoned the city on the night of September 1. During the two-and-a-half months Johnston practiced his defensive strategy, he suffered about 8,000 casualties. Hood's offensive tactics cost his army almost 19,000 soldiers in about a month and a half. These were more casualties than Sherman suffered during the whole campaign. By the end of the year, Hood's aggressive strategy would all but destroy his army.

Washington, D.C., Under Threat

Back East, hoping to force Grant to weaken his grip on Petersburg, Lee sent General Jubal Early with his 2nd Corps into the Shenandoah Valley. Meeting little resistance, Early marched down the valley into Maryland. He brushed aside federal opposition at

A string of field obstructions in this photo are shown protecting a Confederate sandbagged redoubt near the Potter homestead outside of Atlanta, Georgia. Chevaux-de-frise (spiked timber) and palisades (wooden slats driven into the ground) were constructed along this line. Some of the wood came from the stripped outbuildings that can be seen near the fortifications.

APRIL 23
Troops clash in a spirited engagement at Monett's Ferry, Louisiana, as Banks continues his retreat from the Red River.

APRIL 25
Rebels defeat part of General Frederick Steele's army at an engagement at Marks' Mills, Arkansas, as it retreats toward Little Rock.

APRIL 30
Jefferson Davis's five-year-old son Joe dies after a fall from the veranda of the Confederate White House.

This Kurz & Allison lithograph shows Union troops attacking Confederate defenses along Kennesaw Mountain, Georgia, on June 27, 1864. Following a 30-minute artillery barrage, the Federals advanced. "As if by magic," one Confederate officer observed, "there sprang from the earth a host of men, and in one long, waving line of blue the infantry advanced." Less than three hours later, the Federals were repulsed, leaving more than 2,000 casualties behind.

General Steele's retreating column fends off pursuing Confederates in an engagement at Jenkins' Ferry, Arkansas.

MAY 5
CSS *Albemarle* engages Union ships in Albemarle Sound at the mouth of the Roanoke River in North Carolina.

William W. Averell's Union cavalry begins a raid against the Virginia & Tennessee Railroad.

MAY 5–6
The Battle of the Wilderness,

Nathan Bedford Forrest

A self-made millionaire with little formal education and no military training prior to the start of the war, Nathan Bedford Forrest developed into one of the conflict's greatest tacticians. He rose from the rank of private to lieutenant general, commanding most of the Confederate cavalry in the West.

In February 1862, when it became apparent that Fort Donelson would fall to Union troops, Forrest declared, "I did not come here for the purpose of surrendering my command," and proceeded to lead his 700 horse soldiers to safety. His unit then covered the Confederate retreat from Shiloh two months later. Throughout the first two years of the war, Forrest fine-tuned the raiding tactics he would later use to hamper the Union campaigns in Tennessee and Georgia.

His most infamous action was what came to be called "The Fort Pillow Massacre." In April 1864, Forrest's soldiers attacked the federal garrison at Fort Pillow, Tennessee, which was defended by black and Southern white troops loyal to the Union. When the Union commander refused to surrender, Forrest's troops overran the fort. The rebels were later accused of murdering many of the defenders, primarily the black troops, attempting to surrender. Confederates denied the charges as being the result of federal propaganda, although Forrest later stated, "The river was dyed with the blood of the slaughtered for 200 yards."

During Sherman's Atlanta campaign, Forrest's raids on federal supply lines in Tennessee and Mississippi led the Union commander to declare, "Forrest is the very devil." In the same letter, Sherman expressed his wish that the Army "go out and fol-low Forrest to the death, if it cost 10,000 lives and breaks the Treasury." Forrest believed "war means fighting, and fighting means killing."

A successful businessman at the start of the war, Nathan Bedford Forrest joined the Confederate army and quickly advanced to the rank of major general. He was known for his strategic strikes against Union supply lines and strongholds. After the war his antagonist, General William T. Sherman, said he believed Forrest to be "the most remarkable man our Civil War produced on either side."

Virginia, takes place between Union troops led by Generals Grant and Meade and General Lee's Army of Northern Virginia. The inconclusive fighting results in at least 8,000 Confederate casualties and a Union loss of 17,666.

MAY 7
General Sherman's Union armies set out on their southward march as the Atlanta Campaign begins. Sherman's opposition is General Johnston's Army of Tennessee, in position to cover its base at Dalton, Georgia.

One of Kurz & Allison's prints shows Major General Philip Sheridan, at center, leading his army to victory over Jubal Early's Southern troops at the Battle of Cedar Creek, Virginia, on October 19. This print is inaccurate and stylized, but scores of such battle art translated the actual war into illustrations for the public.

MAY 8–12

Sherman's soldiers skirmish with Johnston's defenders in a series of engagements at Rocky Face Ridge, Georgia, with fighting at Mill Creek Gap, Dug Gap, and Snake Creek Gap.

MAY 8–19

For 12 days, Grant and Lee fight around the village of Spotsylvania, Virginia. Casualties total about 18,000 Union and 12,000 Confederate.

MAY 11

In the cavalry Battle of Yellow Tavern, Virginia, Union horse soldiers strike north of Richmond. The famed Jeb Stuart is mortally wounded in the fighting.

After arriving in sight of the Capitol dome in an 1864 raid designed to draw Federal troops from Petersburg, 47-year-old Confederate General Jubal Early realized that storming the ring of forts around Washington would be futile. "We haven't taken Washington," explained the disappointed Early, "but we've scared Abe Lincoln like hell!"

Monocacy, Maryland, on July 9, and on July 11, Early's force of almost 15,000 approached the outskirts of Washington, D.C. Union reinforcements arrived just in time, however, to discourage a Confederate attack on the capital, causing Early to withdraw into Virginia.

Unable to leave a rebel army free to roam the valley and invade Northern states at will, Grant sent Major General Philip Sheridan and 43,000 troops to destroy Early's command. Successive Union victories in mid-September at Winchester and Fisher's Hill drove the Confederates up the valley, leaving it open to Sheridan's "scorched earth" policy, which destroyed much of the Shenandoah Valley's resources. Reeling from two major defeats in less than a week, Early received reinforcements and a note from Lee encouraging him to continue to resist Sheridan. "You must not be discouraged, but continue to try," Lee wrote.

Before dawn on October 19, Early launched a surprise attack against a much larger Union force along Cedar Creek. Achieving unparalleled results in the morning's fight, Early failed to press his victory and let the Federals regroup under the leadership of Sheridan, who had been absent from the field when the fight began. When Sheridan galloped down the highway toward the fighting, his defeated force cheered. Sheridan reproached them not to cheer him but to fight for themselves. The general's example gave them the push they needed to turn the tables. By the end of the day, Early's army had ceased to exist as a threat in the valley.

In September, west of the Mississippi, Confederate Major General Sterling Price led about 20,000 soldiers into southeast Missouri with the intention of capturing St. Louis and invading Illinois. Federal reinforcements in St. Louis, however, forced Price to change his plan. The rebels instead moved westward along the south bank of the Missouri River, destroying sections of railroad as it went. But this plan was thwarted as well when a string of Union victories between October 23 and October 28 forced Price to withdraw his exhausted command back to Arkansas. This campaign ended organized Confederate resistance in the Trans-Mississippi Theater.

This August 1864 political cartoon shows General George B. McClellan, the Democratic candidate, trying to compromise with the warring North and South and their uncompromising presidents. McClellan advocated peace with union.

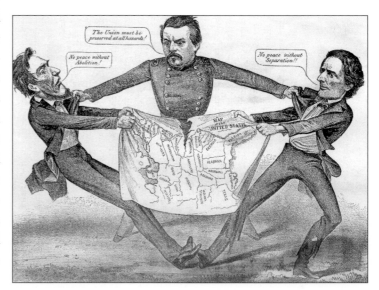

MAY 12–13
An improvised dam across the Red River raises the water level enough to free trapped Union ships previously caught when the water level dropped.

MAY 13
Johnston evacuates his position at Dalton, Georgia, to prevent Sherman from outflanking him.

MAY 14–15
Johnston stands and fights for two days at the Battle of Resaca, Georgia, before retreating again when Sherman tries to outflank his position.

The Presidential Election

Throughout 1864 resistance to Lincoln's reelection grew. Weary of war and the growing number of casualties, many Northerners were ready for peace. Well into the summer, battlefield news had not been encouraging. Grant gained the nickname "The Butcher" for having sacrificed many lives in his fight against Lee's army. Anxiety near the nation's capital had also been heightened as Jubal Early roamed dangerously close. In Georgia, Sherman's army was stalled before Atlanta. By mid-August, even Lincoln did not expect to remain in office. "This morning, as for some days past, it seems exceedingly probable that this Administration will not be re-elected," Lincoln told his Cabinet.

As late summer and early autumn progressed, the President's luck quickly turned, beginning with the fall of Mobile Bay on August 23 and following with Sherman's success at Atlanta and Sheridan's rout of Early's army at Cedar Creek. These major victories practically ensured Lincoln's reelection against his Democratic opponent, former Union commander George McClellan. Lincoln won an overwhelming victory in the electoral college, with McClellan only carrying three states. Final results showed that soldiers voted three to one in favor of the President. They had fought under this man for three years and, now that victory seemed within sight, they wanted to see it through to the end.

Sherman's March to the Sea

After Atlanta fell, Sherman began stocking supplies for a march through eastern Georgia to the Atlantic. Before his army could begin, however, he learned that Hood was

The 1864 Democratic presidential ticket, shown on this Currier & Ives poster, consisted of George B. McClellan and George H. Pendleton. Favorable news from the battlefront in the fall of 1864 enabled President Abraham Lincoln to be reelected with 55 percent of the popular vote.

Having driven the Confederate Army of Tennessee from its position outside of Nashville on December 15, Major General George Thomas's force attacked the rebels south of town in their hastily constructed line in mid-afternoon of the next day. Union troops occupying the defenses around the city, like those pictured here on the afternoon of December 16, could only listen and wonder about the fight's progress.

MAY 15
Cadets from the Virginia Military Institute join a force of Confederates to help defeat Franz Sigel's Union force at the Battle of New Market in the Shenandoah Valley.

MAY 16
Benjamin Butler's Army of the James is defeated at the Battle of Drewry's Bluff, Virginia, by Confederate troops led by P.G.T. Beauregard.

MAY 18
An engagement at Yellow Bayou, Louisiana, is the last major fighting of the Red River Campaign.

A force of 32,000 commanded by federal General John M. Schofield engaged John Bell Hood's Army of Tennessee in a battle at Franklin, Tennessee, on November 30. The combat included much bloody hand-to-hand fighting and resulted in the death of no less than six Confederate generals.

heading north into Tennessee. The rebel commander's original plan had been to draw Sherman back over the same terrain north of Atlanta where the Union had driven Johnston south. If Sherman followed, Hood intended to withdraw into the mountains of northern Alabama. On the other hand, if Sherman proceeded to the sea, Hood would pursue and attack the Federals from the rear. Confederate President Davis divulged the plan in several speeches, however, which forced Hood to abandon his strategy and march instead toward Franklin and Nashville.

MAY 23–25
General Lee repels Grant's attacks at the Battle of the North Anna River in Virginia.

MAY 26
Congress creates the Montana Territory.

MAY 28
Maximilian of Austria lands in Mexico at the invitation of the French occupiers to become emperor of that country.

Sherman sent a portion of his command to Nashville under Major General George Thomas and, on November 15, Sherman himself set out with the rest of his army toward Savannah, about 300 miles away. Practically unmolested, Sherman's troops cut a destructive 60-mile-wide swath through the heart of Georgia, inflicting an estimated $100 million in damage. Diarist Mary Chesnut wrote, "They say no living thing is found in Sherman's track, only chimneys, like telegraph poles, to carry the news of Sherman's army backward."

After Sherman's Army Passed

"About three miles from Sparta we struck the 'burnt country,' as it is well named by the natives, and then I could better understand the wrath and desperation of these poor people.... There was hardly a fence left standing all the way from Sparta to Gordon. The fields were trampled down and the road was lined with carcasses of horses, hogs, and cattle that the invaders, unable either to consume or to carry away with them, had wantonly shot down, to starve out the people and prevent them from making their crops. The stench in some places was unbearable; every few hundred yards we had to hold our noses or stop them with the cologne Mrs. Elzey had given us, and it proved a great boon. The dwellings that were standing all showed signs of pillage, and on every plantation we saw the charred remains of the ginhouse and packing screw, while here and there lone chimney stacks, 'Sherman's sentinels,' told of homes laid in ashes."

Eliza Andrews on what she saw in Georgia after General Sherman's army marched to the sea in the fall of 1864

The rising fortunes of the North translated into greater hardships for the citizens of the Confederacy. The concerns of rebel soldiers on the front were only exacerbated by desperate letters from home. "We haven't got nothing in the house to eat but a little bit o' meal," one woman wrote to her spouse. "Try to get off and come home and fix us all up some and then you can go back. If you put off coming t'wont be no use to come, for we'll all . . . be out there in the garden in the graveyard with your ma and mine." Such letters were received daily by soldiers who were finding it difficult to remain committed to the country they helped form less than four years earlier.

With Lee's army penned up in Petersburg, Hood was the South's last hope to end the year with some measure of military success. He would dash those hopes, however, on bloody Tennessee battlefields. Hood lost more than 6,000 soldiers, including six generals killed or mortally wounded, in his defeat at the Battle of Franklin on November 30. Instead of falling back to allow his army to rest, he pushed them to the outskirts of Nashville, where they were routed on December 15 and 16. "Wagon trains . . . artillery, cavalry and infantry were all blended in inextricable confusion," recalled a Confederate private. General Thomas's defenders crushed the Army of Tennessee by the evening of December 16. The war in the Western Theater was nearly at an end.

The Tennessee state capitol in Nashville overlooks the railroad depot under federal control. The city had been protected from Confederate attack in a December battle that marked the end of rebel activities in the area.

Cavalries battle at Haw's Shop, Virginia, as Sheridan's troops probe for Lee's right flank while Grant moves from the North Anna toward Cold Harbor.

MAY 30
John Hunt Morgan's Confederate cavalry heads north into Kentucky in a raid against federal supply lines.

Grant orders Meade to shift his troops toward Lee's right flank, resulting in an engagement at Bethesda Church, Virginia.

The Battle of Spotsylvania

General George G. Meade's Union Army of the Potomac ended a brutal battle with Robert E. Lee's Army of Northern Virginia on May 6. The rebels had struck the army in the thick underbrush of the Wilderness and inflicted more than 18,000 casualties, suffering only about half that number themselves. As the fighting in the Wilderness ended, most Union veterans assumed they would follow their normal pattern after engaging Lee's army and fall back to regroup. However, their new commander, General Grant, had no intention of relinquishing the offensive. Early on the morning of May 7, he forwarded this order to General Meade: "Make all preparations during the day for a night march, to take position at Spotsylvania Court-House with one army corps." Grant sought to gain a strategic advantage by placing his army between Lee and Richmond, thus forcing the Confederates to attack his entrenched troops. So at a dusty crossroads east of the Wilderness battleground, federal forces took the highway leading south toward Spotsylvania Court House.

Alerted to Grant's flanking maneuver, Lee quickly advanced his own command on the 12-mile trek to Spotsylvania. Marching all night by the shortest possible route, weary Confederate troops arrived, beating the enemy to the strategic crossroads village. Failing in his attempt to outflank Lee, Grant was determined to force his way through the Confederate entrenchments north of the village. But as Lee's troops arrived throughout May 8, he had them build a series of earthworks. One part, called the Mule Shoe because of its shape, would later earn the name "Bloody Angle" for the fierce fighting that took place there. Over 50,000 Confederate troops defended this five-mile line.

Fierce fighting raged around Spotsylvania Court House, Virginia, for nearly two weeks in May. One of the most ferocious attacks of the entire war took place on May 12, when thousands of Union troops launched a massive surprise assault near the center of the Confederate line. The action resulted in thousands of casualties and became known as the "Bloody Angle."

The body of Union Major General John Sedgwick is surrounded by his staff northwest of Spotsylvania Court House, Virginia, on May 9. Captain Richard Halstead desperately checks for a pulse and heartbeat while two other officers gesture for help.

When Grant launched his attack on the Confederate left flank on the morning of May 8, neither army had their full complement of troops on the field. As more units arrived, Grant threw them into the attack, but the Confederate line held throughout the day. By nightfall, Lee had his army in place, but elements of Grant's 100,000-strong force would continue to arrive throughout the next day.

The two armies engaged in light fighting the next day, but a single enemy bullet caused what was perhaps Grant's greatest loss of the campaign. Major General John Sedgwick, commander of the 6th Corps, rode out to inspect his line that morning. He saw soldiers near the center of the line cowering from Confederate sniper fire. Assuming a bold front to encourage his troops, Sedgwick looked toward the distant enemy position, laughed, and said, "They couldn't hit an elephant at this distance." Moments later he was struck below the left eye by a Confederate bullet. "His loss was a severe one to the Army of the Potomac and to the Nation," Grant later wrote.

Reports reached Grant that Lee had weakened his left flank. The federal commander, therefore, planned a coordinated series of attacks on May 10 along the enemy's left and left center. Lack of coordination, however, resulted in series of piecemeal assaults that were repulsed with murderous small arms and artillery fire. Grant suspended his offensive the next day due to unseasonably cold weather accompanied by wind, rain, and hail. But the Union army was not idle. Major General Winfield Hancock's 2nd Corps was ordered to move into position to attack the Mule Shoe at first light the next morning. Anticipating another movement by Grant around his right flank, Lee ordered most of his artillery pulled from the area around the Mule Shoe. At 4:30 A.M., a solid rectangular mass of screaming Federals stormed into the startled Confederate defenders. The Mule Shoe collapsed within minutes, and Lee's army, split in two, faced destruction.

Confederate reinforcements, personally led forward by Lee, recovered the lost ground, driving the enemy back to a thin wall of logs and fresh earth. Fierce combat at point-blank range lasted almost until dawn of the next day and ravaged both forces. Lee finally drew the center of his line back half a mile to hastily constructed fortifications. When the battle was over, one Northern soldier observed, "Hundreds of Confederates, dead or dying, lay piled over one another in those pits. The fallen lay three or four feet deep in some places, and . . . they were shot in and about the head." Conditions were not much better on the Union side.

A lull settled over the battlefield for the next few days, with only minor skirmishing taking place. A final federal attempt to crack Lee's center died before the muzzles of massed Confederate artillery on May 18. Two days later, after repulsing a weak Confederate counterattack on May 19, Grant pulled his army away from the frightful carnage at Spotsylvania. Roughly 18,000 federal soldiers and about 12,000 Confederates were victims of the bloody stalemate. Grant's campaign was only 15 days old but had already cost him more than 36,000 troops.

Commissioned in November 1861, the sloop of war USS Housatonic *was stationed along the South Carolina coast when it was sunk by a 90-pound torpedo carried by the CSS H. L. Hunley on February 17. The Confederate submarine sank, killing the 8 sailors aboard, but the rigging of the* Housatonic *remained above the water, providing refuge for most of its crew.*

By the winter of 1863, food and other supplies in the South were so scarce that federal troops had to support Southern civilians in occupied areas. This sketch by Edwin Forbes shows a Southern family traveling to the Union commissary for rations in February 1864.

The Battle of Olustee is depicted in this Kurz & Allison print. More than 5,000 federal troops crossed the Florida penin- sula in February 1864 to isolate the state from the rest of the Confederacy. Roughly 5,000 Confeder- ates blocked their path at Olustee, precipitating the battle on February 20. In the only major engagement fought in Florida, the Fed- erals were driven from the field with 1,800 casual- ties. The Union made no further attempts to gain control of the state.

JUNE 1–3
The Battle of Cold Harbor, Vir- ginia, is a Union defeat. Attacks against entrenched Confederates fail, resulting in 12,000 Union casualties over three days of fighting.

JUNE 5
A Union army led by General David Hunter in the Shenandoah Valley defeats a defending Con- federate force in the Battle of Piedmont.

JUNE 8
Meeting in Baltimore, the National Union convention (essentially the Republican party convention) nominates Lincoln for a second term, with Andrew Johnson as his running mate.

A group of Southern women, their faces veiled, ride to the U.S. commissaries for provisions. This became a very common sight in federally occupied territories.

Built in February 1864 to hold about 10,000 prisoners, more than 32,000 Federals were crowded into the 26 acres of Andersonville prison by July 1864. Their primary source of water was a single stream, ironically called "Sweet Water Branch," which the prisoners used for drinking and bathing. Adjacent to it was a trench latrine, pictured here, whose sewage would regularly seep into the stream.

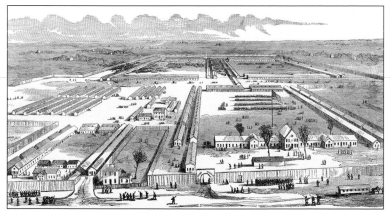

First constructed as a training camp outside Chicago, Illinois, Camp Douglas was converted into a prison for Confederates in 1862. Its 60 acres contained rows of barracks, as pictured here. While prisoners were provided shelter and ample space, the lack of adequate sanitation caused the death rate to rise to more than 10 percent by early 1863 before a drainage system was installed. The camp remained active until November 1865.

At a ceremony in the White House on March 9, Ulysses S. Grant received his commission as lieutenant general from President Abraham Lincoln. "The nation's appreciation of what you have done," said Lincoln, "and its reliance upon you for what remains to be done in the existing great struggle, are now presented, with this commission."

JUNE 10
Nathan Bedford Forrest's Confederate troops defeat Union General Samuel D. Sturgis at the Battle of Brice's Crossroads in Mississippi. There are 2,610 Union

casualties against only 495 for Forrest.

John Hunt Morgan's rebel troops enter Lexington, Kentucky.

JUNE 11–12
Phil Sheridan's Union cavalry, moving west to join Hunter in the Shenandoah Valley, is defeated in the Battle of Trevilian Station, Virginia.

Federal infantry and navy set out up the Red River in March 1864 to capture Shreveport, Louisiana. Standing in the way of the advance was the rebel stronghold Fort DeRussy, an earthen work on the river's western bank. Two Union corps under General A. J. Smith landed south of the fort to approach it from the rear. As federal infantry stormed the fortification, the navy shelled it from the river. Ten guns and 350 rebels were captured.

Mustered into volunteer service in May 1861 as a major general, Nathaniel Banks had no military experience prior to the start of the war. Confederates under General Stonewall Jackson defeated Banks in the Shenandoah Valley and at Cedar Mountain, Virginia, in 1862. Placed in command of the Department of the Gulf, Banks was ineffective in the Vicksburg Campaign and led the aborted Red River Campaign of 1864, after which he resigned his commission.

A soldier who fought in the Wilderness on May 5 and 6 wrote: "It was a blind and bloody hunt to the death, in bewildering thickets, rather than a battle." Another survivor called it "simply bushwacking on a grand scale." The bloody and confusing two-day battle between the forces of Ulysses Grant and Robert E. Lee inflicted about 18,000 Union and 10,000 rebel casualties.

JUNE 14
Confederate General Leonidas Polk is killed by artillery fire on Pine Mountain, Georgia.

JUNE 15
The House of Representatives votes against a joint resolution to approve the 13th Amendment.

JUNE 15–18
Union troops attack the defenses of Petersburg, Virginia, capturing the outer defenses but failing to achieve a decisive breakthrough. By the time the attacks end, Lee

This thick, overgrown vegetation is typical of the Wilderness. Soldiers fighting here were often on their own, as it was difficult to see very far or keep troops in any kind of organized line.

Right: *Soldiers of the 170th New York Infantry pose ready for battle. This regiment of Irish Americans suffered heavy casualties during fighting along the North Anna River. At one point, after the soldiers had run out of ammunition, Colonel Michael C. Murphy kept the regiment on the field rather than allow a retreat. He was rewarded with a Congressional Medal of Honor.*

Left: *Federal troops, including General James Wadsworth's division, deployed across the Orange Plank Road in the Virginia Wilderness on May 6 to halt the advance of Confederate troops. Attempting to rally his command, Wadsworth approached close to the rebel line and was mortally wounded in the head. His troops were soon driven from their position, leaving their commander in Confederate hands. He died two days later.*

has moved his army into the city's defenses. Grant begins a siege of the city that will last until April 1865.

JUNE 19
The USS *Kearsarge* sinks the Confederate commerce raider CSS *Alabama* off the coast of France.

JUNE 22
Sherman repels an attack by John Hood at Kolb's Farm, Georgia, but fails to outflank Johnston's strong position on Kennesaw Mountain.

The U.S. Sanitary Commission was a civilian organization formed to provide services to soldiers that the government was unable to supply. It maintained more than 7,000 aid societies distributing more than 15 million dollars' worth of supplies during the war. One of its services was preparing healthy meals to supplement a soldier's diet, too often high in calories and low in vitamins. One of their cooking tents in Fredericksburg, Virginia, is pictured here in May 1864.

Federal soldiers from the 1st Massachusetts Heavy Artillery are pictured resting while carrying a Confederate soldier for burial the day after the fight around the Alsop farm during the Spotsylvania Court House Campaign on May 19. The soldier to the left can be seen wearing the type of mask typically used by burial details. The soldier to the right appears blurred, having moved during the required 5 to 10 seconds of exposure time.

After two days of savage fighting in the Wilderness, most Federals expected a retreat across the Rapidan River to lick their wounds. Instead, their new commander, Ulysses S. Grant, turned his army toward the enemy. His staff officer, Horace Porter, remembered that the soldiers "swung their hats, tossed up their arms, and pressed forward to within touch of their chief, clapping their hands." Edwin Forbes captured that moment in this sketch.

General James H. Wilson's Union cavalry begins a lengthy raid against Petersburg railroads in Virginia.

JUNE 22–23
At the Battle of the Weldon Railroad, Virginia, Lee's troops defeat a Union flanking movement to seize control of that rail line.

JUNE 27
Sherman launches a frontal attack on Johnston's position on Kennesaw Mountain, Georgia, but fails.

Having formed his line in the pre-dawn hours of May 12, Union General Winfield Hancock launched 20,000 troops against the Confederate Mule Shoe outside of Spotsylvania Court House, Virginia. "Just as the day was breaking," one survivor remembered, "Barlow's and Birney's divisions of Hancock's corps pressed forward upon the unsuspecting foe, and leaping the breastworks after a hand-to-hand conflict with the bewildered enemy, in which guns were used as clubs, possessed themselves of the intrenchments." After initial federal success, Confederate reinforcements reclaimed the position.

In their push south following the Battle of Spotsylvania Court House, Ulysses Grant, George Meade, and their staffs stopped at Massaponax Church. Grant had the pews brought into the yard under two shade trees. In this photo, Grant leans over Meade's right shoulder, pointing out a position on an open map.

Flamboyant 31-year-old cavalry leader General Jeb Stuart was mortally wounded during a fight with General Sheridan's cavalry at Yellow Tavern, Virginia, on May 11. His most famous exploit was his ride around the Union army in June 1862.

JUNE 28
Lincoln signs a bill that repeals all fugitive slave laws.

JUNE 30
Lincoln accepts Treasury Secretary Salmon P. Chase's resignation from the Cabinet.

JULY 3
A Union amphibious attack on Fort Johnson, Charleston Harbor, South Carolina, is repelled.

JULY 6
A Union prisoner of war camp opens in Elmira, New York.

The Siege of Petersburg

When General Grant launched his Overland Campaign in May 1864, his objective was to destroy the Confederate Army of Northern Virginia. To accomplish this feat, he intended to maneuver the 120,000 soldiers of the Army of the Potomac between the rebels and the Confederate capital of Richmond, Virginia. If all went to plan, Confederate General Lee would be forced to attack, leaving his army open to destruction.

The Union army exercised a number of flanking movements around Lee's army of 66,000, but each attempt failed to get between the rebels and Richmond. The Federals, instead of the Confederates, were forced to attack the enemy's entrenched positions. After more than a month of almost constant combat across the face of eastern Virginia, the federal army advanced to Cold Harbor, a village on the outskirts of Richmond. After another costly attack against rebel fortifications, Grant rethought his strategy and decided to isolate the Confederate capital by capturing the vital railroad and communication center at nearby Petersburg.

By midnight of June 14, the Federals had ferried one corps across the James River and began to march the rest of the army over a pontoon bridge more than 2,000 feet in length to strike the lightly defended Petersburg. Several feeble attempts were repulsed by a hastily assembled group of defenders under Confederate General P.G.T. Beauregard. Federal assaults over three days failed to break the Confederate line, which had been bolstered by reinforcements sent by Lee. Realizing that further direct attacks would be costly and ineffective, Grant prepared for siege warfare.

Lee arrived with the bulk of his command on June 18, just in time to assist Beauregard's exhausted troops in repulsing a series of uncoordinated federal attacks. His army then settled into the ten-mile-long chain of trenches, breastworks, and re-doubts that had been constructed around Petersburg earlier in the war. The crescent series of works extended south of the city and were anchored by the Appomattox River on the east and west.

Union troops began constructing a network of fortifications directly opposite those of the rebels. Grant's plan was to gradually extend his line west, parallel to the Confederates,

As General Grant pushed his forces ever westward in an attempt to cut off Petersburg from the rest of the South, Confederate soldiers constructed earthworks and barriers wherever they went. By the end of the siege, the landscape was scarred for miles around the city.

until his troops were able to sever the major roads and two remaining railroads that linked Petersburg with the rest of the Confederacy.

Grant's first target for a thrust around the southern outskirts of the city was the Weldon Railroad, which ran from Petersburg to Wilmington, North Carolina, one of only a few ports still open to Southern blockade runners. Union troops began destroying a portion of the tracks on June 21, but they were driven away the next day by three rebel brigades who had used a hidden ravine to launch a surprise attack. "The attack," one Union soldier wrote, "was to the Union troops more than a surprise. It was an astonishment."

Union Lieutenant Colonel Henry Pleasants, a mining engineer prior to the war, developed a plan to blow up a key Confederate position by digging a mine below it. Receiving enthusiastic support from his corps commander, General Ambrose Burnside,

As the siege of Petersburg dragged on, officers and enlisted soldiers alike burrowed into the ground for protection from enemy bombardment and snipers. Soldiers in both armies constructed a variety of ingenious shelters, making use of whatever material was at hand. This is the interior of a Confederate fortification.

miners of the 48th Pennsylvania began constructing the mine on June 25. They finished almost a month later on July 23. The plan was to blow a hole in the Confederate line and attack amid the confusion that followed. After a false start and a relit fuse, the explosives were detonated at 4:45 A.M. on July 30, tearing apart the enemy line above it. But bumbling federal leaders and stiff rebel resistance caused the attacking federal troops, including a division of black soldiers, to get trapped inside the crater formed by the blast. Forced to advance up the newly formed hill after charging into the hole, virtually the entire assault force was annihilated. In

a report to General Halleck, Grant wrote, "It was the saddest affair I have witnessed in the war."

As the scorching summer wore on, disease, boredom, and constant skirmishing took their toll on both armies. Grant's trench works edged steadily westward. While he failed to inflict a decisive blow against Lee's army, attrition stretched Confederate manpower to the limit. By October, the Weldon Railroad was in federal hands, leaving Lee with a single, rickety rail line to supply his army, as well as the city of Petersburg, through the bitter winter months. The standoff did not substantially change through the end of the year.

Famed Confederate cavalry General Jeb Stuart wore this slouch hat, carried this cavalry saber, and wore the gauntlets pictured here. They were photographed atop his saddle.

Taken from a sketch by Edwin Forbes, this woodcut depicts Union troops advancing at Cold Harbor. Although the Federals made small breakthroughs into the Confederate lines, they fell back before the end of the day with devastating losses.

During the fighting on May 15 at New Market, Virginia, 225 cadets from the Virginia Military Institute charged a federal battery. "A wild yell went up," a Confederate officer wrote, "when a cadet mounted a caisson and waved the Institute flag." Eight cadets were killed and 46 were wounded in the successful attack.

Forced to abandon their position on Rocky Face Ridge, Georgia, by a federal flanking movement, Confederate General Joseph E. Johnston entrenched northwest of Resaca, Georgia. The Union army unsuccessfully attempted to drive the enemy from its position on May 14 and 15. This sketch by Alfred Waud depicts Confederate General Thomas Hindman's division repelling a federal attack.

JULY 8
Sherman's army begins crossing the Chattahoochie River in Georgia, forcing Johnston to fall back closer to Atlanta.

JULY 9
Jubal Early's Confederates, advancing on Washington, meet Union troops under the command of Lew Wallace at the Battle of Monocacy, Maryland.

The rebels triumph, but they are delayed for a day, which allows federal reinforcements to reach the capital.

This Kurz & Allison lithograph depicts the Battle of Resaca, Georgia, on May 14 and 15. Advancing down the Western & Atlantic railway line linking Chattanooga and Atlanta, General Sherman's federal forces defeated General Johnston's Army of Tennessee in this early battle of the Atlanta Campaign. "We have had a heap of hard fiten [sic]," one Confederate summed up the battle, "and have lost a heap of men and kild [sic] a heap of Yankees."

JULY 11–12
Early and his Confederates probe the defenses of Washington, D.C. President Lincoln comes under fire at Fort Stevens on July 12, when a sharpshooter hits one of the President's companions.

JULY 14
Union General Andrew J. Smith's troops repel Nathan Bedford Forrest's attacks at the Battle of Tupelo, Mississippi.

JULY 17
General John B. Hood replaces General Johnston in command at Atlanta.

During the fighting at Cold Harbor, Virginia, on the first three days of June, Grant lost another 12,000 Union troops during frontal attacks on Lee's entrenched Confederates. The June 3 assault claimed 4,600 of these casualties, which later compelled Grant to write, "I have always regretted that the last assault at Cold Harbor was ever made."

JULY 20
Hood launches an attack on advancing Union troops but is repelled at the Battle of Peachtree Creek, Georgia. Union losses are 1,779, Confederate losses 4,796.

North of Winchester, Virginia, Union troops defeat part of Jubal Early's troops at Stephenson's Depot.

JULY 22
Hood launches a major attack on Sherman's troops east of Atlanta. Known as the Battle of Atlanta, this engagement costs Hood at least 7,000 casualties while inflicting 3,722 on Sherman's army.

Joseph E. Johnston

"**M**y small force is melting away like snow before the sun," wrote Confederate General Joseph E. Johnston as his army futilely attempted to stop the advance of General William Tecumseh Sherman's Union juggernaut through the Carolinas. Although Johnston was considered one of the Confederacy's most talented generals, petty disputes with President Jefferson Davis had hampered his contribution throughout the course of the war.

A West Point graduate, Johnston received several brevets in the Seminole and Mexican Wars and was twice wounded in Mexico. Quartermaster general of the Army when the Civil War began, Johnston resigned his commission once Virginia seceded from the Union.

Following the federal defeat at the First Battle of Bull Run, he was one of five officers promoted to the rank of full general, placed fourth in seniority. He had outranked the others in the U.S. Army, so Johnston believed he merited the highest position in the Confederate Army. However, his protests merely set off the first of several conflicts with Davis. He was severely wounded in the Battle of Fair Oaks, but after six months of recovery, was given command of the Department of the West. After the Confederate defeat at Chattanooga, Johnston replaced General Braxton Bragg in command of the Army of Tennessee, where he had the dubious task of halting Sherman's advance on Atlanta. Due to his strategy of tactical withdrawals, Johnston was relieved of his duties by Davis, but after Hood's failure, he quickly reassumed command of the hopelessly outnumbered rebel army in the Carolinas in early 1865. He surrendered his force to Sherman on April 26, 1865.

Virginian Joseph E. Johnston, a great-nephew of Patrick Henry, was called "Uncle Joe" by his soldiers. This did not, however, prevent him from being a strict disciplinarian.

Soldiers of the 7th New York Heavy Artillery surge into the Confederate defenses during the fighting at Cold Harbor, Virginia, on June 3. The regiment seized rebel artillery and captured some prisoners, but a counterattack drove them back and restored the line. The 7th suffered 418 casualties at Cold Harbor, which included the death of Colonel Lewis O. Morris.

"We must destroy this army of Grant's before he gets to the James River," General Lee stated in the spring of 1864. As the federal army stalled before Richmond, U. S. Grant decided to cross the James and capture the rail center at Petersburg. It took about eight hours on June 14 for his engineers to span the river with a pontoon bridge of more than 2,000 feet anchored in the middle by three schooners. Meade's Army of the Potomac began crossing the James later that night.

Three Union corps crossed the James River on this 2,100-foot-long bridge at Weyanoke Point beginning on June 14 in an attempt to capture Petersburg before the city's small garrison could be reinforced by rebel troops from entrenchments around Richmond. Failing to capture the city, the Federals settled into a siege that lasted more than nine months.

In contrast to its Confederate opponent, the Union increased ordnance production throughout the war. In fiscal 1864 alone, the federal government spent $38.5 million on military supplies, including more than 800,000 small arms, 8 million pounds of powder, 1.7 million cannon shells, and more than 169 million rounds of small arms ammunition.

William T. Sherman

Named for Tecumseh, a famous Shawnee chief, federal Major General William Tecumseh Sherman became a renowned warrior himself.

Sherman secured an appointment to West Point at the age of 16 due to the influence of Thomas Ewing, an Ohio politician who took the boy into his home after the death of Sherman's father. Following his graduation, Sherman served at several army posts throughout the South. Upset when he did not have a chance to fight in the Mexican War, he wrote his future wife, "I feel ashamed having passed through a war without smelling gunpowder."

Retiring with the rank of general of the Army, William Sherman remained active in veteran's affairs until his death in 1891.

Discouraged by low pay, meager opportunity for promotion, and his lack of combat experience, Sherman resigned from the Army in 1853. Subsequent endeavors in banking, law, and investment ventures provided little success. "I am doomed to be a vagabond, and shall no longer struggle against my fate," Sherman wrote.

He finally found success as superintendent at a private military academy near Alexandria, Louisiana, before the start of the Civil War. Leaving his post to remain with the Union, Sherman rose from colonel to major general within a year. The next three years featured a string of battlefield successes for the aggressive general, capped by his unprecedented march through Georgia and the Carolinas. When Sherman assumed command of the Western Theater in the spring of 1864, he realized that his objective was not limited to the military force opposing his vast army. "War is cruelty...," he stated, "and those who brought war...deserve all the curses and maledictions a people can pour out."

Opened in July 1864, the Elmira prison became notorious for the conditions its Confederate inmates were forced to endure. Wooden barracks erected to replace the tents as winter approached failed to ease a death rate of nearly 25 percent among prisoners.

This view of the prison at Elmira shows the wooden barracks that had been erected to replace the scores of tents in the photo at left. Nevertheless, Southern prisoners continued to suffer the effects of the harsh northern weather conditions.

A graduate of the West Point class of 1836, Montgomery C. Meigs was promoted to brigadier general in May 1861 and at the same time appointed quartermaster general of the U.S. Army, a position he held until 1882. He oversaw both the development of a supply system able to support more than a million soldiers in the federal Army and the spending of $1.5 billion during the war, the largest military budget up to that time.

A group of Confederate prisoners are surrounded by Union guards and observers. More than 200,000 soldiers on both sides were captured during the course of the war. About 26,000 Confederates and 22,000 Federals died as prisoners.

JULY 23
Voters who have taken the oath of allegiance in Union-held Louisiana adopt a new constitution.

JULY 24
Early's troops defeat a Union force at Kernstown, Virginia.

JULY 27
General George Stoneman's

Union cavalry begins a raid near Atlanta.

JULY 27–29
North of the James River at Deep Bottom, Virginia, Union General

Federal officers were imprisoned here at Libby Prison, located along the James River in Richmond. When federal raids reached the outskirts of Richmond by mid-1864, prisoners were permanently transferred to prisons farther south.

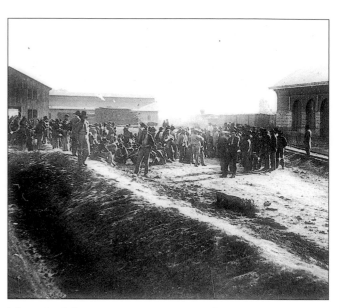

These Confederate prisoners are waiting to be transported north from Chattanooga. Prison populations overflowed on both sides once General Grant suspended prisoner exchange in April. "Every man we hold," Grant wrote, "when released on parole or otherwise, becomes an active soldier against us at once.... If we commence a system of exchange which liberates all prisoners taken, we will have to fight on until the whole South is exterminated."

William Waud drew this 1864 sketch of returned prisoners of war exchanging their rags for new clothing. The artist wrote: "The figures on the right are coming in with the new clothing, in the Centre pitching the old rags overboard, & going out on the left to get their rations."

Because of the unpopularity of the draft, bounties were offered to new recruits who volunteered and to soldiers who reenlisted. This sketch by George Law for Harper's Weekly shows recruiting in New York City in 1864.

Winfield Hancock's army stages a diversion against Richmond.

JULY 28
Hood attacks again, this time west of Atlanta, resulting in the

Battle of Ezra Church. Sherman loses less than 600, but Hood suffers an appalling loss of 5,000 soldiers.

JULY 30
At 4:45 A.M., a huge blast from a gunpowder-packed tunnel under a Confederate fort at Petersburg launches a day of fighting as Union troops try to crack the

Correspondent and sketch artist Frank Vizetelly covered the war for the Illustrated London News. *He returned to London for a short visit in 1864 and sailed back to Wilmington, North Carolina, on the blockade runner CSS* Lillian *on June 4. He captured the* Lillian *running the blockade in this sketch.*

Less than a month after it was commissioned, the CSS Albemarle *met seven wooden Union ships at the mouth of the Roanoke River on May 5. One of them, the USS Sassacus, rammed the Confederate ironclad. "With a crash that shook the ship like an earthquake, we struck full and square on the iron hull," wrote assistant surgeon Edgar Holden of the* Sassacus, *"careening it over and tearing away our own bows, ripping and straining our timbers at the water-line." After a brief fight, both ships limped away.*

The CSS Alabama *was one of 12 Confederate cruisers that inflicted almost $20 million in damages to U.S. shipping on the high seas. Eluding federal warships for almost two years, the* Alabama *was cornered by the USS* Kearsarge *in Cherbourg Harbor, France, in June 1864. The two mighty vessels dueled at close range for more than an hour on June 19 until an exploding shell destroyed the engine room of the* Alabama, *sinking the Confederate raider.*

rebel lines. The Battle of the Crater, however, is another Union failure.

July 31
Stoneman's raid ends in failure.

August 1
General Philip H. Sheridan is placed in command of the Middle Military Division, primarily troops in the Shenandoah Valley, to drive out Jubal Early's force.

August 5
Union Admiral David G. Farragut leads his fleet past defending rebel forts and ships in the naval Battle of Mobile Bay, Alabama.

Captain John A. Winslow and his officers are pictured on the USS Kearsarge. Following his victory over the infamous Confederate raider CSS Alabama, Winslow was promoted by Congress to the rank of commodore, the effective date set at June 19, 1864, the date of the battle.

Union dead began to be buried at Lee's Arlington estate in June 1864. Brigadier General Montgomery C. Meigs wanted soldiers buried as close to the mansion as possible to discourage the Lees from ever returning to live there. Robert E. Lee and his wife did not attempt to reclaim the property, but their oldest son, George Washington Custis Lee, did. In 1882, the U.S. Supreme Court ruled the property had been confiscated illegally and demanded it be returned. Congress bought the property from Lee the following year.

The Arlington estate of Robert E. and Mary Custis Lee had been occupied by Union forces since the war began. On one part of the property, Freedman's Village, a model settlement for freed slaves, was established. Other estate grounds were set aside for a national cemetery on June 15.

General Ulysses S. Grant and his staff pose for this portrait in June 1864, just prior to the beginning of the siege of Petersburg. His Army of the Potomac had just completed a seven-week campaign in which it had suffered an appalling 55,000 casualties. In exchange for these numbers, it had bottled up Robert E. Lee's Army of Northern Virginia in a place from which it could not escape.

AUGUST 6–7
Outside Atlanta, Sherman and Hood tangle again at Utoy Creek, Georgia.

AUGUST 9
Confederate agents place a bomb at the Union supply base of City Point, Virginia. The resulting explosion kills 43, injures 126, and causes much property damage.

AUGUST 10
General Joseph Wheeler's Confederate cavalry sets out on a monthlong series of raids against Sherman's supply lines in Georgia and Tennessee.

Hand grenades were used by both armies. This sketch shows the reaction of Union troops as a Confederate shell lands within their lines during the siege of Petersburg. Knowing that it will explode in seconds, the horrified soldiers attempt to dodge for safety.

The long line of black troops rushed toward the Confederate works along the Petersburg, Virginia, front on June 16. "I never saw troops fight better, more bravely, and with more determination and enthusiasm," one officer recounted of the charge of the 22nd United States Colored Troops. Organized only six months earlier, the regiment would lose 72 troops in battle by the end of the war.

Sharpened timber stakes angled toward the enemy, called fraise, *jut from the earthen walls of Union Fort Sedgwick outside Petersburg. It was built about 1,500 feet from the Confederate Fort Mahone and spanned the Jerusalem Plank Road south of the city. Union troops dubbed Sedgwick "Fort Hell" due to the constant danger of enemy picket and artillery fire. Its designer was Major Washington A. Roebling, one of the future builders of New York City's Brooklyn Bridge.*

A crescent line of entrenchments extending for miles around Petersburg was built by both sides. Earthen bunkers were made as comfortable as possible, even with chimneys. One Federal viewed these ditches as "an immense prairie dog village." Plagued by artillery shells, enemy pickets, insects, rats, the ditches' un-inhabitable living conditions made them a death trap for many. "Men were killed in their camps, at their meals, and . . . in their sleep."

AUGUST 18
General Judson Kilpatrick's Union cavalry begins a raid around Atlanta to interdict Confederate supplies.

AUGUST 18–21
The four-day Second Battle of the Weldon Railroad, Virginia, leaves Union troops in control of the Weldon Railroad connection to Petersburg.

AUGUST 23
Fort Morgan, controlling the entrance to Mobile Bay, surrenders to Union troops.

The Atlanta Campaign

Less than a month after taking command of the western armies, General William T. Sherman received a communication from General Grant, his personal friend, directing him "to move against Johnston's army, to break it up and to get into the interior of the enemy's country as far as you can, inflicting all the damage you can against their war resources."

Sherman planned to outflank the vastly outnumbered Confederate Army of Tennessee, commanded by General Joseph E. Johnston, take up a position between that force and Atlanta, and coerce the rebels to attack him. Atlanta was a major rail, factory, and military supply center—four railroads radiated from the city, acting as a lifeline for all rebel armies in the field. Capturing Atlanta would inflict serious damage to the Confederacy's war resources and would give Sherman the opportunity to break up Johnston's army along the way.

Johnston assumed command in December 1863, restoring order to a fighting force that came close to collapse following its defeat at Chattanooga. "One of his first acts," a staff officer wrote, "was to restore the old organization. The order to this effect created unbounded enthusiasm in the division."

Confederate President Jefferson Davis pressed Johnston to attack Sherman's army at Chattanooga. Preferring a strategy of defense, however, particularly when outnumbered almost two to one, Johnston remained at Dalton, Georgia, about 30 miles southeast of the Union strong-

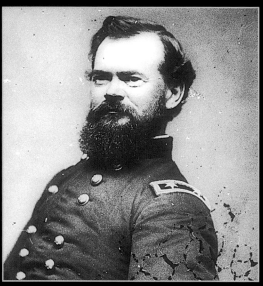

Graduating in the West Point class of 1853, James McPherson began the war as a staff officer. He became a corps commander in January 1863 and played a significant role during the Vicksburg and Meridian Campaigns. Commanding the Union Army of the Tennessee, he led several flanking movements around the Confederate army that drove the rebels from Chattanooga to the outskirts of Atlanta. He was killed on July 22, 1864, during a Confederate counter-attack.

hold, and relied on the rugged, strongly fortified terrain of northern Georgia to block any federal advance.

Sherman marched his army of 110,000 to Dalton on May 7. Avoiding a frontal assault, he feigned attacks north and west of Johnston's position, instead sending Major General James McPherson's Army of the Tennessee to strike the Western & Atlantic Railroad near Resaca. Sherman reasoned that, with his supply line cut, Johnston would be forced to abandon his position.

Normally an aggressive fighter, McPherson stopped a mile short of Resaca when he ran into stiff resistance from a single Confederate infantry brigade. Sherman later noted, "Such an opportunity does not occur twice in a single lifetime." Johnston took the opportunity and successfully withdrew his troops to Resaca by May 13, where he held off federal attacks north and west of the city for the next two days. But concerned that Sherman was once again about to pass around his left flank and cut the railroad line to Atlanta, Johnston vacated his position and headed south.

A succession of Confederate withdrawals ultimately brought both armies to Kennesaw Mountain, northwest of Marietta. Delaying for 16 days, Union troops finally attacked the Confederate position on June 27, fighting for more than three hours as the temperature soared near 100 degrees. Like human battering rams, two columns of federal troops were easy targets as they simultaneously hit several forti-

Union General William T. Sherman defeated Confederate General John Hood in bitter fighting on the outskirts of Atlanta in July. By September, Atlanta had fallen, and Sherman telegraphed to General Halleck: "Atlanta is ours, and fairly won." The news helped turn Lincoln's election fortunes.

fied rebel positions. "By 11:30," Sherman later wrote, "the assault was in fact over, and had failed." Five days later, Sherman moved around Johnston's left flank, forcing the Confederates to fall back to entrenchments along the Chattahoochee River and then to Peachtree Creek, four miles from Atlanta.

Dissatisfied with Johnston's defensive strategy, Davis replaced him with General John Hood on July 17. The battle-scarred 33-year-old was known to be "bold even to rashness." Sherman later wrote, "This was just what we wanted, . . . to fight in open ground, on anything like equal terms, instead of being forced to run up against prepared entrenchments."

As Sherman expected, Hood wasted no time in striking Sherman's army. Discovering a two-mile-wide gap in the Union line at Peachtree Creek, Hood attacked at 4:00 P.M. on July 20. He called off the assault two hours later when he learned that Union troops on another part of the line had advanced within artillery range of Atlanta and were from time to time sending shells into the city. Two days later, Confederate troops struck again, this time against a federal force east of Atlanta. Intense fighting throughout the afternoon resulted in another bloody defeat for Hood.

Federal artillery devastated the city in August as Sherman extended his line southwest of Atlanta to cut the two remaining railroads supplying Hood's army. Desperate Confederate attacks on July 28 at Ezra Church and August 31 at Jonesboro failed to halt Sherman's flanking movement. "We did our best to get up a fight," wrote a Confederate infantry soldier, "but it was no go." Hood destroyed all supplies his army could not carry and marched out of Atlanta on the night of September 1.

In Winslow Homer's Pris-oners from the Front, a Union general examines a group of captured Southern prisoners escorted by a Union guard. The prison-ers range from a young boy to an old man, indicative of the range of ages serving in the Confederate armies.

Federal soldiers relax outside a bombproof shelter. Reinforced with heavy timbers, sand-bags, and several feet of earth, these shelters were erected to protect soldiers, munitions, and supplies from mortar shells and other cannon fire.

A General in Battle

"A deafening roar smote upon the ear, and a storm of bullets and cannister tore through our ranks and around us. The men by this time were well under way, and altho [sic] the line staggered and reeled for a moment, it quickly recovered and went forward.... The pace at which the men were moving slackened; large gaps were visible here and there. The line had lost its regularity, warbling like the movements of a serpent, and things looked ugly, but our supports were coming up in capital style, not more than one hundred yards in rear. The men saw them, and gathered confidence."

Brigadier General
Arthur M. Manigault, CSA,
describing his brigade's advance during the Battle of Atlanta, July 22, 1864

AUGUST 25
A. P. Hill's Confederate corps attacks and defeats the Union 2nd Corps in the Battle of Ream's Station, Virginia.

AUGUST 31
The Democratic national con-vention in Chicago nominates George B. McClellan as its presi-dential candidate.

Sherman defeats Hood's forces at Jonesboro, Georgia, south of Atlanta, ending Hood's ability to defend the city.

Because of its importance to the defense of Richmond, capital of the Confederacy, Petersburg itself was surrounded by fortifications. Named after its builder, Confederate Captain Charles H. Dimmock, the "Dimmock Line" consisted of a chain of more than 50 earth-and-timber forts linked by trenches and armed with a variety of cannons.

To avoid Confederate guns along a five-mile stretch of the James River, federal General Benjamin Butler decided to dig a canal across a 174-yard stretch of land called Dutch Gap, Virginia. Construction began on August 10, 1864, and continued to January 1, 1865, when the northern end of the canal was blown open. The canal was not available to river traffic until April 1865, too late for any military advantage. This view was taken during the construction in November.

One of Mathew Brady's staffers took this picture of the famous photographer on June 20, 1864, observing the effects of the 12th New York Battery firing from a captured Confederate earthwork in the defenses around Petersburg, Virginia. Standing in the center of the photograph wearing his trademark straw hat, Brady took few field pictures himself due to failing eyesight. Two days after this photograph was taken, the 12th New York Battery was captured by Confederates.

Commissioned in March 1864, the USS Onondaga patrolled the James River during the Petersburg Campaign. Only one of two double-turreted iron monitors in the federal Navy, the 1,250-ton ship boasted two 150-pound Dahlgren rifles and two 15-inch smoothbores. It is pictured here at Aiken's Landing, Virginia, a port on the James.

SEPTEMBER 1
Hood evacuates Atlanta rather than risk being surrounded.

SEPTEMBER 2
Union troops occupy Atlanta.

SEPTEMBER 4
Confederate raider John Hunt Morgan is killed in fighting at Greenville, Tennessee.

SEPTEMBER 16
General Wade Hampton raids behind Union lines at Petersburg and brings back 2,400 head of cattle.

Union sailors and marines aboard the gunboat USS Mendota pose for the photographer. Commissioned in May 1864, the Mendota was stationed in the James River, Virginia, where it engaged Confederate shore batteries.

Union and Confederate soldiers spent more time in camp than on campaign. Disease and boredom were the primary enemies in this unsanitary and stagnant environment. When not drilling or on guard duty, soldiers spent time cooking, writing letters home, or playing cards and other games. Singing was also a favorite pastime. Many soldiers and sailors found comfort in religion and attended services whenever possible. Here, sailors worship on the deck of the federal monitor Passaic in 1864.

The U.S. Marine Corps saw limited action during the Civil War. While they participated in one major amphibious operation, the unsuccessful assault on Fort Fisher, North Carolina, in January 1865, they were primarily deployed as gun crews on ships. By the war's end, 148 marines had been killed in action. Here a marine battalion poses for the camera in the Washington Naval Yard in 1864.

Throughout the war, the Adams Express Company delivered letters and packages to and from soldiers in the field through offices like this one in Bermuda Hundred, Virginia. Soldiers came to trust the reliability of Adams Express and often used the service to send part of their pay home. Both Northern and Southern governments employed the company as the paymaster for the armies.

Forrest's cavalry begins a raid against Sherman's communications in northern Alabama and middle Tennessee.

SEPTEMBER 19
Sheridan's troops attack General Early in the Third Battle of Winchester, Virginia. Although the Federals lose 4,108 as opposed to Early's 3,921, Early retreats in the face of superior numbers.

Confederate General Sterling Price's troops invade Missouri.

A Confederate attempt to free prisoners at Johnson's Island on Lake Erie in Ohio fails.

The Battle of Mobile Bay

Throughout the first three years of war, Mobile Bay was not only a popular haven for Confederate blockade runners, it also protected the water route to the rebel stronghold at Mobile, Alabama. Federal naval forces were not able to mount an attack on the bay until the summer of 1864. Protecting the waterway were three Confederate forts, piling obstructions, floating torpedoes, a massive ironclad ram, and three wooden gunboats. A narrow torpedo-free channel passed close to the largest of the three forts, Fort Morgan.

On August 5, 63-year-old federal Rear Admiral David G. Farragut began the assault with 14 wooden warships, four ironclad monitors, and an infantry force of 1,500. The monitors were used to shield the wooden ships as they passed under the guns of Fort Morgan. Farragut's leading monitor, the *Tecumseh*, was struck and sunk by a floating mine. Thinking he saw other torpedoes ahead, the commander of the foremost Union ship halted, blocking the advance of the ships behind it. Fort Morgan's guns blasted into the stalled federal vessels, particularly Farragut's flagship, the *Hartford*. Legend has it that, to escape the enemy guns, Farragut mounted and lashed himself to the *Hartford*'s rigging and ordered, "Damn the torpedoes! Full speed ahead!"

The Union fleet neutralized the enemy gunboats and, after an hour-long fight, disabled the rebel ironclad *Tennessee*. Fort Morgan finally fell into Union hands after a 14-day siege begun after the Federals captured the bay's other forts. Union troops did not capture the city of Mobile until April 12, 1865.

Four Union monitors shield Rear Admiral David G. Farragut's 14 wooden ships from the guns of Confederate Fort Morgan in Mobile Bay on August 5. The Confederate ironclad ram CSS Tennessee *and two of three rebel gunboats can be seen advancing on the federal fleet as the Union monitor* Tecumseh *founders on its side after striking a mine. By day's end, Farragut had captured three enemy ships, including the* Tennessee. *Fort Morgan fell 18 days later.*

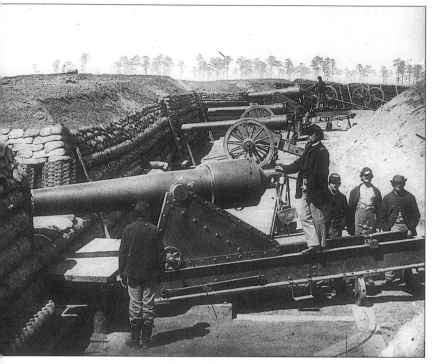

One of two 100-pound Parrott rifles deployed at Fort Brady is shown in this photograph. The fort sat on Signal Hill on the northern bank of the James River opposite Bermuda Hundred Peninsula, Virginia. Captain H. H. Pierce of Company C, 1st Connecticut Heavy Artillery, is seen standing on the gun's carriage.

"I shall never forget the terrible and magnificent sight," Major Charles Houghton of the 14th New York Heavy Artillery later wrote of the July 30 explosion at Petersburg. "The earth around us trembled and heaved—so violently that I was lifted to my feet. Then the earth along the enemy's lines opened, and fire and smoke shot upward seventy-five or one hundred feet. The air was filled with earth, cannon, caissons, sand-bags and living men, and with everything else within the exploded fort."

Two young federal telegraph operators pose at a headquarters camp near Petersburg, Virginia, in August. By 1864 the federal armies had laid more than 6,500 miles of telegraph wire to create vital communication links between the various commands. The overall casualty rate of telegraph operators during the war was nearly 10 percent.

Visual signaling, using flags in daylight or flames at night, was a crucial method of communication during the Civil War. The construction of lofty platforms such as the Union tower pictured here at Bermuda Hundred, Virginia, made signals visible over greater distances.

SEPTEMBER 22
At the Battle of Fisher's Hill, Virginia, General Jubal Early suffers another defeat, with 1,235 casualties.

SEPTEMBER 27
In Missouri, Confederate guerrillas led by Bill Anderson murder unarmed Union soldiers at Centralia, then defeat reinforcements, killing 140 Yankees overall.

At Pilot Knob, Missouri, the Union defenders of Fort Davidson desperately repel Price's attacks before evacuating the fort under cover of darkness.

Soldiers indulged in games while off duty and lounging in camp. Here can be seen a portable chess set, dice, and playing cards. Although many officers frowned on gambling, far too often the enlisted troops could not resist the roll of the dice or playing popular card games such as euchre. The more religious soldiers often threw away evidence of their vices before going into battle. Luckily, if they survived, the ever-present sutler was there to resupply their needs.

Officers and army regulars on both sides of the fortifications around Petersburg spent their free time in a variety of pastimes. This August 1864 photograph shows four officers of the 114th Pennsylvania Infantry playing cards, smoking, and drinking bottles of wine brought by camp servants. Gambling was most prevalent when the paymaster arrived.

Federal soldiers form a three-sided square around a gallows for the hanging of one of their own in Petersburg in August. The pile of earth to the right of the scaffold was the site of the prisoner's grave. Over 260 Union soldiers were executed during the war for various offenses, about half of those for desertion.

More than 2,300 chaplains of all denominations served in the federal Army during the war. Of these, 66 died in service, and three were awarded the Congressional Medal of Honor. One chaplain remarked that he and his fellow clerics were "a supernumerary, a kind of fifth wheel to a coach, being in place nowhere and out of place everywhere." In this photo, eight chaplains from the Union 9th Corps sit in front of their tent at Petersburg in October 1864.

Soldiers often craved religion when faced with death in battle or from disease. Camp life spawned many religious revivals, but some soldiers tended to deal with religion in their own private way. The American Tract Society and the U.S. Christian Commission handed out tens of thousands of Bibles and religious tracts such as those shown here.

SEPTEMBER 29–OCTOBER 2
A Union offensive at Petersburg results in fighting at New Market Heights and Poplar Springs Church, allowing General Meade to extend his line farther into Confederate territory.

OCTOBER 2
A Union column in southwestern Virginia headed toward Saltville is defeated and forced to retreat.

OCTOBER 5
Hood attacks Sherman's supply line in the Battle of Allatoona, Georgia, but is repulsed.

This church was built by the 50th New York Volunteer Engineers at Poplar Grove near Petersburg. It was constructed with pine logs cut down to make the clearing for the church and other regimental buildings. The logs were stripped and squared on three sides but left unfinished on the outside for their rustic look. Saplings were used in building the steeple. The engineering unit's insignia can be seen above the front door.

Through political connections, Lewis Wallace rose from colonel to major general in less than seven months. He drew criticism from Ulysses Grant for incompetent handling of his division during the Battle of Shiloh in April 1862. He led a patchwork command against an invading Confederate army at Monocacy, Maryland, on July 9, 1864, delaying them long enough to allow Grant to reinforce the defenses of Washington before the rebels arrived. He is best known as the author of Ben Hur.

Confederate General Jubal Early was impressed with the formidability of Fort Stevens. He later wrote: "Timber had been felled within cannon range all around and left on the ground, . . . and every possible approach was raked by artillery. . . . The position was naturally strong." Having reached the northern outskirts of Washington during his invasion of Maryland in July, Early decided not to test the strength of the fort's guns. The 3rd Massachusetts Heavy Artillery garrisoned the fort after Early's withdrawal.

In order to alleviate a shortage of workers, the U.S. War Department began in 1863 to organize units of troops deemed unfit for combat—generally wounded and convalescing soldiers. These companies of soldiers performed garrison and escort duty in the rear areas, thus freeing other units to join the main armies. Units skirmished with John Mosby's Partisan Rangers in northern Virginia and staffed fortifications during Jubal Early's July 1864 attack on Washington.

OCTOBER 7
Fighting erupts on the Darbytown and New Market roads in Virginia as Southern troops try to push back Union forces operating near Richmond's outer defenses. The attack is repulsed.

OCTOBER 12
Admiral David D. Porter assumes command of the North Atlantic Blockading Squadron, while Admiral Samuel P. Lee is transferred to command of the Mississippi Squadron.

OCTOBER 13
Voters in Maryland approve a new state constitution that abolishes slavery.

Philip H. Sheridan

On October 19, Confederate General Jubal Early launched a pre-dawn surprise attack on General Philip Sheridan's Army of the Shenandoah as most of the Federals slept along Cedar Creek. Sheridan was 15 miles away when he heard the distant guns. As he raced to his army, he saw "the appalling spectacle of a panic-stricken army...all pressing to the rear in hopeless confusion." Reforming the broken ranks, he ordered them to follow him as he charged to the front. Rallying other units he met along the way, he mounted a counterattack at 4:00 P.M. that shattered Early's force. His presence proved the difference between defeat and victory. Such was the power of this dynamic young general.

In only ten months, from May 1862 to March 1863, Sheridan's spectacular performance in the field resulted in his meteoric rise from colonel to major general of volunteers. When Grant took command of the Union Army, he placed Sheridan in command of the Army of the Potomac's cavalry corps. Sheridan later commanded the Middle Military Division and defeated Early at the battles of Winchester and Fisher's Hill before the Confederate surprise attack at Cedar Creek. Destroying Early's army, he ordered the devastation of the Shenandoah Valley so its resources could not be used by Robert E. Lee's besieged force at Petersburg. His victory at the Battle of Five Forks in April 1865 was a major factor leading to Lee's decision to surrender at Appomattox Court House eight days later.

Major General Philip Sheridan began the war as chief quartermaster and commissary of the Army of Southwest Missouri. Barely escaping a court martial for violating regulations, he received his first field command as colonel of the 2nd Michigan Cavalry on May 25, 1862.

The Veteran Reserve Corps was organized into two battalions and originally called the Invalid Corps. The name was changed in March 1864. The corps' members first wore sky-blue uniforms, which were also later changed to regulation military uniforms. Members of Company B, 10th Veteran Reserve Corps are pictured here at Washington Circle.

Members of Company E, 4th U.S. Colored Troops pose at Fort Lincoln, one of the many strongholds surrounding Washington, D.C. The regiment was active first in the siege of Petersburg then in actions in the Carolinas, including the assault on Fort Fisher in January 1865 and the campaign leading to Confederate General Johnston's surrender on April 26, 1865.

"Give them a chance," proclaimed abolitionist Frederick Douglass, urging the acceptance of black troops. "I don't say that they will fight better than other men. All I say is, Give them a chance!" Almost 200,000 blacks enlisted in the Union Army during the war, and over 32,000 gave their lives for the cause. Ulysses S. Grant wrote, "By arming the Negro we have added a powerful ally." A formal flag presentation to a black regiment is depicted in this drawing.

Wartime Medical Service

When President Lincoln called for 75,000 volunteers following the fall of Fort Sumter, the U.S. Medical Department consisted of an aged surgeon general, 30 surgeons, and 83 assistant surgeons. This small force was woefully inadequate for the task ahead. To accommodate the medical care for the growing number of volunteer regiments, the War Department mandated state authorities to commission one surgeon and one assistant surgeon per regiment.

In 1861, the newly formed Confederacy created a medical department similar to that of the United States. As they did in many areas, however, Confederate regiments experienced a shortage of surgeons throughout the war.

Union and Confederate boards of examiners were established to review surgeon qualifications. Those with political connections, however, often passed the board whether they were competent or not. One veteran wrote, "While there were some noble, humane, and self-sacrificing physicians in the army... unfortunately these formed a minority to the unskilled quacks whose ignorance and brutality made them objects of detestation to the soldier.... They helped to fill many graves where our army marched." Medical inspectors were eventually named to oversee the treatment given to sick or injured soldiers in the field. Union General Emory Upton wrote in his memoirs, "The ablest as well as the most ignorant practitioners in the land were eligible for appointment... until, found incompetent; or, detected in malpractice, they were at last brought before a board and dismissed from service."

Regulations specified that all enlistees had to undergo a medical examination to make sure they were fit for service. The haste to quickly raise commands with full complements of recruits frequently, however, resulted in cursory physical exams at best. Of the one million enlistees who joined the Union volunteer army in 1861 and 1862, some 200,000 received disability discharges prior to the end of their term of enlistment.

Several nurses among their patients pose for the camera inside Washington Square Hospital. A sign at the far end of the ward read, "The true characteristic of a perfect warrior should be fear of God, love of country, respect for the laws, preference of honor to lawlessness, and to life itself."

Once regiments were assembled in camp, soldiers in both armies became targets of communicable diseases that quickly spread throughout an encampment. Sanitation was universally nonexistent due to ignorance of the importance of hygiene. Each camp had latrines, but soldiers often relieved themselves wherever they wished. Human waste, garbage, and the remains of slaughtered animals attracted millions of disease-carrying flies and mosquitoes, particularly during the spring and summer months.

More than 400,000 soldiers died of disease during the war. Over 57,000 Federals died of dysentery and diarrhea alone, amounting to about 10,000 less than were killed in battle. While the figures for Confederates are unknown due to inadequate record keeping, the lack of surgeons and the shortage of medicines and supplies contribute to the belief that deaths due to disease were much higher for rebel soldiers.

Surgeons had their own individual methods for dealing with disease. Favorite medicines for camp illnesses included turpentine, calomel, castor oil, blue mass (a mercury and chalk compound), whiskey, and quinine. Treatment for wounds was also crude and ineffective. As regiments entered battle, the medical staff set up field hospitals as near the front lines as safely possible. Under the direction of assistant surgeons, stretcher bearers, who were generally made up of noncombatant personnel, combed the fields in search of the wounded. Soldiers gathered from the battlefield and taken to field hospitals were divided into two groups: those who would probably survive and those who would not. In the latter cases, wounds of the abdomen and chest were fatal three-quarters of the time, whereas head wounds, especially if the bullet penetrated the bone, resulted in a death rate of 85 percent. Soldiers with these wounds were put aside and tended to only when time permitted.

Surgeons often examined flesh wounds by probing for bullets with their fingers and then generally treated them with cold-water compresses and opiates or liquor to ease the pain. Most soldiers with these types of wounds survived, but the risk

An 1864 image taken at Fort Monroe, Virginia, shows Union surgeons about to amputate the leg of a wounded soldier. One surgeon holds a saw while another, to his left, steadies the leg with a forked retractor. Any blood that results will fall into the basin placed below the leg. Because of the long exposures needed for photography at the time, a photograph like this would have to be posed.

of infection was always present—gangrene would attack even the most minor wound.

Those with shattered bones in an arm or leg faced an uncertain fate in field hospitals. Setting bones was time-consuming, very risky, and often made impractical by the large amount of splinter damage caused by lead bullets. Instead, surgeons resorted to wholesale amputations to save lives. "The surgeons and their assistants," one soldier recalled, "stripped to the waist and bespattered with blood, stood around, some holding the poor fellows while others, armed with long, bloody knives and saws, cut and sawed away with frightful rapidity, throwing the mangled limbs on a pile nearby as soon as removed."

On June 10, General Sherman's army faced Confederate entrenchments on Kennesaw Mountain northwest of Marietta, Georgia. He decided on a frontal attack against the rebel position on June 27. "Our losses in this assault were heavy indeed," one of Sherman's corps commanders wrote, "and our gain was nothing. We realized now, as never before, the futility of direct assaults upon intrenched lines already well prepared and well manned."

Rear Admiral David G. Farragut is in the rigging of his ship, the Hartford, during an extremely close-quarters battle with the CSS Tennessee in this painting by W. H. Overend. The Hartford went on to defeat the Tennessee and its fellow defenders of Mobile Bay, shutting down one of the last outposts for Confederate blockade runners.

OCTOBER 19
At dawn, Jubal Early's Confederates launch a surprise attack on Sheridan's army in their camps along Cedar Creek, Virginia. After initial success, Sheridan regroups and heads a devastating counterattack that forces the Confederates to retreat.

Confederate soldiers invade St. Albans, Vermont, from Canada, robbing three banks and terrorizing the civilians before retreating back across the border.

Located where the James and Appomattox Rivers meet, City Point, Virginia, was General Grant's headquarters and main supply depot during his nearly ten-month siege of Petersburg. Beginning in June 1864, Federals converted City Point from a sleepy little village to a major communication and transportation hub. Until the fall of Petersburg, more than 200 ships docked at City Point each day.

Confederate agent John Maxwell and an accomplice concealed a primitive time bomb on a munitions barge docked off City Point, Virginia, to damage the Union's major supply base during the Petersburg Campaign. The explosion of Maxwell's "horological torpedo" on August 9 destroyed more than 180 feet of the wharf and $2 million of supplies, killed 43, and injured 126. Although General Grant escaped injury, an orderly was killed and a staff officer wounded.

Union troops under General Winfield Scott Hancock were ordered on August 24 to destroy about 14 miles of the Weldon Railroad south of Petersburg. But Confederate troops attacked the next day near Ream's Station. The once-proud Union 2nd Corps was routed, fleeing back to entrenchments along the Jerusalem Plank Road. Humiliated by the performance of his command, Hancock told an aide, "I do not care to die. But I pray God I may never leave this field."

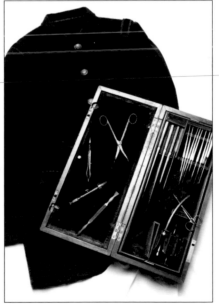

A Civil War surgeon's kit included knives and saws for amputating damaged limbs. Seen here on edge, they seem less intimidating than they were. A skilled surgeon could remove an arm or leg in 15 minutes. Such speed could save a soldier's life if infection did not set in.

Forrest's troops leave Mississippi on a raid into Tennessee to cooperate with Hood's advancing army.

OCTOBER 21
Price's Southern troops in Missouri push back Union defenders during the Battle of the Little Blue River.

OCTOBER 23
Missouri's largest battle of the war occurs at Westport. Price's troops manage to hold off two numerically superior Union forces before retreating.

Medical officers wore a kepi with the emblem of the medical service affixed, as shown here. The gold braid on the crown identified the wearer as a general officer, while the M. S. within a wreath on the front clearly indicated the man was a physician.

Ambulances, despite their names, were little more than simple wooden wagons pulled by horses or mules. The wagons had no springs, and the wounded suffered untold agonies bouncing along rutted dirt roads toward rear-area hospitals. The Union Zouaves pictured staged this photograph.

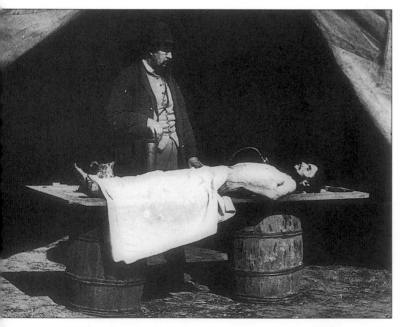

While embalming methods were well known in the 1860s, most soldiers slain in battle were buried in trenches on the battlefields or in more proper cemeteries with marked headboards for identification. The decomposition that soon set in made it imperative that bodies be buried immediately or embalmed for the long trip home to a local cemetery.

The Military Vote in the Election of 1864

The 1864 presidential election occurred in the midst of the Civil War. A major question prior to the election was how Union soldiers would be able to vote. Many states—California, Iowa, Kentucky, Maine, Maryland, Michigan, New Hampshire, New York, Pennsylvania, Rhode Island, Vermont, and Wisconsin—allowed their soldiers to cast votes from wherever their units were stationed or from hospitals where they were convalescing. In other states, such as Illinois and Connecticut, any soldiers who voted went home to do so, and their ballots were tallied along with those of their fellow citizens.

Charges of voting irregularities were lodged against the administration. New York Democratic commissioners were thrown in prison, and only Republicans visited the regiments in the field. In Ohio camps, there were shortages of Democratic ballots. In the end, more than 116,000 soldiers voted for Lincoln; only 33,748 votes went to his Democratic opponent, George B. McClellan.

This engraving, published in Harper's Weekly *on October 29, 1864, is from the sketch "Pennsylvania Soldiers Voting," by William Waud. The home states of these soldiers allowed absentee military votes. The President asked General Sherman to provide leave for soldiers from other states to return home to vote.*

Shown in later life, Mary Anne Ball Bickerdyke supervised the building of about 300 field hospitals during the Civil War. She accompanied General Sherman on his march to the sea. After the war, she served as a pension attorney for veterans.

Early in the war, the U.S. Sanitary Commission worked with the federal government to improve the manner in which wounded soldiers were carried from the field. Dr. Elisha Harris devised a method for mounting stretchers in railroad cars using bands of rubber. This scene depicts a hospital steward overseeing the transportation of wounded to Nashville in 1864. About 225,000 soldiers were carried to the rear on these special trains.

These women are members of the Soldiers Aid Society of Springfield, Illinois. Desiring to make a difference while remaining on the home front, women such as these across the North banded together in aid groups to make or collect items of use for their loved ones in blue. These supplies often included such things as bandages, clothing, writing paper and implements, and food.

Once they left Chattanooga, the Union army took less than two weeks to drive the Confederate Army of Tennessee to the Etowah River, more than halfway to Atlanta. In a wire to a staff member, Sherman called the Etowah "the Rubicon of Georgia." Continuing, he wrote, "We are now all in motion like a vast hive of bees, and expect to swarm along the Chattahoochee in five days." As they neared Atlanta, they were met with Confederate defenses such as these palisades and chevaux-de-frise.

OCTOBER 25
At Mine Creek, Kansas, the pursuing Union cavalry mauls Price's rearguard and forces the rebels to burn a third of their supply train as they retreat.

OCTOBER 27
The CSS *Albemarle* is destroyed in Roanoke River, North Carolina, by a raiding party led by Lieutenant William B. Cushing of the U.S. Navy.

OCTOBER 27–28
The Battle of the Boydton Plank Road, Virginia, results in a Union defeat as the Yankees attempt to interdict the South Side Railroad.

John Logan, a member of Congress from Illinois, fought at the First Battle of Bull Run as a civilian volunteer before being named colonel of the 31st Illinois Volunteer Infantry in September 1861. Wounded in the Battle of Fort Donelson, he was promoted to brigadier general in March 1862 and major general a year later. Named to command the Union Army of the Tennessee in July 1864, he was replaced five days later with a West Pointer, an action that embittered Logan toward West Point for the rest of his life.

This is the Western & Atlantic Railroad depot through which many of General Hood's supplies flowed. Atlanta was a major communication and transportation center for the South, which made it vital for the Federals to capture the city.

General Sherman observes the artillery bombardment of Atlanta in this lithograph. Determined, as Sherman wrote to Halleck, to "make the inside of Atlanta too hot to be endured," the army shelled the city for more than two weeks. "Women and children fled into cellars," Confederate General John Hood later recalled. Elsewhere in his memoir, he continued, "The bombardment of the city continued till the 25th of August; it was painful, yet strange, to mark how expert grew the old men, women, and children in building their little underground forts."

"It is astonishing to see what fortifications they had on every side of the city," wrote a federal soldier after surveying the abandoned Confederate positions ringing Atlanta when the city fell. "All in vain for them, but quite convenient now for us." General Sherman had avoided a direct assault on forts like the one pictured here by exercising a series of flanking movements that eventually forced the Confederates to abandon the city.

OCTOBER 28
Price's soldiers hold off pursuing Union troops at Newtonia, Missouri, until federal reinforcements force Price to continue his retreat.

OCTOBER 31
Nevada is admitted to the Union as the 36th state.

Union troops recapture Plymouth, North Carolina.

NOVEMBER 2–4
Forrest engages Union land and naval troops at Fort Henry and Johnsonville, Tennessee.

Sherman's March to the Sea

"If the North can march an army right through the South," William T. Sherman wired General Ulysses S. Grant, "it is proof positive that the North can prevail." With Grant's blessing, General Sherman launched his army of 60,000 on its infamous march from Atlanta to the Atlantic Ocean on November 15. His target was Savannah, Georgia, an important Confederate port almost 300 miles to the southeast.

Unable to supply his army due to the distances involved, Sherman boldly planned to live off the land. "The skill and success of the men in collecting forage," he later recalled, "was one of the features of this march." As it advanced, the army destroyed all cotton gin factories, railroad tracks, bridges, and military storehouses on its way. Sherman's purpose was to split the South and cut the flow of supplies to Confederate armies throughout the area. He also intended to carry the war to Southern civilians, breaking their will to continue the fight for independence.

The Federals faced little opposition as they cut a destructive path through Georgia. Confederate General John Bell Hood invaded Tennessee with his army in a futile effort to divert the Union advance on Savannah. Only weak militia units comprised of old men and young boys stood in Sherman's way.

It took Union Brigadier General William B. Hazen's division about 15 minutes to charge through wooden obstructions and over land-mined terrain to capture Fort McAllister on December 13. The log-and-earthen fortress had kept federal ships away from Savannah, Georgia, since the start of the war. Fort McAllister's fall marked the end of General Sherman's month-long march to the sea and enabled his troops to be reoutfitted by federal supply ships.

His force reached the outskirts of the Southern port on December 10. After a ten-day siege, the city surrendered. On December 22, Sherman wired President Abraham Lincoln, "I beg to present you, as a Christmas gift, the city of Savannah."

With Atlanta in flames behind him, Union General William T. Sherman embarked on his march to the sea on November 15. Intent on destroying the deep South's ability to wage war, Sherman's army left in its wake a trail of wreckage 60 miles wide.

The Battle of Nashville

Having failed to stop federal General John Schofield's corps from reaching the defenses of Nashville, Confederate General John Bell Hood advanced his fatigued Army of Tennessee to the outskirts of the city on December 2. He had suffered the loss of almost a quarter of his command at the Battle of Franklin only two days earlier. Unable to mount an assault on the strong Union position, Hood erected breastworks, hoping to pressure the 70,000 soldiers in the army of General George Thomas to attack.

The thought of a large Confederate force operating north of General Sherman's army in Georgia concerned Ulysses S. Grant. He ordered Thomas to attack, but due to the lack of adequate cavalry support, the Union commander delayed his assault.

"Attack Hood at once, and wait no longer for a remount of your cavalry," Grant wired from his headquarters in Virginia.

Freezing rain and snow further delayed Thomas's attack until the morning of December 15. He sent a division against the Confederate right while launching the main assault at noon against the enemy's left flank. Thomas's command drove the Confederates from their position in fighting that lasted until nightfall.

Constructing new breastworks throughout the night, Hood's left flank quickly disintegrated the next afternoon in the face of a vastly superior Union force. The remnants of the rebel Army of Tennessee retreated toward Franklin. Hood asked to be relieved of his command less than a month later.

A two-to-one superiority in numbers helped federal troops commanded by General George Thomas break the back of John Bell Hood's Army of Tennessee in the important Battle of Nashville on December 15 and 16.

Confederate General Early's heavily outnumbered command was on the verge of routing General Sheridan's Army of the Shenandoah outside of Winchester, Virginia, on September 19. Then, in the afternoon, two divisions of federal cavalry struck the rebel line, driving Early's army through the city. In his report of the action, General George Custer described, "One moving mass of glittering sabers. This, combined with the various and bright-colored banners and battle flags, . . . furnished one of the most inspiring as well as imposing scenes of martial grandeur ever witnessed upon a battle-field."

Six weeks into his campaign to clear the Shenandoah Valley, Philip Sheridan's 37,000 troops fought and defeated 15,000 Confederates commanded by Jubal Early at Winchester, Virginia, on September 19. Widely celebrated in the North, the victory was immensely beneficial to the political aspirations of Abraham Lincoln, who was seeking reelection in November.

NOVEMBER 8
Lincoln is reelected President, receiving 55 percent of the popular vote, 400,000 more votes than McClellan. The Electoral College total is 212 for Lincoln and only 21 for McClellan.

NOVEMBER 15
Sherman leaves Atlanta to advance on Savannah, Georgia. This comes to be known as Sherman's March.

NOVEMBER 21
General Hood's Confederate Army

of Tennessee leaves Alabama to invade Tennessee.

NOVEMBER 22
Sherman's army occupies Milledgeville, the temporary capital of Georgia.

When federal General Philip Sheridan reached Cedar Creek, Virginia, on the morning of October 19, a rebel surprise attack had already routed his army. Sheridan wrote in his memoirs that as his command formed for a counterattack, it was decided that he should "ride along the line of battle before the enemy assailed us, for although the troops had learned of my return, but few of them had seen me. . . . I started in behind the men, but when a few paces had been taken I crossed to the front, and hat in hand, passed along the entire length of the infantry line."

John Bell Hood's Confederate army was crippled almost beyond repair following the fall of Atlanta. By November, when Hood led his army into Tennessee, combat wounds had cost him a leg and the use of an arm. His army was demolished at the Battle of Nashville, and Hood resigned his command a few weeks later.

Prior to leaving Atlanta on November 15 for Sherman's March, federal soldiers destroyed anything that could be used by the enemy. "Wrecked engines, bent and twisted iron rails, blackened ruins and lonesome chimneys saddened the hearts of the few peaceful citizens who remained there," observed one of Sherman's corps commanders, General Oliver O. Howard. To ensure that the railroad ties could not be reused, Sherman's troops often wrapped them around trees.

NOVEMBER 25
John Wilkes Booth and his brothers Edwin and Junius appear together in *Julius Caesar*.

A Confederate plot to burn New York City fails.

NOVEMBER 29
Union volunteers attack a Cheyenne and Arapaho village at Sand Creek, Colorado Territory, massacring as many as 600 men, women, and children.

NOVEMBER 30
Hood catches up to retreating Union troops at Franklin, Tennessee, and launches a massive frontal attack in the afternoon. The Yankees abandon their strong position and march north

Following the fall of Atlanta, the Confederates turned their attention to Sherman's supply line north of the city. Union Brigadier General John Corse was sent to Allatoona, Georgia, to protect the railroad. Arriving with a division on October 5, Confederate Major General Samuel French demanded Corse's surrender "to avoid a needless effusion of blood." The federal general replied: "We are prepared for the 'needless effusion of blood' whenever it is agreeable to you." The Federals fell back to Allatoona Pass, where they successfully rebuffed the rebel attacks.

Soldiers of the 21st Michigan Infantry, who marched with Sherman through the heart of the Confederacy, became ravagers of Georgia and the Carolinas. The armies under Sherman's command were composed largely of Midwesterners like these. Known as tough if somewhat unruly fighters, they took considerable pleasure in wreaking havoc on the Confederacy.

toward Nashville at night. Union casualties are 2,326. Hood's army suffers six generals dead among the 6,252 killed, wounded, and missing.

Union troops from Hilton Head, South Carolina, move to cut the Charleston and Savannah Railroad but are repelled in fighting at Honey Hill.

DECEMBER 6
Lincoln names Salmon P. Chase as Chief Justice of the U.S. Supreme Court.

By the end of the war, soldiers of both armies had become experts at living off the land, particularly in enemy territory. When supply lines had to be cut loose for the 60,000 federal troops during their march through Georgia, many supplemented their meager provisions by breaking into homes and plantations to steal food or valuables, as depicted in this drawing. "No doubt, many acts of pillage, robbery, and violence were committed by these . . . bummers," General Sherman wrote, acknowledging the behavior of his soldiers.

"Jeff Davis's November Nightmare" was Abraham Lincoln being elected for a second term. Southerners hoped that Democratic candidate George B. McClellan, who might extend an olive branch to the South, would defeat Lincoln in the 1864 election. However, Lincoln triumphed overwhelmingly and continued to press for total victory.

A highly respected acting family, the Booth brothers only performed together once. Edwin Booth was considered the greatest Hamlet of his day, and his younger brother John Wilkes was not far behind. With their brother Junius, they appeared in a benefit performance of Shakespeare's Julius Caesar on Broadway in November. Left to right are John Wilkes as Mark Antony, Edwin as Brutus, and Junius as Cassius.

DECEMBER 10
George Stoneman's Union horse soldiers leave from Knoxville, Tennessee, on a raid into southwestern Virginia to disrupt Confederate salt and supply depots.

DECEMBER 13
General Sherman's troops capture Fort McAllister, Georgia, near Savannah.

DECEMBER 15–16
General George H. Thomas launches a carefully planned attack on General Hood's outnumbered troops at Nashville. In two days of fighting, Hood's army is completely defeated and

As the mixed village of unarmed Cheyenne and Arapaho slept, almost 1,000 federal troops prepared to attack their camp at Sand Creek, Colorado Territory, on November 29. The American Indians had assembled to negotiate peace, but General Samuel Curtis, an advocate of Indian annihilation, felt they had not been appropriately punished for attacks against whites. When the slaughter ended, up to 600 American Indians had been killed, including many women and children.

Fort Monroe, a stronghold at the tip of the Virginia peninsula, served as headquarters of the North Atlantic Blockading Squadron. Heavily fortified with federal troops and guns, it never fell into Confederate hands. The 3rd Pennsylvania Heavy Artillery (152nd Volunteers) is pictured on the fort's parade ground in December 1864. The unit's batteries served in many actions along the coast. While 19 soldiers were killed or mortally wounded in battle, 215 died of disease.

The army of Confederate General John Bell Hood had been strengthening its entrenchments outside of Nashville since December 2. Federal troops finally attacked the works on December 15. Colonel Sylvester Hill's brigade charged one of the rebel artillery placements, Redoubt #3, near the Hillsboro Pike. Before reaching the enemy position, Hill fell dead, a bullet through the head. His troops overwhelmed the rebels, capturing their guns.

heads south, pursued by Union cavalry. Thomas loses 3,061, while Hood sees more than 4,500 of his troops captured, with at least 6,000 total Confederate casualties.

DECEMBER 21
Union troops occupy Savannah, Georgia.

Lincoln signs a bill creating the rank of vice admiral in the Navy, which is immediately awarded to David G. Farragut.

DECEMBER 24–25
Union forces led by General Benjamin Butler and Admiral David Porter attack Fort Fisher, North Carolina, by land and sea. The attack is unsuccessful.

1865

THE DOWNFALL OF THE CONFEDERACY

THE SOUTH AND THE NORTH EACH CONFRONT LOSS

New Year's Day 1865 dawned with an increasing loss of hope for the struggling Confederacy. Sherman's army was ensconced on the Georgia coast at Savannah, preparing for a northward march into the Carolinas. In Mississippi, Hood's battered Army of Tennessee was demoralized and weakened following the disaster at Nashville. Lincoln had won reelection in the November voting based on a campaign that promised

Given the ferocity of fighting between North and South over the previous four years, Robert E. Lee's surrender to Ulysses S. Grant at Appomattox Court House, Virginia, was a decidedly low-key affair. Lee was dressed in what appeared to be a new uniform and brought only one assistant. Grant, who had not expected surrender to come so quickly, was dressed in a private's jacket with his own bars to identify his rank and boots muddy from riding. Accompanying him, as depicted here, were several members of his staff.

Photographer Timothy O'Sullivan took this image of Fort Fisher shortly after its capture by Union troops in January. The scene shows the fort's bombproof, which troops called "The Pulpit." A bombproof was a heavily protected area excavated into one of the fort's thick sand walls. During the heavy naval bombardment that preceded the land attack with a storm of lead projectiles, members of the garrison took shelter here.

to bring a victorious conclusion to the war. In the federal Congress, discussion centered on postwar reconstruction of the South as well as the proposed constitutional abolition of slavery. Representative J. M. Ashley of Ohio addressed the House on the proposed amendment, which needed Democratic support to pass. Speaking on January 6, Ashley said, "Mr. Speaker, if slavery is wrong and criminal, as the great body of enlightened Christian men admit, it is certainly our duty to abolish it, if we have the power." On the last day of January, the House passed the 13th Amendment on a vote of 119 to 56, with 8 abstentions. Already passed by the Senate, the amendment could now be sent to the states for ratification.

The Desperate Confederate Government

In Richmond, the Confederate Congress wrestled with deteriorating political and military situations. The Congress passed a law placing General Lee in command of all Confederate troops, but it was far too late for Lee to have any effect on the situation.

THE GENIUS WHICH OUR SOLDIERS DISPLAYED IN DESTROYING RAILROADS SEEMS REMARKABLE.

Journalist Sidney Andrews

James A. Seddon resigned as secretary of war on February 6, replaced by former U.S. vice president and presidential candidate John C. Breckinridge. The Confederate Congress also debated the idea of arming slaves to help fight the Yankees—indeed, on March 13, such a bill passed, but it was also too late to be of any use. A new national flag came

1865
JANUARY 7
Major General Edward O. C. Ord replaces Benjamin Butler as commander of the Department of Virginia and North Carolina.

JANUARY 12
Secretary of War Edwin Stanton meets with a group of free blacks in Savannah, Georgia, to discuss the future. The consensus is blacks would prefer to live separately than among whites.

JANUARY 15
Union troops capture Fort Fisher, North Carolina, closing the previously porous port of Wilmington to blockade runners.

into being in March, replacing the Stainless Banner, which to some looked too much like a white flag of surrender.

Naval Assault in the Southeast

Winter effectively shut down most military operations, but the Yankee war machine continued to press forward. General Benjamin Butler, having failed to capture Fort Fisher in December, was relieved of command of the Department of Virginia and North Carolina and replaced by General Edward O. C. Ord. The new general immediately readied another expedition to attack Fort Fisher. On January 13, Admiral David D. Porter's armada began a two-day bombardment of the fort as the army landed troops. The ground assault rolled forward and swamped the outnumbered defenders on January 15. The fall of Fort Fisher effectively shut down Wilmington, North Carolina, neutralizing the last major rebel port.

Even as Fort Fisher fell, the Union high command began transferring troops to the Carolinas. From Tennessee, the 23rd Corps went by rail to the East Coast, then by

Standing at the center of this photograph is Admiral David D. Porter, commander of the North Atlantic Blockading Squadron, aboard his flagship, the USS Malvern, in December 1864. Porter had gone to sea at age ten, and during the Civil War his service included New Orleans, Vicksburg, and the Red River before he was transferred to the Atlantic Coast. William B. Cushing, the daring lieutenant who destroyed the CSS Albemarle, stands on the left of this image.

The Union 23rd Army Corps starts moving by water and rail from Clifton, Tennessee, to the vicinity of Wilmington, North Carolina, in preparation for a move inland to support Sherman's advance.

JANUARY 16
Sherman issues Special Field Order Number 15, intended to set apart temporarily land on the Sea Islands of South Carolina and Georgia for exclusive black settlement.

JANUARY 19
Sherman's army begins to leave Savannah, Georgia, and move into South Carolina.

This contemporary woodcut shows Major General William T. Sherman entering Columbia, the capital of South Carolina, on February 17. The city suffered extensive damage from fires likely set by retreating rebel cavalry who burned cotton and military supplies stashed in the city.

sea to North Carolina. This new concentration of troops along the coast would be ready to aid Sherman when he marched north. On January 19, Sherman's troops began moving out of their camps around Savannah and crossed the border into South Carolina.

Consolidating Union Victory

On the Confederate side, General Hood resigned as army commander and was replaced by Lieutenant General Richard H. Taylor. But Taylor was instructed to send the bulk of his troops eastward across Sherman's rear to reinforce the few Confederates confronting the Union veterans. On February 22, General Joseph Johnston was placed in command of the Confederates in North Carolina, but by then the situation had deteriorated. Union troops had marched into Columbia, South Carolina, on February 17 and into an empty Charleston the next day.

Sherman's Federals swarmed into North Carolina as Union troops from New Bern began to drive inland. Although Southern foot soldiers stalemated General John M. Schofield's troops near Kinston on March 8–10, and Confederate cavalry initially bested their counterparts on March 9 at Monroe's Crossroads, there were simply too many Yankees to oppose. Johnston's forces engaged Sherman's advancing columns at Averasboro and Bentonville, but in the end Johnston was forced to withdraw. The Yankees united near Fayetteville on March 23, whereupon Sherman called a halt to rest and reequip his tired army.

Elsewhere across the South, advancing Union columns demonstrated that the enemy was faltering, that the Confederacy was an empty shell. On March 17, two Union columns, one from Pensacola, Florida, and one from the mouth of Mobile Bay, began to move against the Confederate defenders of Mobile, Alabama. After a brief campaign highlighted by successful assaults on Spanish Fort and Fort Blakely, Union troops marched into the city on April 12. On March 22, General James H. Wilson's cavalry corps left its camps in Tennessee and headed south toward Selma, Alabama, to coordinate with the Mobile offensive. Wilson's horse soldiers swarmed over Selma's outnumbered defenders, led by the famed Nathan Bedford Forrest, on April 2. Ten days later,

JANUARY 23
Confederate General Richard Taylor replaces John B. Hood in command of the Army of Tennessee.

President Davis signs a bill creating the position of a Confederate general in chief, which is given to General Lee.

JANUARY 23–24
A naval engagement on the James River in Virginia pits Union and Confederate ironclads against each other. The Confederate squadron attempts to break

Wilson's troops rode into Montgomery. The corps then ranged across Alabama into Georgia, wreaking even more havoc and destruction on the dying Confederacy. Yet another cavalry raid, this one led by George Stoneman, left eastern Tennessee and swept across the Great Smoky Mountains into North Carolina against minimal opposition.

Wearing Down the Army of Northern Virginia

Lee himself, now advanced to the command of the Confederacy's entire armed forces, saw the deteriorating situation and determined that his troops must break out of Petersburg, move south to join Johnston, defeat Sherman, and then turn back on Grant. On March 25, Confederate troops launched a surprise dawn attack and captured Fort Stedman, temporarily punching a hole in the Union trench system near Petersburg. But Union reinforcements quickly deployed and launched a devastating counterattack, inflicting more than 4,000 casualties on the rebels, primarily captured.

In the midst of these federal moves, President Lincoln went to City Point, Virginia, where he conferred with Generals Grant and Sherman and Admiral Porter on March 27 and 28. Grant told the President that only one more campaign would be needed to

This image of Charleston, South Carolina, is merely one of dozens of photographs taken by Yankee photographers in April 1865. It shows the effect of almost two years of warfare that included day after day of artillery bombardment, which wrecked much of the city.

through the blockading Union vessels, but four of eleven Southern ships run aground, forcing a halt to the attack.

JANUARY 31
The House of Representatives passes the 13th Amendment, which is sent to the states for ratification.

FEBRUARY 1
Illinois becomes the first state to ratify the 13th Amendment.

The Ruined South

"The marks of the conflict are everywhere strikingly apparent.... The city always had a mushroom character, and the fire king must have laughed in glee when it was given over into his keeping. There is yet abundant evidence of his energy, not so much in crumbling walls and solitary chimneys as in thousands of masses of brick and mortar, thousands of pieces of charred timber, thousands of half-burned boards, thousands of scraps of tin roofing, thousands of car and engine bolts and bars, thousands of ruined articles of hardware, thousands upon thousands of tons of debris of all sorts and shapes. Moreover, there are plenty of cannonballs and long shot lying about the streets, with not a few shell-struck houses in some sections, and from the courthouse square can be seen a dozen or more forts and many a hillside from which the timber was cut so that the enemy might not come upon the city unawares."

*Journalist **Sidney Andrews**,*
describing Atlanta in the fall of 1865

finish the Confederacy and that the troops concentrated around Petersburg and Richmond would launch that offensive in a couple of days. Grant had been waiting for the winter mud to dry up and enable his troops to deal a crippling blow to Lee's outnumbered forces. The rebels' failure at Fort Stedman convinced Grant that Lee's army was now ripe for a major blow against it.

That blow began on March 29, when General Philip Sheridan's cavalry, supported by two infantry corps, edged toward Lee's weak right flank southwest of Petersburg. Lee countered by sending General George Pickett with reinforcements to contain the more numerous Yankees. Fighting along the Quaker Road slowed as rain set in by nightfall. The wet weather again hampered movement on March 30, but on the last day of March, Sheridan, with a five-to-one superiority, moved forward near Dinwiddie Court House, where Pickett's gray-clad infantry checked his advance. But Pickett realized the advancing Union infantry on the White Oak Road endangered his troops, so he pulled back into a defensive position around a crossroads named Five Forks.

General Joseph A. Mower's division of the 17th Corps assails the left flank of Johnston's army during the fighting at Bentonville, North Carolina, on March 21. Mower's troops flanked the enemy but were recalled by Sherman, who wished to avoid more fighting.

FEBRUARY 3
A peace conference at Hampton Roads between Vice President Alexander H. Stephens, Assistant Secretary of War John A. Campbell, and former Secretary

of State Robert M. T. Hunter for the Confederacy and President Lincoln and Secretary of State William Seward for the Union fails to resolve a peaceful end to the conflict.

FEBRUARY 5–7
The Battle of Hatcher's Run, Virginia, results in another lengthening of the already extensive Union siege lines at Petersburg.

After service on Grant's staff, General James H. Wilson led a cavalry division in the 1864 Virginia Campaign before being transferred to Nashville to command the cavalry corps assembling there. Wilson's horse soldiers fought at Nashville then raided through Alabama and Georgia in 1865.

General Sheridan and his cavalry assail the Confederate line at Five Forks. The three infantry divisions of the 5th Corps crushed General George Pickett's left flank, cut off his retreat route, and forced the rebels westward. By nightfall, more than 5,000 Southern troops had been captured.

FEBRUARY 6
John C. Breckinridge becomes the last Confederate secretary of war, replacing James A. Seddon, who resigned.

FEBRUARY 12
The Reverend Henry H. Garnet of New York is the first black person to speak in Congress.

FEBRUARY 17
Union troops occupy Columbia, South Carolina. Fires are set that quickly rage out of control and burn a portion of the city. Controversy remains over whether

The Falls of Petersburg and Richmond

As a result of the smashing victory at Five Forks, Grant ordered an attack on Petersburg's defenses on April 2. Troops of Horatio G. Wright's 6th Corps broke through on a narrow front and then widened the gap as elements of the 9th Corps also gained ground. Lee desperately attempted to bring order during the day as his outnumbered troops tried to withdraw. Two forts—Gregg and Alexander—repelled John Gibbon's 24th Corps until they were finally overwhelmed late in the day. Confederate General A. P. Hill, Lee's 3rd Corps commander, was slain during the confused fighting. After nightfall, Lee's battered troops managed to retreat from the doomed city.

Farther north, General Ewell, in charge of the Richmond defenses, learned that Lee was withdrawing and ordered the destruction of all military stores prior to his own evacuation of that city. Confederate naval vessels in the James River were blown up to prevent capture. As the troops withdrew, looters appeared and added to the fires and chaos in the city. Before Union troops entered Richmond on April 3 and helped quell rioters and assist in putting out blazes, more than 900 buildings in 20 blocks went up in flames. All bridges across the James had also been destroyed to prevent their use by the Yankees.

President Lincoln, who had been visiting Grant's headquarters at City Point, Virginia, came to visit the ruined capital of the Confederacy on April 4. He was greeted by jubilant blacks but not many white citizens.

During the campaign against Petersburg and Richmond from June 1864 through April 1865, Union casualties totaled perhaps 61,500, with Confederate losses of at least 38,000.

This is a view of the Tredegar Iron Works, situated on the James River in Richmond, Virginia, as it looked in April 1865. The South's only rolling mill capable of producing cannon and railroad rails, the firm expanded from 900 to more than 2,500 workers during the war but faced chronic shortages of raw materials.

Lee told Pickett to "hold Five Forks at all hazards." But outnumbered as he was, Pickett was doomed. As Sheridan's dismounted cavalry held the graycoats' attention in front, the infantry of General Gouverneur K. Warren's 5th Corps assailed the Confederate left and outflanked the enemy. Conflicting messages between Warren and Sheridan, in charge of the operation, delayed the assault and later led Sheridan to relieve Warren from command. But the Yankee infantry smothered Pickett's troops. By day's end, more than half of Pickett's force had become casualties, mostly captured by the Yankees.

As a result, Grant ordered a large-scale assault on the Petersburg entrenchments for April 2. Covered by a heavy ground fog, the attacking 6th Corps breached the enemy defenses near the South Side Railroad, while 9th Corps troops clung to footholds elsewhere along the lines. The Union success meant Lee was unable to move directly south toward Joe Johnston's troops in North Carolina. Instead, he evacuated the Petersburg fortifications and withdrew northward across the Appomattox River before turning west in an effort to move beyond the Yankees and then head south.

After four years of war and several unsuccessful Union campaigns to take the Confederate capital, Richmond fell on the night of April 2. As soldiers and civilians fled the city, fire erupted about 3:00 A.M. Flames and explosions destroyed much of the city between the capitol and the James River. In this painting, refugees flee on a bridge over the James River.

---

retreating Confederates or invading Federals started the fires.

FEBRUARY 18
Union troops occupy Charleston, South Carolina.

FEBRUARY 21
Confederate partisan rangers led by Jesse McNeill enter Cumberland, Maryland, and capture Union generals George Crook and Benjamin Kelley.

FEBRUARY 22
Union troops occupy Wilmington, North Carolina.

Joseph E. Johnston is placed in command of all Confederate

Photographer Thomas Roche visited the abandoned Confederate defenses of Petersburg on April 3, a day after they had been captured by the Army of the Potomac. This photograph, one of a number taken in Fort Mahone (nicknamed "Fort Damnation"), shows one of the dead left behind when the Confederates retreated. Fort Mahone had been garrisoned by the 53rd North Carolina.

Richmond Falls

Lee informed President Davis that Richmond must also be evacuated. By midnight, the Confederate government had fled westward. Military storehouses and installations were set afire, and looting began in the capital. The next morning, April 3, Union troops from the Army of the James marched into Richmond and began restoring order. Meanwhile, Lee's army retreated toward the west, pursued by Union troops on a parallel course to the south led by Grant, Meade, and Sheridan. On April 4, President Lincoln himself

THE SURRENDER WAS ACCOMPLISHED. THERE WAS NO THEATRICAL DISPLAY ABOUT IT.

Colonel Charles Marshall, assistant to Robert E. Lee, on the Confederate surrender

visited the ruined capital of the Confederacy. Escorted by Admiral Porter and a small number of armed sailors, Lincoln walked through the streets to the Confederate White House. Crowds of freed blacks cheered their liberator before he returned to a vessel anchored in the James River.

troops in the Carolinas, Georgia, Florida, and Tennessee.

Tennessee voters abolish slavery by adopting a new constitution.

MARCH 2
The Battle of Waynesborough, Virginia, is the last major engagement of the war in the Shenandoah Valley. General Jubal Early's Confederate force is attacked and

dispersed by Sheridan's cavalry, led by George A. Custer.

MARCH 3
Congress creates the Bureau of Refugees, Freedmen, and Aban-

Lee continued heading west, hoping to outdistance his pursuers and finally turn south in a last effort to link up with Johnston. Lee regrouped his army at Amelia Court House even as Lincoln toured Richmond. The general had hoped to receive supplies there, but his soldiers found nothing. The general then turned his column toward Farmville and sent messages for supplies to be brought there via railroad from Lynchburg.

Surrender at Appomattox

Federal troops caught up with Lee's army as it neared the Appomattox River. Sheridan's cavalry and the infantry of the 6th Corps mauled Richard Ewell's rearguard at Saylor's Creek, capturing perhaps 8,000, severely depleting Lee's diminishing army. Knowing the rebels were being hemmed in, Grant opened communications with Lee on April 7, hoping to prevent further bloodshed. Delays the rebels experienced crossing the river enabled Sheridan to get ahead of Lee and block his path beyond Appomattox

This depiction of Lee's surrender to Grant, painted in about 1870 by Alonzo Chappel, may accurately portray the simplicity of Wilmer McLean's parlor, but it significantly underplays Grant's entourage. Grant was not dressed as formally as pictured here, and he was accompanied by several more members of his staff. Lee's portrayal is more correct. He presented himself in formal military attire and had only one assistant present, Colonel Charles Marshall.

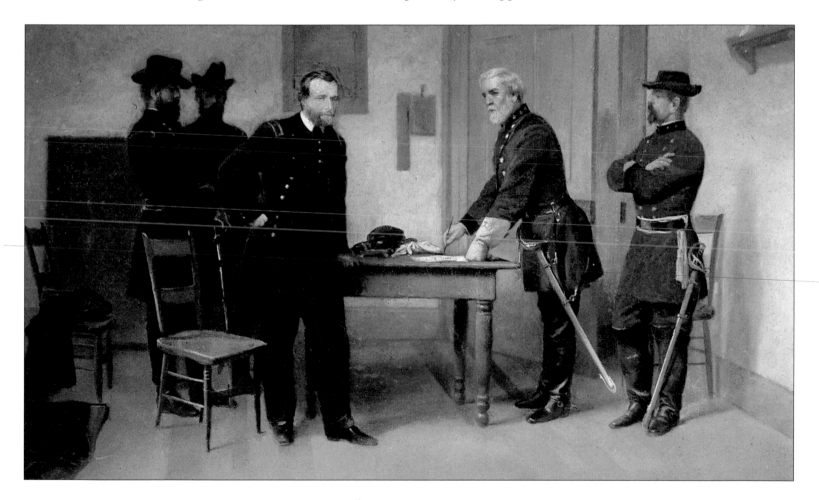

doned Lands, better known simply as the Freedmen's Bureau. This federal agency would be in charge of resettling and taking care of newly freed slaves.

Congress adjourns until December 4. The Senate will convene a special session for one week in March.

MARCH 4
Lincoln is inaugurated for his second term as President.

The Confederacy adopts a new national flag.

Court House. On April 9, after a day of stalled negotiations, Lee attacked the Yankees in his front. Union cavalry troops were pushed back to reveal long battle lines of blue infantry, as even more Union troops closed in on Lee's rear.

Thus surrounded, Lee met Grant that afternoon in a house in the small village of Appomattox Court House. The end result was that Lee accepted Grant's generous terms and surrendered the entire Army of Northern Virginia. Three days later on April 12, the formal surrender took place when Confederate soldiers stacked their arms and surrendered their flags. Each soldier was paroled and allowed to go home, officers taking their swords and troops with horses allowed to keep their animals for spring planting.

Assassination

The North went wild with enthusiasm as word spread that the great Lee had surrendered his troops. But this mood did not last long. On the evening of April 14, President Lincoln, accompanied by his wife and another couple, visited Ford's Theatre in Washington to attend the showing of the play *Our American Cousin*. While Lincoln watched the play, actor and Southern sympathizer John Wilkes Booth stole into the theater, opened the door to Lincoln's booth, and fired his derringer point-blank into the back of Lincoln's head. The assassin leapt down 12 feet from the President's box to the theater stage, breaking his leg in the process, and managed to escape during the ensuing chaos. He was eventually hunted down and slain in a barn near Bowling Green, Virginia, on April 26. Another would-be assassin wounded Secretary of State William Seward during the same night.

The mortally wounded President was carried across the street to a boarding house, where he died the next day. Lincoln's formal funeral took place in Washington on April 19. The casket was then placed aboard a special train that went to Harrisburg, Philadelphia, New York, Rochester, Buffalo, Cleveland, Columbus, Indianapolis, and Chicago before steaming to Springfield, Illinois, for burial on May 4.

A New President at War's End

Following Lincoln's unexpected death, Vice President Andrew Johnson was sworn in as President as the war wound down. Once General Johnston received word of Lee's surrender, he opened negotiations with Sherman and eventually surrendered his own army on terms similar to those granted to Lee. On May 4, General Richard Taylor surrendered the troops under his command in Alabama as the Confederacy collapsed. Confederate troops west of the Mississippi laid down their arms on May 26. By month's end,

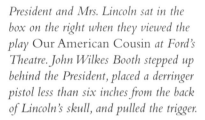

President and Mrs. Lincoln sat in the box on the right when they viewed the play Our American Cousin *at Ford's Theatre. John Wilkes Booth stepped up behind the President, placed a derringer pistol less than six inches from the back of Lincoln's skull, and pulled the trigger.*

MARCH 5–6
At an engagement at Natural Bridge, Florida, a Union expedition aimed at capturing the port of St. Marks is turned back.

MARCH 8–10
Confederate troops under the command of Braxton Bragg assail Union forces advancing inland from New Bern at the Battle of Wise's Forks, North Carolina.

Bragg withdraws after three days of inconclusive fighting.

MARCH 9
Confederate cavalry surprise Sherman's horse soldiers in an

Part of Lincoln's funeral procession travels down Pennsylvania Avenue in Washington on April 19. A wing of the Capitol appears at the upper right of this image.

James Bennett's log home near Durham Station, North Carolina, is not as famous as its counterpart at Appomattox. Generals Sherman and Johnston met here on April 17 to discuss Johnston's surrender. Sherman also handed his foe news of Lincoln's assassination. Johnston formally surrendered his army the next day.

all organized resistance to Union troops had ended. Ironically, the last major engagement of the war, Palmito Ranch, Texas, on May 12 and 13, ended in a Union defeat.

After authorizing Johnston to open negotiations with Sherman, Jefferson Davis, intending to escape the country, headed farther south as his cabinet members drifted away, each attempting to make his own way to freedom. Many feared Union officials would put them on trial for treason. Davis was captured by one of Wilson's cavalry regiments near Irwinville, Georgia, on May 10. He was taken to Fort Monroe, Virginia, and incarcerated as government officials considered how to go about putting him on trial.

Another more important trial opened in Washington on May 9. Following Lincoln's assassination, investigators rounded up seven men and one woman accused of helping Booth plan the murder. The lone woman was Mary Surratt, owner of the boarding house where some of the conspirators met. One of those rounded up was

engagement at Monroe's Crossroads, North Carolina, but withdraw after the Yankees reorganize and counterattack.

MARCH 11
Sherman's army captures Fayetteville, North Carolina, and destroys the Confederate arsenal there.

MARCH 13
The Confederate Congress authorizes the arming of slaves as soldiers.

Frank Leslie's Illustrated Newspaper *printed this cartoon of a fugitive Jefferson Davis running off with the Confederacy's gold. When Davis left Richmond in 1865, he fled south with some of his cabinet members and was captured in Georgia in May. Northern papers made political hay with their satires of Davis, who was rumored to have been taken while wearing women's clothes as a disguise.*

Dr. Samuel Mudd, a doctor who set Booth's broken leg. After a lengthy trial, all eight were found guilty. Three received life sentences, and one was sentenced to only six years. The others—David Herold, Lewis Powell (who used the aliases *Payne* and *Paine*), George Atzerodt, and Mary Surratt— were sentenced to be hanged. The public hanging took place at the old federal penitentiary in Washington on July 7. President Johnson was besieged by requests that he pardon Mrs. Surratt. The officer in charge of the hanging, Major General John F. Hartranft, hoped to the last for a pardon, but none was forthcoming. The four conspirators given life in prison were sent to Fort Jefferson, Florida, where one died of yellow fever and the other three were pardoned in 1868 and 1869.

Celebrating Victory

The rapid collapse of the Confederacy was followed by an equally rapid demobilization of the Union army. Philip Sheridan was sent to the Mexican border with a force of troops to monitor unrest in that country caused by French occupying forces. The armies of Meade and Sherman put on a "Grand Review" of their forces in Washington on May 23 and 24 before going into camp outside the city, where they were mustered out of service and sent home. Regiments with more time to serve were distributed across the defeated Southern states as occupying and guard forces until law and order could be reestablished.

President Johnson issued a proclamation on May 10 declaring that armed resistance was "virtually at an end," and on June 23 he lifted the blockade of Southern ports. The disintegration of the Confederacy was startlingly quick in April and May. Most soldiers followed Lee's example and quietly went home to resume their prewar careers or businesses. A number of unreconstructed rebels fled abroad, some fearful of being indicted for treason, others unwilling to live under Yankee rule. The last surrender took place in November, when the commerce raider CSS *Shenandoah* steamed into Liverpool, England. Captain James I. Waddell had finally seen newspaper reports of the Confederacy's demise and decided to head for England from the northern Pacific, where his vessel had devastated the American whaling fleet.

MARCH 16
Sherman's left wing attacks part of Johnston's army at the Battle of Averasboro, North Carolina, forcing a Confederate retreat.

MARCH 17
The Union land campaign against Mobile, Alabama, begins as Union troops from Pensacola advance to support other troops moving north against the city from the mouth of Mobile Bay.

MARCH 19–21
In the three-day Battle of Bentonville, North Carolina, Johnston assails Sherman's left wing but is repelled. He withdraws completely when Sherman's

A Union cavalry regiment approaches the presidential reviewing stand during the Grand Review on May 23. Apparent in this image are some umbrellas in the crowd and widely spaced guards along Pennsylvania Avenue to maintain crowd control.

Headed by its mounted commander and drummer boys, an infantry regiment with fixed bayonets marches with its weapons at the "right shoulder shift" in the Grand Review. Ambulances follow the unit.

entire army unites in his front. Johnston suffers 2,600 casualties as opposed to Sherman's 1,500.

MARCH 20
Union General George Stoneman

leads a cavalry raid that starts in Tennessee and goes into North Carolina.

MARCH 22
Major General James H. Wilson's

Union cavalry begins a raid across Alabama and Georgia.

MARCH 25
Lee's attempts to break through Grant's Petersburg lines at the

In this Louis Prang lithograph, Confederate soldiers defending Fort Fisher pour a withering fire into the faces of the U.S. marines and sailors assaulting the fort from the ocean beach. Delayed by having to break through the wooden palisade in front of the fort, the attackers were shot down like a "covey of partridges." Although this attack failed, it created enough of a diversion for the main army attack on the fort's north front to succeed.

Admiral Porter's naval bombardment of Fort Fisher consisted of a front line of ironclad monitors supported by a lengthy second line of wooden warships. Finally, a third line was held in reserve to be used in battle only if needed. The bombardment started on January 13 and lasted until land troops captured the bastion on January 15.

Battle of Fort Stedman are unsuccessful.

MARCH 27–28
President Lincoln meets with Generals Grant and Sherman and Admiral Porter in a conference at City Point, Virginia. These discussions allow the North's top leaders to plot and understand their overall strategy.

MARCH 29
Grant's troops, led by Phil Sheridan and General Gouverneur K. Warren, move to Lee's right flank near Petersburg, resulting in an engagement at the Quaker Road in Virginia.

The January 15 capture of the North Carolina bastion Fort Fisher was accomplished by a combined assault of federal army troops, sailors, and marines. The fort's loss was a heavy blow for the struggling Confederacy—it enabled the North to seal off the port of Wilmington, which had been a primary destination for Southern blockade runners. Deprived of the supplies that entered this port, the Army of Northern Virginia was presented with critical shortfalls in food and ammunition.

MARCH 31
More Union advances at Petersburg lead to fighting at the White Oak Road in Virginia.

APRIL 1
At the decisive Battle of Five Forks, Virginia, Sheridan and Warren's troops overwhelm George Pickett's defenders. Estimates in official accounts of the number of Confederates captured run from more than 1,000 to 5,000 or 6,000.

Florida Governor John Milton commits suicide.

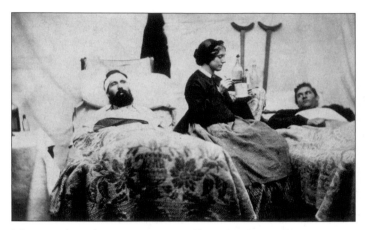

This rare photo shows Nurse Anne Bell posed with two of her patients, probably in Nashville late in the war. Two crutches and a few medicine bottles can be seen behind her.

The nation's capital hosted a huge complex of war-related industries by 1865. This "Ambulance Shop" both repaired and outfitted army ambulance wagons. With the burgeoning casualty lists late in the war, such wagons were always in urgent need.

By war's end, the Union Army was perhaps the best equipped and supplied of any of the world's armed forces. This view shows a virtual mountain of supply boxes stacked at the commissary depot at Cedar Level, Virginia. The Confederacy could not have hoped to match such an economic output in support of its Army.

The Wandering Newspaper

Unlike their counterparts throughout the North, Southern newspapers were constantly under threat of Union occupation as federal troops invaded the South and seized large chunks of territory. This is one of the reasons that many newspaper titles once published during the Civil War are no longer available for inspection.

One such paper was the *Memphis Appeal,* a paper that had started publication in 1840 and by 1861 was the largest daily newspaper in Tennessee. Although it advocated compromise in 1861, the paper's editorial slant became staunchly pro-Confederate when Tennessee left the Union.

The *Appeal's* press and other equipment left Memphis by rail just before the city was occupied by Union troops in June 1862. The editors set up shop in Grenada, Mississippi, only to flee again in November when soldiers from Ulysses S. Grant's army moved into that town. Until May 1863, the *Appeal* published in Jackson, Mississippi's state capital, moving to Atlanta when Grant's troops seized Jackson. In Atlanta, circulation topped 14,000 for the paper's two daily editions. But the *Appeal* had to move again when Sherman's army captured Atlanta in September 1864. At that time, the paper moved 167 miles to the west to set up in Montgomery, Alabama, where it remained until April 1865, when Yankee troopers from James H. Wilson's cavalry corps seized the city.

The paper's staff continued to elude capture, however, by moving to Columbus, Georgia, where their luck ran out. Many staffers were taken prisoner and some of the equipment wrecked. Editor Benjamin F. Dill was brought before General Wilson. "Have we caught the old fox at last?" exclaimed the general. "Well, I'll be damned." After some laughter and backslapping, the general and editor drank whiskey together. The press survived and was returned to Memphis, where the paper resumed publication in November. Today, the *Memphis Commercial Appeal* continues the tradition of its earlier name.

This woodcut depicts a common scene in Sherman's army as it destroyed Confederate railroads during the march to the sea and into the Carolinas. Entire regiments would take sections of track and rip up the rails wholesale as shown here. Often, the iron rails would be heated over hot fires and then taken and wrapped around trees to ensure they could not be reused.

William T. Sherman, seated at center, poses with the subordinates who led his troops across Georgia and into the Carolinas. One-armed Oliver O. Howard (left) led the Army of the Tennessee, and Henry W. Slocum (seated at right) led the Army of Georgia. The others in this image are 15th Corps commander John A. Logan (seated at left); William B. Hazen, commander of one of Logan's divisions (standing left); 14th Corps leader Jefferson C. Davis (standing right); and Joseph A. Mower, division commander in the 17th Corps (standing far right).

Sherman's army works their way through a South Carolina swamp. Soggy terrain such as this, without clear pathways, slowed Sherman's advance across the state. In this picture, they are also met with return fire. However, as one Pennsylvania veteran recalled, the local citizens finally stopped burning the bridges ahead of these soldiers to make it easier for them to pass. The locals apparently decided to help the Union troops and make sure they moved out of the state more quickly.

APRIL 2
Union troops attack and break the Confederate lines at Petersburg, forcing Lee to begin evacuation procedures from Petersburg and Richmond.

Wilson's Union cavalry attacks and captures Selma, Alabama.

APRIL 3
Union troops occupy Petersburg and Richmond.

APRIL 4
President Lincoln visits Richmond.

APRIL 5
William G. Brownlow is inaugurated as Tennessee governor.

Appomattox

By the morning of April 9, the federal armies commanded by General Ulysses S. Grant had been on the heels of Robert E. Lee's retreating Confederates for a week. Since the fall of both Richmond and Petersburg, Lee had moved west, hoping to beat Grant's pursuing army to waiting supplies at Appomattox Station. From there he intended to turn south to unite with Joe Johnston's army. During his flight west, Lee lost a large portion of his command each day to fatigue or capture.

Palm Sunday, April 9, dawned with the Federals in possession of the train station at Appomattox, blocking the Confederate avenue of retreat. "There is nothing left me but to go and see General Grant," Lee has been quoted as saying, "and I had rather die a thousand deaths."

The two generals and some of their staff officers met in the home of Wilmer McLean, who had moved his family from Manassas Junction, site of the First Battle of Bull Run, to a safer place as he continued his business dealings. The generals talked briefly before Lee agreed to Grant's generous surrender terms. As word spread of Lee's surrender, soldiers who had fought each other for four years could hardly believe it. As Lee rode through his army, "Whole battle lines rushed up to their beloved old chief," recorded an onlooker, "and struggled with each other to wring him once more by the hand. Not an eye that looked on that scene was dry."

The reaction was much the same on the Union side. "Such yelling and cheering I never heard," wrote General Meade's son George to his mother. Meade's chief of staff, General Alexander S. Webb, happily gathered in the scene as soldiers in blue wept, yelled for all they were worth, and screamed Meade's name as the general rode through the victorious army.

On Monday, April 10, Meade and his staff passed through the enemy line in search of General Lee. Seeing Lee approaching on horseback, Meade bowed and removed his cap. Lee, who had not seen Meade in 18 years, at first did not recognize him. His first question was "What are you doing with all that gray in your beard?" Meade responded, "You have to answer for most of it." The two generals then spent some time in Lee's tent discussing the recent operations at Petersburg.

Meade also found his brother-in-law, former Virginia governor and Confederate General Henry A. Wise. After the two in-laws briefly conversed, Meade loaned Wise 50 dollars and ordered two mules and an ambulance loaded with supplies to be sent back to the Wise family, still in Richmond.

Wilmer McLean's family left Manassas, Virginia, after the first major battle of the war took place there in 1861. They settled in this house in the small village of Appomattox Court House to get away from all the fighting. And yet, on April 9, 1865, the war in Virginia came to an end in McLean's parlor, where Lee and Grant met to make peace.

The Formal Surrender at Appomattox

"At the sound of that machine-like snap of arms, General Gordon started, caught in a moment its significance, and instantly assumed the finest attitude of a soldier. He wheeled his horse, facing me, touching him gently with the spur, so that the animal slightly reared, and, as he wheeled, horse and rider made one motion, the horse's head swung down with a graceful bow, and General Gordon dropped his sword-point to his toe in salutation.

"By word of mouth, the general sent back orders to the rear that his own troops take the same position of the manual in the march past as did our line. That was done, and a truly imposing sight was the mutual salutation and farewell.

"Bayonets were affixed to muskets, arms stacked, and cartridge-boxes unslung and hung upon the stacks. Then, slowly and with a reluctance that was appealingly pathetic, the torn and tattered battle-flags were either leaned against the stacks or laid upon the ground. The emotion of the conquered soldierly was really sad to witness. Some of the men who had carried and followed those ragged standards through the four long years of strife rushed, regardless of all discipline, from the ranks, bent about their old flags, and pressed them to their lips."

Brigadier General Joshua L. Chamberlain, describing the formal Confederate surrender at Appomattox, April 12, 1865

On February 21, the 55th Massachusetts regiment marched into Charleston, South Carolina. Jubilant freed slaves greeted their brothers in arms as this regiment of free blacks from the North marched in singing "John Brown's Body." The mounted officer is Colonel Charles B. Fox, the unit's white commander.

This scene, taken by photographer George Barnard, merely hints at the widespread destruction that took place in Columbia, South Carolina, in February 1865. Fire devastated the city as it changed hands from Confederate troops to federal forces. Controversy over whether the fires were started by retreating rebel horse soldiers or by occupying Yankees still continues.

As the Civil War progressed, it became as much a struggle against the people and the economy of the South as it was against Confederate armies. By 1864 it became the goal of Union leaders to destroy the Southerners' willpower and ability to continue the war. These ruins of Charleston, South Carolina, graphically illustrate how this "total war" policy was put into effect.

APRIL 6
At the Battle of Saylor's Creek, Virginia, Lee's rearguard is attacked and decimated, with 8,000 captured by Union troops.

APRIL 7
Lee's retreating army fights off a Union attack at Farmville, Virginia.

APRIL 8
Union troops assault and capture Spanish Fort, outside Mobile, Alabama.

APRIL 9
Lee surrenders his troops to Grant

This dramatic representation of the hardships faced by the South shows a family who once possessed great wealth reduced to abject poverty. In this sketch the blacks, who before emancipation were owned by this grieving woman, remain with her to care for her family.

Lincoln's Assassination

"At about 10 o'clock, while sitting in the front parlor reading, I heard a commotion in front of the house. Going to the window I saw the provost guard running up and down the street as though looking for someone, and the audience rushing out of the building. Everybody seemed panic stricken, and I raised the window and sang out, asking of those below what was the matter, and they replied that the President had been shot.

"I was soon down at the door and across the street and edging my way through the crowd half way into the theater, and finding it impossible to go further, as everyone acted crazy or mad, I retreated to the steps of the house, and some five minutes later when the bearers of the body had brought him nearly across the street one of the leaders asked: 'Where can we take him?' As there was no response from any other house I cried out: 'Bring him in here.'"

Henry S. Safford, a boarder at the Petersen House, across the street from Ford's Theatre

The USS Linda *on the James River lands a detachment of sailors ashore. Even though the Navy controlled the river from its mouth to as far inland as the Richmond defenses, bands of Confederate irregulars roamed the banks beyond Union camps, sniping at exposed sailors on shipboard. As a result, irritated ship captains sometimes sent small parties ashore to flush out troublesome enemies. The prow of this steam tug contained a spar on which was rigged a 150-pound torpedo. If needed, the* Linda *would attack by lowering the torpedo into the water and running alongside an enemy vessel. The torpedo would be detonated by pulling a lanyard.*

United States Navy sailors wore this type of summer uniform, which replaced the traditional navy blue color. The straw hat shown here was widely used during the hotter summer months rather than the normal visorless cloth cap.

at Appomattox Court House, Virginia.

A Union attack seizes Fort Blakely, another of Mobile's major defensive forts.

APRIL 10
Celebrating the recent surrender, a crowd of people, accompanied by a brass band, parade through the streets of Washington to the White House. After offering a few words, President Lincoln requests that the band play "Dixie."

APRIL 12
Union cavalry occupies Montgomery, Alabama.

The Lincoln Assassination

In anticipation of President Abraham Lincoln's attendance, the performance of *Our American Cousin* at Ford's Theatre on the evening of April 14 was sold out. Major Henry Rathbone and his fiancée, Clara Harris, accompanied the President and Mrs. Lincoln to the theater.

John Wilkes Booth, a staunch Confederate supporter, also entered the theater. A member of a nationally respected dramatic family, Booth was well known to the theater staff. Having appeared in this play several times, Booth knew when the audience would be most distracted by the actions onstage.

As laughter filled the theater, Booth took only 30 seconds to slip into the President's box, shoot Lincoln in the back of the head with a single-shot derringer, slash Rathbone in the arm, break his own left leg leaping to the stage, and limp out of the theater exclaiming, "*Sic semper tyrannis!*"—"Thus be it ever to tyrants," Virginia's state motto.

Lincoln died the next morning. The lives of everyone else in the box that evening would be dramatically changed, as well. Booth was captured and killed 12 days later. Mary Todd Lincoln was declared insane in 1875 and spent several months in an asylum. Although Rathbone and Harris married two years later, his inability to save Lincoln helped drive Rathbone insane. He murdered his wife several years later and spent the rest of his life in a criminal asylum.

Immediately after Lincoln was shot by John Wilkes Booth, he was carried unconscious to a house across the street from Ford's Theatre. He died at 7:22 the next morning in the bed shown here. Upon the President's breathing his last, Secretary of War Stanton, standing at his bedside, said, "Now he belongs to the ages."

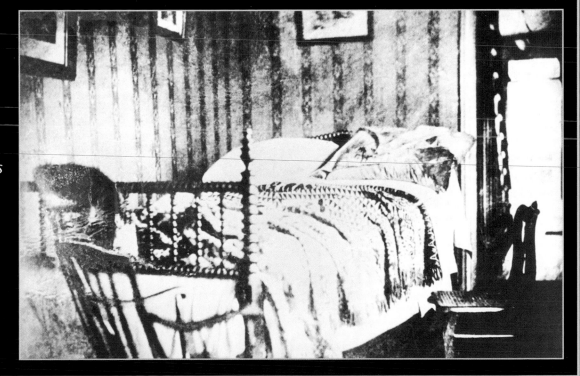

Mobile, Alabama, is occupied by Union troops.

Stoneman's Union cavalry captures Salisbury, North Carolina.

The formal surrender of Lee's army takes place at Appomattox. Neither Lee nor Grant are in attendance.

APRIL 13
Sherman's troops enter Raleigh, North Carolina.

APRIL 14
General Robert Anderson raises a

Meeting in President Lincoln's cabin on board the River Queen, anchored off City Point, Virginia, Generals Grant and Sherman and Admiral Porter discuss strategy with the President and learn what was to be done after the Confederacy collapsed. "Let them surrender and reach their homes, they won't take up arms again. Let them go, officers and all. I want submission and no more bloodshed," said the President.

Confederates of John B. Gordon's command storm Fort Stedman just before dawn on March 25, chopping through the federal abatis—felled trees with their limbs made sharp—placed to slow down attackers. Confederates pretending to be deserters managed to neutralize many Yankee pickets, which allowed the storming column to get close to Union lines before the alarm was given.

The Capitol provides the venue for Lincoln to deliver his second inaugural address on March 4. The President is in the center behind the podium, reading from a sheet of paper he holds in both hands. Pledging to prosecute the war to a successful conclusion, he calls for a peace that will provide "malice toward none . . . charity toward all."

U.S. flag over Fort Sumter, the same flag he had lowered in April 1861.

Lincoln is shot by John Wilkes Booth while watching the play

Our American Cousin at Ford's Theatre in Washington.

APRIL 15
President Lincoln dies in the Petersen House, across the street

from Ford's Theatre. Andrew Johnson is sworn in as President.

APRIL 16
Wilson's cavalry captures Columbus and West Point, Georgia.

Once the Confederates seized Fort Stedman and some trenches on either side of it, they were unable to move any farther. Union Brigadier General John F. Hartranft, in command of the Third Division, 9th Corps, assembled his six regiments of untried Pennsylvanians and contained the rebel advance. This painting, displayed at Petersburg National Battlefield Park, shows Hartranft's troops advancing to recapture the fort. Hundreds of Confederates chose to surrender rather than attempt to retreat to their own lines, having to cross land that was now swept by Union artillery fire.

This view of Confederate defenses of Petersburg, probably taken in April 1865, shows the log-reinforced trenches and, in the distance, the sharpened stakes of chevaux-de-frise, impediments to both infantry and cavalry attack.

Fort Stedman was temporarily captured by John B. Gordon's Confederates on March 25. Timothy O'Sullivan photographed the interior of the fort, which was a typical earthwork fortification in the lines around Petersburg.

General Philip Sheridan receives information from a black messenger, Thomas Laws, about enemy troop movements. Sheridan's cavalry gathered information from a variety of agents and often passed it up the ranks to his commanders. Many black agents, such as Laws, could pass through military lines without undue notice.

APRIL 18
Sherman and Johnston sign a surrender agreement near Durham, North Carolina. When sent to Washington, the agreement is refused as too lenient.

APRIL 19
Formal funeral proceedings are held for President Lincoln in Washington. His body is then placed in the Capitol rotunda for public viewing.

APRIL 21
Lincoln's funeral train leaves Washington for Springfield, Illinois, traveling through Harrisburg, Philadelphia, New York, Rochester, Buffalo, Cleveland,

The Human Cost

The Civil War was the bloodiest conflict in American history. If we combined all the deaths from all conflicts in U.S. history, nearly half would come from the Civil War. But because of fragmentary records, we will never know precisely how many people served in the war or how many were killed, wounded, or captured.

Officially, the Union Army recorded 2,778,304 enlistments, although many soldiers enlisted more than once in different regiments. Of this total, 178,975 were black and 3,530 were American Indian. The Navy and Marine Corps enlisted 105,963.

Northern casualties can be tallied as follows:
Total deaths	359,528
Killed in battle	67,088
Mortally wounded	43,012
Died of disease	199,720
Died as prisoners of war	24,866
Killed by accident	4,114
Died from other causes	20,728
Wounded	275,175
Navy killed and mortally wounded	1,804
Navy died of disease and accidents	3,000
Navy wounded	2,226

The headstones at Richmond's Hollywood Cemetery, shown here in April 1865, were generally wooden slats or boards inscribed with the name of the body buried beneath. Over the years, more permanent markers were erected as time and money permitted.

Macabre scenes such as this were all too common on old battlefields of the war. Faded fragments of clothing and brass buttons would often help burial details figure out at least whether the remains of the body had been clothed in blue or gray.

Since many Confederate records were burned when Richmond fell or were otherwise misplaced or destroyed during the war, exact numbers of Southern enlistments and casualties will never be fully accurate. Confederate enlistments fell somewhere between a low of 600,000 and a high of 1.4 million, with a widely accepted estimate being 1 million. The gray armies included more than 1,000 regiments, battalions, independent companies, and artillery batteries.

The best estimate of Southern deaths include 94,000 killed in battle or mortally wounded, with another 164,000 deaths from disease. An incomplete summary of the wounded included 194,026 names. The number who died in Northern prison camps has been estimated to be somewhere between 26,000 and 31,000. Figures for losses in specific battles change over the years, however, as historians find new muster rolls or casualty lists and revise earlier research.

Statisticians adding up the fighting in the war came up with 1,882 incidents in which at least one regiment was engaged. In 112 of these battles, one of the two sides had at least 500 combatants killed or wounded.

Federal troops commanded by Philip Sheridan scored a smashing victory over the Confederates at the Battle of Five Forks, Virginia, on April 1. George Pickett commanded the Confederates. The battle occurred when Sheridan's cavalry made a move to turn by Lee's right flank just south and west of Petersburg. Lee ordered Pickett to hold them "at all costs," which Pickett attempted with two depleted infantry divisions plus some cavalry. Outnumbered and outgunned, the rebels never stood a chance.

This is a pair of U.S. regulation cavalry boots, blackened leather with pull straps at the top. The trooper who wore these boots replaced the regulation rounded-tip spurs with a nonregulation pair that featured an eagle's head at the tip of each spur.

Outnumbered ten to one, the Mississippi troops of General Nathaniel Harris's brigade defended Fort Gregg and Battery Whitworth against the attacking columns of John Gibbon's 24th Corps on the afternoon of April 2. Of the fort's 214 defenders, 55 were killed and 129 wounded as the swarms of soldiers in blue finally won the fort. But Harris's stand bought time for Lee's army to retreat from Petersburg.

Columbus, Indianapolis, and Chicago.

APRIL 23–24
The ironclad CSS *Webb* dashes through the Union fleet from the Red River to below New Orleans before being beached and destroyed.

APRIL 26
General Joseph E. Johnston surrenders his troops to General Sherman in an agreement acceptable to Washington.

John Wilkes Booth is killed in a barn near Bowling Green, Virginia.

The ten-month siege of Petersburg ended when Ulysses S. Grant ordered an all-out assault on Confederate lines after the federal victory at the Battle of Five Forks. Having weakened his ranks to support his right flank at Five Forks, Robert E. Lee did not have the army to withstand an attack. On the night of April 2, he led his troops out of Petersburg toward the town of Amelia Court House. Richmond, left defenseless by this move, fell the next day.

Union soldiers of the 9th Corps push aside chevaux-de-frise and charge toward Confederate Fort Mahone in the enemy lines around Petersburg on April 2. Vicious fighting erupted along the 9th Corps front as troops battled their way by inches at times. By nightfall, the Union attacks had broken through in several places, and Lee was forced to retreat.

Attributed to photographer James Reekie, this image portrays one of the endless Union supply trains heading through Petersburg to catch up with Grant's troops pursuing Lee to Appomattox.

Jefferson Davis meets with his cabinet for the last time in Charlotte, North Carolina.

APRIL 27
The USS *Sultana* explodes on the Mississippi River. This overcrowded steamer's demise results in the deaths of at least 1,238 crew members and soldiers, the worst maritime loss in U.S. history.

MAY 3
Lincoln's funeral train arrives in Springfield.

The Grand Review

The Grand Review of Union troops, held May 23 and 24 in Washington, D.C., is shown here. The view is that of Pennsylvania Avenue, looking toward the Capitol. Even the assassination of President Lincoln a month earlier could not dampen the wild outpouring of joy and excitement that characterized this event.

On May 23 and 24, more than 160,000 Union soldiers paraded before President Andrew Johnson, his Cabinet, a host of dignitaries, and thousands of civilians lining Pennsylvania Avenue in Washington. Government employees and school children were given the day off—even the trial of the Lincoln conspirators was suspended for this military pageant. At 9:00 A.M. on May 23, a signal gun heralded the start of the review. General George G. Meade appeared, riding alone in front of his massed Army of the Potomac. For the next six hours, rank upon rank of soldiers of this veteran army marched up Pennsylvania Avenue to the cheers of the large crowd on both sides of this wide street.

May 24 was the date for General William T. Sherman and his western veterans to receive their share of the adulation. Sherman himself rode up to the reviewing stand and shook hands with Johnson and his Cabinet. He refused the hand of Secretary of War Edwin Stanton, however, as he was still angry over Stanton's criticism of the general's negotiations with General Joseph Johnston in North Carolina. But Sherman's veterans put on a show for the crowds massing along the parade route. The ragged, dirty appearance of these soldiers contrasted with the spit and shine of the Army of the Potomac the previous day. Following each brigade were the famed bummers, the army's very effective foragers, mounted on mules and carrying all sorts of plunder they had taken from the South. Even black contrabands accompanied the soldiers of the western army. This two-day demonstration for the nation was a fitting end to the contributions the Union soldiers made to victory.

Richmond photographer Charles Rees took several wartime photographs of the city. His images were found in 1865 and appropriated for use by Northern publishers. In this view, Rees captured the infamous Libby Prison, with its commandant, Thomas P. Turner, standing at center of the group in the foreground.

Alexander Gardner captured this view of Richmond's "Burnt District" on April 6, 1865. Retreating Southern troops set fire to everything that might be of value, and as a result, perhaps 1,200 buildings went up in flames—the arsenal, tobacco warehouses, railroad bridges, commissary depot, and other buildings. The conflagration smoldered for more than two months.

Richmond's devastation in April 1865 is readily apparent in this Alexander Gardner photograph. Scenes such as this were all too common across the South. The war had been fought on Southern territory, and destruction of homes, factories, railroads, and farms was widespread.

MAY 4
General Richard Taylor surrenders Confederate troops at Citronelle, Alabama.

Lincoln's body is interred at Springfield.

MAY 9
The trial of the conspirators in the Lincoln assassination begins in Washington.

MAY 10
Union cavalry captures Jefferson Davis near Irwinville, Georgia.

President Andrew Johnson declares that armed resistance is at an end.

This is how Richmond looked in 1865 and, indeed, throughout much of the war. The capital of the Confederacy was situated in a state that had much to offer the Southern cause. Among its resources were shipbuilding facilities, iron works, and a sizable population that produced some of the South's ablest soldiers.

Richmond is seen across the James River. The Virginia state house, which was also the Confederate Capitol, now has an American flag flying over it. In the foreground are the remains of burned-out commercial buildings that went up in flames the night the Confederate Army evacuated the capital.

In 1866, artist Dennis Carter produced this view of President Lincoln's visit to Richmond on April 4 of the previous year. In the carriage with the President is Admiral Porter, who provided the guards for the visit. Carter chose to show both whites and blacks in the crowd of well-wishers around the carriage.

MAY 12
Johnson appoints General Oliver O. Howard to head the newly created Freedmen's Bureau.

MAY 12–13
The last major military action of the war takes place at Palmito Ranch, Texas. Ironically, it ends in a Confederate victory.

MAY 22
Jefferson Davis is imprisoned in solitary confinement at Fort Monroe, Virginia.

What to Do with Jefferson Davis

Following his capture near Irwinville, Georgia, on May 10, 1865, the erstwhile president of the Confederacy was incarcerated in a casement at Fort Monroe, Virginia, with a 24-hour guard on suicide watch. For the first five days, he was even manacled with a ball and chain. By August, he was allowed to write to his wife, Varina, but she was not permitted to visit until April 1866.

The federal government worked diligently to find a conspiracy that involved Davis in Lincoln's death. The trial of the assassination conspirators, however, did not turn up any evidence that Davis was a part of their plot, and such charges were dropped. Secretary of War Stanton and others instead attempted to try Davis for treason. Lawyers reasoned that such charges would revolve around interpretations of the Constitution and that those might lean in Davis's favor. Eventually those charges were also quietly dropped.

Varina worked ceaselessly to secure her husband's release. In May 1867, a federal court in Richmond ordered the former Confederate president freed on $100,000 bond to guarantee his appearance at a future trial. Penniless, Davis was unable to post bond until three Yankees—*New York Tribune* owner Horace Greeley, abolitionist Gerrit Smith, and financier Cornelius Vanderbilt—came to his rescue and put up the money.

Jefferson Davis's complaints about the food he received while imprisoned at Fort Monroe are mocked in this cartoon. Union soldiers here tell the former president that rotten pork, moldy hardtack, and a pint of cornmeal were standard fare for Northern prisoners incarcerated in Southern prison camps.

MAY 23–24
The Grand Review of Union armies takes place in Washington.

MAY 26
Confederate troops west of the Mississippi agree to surrender at New Orleans.

MAY 29
The President issues a general amnesty and pardon to Confederates, including many rebel leaders.

Timothy O'Sullivan took this view looking across High Bridge, which carried the South Side Railroad across the Appomattox River. At this locale on April 7, Confederates attempted to destroy the bridge and compel Union forces to end their pursuit. The engagement was inconclusive—Union troops were repulsed, but the rebels failed to destroy the bridge.

W. T. Sheppard depicts General Edward Porter Alexander, Longstreet's chief of artillery, organizing the last Confederate line of defense at Appomattox. The troops deployed in an apple orchard to face oncoming Union soldiers of the 2nd Corps, but not a shot was fired, Alexander recalled. Lee and Grant were already negotiating surrender.

A sad Robert E. Lee rides away from Appomattox after surrendering his army to Grant. When he returned to his troops, recalled a witness, "hundreds of his devoted veterans pressed around the noble chief, trying to take his hand, touch his person, or even lay a hand upon his horse, thus exhibiting for him their great affection."

Richard Norris Brooke painted this view of tearful Confederate soldiers rolling up their precious regimental flag during the formal surrender proceedings at Appomattox. The War Department kept most surrendered flags until 1905, when they returned the flags to their states of origin.

JUNE 8
The Union 6th Army Corps holds its own review in Washington.

JUNE 10
Monuments to the Union dead of the First and Second Battles of Bull Run are dedicated on the battlefield.

JUNE 16
Grant supports Robert E. Lee's application for a presidential pardon and amnesty.

JUNE 23
President Johnson declares the blockade of Southern ports to be at an end.

This image of Robert E. Lee is the last photograph of the great Confederate general in his uniform. Mathew Brady took this view on April 16 at Lee's Richmond home. Just visible between the general's legs is the bottom of a stand that period photographers used to prop up and steady their living subjects. Any slight movement they might make after the lens was opened would mean a blurred and ruined image.

On April 14, retired Union General Robert Anderson returned to Fort Sumter and, in a moving but solemn ceremony, raised the same flag he had lowered when he surrendered the fort in 1861. This view shows the assembled crowd at the base of the high flagpole.

Around 5,500 black soldiers from Arkansas are estimated to have served in the U.S. Colored Troops. The first regiment was organized in the summer of 1863—six regiments of infantry and one of artillery were formed in all. This sketch shows a regiment returning to Little Rock after its service, a scene that was repeated in countless Northern towns while defeated Confederates struggled home in small groups as best they could.

JUNE 28
Still disrupting Northern shipping interests, the CSS *Shenandoah* captures 11 whalers in the Bering Strait.

JUNE 30
All eight Lincoln conspirators are found guilty—three receive life sentences, one is given six years, and four are sentenced to be hanged.

JULY 7
Four Lincoln conspirators are hanged in Washington.

Regimental Mascots

During the course of the war, many regiments brought along or acquired mascots who helped the soldiers pass the time in camp and generated regimental pride in time of battle. In the Union army, for example, the 11th Pennsylvania had "Sallie" and the 102nd Pennsylvania "Dog Jack." Both of these dogs failed to survive the war; Sallie was killed in battle, and Jack mysteriously disappeared while the 102nd was home on furlough. The 8th Wisconsin had "Old Abe," a pet eagle that perched atop a specially made platform carried alongside the regimental color guard. In time of battle, Old Abe flew aloft and survived the unit's many engagements. The 159th New York acquired a black bear cub during its service in Louisiana in 1863. This animal loved to wrestle with the soldiers, ate army food, and drank from canteens. The bear went along by ship to Virginia in 1864, survived the Shenandoah Valley Campaign, and marched in the Grand Review.

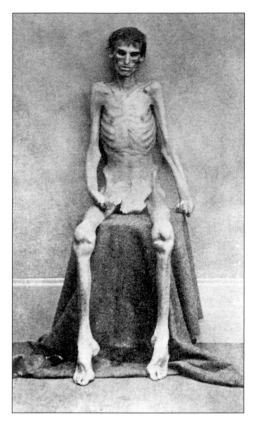

This photograph of a Union soldier after his release from Andersonville speaks eloquently about the terrible conditions at that notorious prison camp. A Union survivor wrote, "It is hardly possible to conceive of greater accumulation of woes…than fell to the prisoners at Andersonville."

Old Abe, the battle eagle mascot of the 8th Wisconsin, got a fair amount of fame. The eagle survived the war and died a natural death. His remains were stuffed and went on display in the Wisconsin state capitol in Madison, as part of the Grand Army of the Republic display there. Alas, when the building burned in 1904, so did Old Abe.

After the war was over, many battlefields still had to be cleaned up. Scenes such as this were commonplace for the workers hired to perform that task. Pigs and other animals rooted up hastily buried corpses, some of which were also exposed by rain and other natural processes. This scene shows the remains of soldiers who had been killed on the Gaines' Mill battlefield.

This immediate postwar view of Washington focuses on what would become the mall area. The Treasury Building is on the right, with the top of the White House visible above the trees at left. Cattle graze on lush grass beside a canal that runs through the flat land of the nation's capital.

This photograph, Abraham Lincoln's last, was taken on April 9—the day Lee surrendered his army to Grant at Appomattox Court House. By comparing this image with earlier photographs of Lincoln, it is possible to see the toll the war years took on him.

Below: A pistol shot cut through the laughter of Ford's Theatre the night of April 14. An instant later, a dark figure plunged to the stage from the President's box. A 27-year-old actor from a famous theater family and a passionate Southern sympathizer, John Wilkes Booth had played his final role—the assassin of President Abraham Lincoln.

Above: A manacled Lewis Powell (also known as Lewis Paine) poses for the camera sometime in April 1865, after his capture and incarceration. The conspirators to the Lincoln assassination were at first kept on two ironclad monitors anchored at the Washington Navy Yard before they were transferred to prison cells in the capital.

JULY 24
Ulysses S. Grant begins a tour of the East and Midwest that will last two-and-a-half months.

AUGUST 18
As part of his national tour, Grant and his family return to his hometown of Galena, Illinois. The citizens of Galena present them with a house.

AUGUST 23
The trial of Captain Henry Wirz, former commandant of Andersonville Prison, begins.

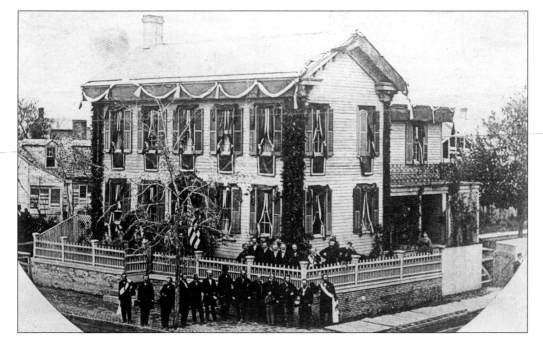

Ford's Theatre, where President Lincoln was assassinated on the evening of April 14, is seen in an exterior view. The site had originally housed the First Baptist Church of Washington. John Ford bought the vacant building in 1861 and opened the theater soon after. A fire gutted the building a year later, and Ford had the current structure built on the site. Ford's Theatre opened in August 1863, with seating for 1,700 people.

The U.S. War Department issued reward posters such as this one, which offered cash sums for information leading to the capture of the Lincoln conspirators. Booth was worth $50,000, with John Surratt and David Herold only $25,000 each.

This is a view of Lincoln's home in Springfield, Illinois. Black crepe is decked all over the outside of the structure to mourn the dead president, whose funeral took place in Springfield on May 4.

OCTOBER 2
Robert E. Lee signs his amnesty oath and is inaugurated president of Washington College.

OCTOBER 11
President Johnson paroles former Confederate Vice President Alexander Stephens.

NOVEMBER 6
The CSS Shenandoah arrives in Liverpool, England, and becomes the last Confederate commerce raider to surrender.

The Trial of Henry Wirz

Following the war, Captain Henry Wirz won infamy as the only Confederate executed for war crimes. The Swiss-born Wirz came to America in 1849 and was a Louisiana resident when war erupted. Wirz joined a Louisiana unit that acted as guards for Union prisoners. His military career included a stint at an Alabama prison before he was assigned to Richmond as the officer in charge of the city's prisons. When Andersonville Prison in Georgia opened in 1864, Wirz became its commander. Modern scholars disagree about how direct Wirz's role was in the resulting 13,000 prisoner deaths. At the time, however, he was held directly responsible. The captain was arrested in May 1865 and incarcerated in the Old Capitol Prison in Washington. He was charged with the murder of prisoners and conspiracy "to injure the health and destroy the lives of soldiers in the military service of the United States." The resulting trial began on August 23 and lasted until October 24. Witnesses numbered 160 and mainly consisted of former prisoners from Andersonville. Wirz was found guilty and hanged on November 10, 1865, as four companies of soldiers chanted, "Wirz—remember—Andersonville."

Convicted of inhuman crimes against prisoners, Heinrich (Henry) Wirz, commandant at Andersonville, was executed on November 10. Offered a last-minute reprieve if he implicated Jefferson Davis in the deaths of Northern prisoners, Wirz responded, "He had no connection with me as to what was done at Andersonville."

NOVEMBER 10
Captain Henry Wirz of Andersonville Prison is hanged in Washington after being found guilty of murdering prisoners under his care.

NOVEMBER 24
Mississippi is the first Southern state to enact black codes.

NOVEMBER 27
At Johnson's request, Grant

begins a two-week tour of the South, stopping in Raleigh, North Carolina; Charleston, South Carolina; and Savannah, Georgia; to a surprisingly warm reception. On his return, he reports that

On April 27, the Mississippi River steamboat Sultana exploded and sank near Memphis, Tennessee. The new steamer, launched in 1863, was overloaded with perhaps 2,100 released Union prisoners of war, 200 civilians, and cargo. Laboring upstream against a rain-swollen current, the ship, whose boiler had been patched in Vicksburg instead of being properly repaired, exploded shortly after two o'clock in the morning. Only 600 passengers survived, with the rest killed or drowned. The loss of life caused by this explosion makes it the worst marine accident in American history.

White-haired Edmund Ruffin, born in Virginia in 1794, had a successful career as a planter, published an agricultural journal, and conducted experiments in soil fertility. A spokesperson for slavery and supporter of states' rights, he was in Charleston, South Carolina, on April 12, 1861, where he was given the honor of firing one of the first shots on Fort Sumter. After the Confederacy collapsed, Ruffin became increasingly depressed. On June 17, he committed suicide rather than continue to live under Yankee rule.

A Brady image captures the Grand Review in Washington on May 23 and 24. This artillery battery rolls along Pennsylvania Avenue away from the Capitol, seen in the distance. Behind the cannon marches a great many more infantry regiments.

Southerners will submit to the U.S. government's authority and backs Johnson's plan for an easy Reconstruction.

DECEMBER 4
The 39th Congress convenes in Washington. This is the first time Congress has been in session since March.

Congress appoints a joint committee of 15 to examine suffrage issues and Southern representation in Congress.

Austrian archduke Ferdinand Maximilian accepted the offer to become emperor of Mexico after French forces occupied the country in 1863. Maximilian came to Mexico in 1864 and ruled only until 1867, when Napoleon III withdrew French troops to appease the United States. The emperor did not leave with the French, and he was subsequently defeated in battle, captured by Mexican revolutionaries, and executed by firing squad.

"In Memory of the Patriots," proclaims the plaque on this battlefield monument, erected in memory of the Union soldiers of the First Battle of Bull Run and dedicated on June 10, 1865. The man in the stovepipe hat to the left of the monument is the ceremony's speaker, Judge Abram B. Olin.

The June 10 ceremony on the Bull Run battlefield included the dedication of two monuments, the Henry Hill Monument for soldiers lost in the first battle and the Groveton Monument for those lost in the second. Photographer William M. Smith captured these images of that day.

DECEMBER 6
In his annual message to Congress, President Johnson announces that the Union has been restored.

DECEMBER 18
Secretary of State Seward declares that 27 states have ratified the 13th Amendment, enough to make it part of the U.S. Constitution.

DECEMBER 21
The state of Louisiana passes a black code.

Confederate Refugees

After the Confederacy's collapse in the spring of 1865, several of its leaders and generals decided they did not wish to live under Northern rule. On July 4 of that year, a column of Confederates and their families crossed the Rio Grande into Mexico. This party included generals John B. Magruder, E. Kirby Smith, Sterling Price, and Joseph Shelby, as well as two state governors. They crossed at the behest of the government of Emperor Maximilian, the Austrian aristocrat installed by France the previous year. Moving to Mexico City, the former rebels were offered land in exchange for military service, a proposal Maximilian quickly withdrew to avoid offending the United States. After the emperor was overthrown in the spring of 1867, most of the Confederates returned to the United States.

Other Southerners fled elsewhere. Confederate Secretary of State Judah P. Benjamin managed to evade capture and settled in England, where he became a highly renowned attorney. Jubal Early went to Mexico and then to Canada, returning to Virginia in 1867 after President Johnson proclaimed general amnesty. Other expatriate rebels settled in Brazil, where their descendants still live to this day.

The dangling, hooded bodies of the Lincoln conspirators are seen shortly after their hangings. From left to right are Mary Surratt, Lewis Powell (also known as Lewis Paine), David Herold, and George Atzerodt.

The Confederate commerce raider CSS Shenandoah destroyed American whaling ships in the northern Pacific in 1865. Lieutenant James I. Waddell, who did not find out the war was over until August, surrendered his ship at an English port after learning the truth.

These five former Confederate generals were photographed in Mexico after fleeing the United States in 1865. Standing are John B. Magruder (left) and William P. Hardeman. Seated are (from left) Cadmus M. Wilcox, Sterling Price, and Thomas C. Hindman.

Until 1877

RECONSTRUCTION

THE NATION REBUILDS AND EXPANDS CIVIL RIGHTS

*E*arly in the Civil War, Congress began to argue with the Lincoln administration about how to treat the postwar South. What was the political status of the seceded states? The President had refused to recognize the independence of the Confederate states and instead treated them as rebellious entities. But many Republicans in Congress thought a stronger position was appropriate. Because the Southern states had seceded,

In 1868, for the first time in American history, the House of Representatives impeached the President. Although the Constitution provides impeachment as a response to "high crimes and misdemeanors," President Andrew Johnson's primary offense was to disagree with Congress. His idea of a lenient Reconstruction conflicted with the desire of radical Republicans to punish the South. This illustration shows Thaddeus Stevens, a leading radical Republican and House impeachment manager, delivering a stern presentation during impeachment hearings.

the radical Republicans believed, they must be punished. After the issuance of the Emancipation Proclamation, the question of what to do about the freed slaves was also discussed in Congress. As early as February 1862, Lincoln was taking an active hand in the reclamation of Southern territory occupied by Union troops. When the Union gained control of Tennessee that year, he appointed Andrew Johnson as military governor. Johnson was also appointed a brigadier general of volunteers and given the task of restoring federal authority across the state. Despised by pro-Confederate Tennesseans, Johnson nevertheless acted with a firm hand and an unswerving devotion to the Union as he sought to establish civil law in a state increasingly occupied by Union soldiers.

In May 1862, Lincoln appointed former Whig Edward Stanly as military governor of North Carolina. Stanly faced a more difficult situation because Union troops occupied only coastal areas of the state. Given orders to uphold existing state laws, Stanly ran afoul of abolitionists in Congress who heard that he tried to return runaway slaves to their owners. In addition, many Union soldiers harassed civilians and more than occasionally ransacked private property, all of which made Stanly's position very tenuous. Confederate authorities in the state routinely ignored Stanly when corresponding with Union

"The 'Rail Splitter' at Work Repairing the Union" is a political cartoon produced after Abraham Lincoln and Andrew Johnson were nominated by Republicans for the 1864 election. Johnson, a tailor by trade, is shown sewing up the nation while Lincoln uses a rail to assist.

1866
Newspaper editor Edward A. Pollard coins the phrase *Lost Cause* in the title of his book *The Lost Cause: A New Southern History of the War of the Confederates.*

FEBRUARY 6
Congress votes to expand the duties of the Freedmen's Bureau.

FEBRUARY 19
President Johnson vetoes the Freedmen's Bureau bill.

MARCH 13
Congress passes the Civil Rights Act, which is designed to protect the rights of newly enfranchised African Americans.

authorities. Stanly, aggravated with his situation and unhappy with emancipation, resigned in March 1863.

Lincoln's Plans for Reconstruction

Lincoln continued to prepare for the postwar era. In December 1863, he announced his plan for reconstructing the Southern states. New state governments would have to meet only two conditions for Lincoln to recognize them as legitimate: Ten percent of the voters registered as of 1860 would have to take an oath of allegiance to the Union, and the state government would have to agree to the emancipation of all slaves in the state. In March and April 1864, voters in Arkansas and Louisiana agreed to Lincoln's plan. However, when representatives from these two states appeared before Congress, they were refused recognition and sent away.

Senator Benjamin F. Wade of Ohio, a leading radical Republican, teamed with Representative Henry W. Davis to sponsor a bill purported to be the Congressional response to Lincoln's leniency toward a defeated South. The Wade-Davis Bill specified that more than 50 percent of the state's voters had to take an oath of allegiance. Further, each state must abolish slavery, prohibit former Confederate officials from holding office, and repudiate its own state wartime debt as well as any Confederate debt. On July 4, 1864, Lincoln answered with a pocket veto of the bill, which led Republicans to issue a manifesto denouncing the President and declaring that Congress would never accept his plan for Reconstruction.

Senator Benjamin F. Wade of Ohio, or "Bluff Ben" Wade, as he was sometimes called, was among the most vocal radical Republicans in Congress. His interest in military affairs earned him the chair of the Joint Congressional Committee on the Conduct of the War. He cosponsored the Wade-Davis Bill that opposed Lincoln's conciliatory policy toward the South and would have succeeded Andrew Johnson as president had Johnson been successfully impeached.

Edward Stanly was appointed by Lincoln as military governor of North Carolina in 1862. A former Whig, Stanly tried to uphold existing state laws and ran into trouble with radical Republicans when he closed two schools for blacks started by a member of the U.S. Christian Commission and tried to return runaway slaves to their masters. Misbehavior by Union soldiers and a lack of loyalist sentiment in the state doomed Stanly's tenure as governor.

Congress Versus Andrew Johnson

Lincoln's assassination in April 1865 completely changed the equation in Washington. Andrew Johnson, a Democrat, was the new president, and Congress was in recess until December. Johnson quickly took action to ensure Lincoln's plan of leniency toward the defeated Confederacy would go into effect. In May, he issued an amnesty proclamation to most former Southern leaders who took an oath of allegiance. Exempted from this proclamation were those Southerners who owned property worth over $20,000 or were among the highest Confederate civil

MARCH 27
President Johnson vetoes the Civil Rights Act.

APRIL 6
The Grand Army of the Republic is founded in Illinois.

APRIL 9
Congress again passes the Civil Rights Act, this time over the President's veto.

MAY
The Ku Klux Klan is organized in Pulaski, Tennessee.

A self-educated tailor, Johnson was a man of the people and proud of it. When he appeared for Lincoln's second inauguration in 1864, Johnson was sick and drank some brandy to clear his throat. Unused to strong drink, an inebriated Johnson berated the Cabinet and embarrassed Lincoln, who hung his head in shame during Johnson's tirade. As a result, Johnson was wrongly labeled as a drunk and earned the wrath of several leading Republicans.

and military leaders—Johnson declared he would examine these petitioners on a case-by-case basis, but he granted amnesty liberally to them, as well. Johnson next called for each state to organize a convention to abolish slavery, repudiate secession and wartime debts, and petition for recognition. By late November, all Southern states except Texas had met Johnson's criteria. In his annual message to Congress that December, the President declared that the Union was restored.

Congress rebelled against Johnson's measures. When they reconvened on December 4, Congressional leaders appointed a 15-member joint committee to examine issues of suffrage and Southern representation in Congress. Just a month earlier, Mississippi had become the first state to enact "black codes" to control the freed slaves. Such codes applied only to blacks and dealt with labor contracts and the punishment of vagrancy and criminal activities. Laws such as these enraged Northern abolitionists, who clearly believed that racist white Southerners were determined to keep blacks as far as possible from their newfound freedom.

The committee reported in June 1866 that former Confederate states were not entitled to representation in Congress. The committee also stressed that Congress, and not the President, held authority over the reconstruction process. These merely pro-

IT IS HARD FOR THE OLD SLAVEHOLDING SPIRIT TO DIE. BUT DIE IT MUST.

Sojourner Truth

vided extra justification to Congress, which had already moved to assert its authority in the postwar South. Southern states had previously sent new representatives to Congress—among them were 74 former Confederate officials, including former CSA Vice President Alexander H. Stephens. Congress simply refused to recognize their credentials and sent them all home. The Freedmen's Bureau, which had been established in

MAY 1–4
A race riot in Memphis, Tennessee, results in the deaths of 46 African Americans and two whites.

JUNE 16
The 14th Amendment is submitted to the states for ratification.

JULY 16
The bill to broaden the powers of the Freedmen's Bureau is passed by Congress over President Johnson's veto.

March 1865, reported that blacks suffered greatly in the postwar South. Pleas for economic aid flooded Congress, which also received reports of antiblack riots in New Orleans and Memphis.

The stage was thus set for a major political battle between the President and Congress over Reconstruction. The first half of 1866 widened the gap between the two branches of government. In February, Congress crafted a renewal of the Freedmen's Bureau, in part enlarging its scope to counter the rise of black codes. It was given the power to appoint military commissions to try people accused of depriving blacks of their civil rights. Johnson vetoed the bill on the grounds that Congress had no power to legislate within 11 states not yet represented in its halls. Johnson also argued that military trials

In April 1866, Congress passed the Civil Rights Act over President Johnson's veto. This cartoon, published shortly after Johnson vetoed the bill, asks the reader whether slavery is really dead. African Americans were treated badly in the South, their rights infringed upon by former Confederates who wished to keep them as virtual slaves.

JULY 24
Tennessee becomes the first former Confederate state readmitted to the Union.

JULY 25
Congress establishes a new military rank above all others, General of the Army. It is immediately given to Ulysses S. Grant.

JULY 30
New Orleans civic leaders foment a race riot against African American and white Republicans meeting in convention. In all, 39 are killed, and many more are wounded.

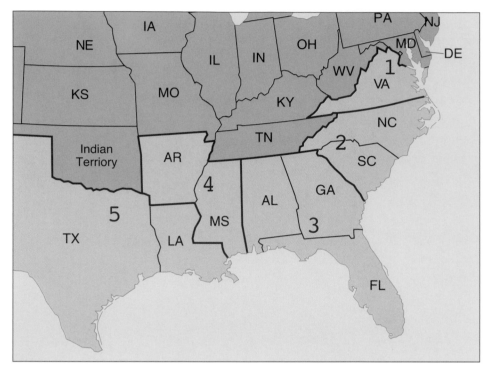

Congress, in the First Reconstruction Act of March 1867, divided most of the former Confederacy into five military districts, each headed by an army general to maintain law and order, protect all people and property, and punish all criminals and those who disturbed the peace. Some generals, such as Dan Sickles, were removed for being too zealous in their duties. Others, such as George Meade, tried to do their duty without partisanship but were attacked by both unionists and former Confederates anyway. Tennessee, already readmitted to the Union, was not included in the districts.

violated the Fifth Amendment. On July 16, Congress assembled enough votes to pass the bill over Johnson's veto.

On April 9, mustering enough votes to counter another Johnson veto, Congress passed the Civil Rights Act, granting citizenship to blacks and bestowing the same civil rights to all people born in the United States, with the exception of American Indians. This bill specified the civil rights involved and included any application to state segregation laws. Worried that this rights bill might be proven unconstitutional, the radicals crafted the 14th Amendment, which would put the rights into the Constitution itself. Congress quickly passed the amendment and sent it to the states. Not surprisingly, Southern states initially rejected the Constitutional change, so Congress responded by making its ratification a prerogative for readmission to the Union. It was enacted into law in July 1868 after 28 of the 37 states had ratified it.

Consolidating Radical Republican Power

The battle between the President and Congress had a profound effect on the midterm elections in November. Southern defiance over the 14th Amendment played into radical Republican hands. Johnson did not help matters when he went on a speaking tour of several Northern cities to drum up support for the Democratic party. His "Swing Around the Circle" turned into a disaster. Hecklers planted in audiences destroyed the President's composure and turned his orations into media circuses. As a result, radical Republicans swept most states, in effect leaving them in control of both the House and the Senate.

The reinforced Republicans moved quickly to assume control of Reconstruction. In March 1867, again over a presidential veto, Congress passed the First Reconstruction Act and then followed it with a second later that month, a third in July, and a fourth in March 1868. These acts divided the South—except for Tennessee, which was declared to have a legal government—into five military districts, each under a general officer responsible to Congress for direction. Each former Confederate state was to call a con-

AUGUST 28
President Johnson begins his "Swing Around the Circle" tour. Intended to help the campaigns of supporters running in congressional midterm elections, the

speaking tour turns into a disaster and severely damages Johnson's political career. The tour ends on September 15.

NOVEMBER
Partially as a result of his poorly received tour, Johnson and his policies are rejected in congressional elections. Johnson's Republican opponents win a two-thirds majority in both houses.

stitutional convention to reestablish its state government, secure black voting rights, and ratify the 14th Amendment. After recognizing that the Southern states would not call such conventions, Congress gave each district commanding officer the power to initiate voter enrollment to ensure that elections would take place. Finally, Congress approved a measure declaring new state constitutions could be put into effect by a majority of votes cast, thus negating boycotts by white voters.

Congress also passed two additional laws in March 1867 designed to curb the power of the president. The Command of the Army Act forbade the president to remove the general in chief from his office without Senate approval. The Tenure of Office Act stipulated that the president could not fire any Cabinet members without Senate approval.

In late 1867, Southern states voted to call the required conventions, all of which met in 1868 and drew up new constitutions. With the assistance of newly registered African American voters, radicals dominated these conventions. Encouraged by this trend, in June 1868 Congress passed an omnibus bill that readmitted the states of Arkansas, Alabama, Florida, Georgia, Louisiana, North Carolina, and South Carolina. Later that year, Georgia voters deprived African Americans of the right to vote after troops were withdrawn, so military rule was reimposed, and the state had to follow Congressional guidelines before being readmitted yet again in July 1870. To further solidify its hold on the reconstructed South, Congress proposed and sent to the states the 15th Amendment, which forbade any state from depriving a citizen of the right to vote regardless of color, race, or previous condition of servitude. When Mississippi, Texas, and Virginia ratified this amendment in 1870, they were readmitted to the Union, as well.

Left: Former Union general Oliver O. Howard was appointed commissioner of the Freedmen's Bureau by President Johnson in May 1865 and remained in that position until the commission was closed in 1872. He was also instrumental in founding Howard University and was its president from 1869 to 1874. Howard tried his best with the Freedmen's Bureau, but lack of staff and funding and the opposition of white Southerners made the agency's job difficult.

Mathew Brady took this photograph of the House impeachment managers. Seated from left to right are former Union general Benjamin F. Butler, Thaddeus Stevens, Thomas Williams, and John A. Bingham. Standing from left to right are James F. Wilson, George S. Boutwell, and another former Union general, John A. Logan.

Impeachment

Meanwhile, Johnson incurred the wrath of Congress in August 1867 when he dismissed Secretary of War Edwin Stanton and replaced him with General Ulysses Grant, then the general in

1867

MARCH 2

Congress passes three laws over Johnson's vetoes—the First Reconstruction Act, the Command of the Army Act, and the Tenure of Office Act—each designed to limit presidential power and enlarge the role of Congress.

Howard University, named after General Oliver O. Howard, head of the Freedmen's Bureau, is chartered in Washington, D.C. It will accept its first students in May.

Impeachment

"It is impossible now to realize how perfectly overmastering was the excitement of these days. The exercise of calm judgment was simply out of the question.... Passion ruled the hour and constantly strengthened the tendency to one-sidedness and exaggeration. The attempt to impeach the President was undoubtedly inspired mainly by patriotic motives, but the spirit of intolerance among the Republicans toward those who differed with them in opinion set all moderation and common sense at defiance. Patriotism and party animosity were so inextricably mingled and confounded that the real merits of the controversy could only be seen after the heat and turmoil of the strife had passed away. Time has made this manifest. Andrew Johnson was not the devil incarnate he was then painted, nor did he monopolize entirely the wrong-headedness of the times. No one will now dispute that the popular estimate of his character did him very great injustice.... The idea of making the question of impeachment a matter of party discipline was utterly indefensible and preposterous."

Representative George Julian (R-Indiana),
commenting in his memoirs on the impeachment of President Johnson

chief of the Army. When Congress reconvened in December, it refused to concur with Johnson's actions and forced him to reinstate Stanton, although the President fired him again on February 21, 1868. That same day, the House introduced a resolution of impeachment against the President, eventually drawing up a list of 11 charges. Three days later, the representatives approved the measure, and Johnson went on trial in the Senate on March 30. By the time the trial finally ended in May, the House managers wound up one vote short of the majority they needed to remove the President from office.

As a result of this experience, Johnson decided against running for reelection in the 1868 presidential race. The Democrats instead chose former New York governor Horatio Seymour as their candidate. Republicans meeting in Chicago elected Ulysses S. Grant to run on their ticket and waved "the bloody shirt of the rebellion" as their main campaign issue. Democrats, they said, would allow former Confederates to hold office and negate the reasons for the Civil War. On November 3, Grant captured 26 of 34 recognized states, with a popular vote plurality of just over 300,000. Thanks to the registration of African Americans across the South, Grant was the nation's 18th President.

Adjusting to New Southern Realities

The political furor over Reconstruction was widespread during this tumultuous period of American history. The war had left much of the South destroyed. Many cities, such as Atlanta, Richmond, and

A group of African American schoolchildren pose with their books outside their log cabin school somewhere in the South during Reconstruction. Despite the turbulence and antiblack feeling of much of the white South, the freed slaves made great strides in education when compared to their overall illiteracy rate in 1865.

MARCH 23
Congress enacts the Second Reconstruction Act.

MARCH 30
Secretary of State William Seward signs a treaty with Russia to purchase the territory of Alaska. The Senate ultimately ratifies the treaty and approves the purchase by only one vote.

MAY 13
Jefferson Davis is released from prison on bail.

As husband and wife tend a cooking fire, a hooded Klan member opens their cabin door and fires a shot at the back of the unsuspecting man of the house. This picture by period artist Frank Bellew vividly illustrates the daily terror that could appear without warning as the Ku Klux Klan and other associated hate groups terrorized African Americans across the South.

Charleston, had suffered heavy damage to their infrastructures. Railroads across the region had been torn up and destroyed. Crops and fields had been ravaged. The civilian population was beset with refugee problems, which were more or less severe depending on where the armies had moved. Trade had been disrupted, and cotton and tobacco, the South's two main cash crops, were all but destroyed for the short term.

THE STATES LATELY AT WAR WITH THE GENERAL GOVERNMENT ARE NOW HAPPILY REHABILITATED.

Ulysses S. Grant, in his second inaugural address

Of course, the South's labor supply had received the most devastating damage. Slavery was now dead, which meant that both white and African American Southerners had to learn how to readjust. African Americans were now free but were not always prepared to survive on their own. Most freed slaves were illiterate and could easily be taken advantage of in contract situations. General Oliver O. Howard, in charge of the Freedmen's Bureau, was responsible for assisting freed slaves in the postwar environ-

JULY 19
Congress enacts the Third Reconstruction Act.

AUGUST 12
President Johnson suspends Sec-

retary of War Edwin Stanton, in apparent violation of the Tenure of Office Act. After appointing Ulysses Grant in his place, Johnson is pressured into reinstating Stanton.

1868
FEBRUARY 21
Johnson fires Stanton again, this time for good.

Thomas Nast caricatured Carl Schurz, a Republican senator from Missouri from 1869 to 1875, as a carpetbagger who could not see the larger carpetbag, the one containing his own faults. Schurz, a strong supporter of African American rights, was a harsh critic of the Republican Reconstruction policy.

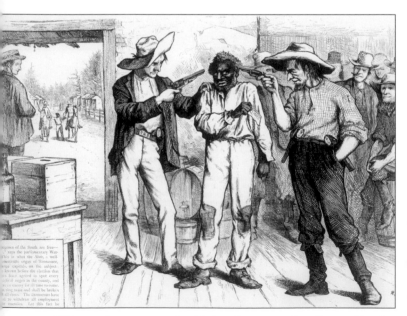

White southerners opposed to black suffrage resorted to all sorts of tactics to prevent African Americans from voting, regardless of the rights guaranteed by the 14th and 15th Amendments. This cartoon is entitled "Of Course He Wants to Vote the Democratic Ticket."

Charles Sumner

Born in Massachusetts, Charles Sumner was a Harvard Law School graduate whose first political affiliation was with the Whig Party. Sumner spoke out for educational and prison reform and advocated the abolition of all military spending and of the U.S. Military Academy at West Point. As a Free Soil candidate in 1851, Sumner was elected senator—his stirring speeches against the evils of slavery earned him many Southern enemies. In 1856, after the senator delivered a particularly inflammatory speech, Preston Brooks, a representative from South Carolina, beat him insensible with a cane. Sumner, convalescing, did not return to the Senate for more than three years.

Once war began, Sumner supported the Union wholeheartedly and called for the abolition of slavery. Immediately after the war, he took up the cause of equal rights for freed slaves and sponsored a lot of legislation to ensure African Americans the right to vote. He also led the attack to impeach Andrew Johnson, delivering one of the trial's bitterest speeches.

Caricatured in 1872, radical Republican Charles Sumner staunchly advocated immediate abolition, opposed reconciliation with the Confederacy, and, after the war, opposed Andrew Johnson's soft stance toward the South.

Sumner's influence was felt in foreign affairs, as well. As chair of the Senate Foreign Relations Committee, he opposed adverse settlement of the *Alabama* Claims with Britain and the U.S. annexation of Santo Domingo. Running afoul of the Grant administration for such positions, he was ultimately removed as chairperson. He served in the Senate until his death in 1874.

Fighting American Indians

"When the two detachments had become so far separated as to be of no assistance to each other, the Indians developed their scheme. Suddenly dashing from a ravine, as if springing from the earth, forty-three Indian warriors burst out upon the cavalry, letting fly their arrows and filling the air with wild war whoops.... The Indians began circling about the troops, throwing themselves upon the sides of their ponies and aiming their carbines and arrows over the necks of their well-trained war-steeds.... The Indians displayed unusual boldness, sometimes dashing close up to the cavalry and sending in a perfect shower of bullets and arrows. Fortunately their aim, riding as they did at full speed, was necessarily inaccurate."

Lieutenant Colonel George A. Custer
describing a Sioux assault on one of his cavalry detachments in 1867

ment. Northern idealists believed that African Americans and whites were equal in God's eyes and thus should be equal under American law. But many white Southerners, although they realized that slavery was over, refused to admit that African Americans were their equals.

The rise of black codes was one answer to the question of color. Another was the creation of a number of organizations whose goals were to establish white supremacy throughout the region and keep the newly freed slaves in a condition of fear. The Ku Klux Klan was the best known of these secret organizations. Other such groups included the Knights of the White Camelia and the Redshirts.

With the former plantation system disrupted by war and the end of slavery, new economic relationships had to be formed before the fields could again be worked. Cash was short across the region and would continue to be until the economy began new production. The two predominant forms of labor that developed were sharecropping and the crop lien system. Sharecroppers did not own their own land—instead, they worked for the land's owner, who provided implements and seed. In return, sharecroppers pledged as much as half the crop to the owner. African Americans who owned their own land could receive credit from a bank or wholesaler to buy seeds and implements, pledging half their crops in payment.

Governing the South

The state governments throughout the region were dominated by three main groups: radical Republicans who went south to help in reconstruction and disparagingly became known as *carpetbaggers*, free African Americans, and sympathetic native Southerners, insultingly called *scalawags*. By 1867, black voters outnumbered registered white voters in many Southern states. The effectiveness of these reconstructed state governments

Oscar White took this photograph of Ulysses S. Grant as President. There were very high hopes for Grant's administration, but a series of scandals and an ineffectual Cabinet destroyed his presidency, although they did not prevent his reelection to a second term. Henry Adams, the great American historian of the time, felt betrayed by Grant's politics. "A great general might be a baby politician," he complained.

FEBRUARY 24
The House of Representatives votes to impeach the President.

MARCH 4
The House managers present the Articles of Impeachment to the Senate. This begins the preliminary phase of the impeachment trial.

MARCH 11
Congress enacts the Fourth Reconstruction Act.

An African American family of share-croppers poses outside their cabin and shed. For many such families, freedom meant hunger, dependence on land owners for seeds and implements, the constant threat of violence from whites, and a lack of hard cash for buying anything. Many still farmed the traditional crops such as cotton.

remains a topic of much controversy among historians. The majority of disenfranchised white Southerners despised their state governments. Regardless of the government's effectiveness or how well it might operate, the simple fact that state governments were in the hands of newly freed slaves and their sympathizers, ultimately backed by the American Army, was anathema to Southern whites. These governments widened public school systems, rebuilt railroads, and in many cases genuinely tried to rebuild communities and reestablish law and order, but enough graft and corruption was apparent to give the legislatures a bad name. Influence peddling, bribery, and scandals were rife and well reported by the press. Although whites benefited from this seamy side of politics more than did African Americans, the existence of empowered blacks blinded white Southerners to the truth. African Americans did not have the influence many of today's observers seem to believe they had. During the Reconstruction era, only 16 African Americans served in Congress—12 were former slaves, while the other four were college educated.

The graft and corruption that came to be so evident during the administration of Ulysses S. Grant, who had been reelected in 1872, were only part of a national pattern after the Civil War, but the issue of race overwhelmed awareness of anything else in the South. As disgust with carpetbag rule grew, honest whites and blacks drifted apart from their governments and sometimes formed third parties. The Democratic party also grew

MARCH 30
Johnson goes on trial in the Senate as House managers begin presenting evidence. The U.S. Supreme Court Chief Justice Salmon P. Chase presides.

MAY 16
On the first charge of impeachment to come to a vote, the Senate decides in Johnson's favor by one vote.

MAY 21
Delegates at the Republican convention in Chicago nominate Ulysses S. Grant for president.

in strength. In 1870, Democrats won back control of Virginia and North Carolina. Georgia followed in 1871. By 1876, only South Carolina, Florida, and Louisiana were still under Republican control.

White supremacists continued their activity and were quite vocal at keeping the freed slaves in their places—election day violence was normal across the region. As a result, Congress passed the Civil Rights Act of 1875 to protect the civil rights of all Americans as guaranteed by the 14th Amendment. This law specified that African Americans should have equal access to hotels, restaurants, and other public accommodations. But in 1883 the Supreme Court declared the law unconstitutional, reasoning that discrimination in public accommodations had nothing to do with slavery. The Court also argued that Constitutional amendments referred to state actions, not private individuals. This decision was followed by Jim Crow laws across the South, which created a theory of "separate but equal," which itself was upheld by the Supreme Court in the decision of *Plessy* v. *Ferguson* in 1896.

The End of Reconstruction

The year 1876 was another presidential election year. Grant chose not to run again, and the Republicans selected former Union General Rutherford B. Hayes of Ohio as their candidate. The Democrats went with Samuel J. Tilden, governor of New York. The voting in November provided no clear winner, as the 19 electoral votes of South Carolina, Florida, and Louisiana, all still controlled by radical Republicans, and one vote in Oregon were in dispute. An electoral commission made up of eight Republicans and seven Democrats was created to investigate the situation. On March 2, 1877, two days before the new president was due to be sworn in, Republican candidate Hayes was given all 20 votes. In return, Hayes removed federal troops from the South, allowing the final three former Confederate states to be surrendered to Democratic party rule. Hayes also promised internal improvements and more railroads to the South.

Reconstruction ended later that year when the last troops were withdrawn from the South. Just 12 years after the end of the war, most Northerners had forgotten about the South and its former slaves. After the Civil Rights Act of 1875 was struck down by the Supreme Court, Congress would enact no significant new civil rights legislation until 1964. The promised freedom and equality the war brought to the freed slaves had failed miserably by the time Reconstruction ended.

Southern Economic Hardships

"There is a scarcity of food everywhere—in many whole counties the merest necessaries of life are all any family have or can afford, while among the poorer classes there is a great lack of even these. Of course this poverty falls most hardly on the negroes.... But the suffering will not by any means be confined to the blacks. Hundreds of the 'cracker' families will have a hard fight to keep the lean wolf of starvation from the doors of their wretched cabins; and not a few of those who before the war never knew any want, will now know that sharpest of all wants—the want of food."

*Newspaper correspondent **Sidney Andrews** writing from Savannah, Georgia, December 4, 1865*

MAY 26
After decisions on two more charges go to Johnson by just one vote, the Johnson impeachment trial ends in the President's acquittal.

JUNE 22–25
Congress enacts the Omnibus Act, in which the Southern states of Arkansas, Alabama, Florida, Georgia, Louisiana, North Carolina, and South Carolina are re-admitted to the Union.

JULY 28
The 14th Amendment becomes law after being ratified by three-fourths of the states.

Andrew Johnson

A North Carolinian by birth, Andrew Johnson was apprenticed to a tailor at age 14 but fled back to his family, who had settled in Tennessee. There he met and married Eliza McCardle, who helped her new husband learn to read and write. Johnson developed fine speaking skills and entered politics,

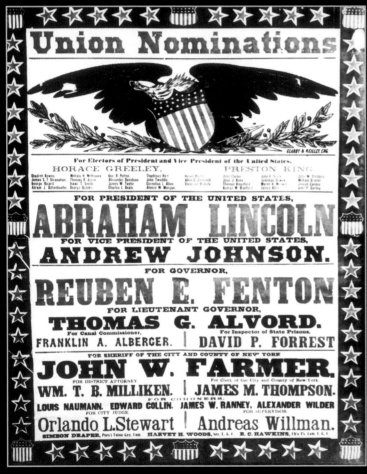

This poster from the 1864 Republican presidential campaign, with Andrew Johnson installed as the vice-presidential candidate, lists the slate of Union party candidates for the state of New York. Reuben E. Fenton, gubernatorial candidate, had been a member of Congress and was a founder of the Republican party. He would later serve as senator from New York. Both he and Thomas G. Alvord, candidate for lieutenant governor, won their respective races in 1864.

first becoming mayor of Greenville, Tennessee, and then a representative to the state legislature. In 1843, Johnson was elected to the House of Representatives in Washington. From that office, he went on to become the governor of Tennessee and followed that with another trip to Washington, this time as a senator. Throughout his legislative career, Johnson championed homestead legislation and public education, and he opposed the developing states' rights doctrine in the South.

Although he supported John C. Breckinridge in the presidential election of 1860, Johnson backed President Lincoln and denounced secession. When his home state voted to secede, Johnson became the only Southern member of Congress who refused to resign his seat and go with his state. Forced by this position to flee to Kentucky, Johnson quickly developed a reputation across the North as a steadfast patriot.

In May 1862, Lincoln rewarded Johnson's loyalty by appointing him military governor of Union-occupied Tennessee. During his three years in Nashville, Johnson dismissed officials who refused to take the oath of allegiance to the Union, squashed newspapers that took a pro-Confederate position, and even arrested clergy who supported the South. In 1864, Lincoln chose Johnson, a Democrat, to be his vice-presidential running mate to create a nonpartisan, prowar ticket.

After Lincoln's untimely death in April 1865, Johnson became president and undertook to carry out the policy of leniency toward the defeated South that Lincoln had begun to practice. But Johnson ran afoul of radical Republicans who believed the South should be punished, and the President and Congress quickly took opposite sides. In 1868, Johnson was impeached and only narrowly avoided being removed from office. Later that year, neither Democrats nor Republicans chose to renominate him. He returned to Tennessee and was again sent to the Senate in 1874. He died shortly after taking the seat the next year.

Appearing in the Harper's Weekly of July 21, 1866, this illustration of life among the ruins of Columbia, South Carolina, suggests the devastation that faced the South after the war. Homes and industry had been destroyed, and there was little with which to pick up the pieces. Blacks and whites shared many of the same hardships during this time.

Andrew Johnson was inaugurated as Lincoln's successor soon after the President died in the Petersen House on the morning of April 15, 1865. Johnson, the only senator who did not resign when his state left the Union, was already on weak ground because he had made some political enemies at Lincoln's second inauguration.

Oaths of allegiance were required of former Confederate citizens before they were allowed to repatriate to the United States. Lincoln's original plan of reconstruction called for rebel states to be readmitted to the Union when 10 percent of voters registered in 1860 took the oath, but radical Republicans in Congress raised the bar far higher.

SEPTEMBER
The Georgia legislature expels African American members from both houses.

NOVEMBER 3
Ulysses S. Grant is elected President of the United States.

1869
The first of what will ultimately be more than 50 former Union and Confederate officers begin service with the Egyptian army. This attempt by the Egyptian

Left: *Attorney General James Speed resigned his Cabinet post in July 1866 to protest President Johnson's lenient Reconstruction policies. Postmaster General William Dennison and Secretary of the Interior James Harlan also resigned at the same time.*

Andrew Johnson is portrayed as a parrot in this cartoon, repeating the same word, "Constitution," over and over. Johnson often tried to fall back on the Constitution to support his forgiving treatment of the states that had recently been in rebellion against the Union.

THE PAROQUET OF THE WH—E HO—E.

In its August 5, 1865, issue, Harper's Weekly *printed this Thomas Nast woodcut of Lady Liberty asking the question "and not this man?" There was much discussion at this time about the voting rights of the newly freed slaves. Lady Liberty shows a wounded black veteran who has lost his leg in defense of the Union—how could this man be deprived of his right to vote?*

army to modernize its forces will continue until 1879.

FEBRUARY 26
Congress passes the 15th Amendment, guaranteeing African American men the right to vote.

MARCH 4
Ulysses S. Grant is inaugurated as the nation's 18th President.

APRIL 12
In the case of *Texas* v. *White,* the Supreme Court states that the Union is indissoluble, making secession illegal.

Thaddeus Stevens

A New Englander by birth, Thaddeus Stevens moved to Pennsylvania to study law. He opened a practice in Gettysburg and developed into a staunch defender of fugitive slaves. He also entered the ironworks business.

In 1833, Stevens was elected on the Anti-Masonic party ticket to the Pennsylvania House of Representatives. He played a key role in establishing the state's public education system. Stevens made an odd figure. Born with a clubfoot, he wore a red wig to cover his bald head and never married. Nevertheless, he was a successful politician. Elected to the U.S. House as a Whig in 1848 and 1850, he helped create the Republican party in Pennsylvania.

Thaddeus Stevens supported equal rights for African Americans and wanted to punish the South for secession. During the 1863 Gettysburg Campaign, Confederate soldiers burned one of his ironworks, located on South Mountain between Chambersburg and Gettysburg.

From 1859 until his death in 1868, Stevens was a member of the U.S. House. During the war, he opposed any concessions to the Confederacy, and afterward he became the ranking House member of the Joint Committee on Reconstruction. He was a prosecuting House manager in the impeachment trial of President Johnson. He also worked tirelessly to upgrade the status of freed slaves by supporting the Freedmen's Bureau, guiding the 1866 Civil Rights Act through Congress, and working to pass the 14th Amendment. More than most of his generation, Stevens was egalitarian in his quest to better the condition of freed slaves, even going so far as to grant them land. In death, Stevens was buried in an all-black cemetery.

This 1866 woodcut shows a white schoolteacher in front of a class of newly freed slaves of all ages, men, women, and children. General Howard, head of the Freedmen's Bureau, believed that education was the most important part of his agency's work. Without education, he felt, African Americans would not be able to survive in their new world of freedom.

Harper's Weekly *printed this political woodcut in its issue of July 25, 1868. In this sympathetic view of the Freedmen's Bureau, the agency is seen as a promoter of racial peace in the occupied South, keeping the peace between agitated white Southerners who want revenge against the freed slaves and the more radical African Americans prepared to defend themselves.*

For the many newly freed slaves, life after emancipation did not change much from what had gone before. Long days in the fields, particularly if they were cotton fields, remained a constant. In the old days, these people would have been forced to pick the cotton. After the war, they had to pick cotton or another such crop in order to survive.

As in the days before the war, the rice crop was the major cash crop of the coastal lowlands in Georgia and South Carolina. This Harper's Weekly woodcut shows freed slaves planting, maintaining, and harvesting this important crop.

Noted artist Winslow Homer entitled this painting "A Visit from the Old Mistress." Here, a former owner visits her ex-slaves in their cabins to inquire about their welfare and perhaps reach a contract understanding between them. In many cases, relations between old masters and freed slaves who had been treated fairly remained cordial, and both parties were able to reach some sort of an agreement in regard to working on the old plantation—sharecropping was usually the result.

MAY 10
The transcontinental railroad is completed in a ceremony at Promontory Point, Utah.

SEPTEMBER 24
The bottom of the gold market falls out when President Grant, intending to thwart a scheme by financiers Jay Gould and Jim Fisk to corner that market, orders

the U.S. Treasury to sell its gold. Prices of the commodity plummet on what comes to be known as "Black Friday."

In many states, the polls were guarded by soldiers, often African American soldiers, to guarantee African American citizens the right to vote without harassment. Poll-watchers were also dispatched to ensure that no irregularities occurred during the voting process.

"The First Vote," an illustration based on a woodcut from Harper's Weekly, shows African Americans lined up to vote for the first time in their lives. The three men—an artisan with his tools in his jacket pocket, a well-dressed city dweller, and a soldier—represent the three main sources of political power for the freed slaves.

Here, African Americans vote in a city election in the nation's capital. Two election officials—one of them black—watch each voter place his ballot in the box. Republicans had enfranchised black voters in the city shortly after the Civil War and were keenly interested in local elections and how African Americans took part.

OCTOBER

Georgia legislator Abram Colby, an African American, is kidnapped by the Ku Klux Klan and tortured. Although threatened with further harm, he refuses to leave the legislature and testifies to Congress about his ordeal two years later.

DECEMBER

In response to rising violence against African Americans, election abuses, and the legislature's refusal to ratify the 15th Amendment, Congress reimposes military rule in Georgia.

Previously forbidden by law from learning how to read and write, newly freed adults also took advantage of the schools established by the Freedmen's Bureau. They would sometimes share classrooms with children. In other cases, teachers would provide night classes so adults could attend after their workday was finished.

Many Northerners went to South Carolina's sea islands to teach African American children shortly after the Civil War. One such teacher, Laura Towne, weathered several storms of controversy and hatred and kept teaching in schools like this one until her death in 1901. Towne was one of the best examples of Northerners who came South to help rather than to get rich.

Religion was a very important element in the lives of African Americans after the Civil War. Many African American leaders rose up through the church to take part in civic affairs, as well. This illustration from 1872 portrays a camp meeting held in the woods. Emotions and religious feelings could run very high on such occasions.

1870
JANUARY–MARCH
Virginia, Mississippi, and Texas are readmitted to the Union.

FEBRUARY 25
Mississippi Senator Hiram Revels becomes the first African American member of the U.S. Senate. He takes the seat formerly held by Jefferson Davis.

MARCH 30
The 15th Amendment to the Constitution is officially declared ratified.

The 13th, 14th, and 15th Amendments

The Civil War spawned three constitutional amendments that forever altered the status of African Americans. Lincoln was especially interested in seeing the ratification of the 13th Amendment. "Neither slavery nor involuntary servitude... shall exist within the United States, or any place subject to their jurisdiction." Simply put, slavery was made illegal. This amendment finished the process begun by the Emancipation Proclamation by freeing all the slaves still in bondage anywhere in the country. The amendment passed the House on January 31, 1865, and was ratified in December, eight months after Lincoln's assassination. Among Northern states, only New Jersey rejected it. The border states of Maryland and Missouri ratified it. Radical Republicans in Congress made Southern states accept the amendment as a condition of readmission to the Union.

The 14th Amendment further solidified the rights of African Americans by stating that all persons born or naturalized within the United States were American citizens. The amendment also forbade any state from passing laws that abridged this right. Furthermore, no state was allowed to deprive any person of life, liberty, or property, nor could any state deny a person equal protection under the law. This amendment also specifically repealed the old three-fifths clause of the Constitution and added penalties against any states that denied citizens the right to vote, proclaiming that such states' representation in Congress would be proportionately reduced. This amendment was ratified in July 1868.

Finally, the 15th Amendment, which was ratified in 1870, expanded on the 14th Amendment, spelling out the voting rights of all citizens and specifically forbidding states from denying those rights to African American citizens.

Following the Civil War, Robert E. Lee returned to his family and civilian life. Declining several lucrative job offers, Lee accepted the post of president of Washington College in Lexington, Virginia, at a salary of $1,500 per year. He died in Lexington on October 12, 1870, at the age of 63. The institution was later renamed Washington and Lee University.

The resistance of many Southerners to the North's reconstruction efforts is the subject of this cartoon. President Ulysses Grant looks on as a white Southerner would rather drown than be rescued by a newly free African American. Race played an overt part in the political process, with many Democrats promoting a "white man's government." Grant won his first presidential election by the margin provided by new African American voters.

The Impeachment of Andrew Johnson

President Johnson's differences with Congress over Reconstruction policy had simmered since he first attained the presidency, with flare-ups from time to time. But they boiled over when the House of Representatives voted to impeach the President in 1868. Secretary of War Edwin Stanton was an outspoken opponent of Johnson, and the President suspended him from his duties on August 12, 1867. Although Johnson wanted to replace him with a controversial nominee, Lorenzo Thomas, he made the more conventional choice of General Ulysses Grant. With the Tenure of Office Act of 1867, Congress had voted itself the power to approve or deny such Cabinet changes, and when the legislative body refused to confirm the switch, Grant stepped out of the position and gave it back to Stanton.

Undeterred, Johnson again removed Stanton on February 21, 1868, but the secretary barricaded himself in his office and refused to leave. Three days later,

the House voted 128–47 to impeach the President. He was charged with 11 articles of impeachment, most of which related to his differences with Stanton and his disobedience against the Tenure of Office Act.

The impeachment trial began in the Senate in March, with Chief Justice Salmon P. Chase presiding. With 54 senators present, 36 votes were needed to impeach the President. To defend himself, Johnson chose former Supreme Court Justice Benjamin R. Curtis and Attorney General Henry Stanberry, who resigned in order to assist the President. Johnson himself refused to appear at the trial.

Representative Benjamin F. Butler, the former Union general, tried to tie Johnson to Lincoln's assassination but failed. Johnson's defense argued that no high crimes had been committed and that the charges arose from differences of opinion, a situation that was protected by the Constitution. Since Stanton was appointed by Lincoln, the defense team argued, the Tenure of Office Act did not apply to him.

On May 16, a vote on the 11th charge of impeachment failed by one vote. Ten days later, voting on two more articles resulted in the same one-vote difference. The remaining charges were never voted on. Seven moderate Republicans had resisted all sorts of threats and voted their consciences instead of following party orders. They did pay a price, however: All seven were booted from office in the next election and never held public office again. In the end, Johnson remained in office, and Secretary Stanton was replaced by General John M. Schofield, a more acceptable choice than was Johnson's original pick, Thomas.

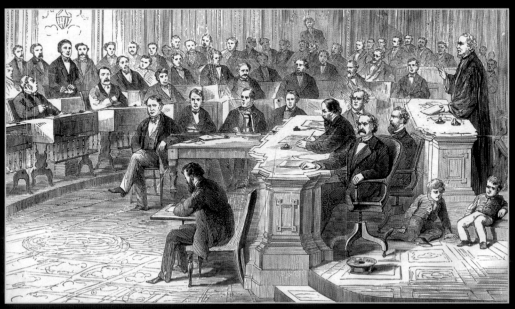

The Senate chamber is tense during the vote in the impeachment trial of Andrew Johnson. Salmon P. Chase, Chief Justice, of the Supreme Court, presides. Although there were 11 counts of impeachment against the President, the Senate only voted on three. Once it became clear that none of the counts would receive a guilty verdict, the House managers allowed the eight remaining counts to lapse.

This early reunion of Civil War generals and others demonstrates how hard feelings were at times set aside fairly quickly. The generals in this photograph, meeting in 1869, include representatives from both the North and the South. Robert E. Lee is seated (second from left), and Lew Wallace (standing fourth from left) stands beside his opponent at Shiloh, P.G.T. Beauregard, on the right. Seated on the right side of the photograph are philanthropists George Peabody and W. W. Corcoran.

It did not take long until white leaders in the South began to put black codes into place, putting any number of restrictions on African Americans. One of the primary functions of these codes was to deny the new citizens their rightful access to the ballot box.

In May 1866, Memphis, Tennessee, was the scene of a race riot that was typical in the postwar South. The actual riot was presaged by increasing troubles between local white police and African American soldiers from a nearby fort in the city on leave. After a street brawl erupted between armed soldiers and police, white mobs roamed the city, attacking African Americans, burning their properties, lynching, raping, and in general terrorizing the local populace. In two days of such violence, 46 African Americans and 2 whites died.

MAY 31
Congress passes the Enforcement Act, forbidding interference with the 15th Amendment.

JULY 15
Georgia is again readmitted to the Union.

OCTOBER 12
Robert E. Lee dies in Lexington, Virginia, at the age of 63.

The Presidency of Ulysses S. Grant

The great Union general won the 1868 presidential election handily on his war record. Once in office, however, Ulysses Grant disappointed many of his supporters. Scandal after scandal blackened the administration and showed that, although he was personally honest, the general was a poor judge of "friends" and showed little ability at running the country. Many of the members of his Cabinet were incompetent and dishonest. Exceptions were Secretary of State Hamilton Fish and Secretary of the Interior Jacob D. Cox, a former general who resigned his Cabinet post in disgust. Secretary of the Treasury George S. Boutwell was a crook. Secretary of the Navy Adolph E. Borie, upon boarding a wooden ship for the first time, was reputedly surprised to learn that it was hollow and not just a big floating log! War secretaries John Rawlins and William W. Belknap were little better than average.

Scandals rocked the eight years of the Grant administration. The 1869 "Black Friday" affair was an attempt by financiers James Fisk and Jay Gould to corner the gold market with the alleged collaboration of the administration. When gold prices rose, Grant ordered Treasury Secretary Boutwell to release more federal gold onto the market. This drove gold prices down and ruined many investors, but did not damage Fisk and Gould. A congressional investigation was unable to acquire sufficient

President Grant is seen with his Cabinet in this woodcut from Harper's Weekly. *Grant is in the center at the end of the table. Secretary of the Interior Jacob D. Cox stands at left, next to Secretary of State Hamilton Fish. Between Fish and Grant is Secretary of War John Rawlins. Seated on the other side of the table are Secretary of the Treasury George S. Boutwell and Secretary of the Navy Adolph E. Borie.*

evidence to convict the two men. The so-called "Whiskey Ring" was exposed in 1875. This group originally diverted liquor tax money into the coffers of the Republican party, but the temptation to skim off profits for individual members themselves was too great. Treasury Secretary Benjamin H. Bristow investigated, and 240 officials were arrested. When some of Grant's friends were among those arrested, Grant used his influence to acquit them. In 1876, Secretary of War Belknap was charged with using his office for personal gain, generally by receiving

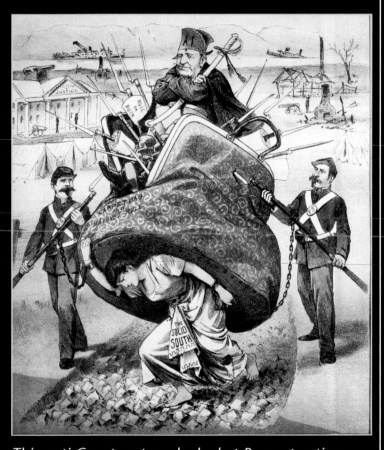

This anti-Grant cartoon looked at Reconstruction from the Southern point of view. The "Solid South" is weighed down by a massive carpetbag, reflecting the rule imposed by the victorious North, backed by the bayonets of Union soldiers. Sitting atop the bag is Grant, bedecked in a Napoleonic-style cockade hat and carrying a sword. Scenes of a prosperous North and a desolated South form an appropriate backdrop for this parody of reality.

bribe money to award contracts to Indian agents. He resigned to avoid indictment.

One of Grant's worst scandals erupted in 1872, when a New York newspaper broke the story of how the vice president of Union Pacific Railroad had created the Credit Mobilier Corporation, which he used to assist the railroad company in its westward expansion. Two members of Congress who had invested in the railroad headed off a congressional investigation of the railroad by allowing their colleagues to purchase Credit Mobilier stock at a fraction of its value and reap profits of as much as 341 percent. When Congress eventually did investigate, no indictments were handed down, but Vice President Schuyler Colfax, among others, was implicated.

In March 1873, Congress passed what disparagingly came to be known as "The Salary Grab Act," which increased the salaries of many government officials. Public indignation forced Congress to repeal the act in January 1874—only the President and Supreme Court justices retained their raises.

Money was also a factor in "the Crime of '73," the Coinage Act that was enacted in February of that year. Silver was removed as a monetary standard, leaving gold as the sole standard in the United States. The administration was heavily criticized. Opponents charged a gold conspiracy, and western advocates of silver, which had recently been discovered in the West, were unable to have the act repealed.

On the positive side, Secretary of State Ham Fish was instrumental in finally putting to rest the *Alabama* Claims during Grant's administration. Fish also worked hard to avoid war with Spain after a Spanish gunboat off the coast of Cuba captured the *Virginius*, a merchant vessel flying the American flag that had been running guns to revolutionaries on the island in 1873. Local authorities executed the entire crew, arousing much war feeling in the United States. An investigation showed that the ship had been flying the U.S. flag illegally. Nonetheless, Fish and the Spanish minister in Washington worked out a payment of $80,000 to families of executed Americans, avoiding a conflict with Spain.

After the Louisiana legislature passed black codes in 1865, some radical Republicans met with African American leaders in New Orleans on July 30, 1866, for a new constitutional convention. In response, a white mob sanctioned by the mayor and including police among its ranks went on a rampage, killing 39 African American and white Republicans. Federal troops arrived too late to offer protection.

The carpetbag became a symbol to bitter Southerners of the repression that came after the war when scores of Northerners—some altruistic, some mere scoundrels—came South to help reconstruct the Confederacy. Cheap travel bags made from carpets came to represent cheap opportunists. Anyone who actually came to help was characterized with the same stereotype.

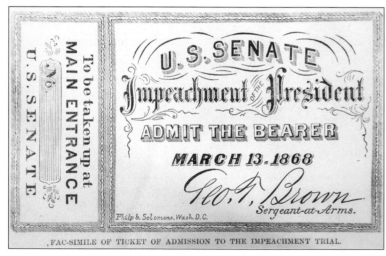

President Johnson's impeachment trial, held in the chambers of the U.S. Senate, was the media event of its time. Limited seating meant that those who wished to have a glimpse of this historic event would have to present a ticket, such as the one shown here, to be admitted to watch the proceedings.

Harper's Weekly printed this editorial woodcut in 1875 to press the view that soldiers needed to remain in the South to protect the rights of the freed slaves from their former masters. Otherwise, African Americans would be denied their rights.

DECEMBER 5
Congress convenes after its mid-year recess. For the first time in a decade, representatives from every state are eligible to be seated.

1871
APRIL 20
Congress passes the Third Enforcement Act, also known as the Ku Klux Klan Act, authorizing the use of military force against all such armed groups.

MAY 8
The *Alabama* Claims Commission negotiates the Treaty of Washington between the United States and Great Britain and agrees to send the matter to an international tribunal.

The Transcontinental Railroad

The dream of a railroad linking the east and west coasts of the growing nation was hampered by the sectional difficulties that preceded the Civil War. Although both Northern and Southern politicians supported the idea, none could agree on a route. In 1854, the Senate ratified a treaty authorizing the expenditure of $10 million to buy land along the border with Mexico to ease the construction of a southern route from Texas to California.

In May 1862, President Lincoln signed into law the Pacific Railroad Act, which chartered the Union Pacific Railroad and specified a route that would link Council Bluffs, Iowa, with Sacramento, California. The plan called for the Union Pacific to begin construction in Nebraska while the competing Central Pacific Railroad would start in California. This act provided government loans for both railroads to help both companies raise the necessary capital, the money variable depending on the terrain. In 1864, Congress doubled the land grants along the right of way for both companies and authorized each to sell its own bonds in amounts equal to the government bonds already being sold. This influx of capital enabled both companies to raise money and keep building.

The Central Pacific's work crews had to overcome the western mountain ranges as well as bitter winter weather. Union Pacific crews had to contend with American Indians. Still, both ends made progress across the 1,775-mile gap. On May 10, 1869, a golden spike was driven at Promontory Point, Utah, signaling the link between East and West was complete.

The Union Pacific railroad was built west from Council Bluffs, Iowa, and the Central Pacific was built east from Sacramento, California. On May 10, 1869, the two railroads met with great ceremony at Promontory Point, Utah, linking the West Coast with the Middle West and East Coast.

As one of the House members who led the impeachment attack on Johnson, Thaddeus Stevens is seen here delivering a speech during the trial. Stevens's health had been failing, and angry over Johnson's acquittal, Stevens never recovered, dying the next November.

Opened with federal support in 1867, Howard University was named after its chief founder, General Oliver O. Howard. The general wanted to educate the free black population of the nation's capital, which swelled after the war as thousands of freed slaves flocked to Washington, seeking a better life.

This painting depicts the American purchase of Alaska from the Russians. Secretary of State William Seward, the man behind the deal, is seated next to the globe. The purchase was controversial, as many could not see the value of extending the country so far to the north.

OCTOBER
In response to violence by the Ku Klux Klan, President Grant suspends the writ of habeas corpus in nine counties in South Carolina. He later follows this action with federal troops for enforcement.

1872
MAY 22
The General Amnesty Act paves the way for many former Confederate leaders to resume their political careers, restoring complete civil rights to all but about 500 Southerners.

JUNE 5
Grant is nominated for a second presidential term by the Republican convention in Philadelphia.

Secretary of State Seward's 1867 purchase of the Alaska territory from Russia for $7.2 million was widely castigated at the time as an unnecessary waste of government funds. "Seward's Folly" and "Johnson's Polar Bear Garden" were only two of the derogatory terms used to ridicule the purchase.

Major General John M. Schofield served as President Johnson's secretary of war after Edwin Stanton but resigned soon after Grant's inauguration. He was superintendent at West Point from 1876 to 1881, president of the review board that exonerated Fitz John Porter, and general in chief of the Army from 1888 until his retirement in 1895.

Horatio Seymour, elected governor of New York in 1852 and again in 1862, supported the war effort despite disagreement with Lincoln over emancipation. In 1868, he accepted the Democratic nomination for president but lost to Grant by about 310,000 votes.

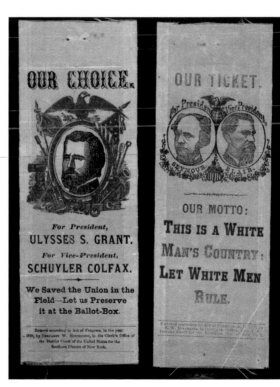

The Democratic campaign ribbon on the right was used by hardcore Southerners to show their feelings in the 1868 presidential election. Former New York governor Horatio Seymour teamed with Francis P. Blair to attack the Republican method of Reconstruction. The ribbon to the left represents Grant and vice-presidential candidate Schuyler Colfax, who won 26 of 34 states.

AUGUST 25
An international tribunal resolves differences between the United States and Britain in settling the *Alabama* Claims.

NOVEMBER 5
Grant is reelected president, defeating Democrat Horace Greeley.

NOVEMBER 28
Troops leave Fort Klamath in Oregon near the California border to move the Modoc people away from new U.S. settlements along the Lost River. Fighting breaks out, initiating the Modoc War.

This anti-Republican broadside suggests how racism was exploited for political purposes during Reconstruction. The subtitle of the sheet, "The Bottom Rail on Top," is a reference to a black Union soldier's description of his reality upon confronting his former master.

Once freed, former slaves could now organize political meetings to discuss candidates and issues. Being able to meet freely without restrictions set by their masters was a new idea. As seen in this picture of the South Carolina legislature, sometimes these candidates won elections. Danger remained, however, from the Ku Klux Klan and other radical groups.

The Ku Klux Klan

Founded at Pulaski, Tennessee, by former Confederate soldiers in 1866, the Ku Klux Klan aimed to intimidate newly freed African American slaves, particularly those active in politics. Former Confederate general Nathan Bedford Forrest was reportedly the Grand Wizard of what was sometimes called the "Invisible Empire," which perhaps had more than half a million members. The group's name is a corruption of its original title, the Greek word *kyklos*, which means circle.

The Klan's activities included cross burnings, wearing white-hooded robes that allowed members to be anonymous, and midnight rides with torches, all of which proved very effective at frightening their victims. Those not so easily scared were oftentimes kidnapped and beaten or tarred and feathered. They might see their houses burned to the ground or male family members lynched.

Forrest, pressured by Klan members who opposed such violence, ordered the organization disbanded in 1869, but many local groups continued to operate. In 1870 and 1871, the government passed two Ku Klux Klan Acts, which made it a crime to attempt by "force, intimidation, or threat" to undermine the right to vote of any American citizen. The 1871 act authorized the use of federal troops against those who continued these tactics of violence.

An unidentified artist presented this view of members of the Ku Klux Klan debating the murder of a white supporter of African Americans. Indeed, the Klan and other such groups spread terror whenever and upon whomever they deemed a threat to their viewpoint.

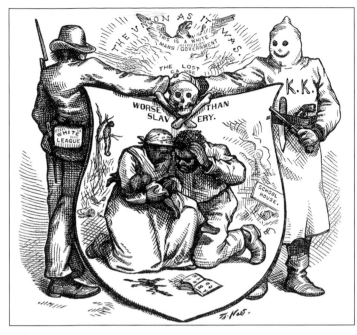

Former Confederate General James Longstreet was a controversial figure after the war. He became a member of the Republican party and dared to criticize the late General Lee's strategy at Gettysburg. As a result, Longstreet became a scapegoat for the Confederate defeat there. The general held a number of federal jobs, including that of postmaster, minister to Turkey, New Orleans surveyor of customs, and Louisiana adjutant general.

Thomas Nast entitled this 1874 political cartoon "Worse Than Slavery." A suffering African American family is beset by the Ku Klux Klan and the White League, who shake hands over a skull. A burned school and a lynched man show the devastating acts such hate groups inflicted on the newly freed slaves. Nast derisively called "The Union as It Was" a "white man's government."

John Roy Lynch was a former slave who entered the Mississippi legislature in 1869, where he ultimately rose to speaker of the house. He served in the U.S. Congress from 1873 to 1877. After losing a congressional race in 1880, he successfully contested the election and took his seat in the House in 1882. Active in national Republican politics, he had a number of jobs behind the scenes. He studied law and was admitted to the Mississippi bar in 1896.

African American citizens were very much underrepresented in postwar Southern state legislatures, regardless of Southern furor over the political role of the freed slaves. Only in South Carolina's lower house, shown here in a derogatory cartoon, did blacks hold a majority for a few years. Many of these new politicians tried hard to advance the cause of their race in spite of the hatred and violence displayed by defeated whites who often spitefully misrepresented the political contributions of African Americans.

1873
APRIL 11
Modoc leader Captain Jack ambushes and kills General Edward R. S. Canby and one other during a meeting to negotiate peace.

APRIL 13
Members of the White League surround a courthouse in Colfax, Louisiana, and kill African American militia and officeholders. Estimates of the dead run from 60 to well over 100. "The Colfax Massacre," as this event came to be called, effectively ends active African American participation in Louisiana government.

The first African American in the Senate, Hiram Revels served only for one year. He entered Jefferson Davis's old seat in the Senate on February 25, 1870, after his state of Mississippi had reentered the Union. Before he could be seated, he had to overcome a challenge to his credentials, but after Senator Charles Sumner spoke on his behalf, the Senate overwhelmingly voted to allow him in.

Louisiana had sugarcane as its specialty crop. As in other areas of the ruined South, freed slaves played an important role in maintaining the crop's viability in the postwar economy. This 1875 scene shows African American workers harvesting the crop.

After Senator Charles Sumner was beaten senseless by Preston Brooks in 1856, he became an implacable foe of the South and called for retribution after the war. He clamored for equal voting rights and voted to impeach President Johnson.

This painting illustrates the kind of ramshackle dwellings available to both African Americans and whites in the postwar South. A freed black family makes do with what they can find, as chickens peck near the cooking pot, which itself is not too far from piles of laundry.

JUNE 1
The Modoc War comes to an end when Captain Jack surrenders at Willow Creek in California.

SEPTEMBER 18
Jay Cooke's financial firm declares bankruptcy, setting off the Panic of 1873.

1874
AUGUST 29–30
Several Republican officeholders in Coushatta, Louisiana, are arrested by white vigilantes and sent out of state. Before they can cross state lines, they are murdered.

The *Alabama* Claims

During the Civil War, the Confederate commerce raider CSS *Alabama* captured 66 Union merchant vessels, costing their owners millions of dollars in damages. Other Confederate raiders caused additional damage to American ships. Since many of these raiders had been built and purchased in Britain, the American minister to Britain, Charles Francis Adams, demanded that the British government pay for the damage these vessels caused. Britain, not surprisingly, refused.

When the English government changed in 1866, Secretary of State William Seward renewed American demands. Negotiators reached an agreement in 1868, but Charles Sumner, chairman of the Senate Foreign Relations Committee, felt the monetary settlement was not large enough. The agreement was

This illustration is based on a Mathew Brady photograph of the five members appointed to the 1871 commission that settled the Alabama *Claims in favor of the United States. Although a number of issues involving trade and fishing were agreed upon, the* Alabama *Claims themselves were turned over to an international commission.*

The British contingent of the Alabama *Claims Commission was made up of prominent political figures from Britain and Canada, shown here with the British minister to Washington, who served as secretary to the delegation. Issues of navigation and trade, particularly those concerning waters shared by the United States and Canada, were negotiated at length. Both sides felt the agreement was fair.*

thus never ratified by the Senate, and the conflict between the two countries remained unresolved.

After Ulysses Grant became president, negotiations again reopened regarding the *Alabama* Claims. Hamilton Fish, Grant's secretary of state, reached an agreement with British diplomat John Ross in 1871 to submit the problem to a ten-member commission made up of members from both countries. The British sent a delegation to Washington to handle the negotiations. In addition to clarifying American fishing rights off Canadian waters and navigation rights on the St. Lawrence River, the Treaty of Washington, ratified by the Senate in 1871, sent the *Alabama* Claims to an international commission composed of representatives from the United States, England, Switzerland, Brazil, and Italy. In 1873, the commission awarded the United States $15.5 million in compensation for the damage caused by these commerce raiders.

President Grant, influenced by moneyed interests in the United States, placed his prestige behind the U.S. acquisition of Santo Domingo (present-day Dominican Republic), an idea that was also promoted by the president of Santo Domingo, Buenaventura Baez, shown here. Grant submitted an annexation treaty to the Senate, which rejected the document on three separate occasions in 1870. Attorney General E. R. Hoar was forced to resign when he protested the treaty.

As a result of violence by the Ku Klux Klan and similar organizations across the South, President Grant uses the Ku Klux Klan Act to impose martial law in South Carolina in 1871. The President was leery of reintroducing military troops into the South, concerned of inflaming passions even further, so he limited his action to nine counties in this state, using military law enforcement and extensive trials of lawbreakers to set an example to the rest of the region.

This anti-Grant cartoon, which appeared late in the President's second term, derides the idea that Grant, burdened by the many scandals and corruption of his presidency, would even think of running for a third term. Grant entertained the idea of another term, but it quickly became clear that this was not a viable option.

Horace Greeley, founder of the influential New York Tribune, was drafted by liberal Republicans as well as Democrats to run against Grant in 1872. The eccentric Greeley, long an active participant in the civil life of the nation, went down in an overwhelming defeat. Greeley's wife had died only a few days earlier. The combination of these events sapped Greeley's strength. He died on November 29, only a few weeks after the election.

SEPTEMBER 14
The White League attacks the Louisiana state house in New Orleans to depose the Republican governor. In what turns into a public relations disaster, the Presi-dent sends federal troops to the city to retake the state house and reinstate the governor.

1875
JANUARY 26
Andrew Johnson is again elected to the Senate by the state of Tennessee.

Financier Jay Cooke, whose expertise had helped finance the Civil War for the North, ran into serious monetary problems in the early 1870s. His attempts to help sell securities for the Northern Pacific Railroad were not well received, and in August 1873 several depositors withdrew their funds from his bank. On September 18, Cooke closed the doors of his firm, precipitating a national financial crisis that was called "The Panic of 1873."

Unbeknownst to most Americans, a large number—perhaps 25 percent—of cowboys on the postwar western frontier were African American. This 1870s-era image shows one such cowpoke posed in traditional western wear for the camera.

The 1872 Louisiana elections resulted in two competing governors claiming legitimacy. A federal court declared the Republican candidate the winner, but white Democrats refused to accept the ruling. They maintained a parallel government, using the White League as enforcement. One notorious incident of such enforcement was the Colfax Massacre, in which the White League surrounded the Colfax courthouse and killed black militia and officeholders inside. Estimates of African American deaths range from 60 to over 100, with many killed as they tried to surrender. Only three white lives were lost.

MARCH 1
Only days from the end of its term, Congress enacts the Civil Rights Act of 1875, legislating against racial discrimination in public areas such as restaurants, hotels, and public transportation.

MARCH 29
The Supreme Court rules on *Minor* v. *Happersett*. The right to vote is "not necessarily one of the privileges... of citizenship," the Court explains, so state law may determine which citizens can vote and which cannot. The 15th Amendment forbids using race to deny citizens the vote, so this ruling is directed primarily to women.

The Presidential Election of 1876

This election is one of the most controversial in American history. The two candidates were Republican Rutherford B. Hayes, a former Ohio governor and Civil War general, and Democrat Samuel J. Tilden, the governor of New York. When the votes were originally counted, Tilden had a popular vote margin of more than 250,000 over Hayes. However, the Democrat had only 184 electoral votes, one shy of the 185 needed to win the presidency. Hayes had 165 electoral votes. There were 20 votes in dispute—19 from South Carolina, Florida, and Louisiana, and one from Oregon. The conflict over votes from the three Southern states was between two different sets of returns.

When neither political party would give in to end this stalemate, Congress established a special commission to investigate and render a verdict on the disputed electoral votes. This commission was to consist of five senators, five House members, and five Supreme Court justices. In an attempt at balance, seven members were Democrats, seven were Republican, and one—Justice David Davis of Illinois—was an independent. After his appointment, however, Justice Davis was elected to the Senate by the Illinois legislature. To replace him, the remaining four justices on the commission chose Justice Joseph P. Bradley, a Republican.

The commission dutifully met on March 2, 1877, two days before the new president, whoever he would be, was scheduled to be sworn in. The commission examined each and every one of the 20 disputed votes. To the surprise of no one, the commission voted 8-7 along party lines on each of them. Hayes was awarded all 20, giving him the 185 electoral votes he needed to win the presidency.

Even before the commission met, political leaders from both parties had worked out a compromise behind closed doors. In return for securing the votes needed to elect Hayes, Republicans promised Southern leaders who favored Tilden that Hayes would withdraw the last federal troops from South Carolina and Louisiana. The Republicans also promised to spend more money on Southern railroads and internal improvements.

Because March 4, the official day set aside for presidential inaugurations, fell on a Sunday, Hayes was inaugurated as President privately on March 3 and publicly on March 5. In April, he issued orders for the remaining troops in Louisiana and South Carolina to be removed. As a result, African Americans in those states were ignored and left to fend for themselves. Southern white supremacists now had a free hand in crafting all sorts of Jim Crow laws that interfered with freedoms guaranteed to all Americans. On the other hand, Hayes did not follow through with the promise of providing more financing for railroads and internal improvements in the South.

Republican presidential candidate Rutherford B. Hayes shares a campaign poster with his running mate, Representative William A. Wheeler of New York.

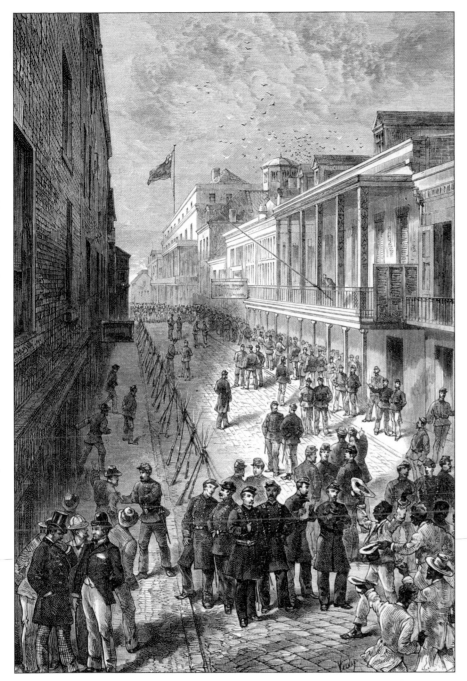

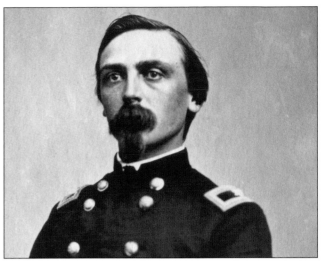

Union General Adelbert Ames was appointed provisional governor of Mississippi in 1868 and elected to the U.S. Senate two years later. In 1874, he was elected governor of Mississippi. In that office, he was unable to stem the violence spreading across the state. Ames requested military help to restore order, but President Grant, after his experience in New Orleans, refused. Ames, avoiding impeachment from the restored Democratic legislature, resigned his office in 1876 and returned north. He died in 1933 at age 97, the last surviving general officer of the Civil War.

In September 1874, when the White League took control of the statehouse in New Orleans, President Grant ordered 5,000 troops to the city to disperse the rioters and bring order. Although federal control was reestablished, the President and Republicans were repudiated in the November elections, which returned Democratic control to the House of Representatives for the first time in 28 years.

In spite of increasing mechanization of American agriculture after the Civil War, many tasks still had to be done by hand. This scene, taken in the 1890s, shows black peanut pickers at work in Virginia. For many of the former slaves and their descendants, conditions were not much better than they had been in 1861.

MAY 1
The Whiskey Ring, a political fund-raising conspiracy, is uncovered. The plot reaches into the White House, as Grant's private secretary, former General Oliver E. Babcock, is implicated.

JULY 31
Andrew Johnson dies at the age of 76 in Tennessee.

1876
JUNE 25
Colonel George Armstrong Custer and his troops at the Little Bighorn River make their last stand against Sioux warriors.

Indian Wars

One result of the Civil War was an increased exodus of Americans to the western frontier in search of new land. The 1862 passage of the Homestead Act, coupled with the increased building of railroads, induced thousands to look west. Many of these settlers were veterans enticed by the land bounties of the 1862 law.

Increased westward expansion also meant increased friction with American Indians who lived in the West. Between 1865 and 1891, the U.S. Army conducted 13 major campaigns against native peoples and fought 1,067 separate engagements. The army suffered 948 killed and 1,058 wounded. Although American Indian losses are more difficult to tally accurately, one compendium lists 4,371 dead, 1,279 wounded, and 10,318 captured.

Most of the army commanders were seasoned veterans of the Civil War. Most had earned generalships in the volunteer service, but afterward, with the reduction in size of the Army, had been rele-

This 1889 lithograph shows a fanciful view of Custer's Last Stand at the Little Bighorn on June 25, 1876. For one thing, the terrain depicted here is wrong. Also, after surrounding the outgunned cavalry, the American Indians actually attacked dismounted.

Harper's Weekly *included this woodcut of the event that climaxed the Modoc War of 1872 and 1873. General Edward R. S. Canby met with Modoc leader Captain Jack and some of his followers to negotiate an end to the fighting in the area near the border between California and Oregon. The general had the Modoc surrounded in a maze of old lava beds, and he wished to avoid more bloodshed by ending the war. But Captain Jack succeeded in his plan to kill the general during the April 11, 1873, parley.*

gated to lesser ranks. One such example is George Armstrong Custer, who rose to major general of volunteers during the war but was given a commission of lieutenant colonel of the new 7th U.S. Cavalry afterward. Some officers, such as General John Pope, were sympathetic to the plight of American Indians, while others, notably General Philip Sheridan, looked down upon them as pests to be erased.

Campaigns ranged up and down the Great Plains, into the Rocky Mountains, and to the Pacific Coast. The Sioux, the most powerful nation of the northern plains, fought the army to a standstill in 1866 and 1867, inflicting a defeat at the so-called "Fetterman Massacre" in 1866. In the end, however, they agreed to live on a reservation. Ten years later, white trespassers discovered gold on Sioux land in the Dakota Black Hills and started a gold rush the Army was unable to stop. The result was another war, this one lasting until 1881. On June 25, 1876, Custer and five companies of his 7th U.S. Cavalry ran into overwhelming numbers of Sioux on the Little Bighorn River and were wiped out, the worst defeat suffered by the Army during the Indian wars. Although American Indians won the battle, they lost the larger war and were forced back onto their reservation.

On the southern plains, the Cheyenne, Arapaho, Kiowa, and Comanche nations engaged cavalry regiments in several entanglements, most notably at Beecher's Island in September 1868, and after Custer attacked peaceful Indians at the Washita on November 27, 1868. Even farther south, the famed Comanche chief Cochise was finally cornered, surrendering to George Crook's troops in 1873.

A minor conflict arose when the Army evicted the Modoc from their home near the border of California and Oregon in 1872 and 1873. Other notable wars developed along the Mexican border with Lipan Apache and Kickapoo that lasted from 1876 until Geronimo surrendered in 1886. In 1877 the Nez Perce left their reservation because of encroachment by whites and tried to flee to Canada. After a 1,700-mile trek, they were halted and forced to surrender.

Life did not become easier for African Americans after the Civil War. Although there was no longer a master, former slaves had to rely on their own work and depend on a landlord to supply the means to work their land—sometimes the landlords even provided the land itself. Husband and wife both worked in the fields to pick enough cotton to survive.

Cotton remained a major crop throughout the South, and growing and picking cotton in the field was not changed much by the war. Many former slaves ended up working for the same master as they always had. Although these workers were now on salary and were responsible for their own food and shelter, life in the cotton fields themselves remained much the same as it always had.

Rutherford B. Hayes was the Republican candidate for president in 1876. His role in the disputed election is still hotly debated. Hayes withdrew federal troops from the South as promised and thus lost much support in his party. He promoted civil service reform during his single term as president. Hayes retired to his estate in 1881 and devoted himself to prison reform, aid to freed slaves, and public education. He died in 1893.

NOVEMBER 7
Disputed results in the presidential election leave no clear winner between Rutherford B. Hayes and Samuel J. Tilden. This leads to the establishment of a special commission of 15 to examine the election results and determine a winner.

1877
MARCH 2
The special commission declares Rutherford B. Hayes president of the United States.

As part of his deal to secure the election in 1876, Rutherford B. Hayes promised to take federal troops out of the South. Less than two months after his inauguration, he had done just that. This cartoon portrays Hayes returning the South, a strayed child, to its Democratic family.

Samuel J. Tilden, the former New York governor who earned a record as a tireless reformer, won the most votes in the 1876 presidential election but lost the electoral college to Rutherford B. Hayes. Embittered by this defeat, Tilden refused the Democratic nomination in 1880 and 1884. After his death in 1886, Tilden left most of his fortune for the establishment of what would become the New York Public Library.

Ulysses S. Grant survived two rocky terms as president, tainted by scandals. After leaving the oval office, Grant and his wife Julia toured Europe and Asia before returning home. Left nearly bankrupt by bad investments, the former president developed throat cancer and set about writing his memoirs, which he finished two days before his death on July 23, 1885. Entitled Personal Memoirs, it became an instant best seller, wiping out his debts and leaving Julia with ample monetary means to live.

MARCH 3
Rutherford B. Hayes is sworn in as the 19th President of the United States.

APRIL 10
Union troops are withdrawn from South Carolina.

APRIL 24
Union troops are withdrawn from Louisiana. They are the last occupation troops to leave the former Confederacy.

The War's
ENDURING LEGACY

THE CIVIL WAR CASTS A
SHADOW OVER U.S. HISTORY

The Civil War, which cost over 600,000 American lives, lasted four years. But its reverberations have been felt ever since throughout American and even world history. Every state in the South witnessed military or naval invasions and scores of skirmishes, actions, engagements, and battles. As a result, the region was wrecked. Economic and social dislocation was widespread. When Southern armies surrendered and were

The Mall in Washington filled with 250,000 people gathering around the reflecting pool separating the Washington Monument from the Lincoln Memorial for the March on Washington for Jobs and Freedom on August 28, 1963. This interracial group came from around the country in this year of the 100th anniversary of the Emancipation Proclamation to demonstrate for civil rights. Many speakers, most prominently Martin Luther King Jr., addressed the crowd from the steps of the Lincoln Memorial.

disbanded, they received no parades or welcome-home speeches. Regiments and batteries ceased to exist wherever they surrendered, and the troops had to find their own ways home. Returning Confederate veterans came home to find desolation. Many could not even find their families, who had fled or relocated ahead of advancing Union armies.

The South's Economic and Political Life Destroyed

Southern economic life was shattered beyond repair. The war freed the slaves and thus destroyed the South's economic underpinnings. The newly freed blacks had to compete with poor whites for land and labor; former plantation owners found their way of life gone forever. Railroads were largely destroyed during the war. What rolling stock that remained was generally in poor condition, its owners unable to find replacement parts as war raged. Telegraph lines had disappeared, and the majority of river traffic had been either sunk or captured.

Most Southern cities had suffered severely. The core of Richmond burned in 1865, as did Charleston and Columbia in South Carolina. Atlanta had been destroyed in 1864. Other cities were overcrowded with refugees from rural hinterlands desperately seeking food and shelter.

The remains of flour mills in Richmond, Virginia, following the Civil War provide a glimpse of the devastation visited upon Southern industry. Any industrial base had to be recreated virtually from the ground up before it could make any contributions to the economic improvement of the region.

1877
George E. Lemon publishes *The National Tribune*, which will grow into the most influential Union veterans' newspaper, eventually becoming *Stars and Stripes*, an official American military paper.

1879
MARCH 19
A court of inquiry issues its report exonerating General Fitz John Porter for his actions at the Second Battle of Bull Run.

1880–1901
The U.S. War Department publishes the 128-volume *War of the Rebellion: A Compilation of the Official Records of the Union and Confederate Armies*.

In addition to the ruin of manufacturing facilities, transportation networks in the South were destroyed, as well. Every aspect of economic life was in need of reconstruction.

Rutherford B. Hayes served in the 23rd Ohio infantry in Maryland, West Virginia, and Virginia, ending the war as a brigadier general of volunteers. He served in Congress and as Ohio governor before being awarded the presidency in the disputed election of 1876. During his term as president, Hayes worked hard to reform the civil service. He remained in office for only one term and then retired to Ohio, where he worked for prison reform, public education, and aid to freed slaves.

The South's political influence in Washington was also destroyed for the remainder of the century. Current or former slaveholders had been president of the United States for 53 of the nation's 72 years prior to 1861. Of the 36 Congresses until that time, 23 had been led by Southern speakers of the House. The Supreme Court counted 20 of its 35 justices as Southern. The war changed that power structure. For 50 years after 1865, only two speakers of the House and three presidents pro tem of the Senate came from a formerly Confederate state. Just 7 of 28 appointed Supreme Court justices represented such states. After Andrew Johnson left office in 1869, all presidents of the United States were Northerners until the 1912 election of Woodrow Wilson, who had been born in Virginia.

OUR CONSTITUTION IS COLOR-BLIND.

Supreme Court Justice John Marshall Harlan

Industrialization and Westward Expansion

In the early days of the republic, two divergent views were held of America's future. Thomas Jefferson took the agricultural view, looking toward small farmers tilling their fields with a minimum of interference from cities, factories, and the federal government. Alexander Hamilton, on the other hand, believed that strong manufacturing interests and a strong central government would enable the United States to grow into a

1881
Tennessee enacts Jim Crow laws establishing separate rail cars for African American riders and segregation in other public places. Other states follow its lead over the next few years.

MARCH 5
Robert Todd Lincoln is appointed secretary of war under James A. Garfield. He continues in that position during Chester A. Arthur's administration.

MAY 21
Clara Barton founds the American Association of the Red Cross.

JULY 4
Booker T. Washington founds Tuskegee Institute.

strong international power. To some, the Civil War settled the direction that America would take. The Northern military victory in 1865 insured that Jefferson's ideal of an agrarian nation gave way to Hamilton's vision of the rise of an industrial power. And indeed, wartime developments in the North laid the foundation for this change, as the Republican-dominated Congress passed the laws that had been defeated by Southern interests prior to 1861. The Legal Tender Act, the Pacific Railway Act, the Homestead Act, the Morrill Act, and other such progressive legislation paved the way for the nation's quick westward expansion after 1865.

The war also created an atmosphere of business and commerce that showed how much money could be made by industrious individuals with drive and ambition. The tycoons who rose after the Civil War generally got their start during the conflict. John D. Rockefeller, J. P. Morgan, Andrew Carnegie, and Cornelius Vanderbilt, among others, rose to prominence on the crest of the forces unleashed by the conflict. But the war did not initiate the rise of industrial America. No great inventions came out of the war effort. To be sure, suppliers developed better canning and packaging methods for the armed forces, steam warships took the place of sail-powered vessels, repeating rifles and cannon showed their killing power, and ironclad vessels began to

In this 1882 editorial cartoon, the New South is seen to be adopting industry as the future and leaving behind "King Cotton," the most lucrative crop in the Old South before 1861. Slavery and its one-crop dominance became a thing of the past—diversity and industry aided the growth of the New South.

The Gilded Age that followed Reconstruction brought great riches to an entrepreneurial few in industry or finance. John D. Rockefeller (left) established Standard Oil and quickly gained control of the vast majority of the U.S. oil refinery business. J. P. Morgan (center) was born to wealth but became the primary industrial financier in the nation. Andrew Carnegie (right), an immigrant from Scotland, rose to become a steel magnate and, at one point, the richest man in the world. During the Civil War, both Rockefeller and Carnegie hired substitutes to fight for them.

1882
A court of inquiry clears most of the charges against General Gouverneur K. Warren for his conduct at the Battle of Five Forks.

1883
OCTOBER 15
The Supreme Court rules that the Civil Rights Act of 1875 is unconstitutional.

OCTOBER 22
The initial version of French artist Paul Philippoteaux's Gettysburg cyclorama opens to the public in Chicago.

replace wooden ships. But the Civil War did not produce inventions of the scale and importance of those produced by the two world wars.

Other factors, such as the creation of larger-scale businesses, a decline in business ethics, and the evolution of social Darwinism, contributed to the postwar economic boom. In effect, the Civil War was a watershed moment in American economic and political history because it destroyed Southern dominance in the federal government and allowed more progressive legislation to be passed, both of which paved the way for the future of America.

The Rise and Fall of Jim Crow

But that future of America was still intimately connected to the events of 1861–65. Perhaps the most important legacy of the war was its unfinished social revolution. Lincoln began it with the Emancipation Proclamation, and Congress moved it along with the 13th, 14th, and 15th Amendments. In total, these developments gave equality and citizenship to all Americans and specifically ensured equal voting rights for African American men. (Women, regardless of race, would not gain the vote for another 50 years—when the 19th Amendment was adopted.)

The disputed election of 1876 proved a virtual death knell for the rights of newly freed African American slaves. Once President Rutherford B. Hayes withdrew the last troops from the South, the war began to fade more and more from the consciousness of everyone but the veterans. The political corruption of the Ulysses S. Grant administration, coupled with widespread economic problems that culminated in the Panic of 1873, resulted in most Northerners turning their backs on the South's African American population.

The chef "Rastus" has been the advertising icon for Cream of Wheat for over 100 years. Although the product used a generic black chef in its ads as early as 1893, the current incarnation of the character is based on a waiter in Chicago who was given five dollars to pose for the company. This portrayal of Rastus has changed little since his first appearance in the 1920s.

The Grand Army of the Republic

"Memorial Day should be observed by every member of the Grand Army of the Republic and his family, not as a holiday but as a holy day. A few days prior to May 30th every school house in the State should be visited by some comrade, or comrades, who would talk to the children in a way which they could understand about the rebellion, the lessons learned from that awful conflict, and the meaning of Memorial Day.

"Comrades should in every way possible discourage the making of this day as a holiday by the citizens at large, and should upon this one day at least remain away from any game of sport, horse racing, or game of chance, thereby by their actions making an object lesson for all mankind."

*Pennsylvania Department **Commander Edwin Walton**, 1904*

1885
JULY 23
Ulysses S. Grant, 63, dies at Mount McGregor, New York.

DECEMBER
The first volume of Grant's *Personal Memoirs* is published by Mark Twain.

1887
FEBRUARY 26
The cyclorama depicting the Battle of Atlanta debuts in Detroit, Michigan.

Homer A. Plessy, a person of mixed race, boarded a train in New Orleans in 1892 and sat in a car designated for whites only. He was arrested. Plessy's lawyer argued that the law calling for the separation of races in railroad cars was unconstitutional, but lost in a trial presided over by District Criminal Court Judge John H. Ferguson. The case eventually went to the Supreme Court, which ruled in May 1896 that laws providing for separate but equal treatment and facilities were reasonable uses of state power. Such laws remained on the books until the legal concept was overturned in 1954.

After Reconstruction, white Southerners retook their state governments and imposed all sorts of Jim Crow laws to keep African Americans at the bottom of the social pyramid. States enacted poll taxes designed to keep African Americans from voting. Literacy tests and residency requirements also inhibited them from voting. The 1896 Supreme Court *Plessy* v. *Ferguson* decision legitimized the "separate but equal" doctrine and allowed whites and blacks in the South to live as separate races. Intermarriage was prohibited. Any blacks rocking the boat were terrorized and often lynched. These new developments were of little concern to the Northern victors.

Such remained the status quo in the South until 1954. In that year, the Supreme Court, in *Brown* v. *Board of Education*, overturned *Plessy* v. *Ferguson* and decreed that separate but equal public schools were unconstitutional. Advocates of civil rights used the *Brown* case to begin overturning the entire "separate but equal" doctrine in all facets of life. African Americans used the law to demand the equal rights they were denied. Sympathetic whites from around the country descended upon the South to help African Americans attain their rights. Feelings on both sides ran high. Violence erupted in cities. Some of the civil rights workers, particularly those encouraging voter registration, were roughed up; a few were slain. But the movement struggled forward, step by step, reclaiming the rights that had been granted during Reconstruction.

The rebirth of civil rights after a hundred years saw an accompanying rise in Southern nationalism. Suddenly, it seemed, the old social order, even the Southern way of life, was under attack. Georgia changed its state flag to include the old Confederate battle flag. That battle flag itself became more and more popular and was taken by civil rights supporters as a symbol of opposition. The old Lost Cause myth was revitalized. Slavery, the dominant underlying cause of the war, was pushed to the side by those

JUNE 7–15
The War Department, backed by President Grover Cleveland, proposes the return of captured Confederate flags. This unleashes a storm of criticism from Northern veterans, and the idea is dropped.

1889
The United Confederate Veterans is founded.

JULY 1
President Benjamin Harrison appoints Frederick Douglass minister resident and consul general to Haiti. He will serve in this post for two years.

Jim Crow was a constant presence in the United States during the first half of the 20th century. African Americans were forced to use separate facilities throughout the South when traveling, eating, going shopping, or even just going to the bathroom. Although signs such as this were commonplace in the South, segregation was also present, if less blatant, in the North.

In March 1965, civil rights leaders led a Freedom March intended to go from Selma to Montgomery in Alabama. On March 7, Alabama State Police and local law officers charged into the nonviolent march at the Edmund Pettus Bridge. The resulting violence captured national attention and increased pressure on Southerners.

espousing the new Southern point of view. White Southerners claimed instead that each side fought nobly for its cause, but when the war was over, the reunified United States was stronger than it had been before. Black participation in the war was slighted in this process of revision. Even during the 1960s centennial of the war, the new Southern viewpoint remained dominant. Since the late 1970s, however, renewed scholarly interest in the war has included more and more work on how the 180,000 black soldiers contributed to the Union victory.

The relative importance of African Americans in the Civil War is indeed a part of how the war has been shaped by collective memory since the 1860s. Northern and Southern apologists each had their own viewpoints to defend. The interpretation of the reasons for civil war have changed with each generation. To some, it was an unnecessary war. To others, the conflict was unavoidable. The eminent historian Charles Beard saw it as a second American revolution. Some historians argued that extremists, particularly the abolitionists, caused the war.

1890
JUNE 27
President Harrison signs the Dependent Pension Act into law.

AUGUST 19
The Chickamauga and Chattanooga National Military Park is established.

AUGUST 30
The privately owned Antietam battlefield is transferred to the federal government. Antietam National Battlefield is established by an act of Congress.

The Flood of Literature

Because of its importance in American history, the Civil War has been the subject of tens of thousands of books, articles, works of fiction, and associated literature. Historians have divided the literature of the conflict into several major groupings to explain how the war has been viewed since the guns fell silent in 1865.

The War of the Rebellion school was dominated by Northern writers who blamed a handful of Southern extremists for the war. Benson J. Lossing, John W. Draper, and others expounded this theory. At the same time, pro-Southern authors such as Edward A. Pollard claimed that economic differences caused the war and that secession was necessary because of the aggressive, commercial North. Those historians discontented with both sides formed a Needless War theory that claimed both sides were belligerent over artificial issues devised by extremists.

From the 1880s through World War I, the Irrepressible Conflict school of thought formed. Both Northern and Southern historians blamed slavery, which they called wrong, but regarded the results of the war as good for the nation. No real blame could be found by historians of this genre. Given the climate of opinion in the years before the war, they believed, the conflict was inevitable. James Ford Rhodes, Frederick Jackson Turner, John Bach McMaster, Edward Channing, and Woodrow Wilson all espoused this school of thought.

The noted Charles A. Beard called the Civil War the Second American Revolution. Mainly a social conflict, as well as fight between two economies, it unified the nation. Marxist historians agreed with Beard's interpretation, faulting Lincoln for not making the war a class struggle.

Beginning in the 1930s, Southern historians began the New Vindication of the South. Their region, they claimed, was misunderstood by outsiders. It really wasn't a bad place, they argued, and slavery did have its good aspects. In their view, the North was responsible for the war, which was generally deemed unnecessary. These historians included Ulrich B. Phillips, E. Merton Coulter, Charles W. Ramsdell, and Frank Lawrence Owsley.

At the same time, largely in response to World War I, another group of revisionists looked at the Civil War and called it the Repressible Conflict. Proponents of this view believed war should have been avoided, but people of the time ignored compromises, listened to abolitionists, and were too extreme in their viewpoints. Both sides, they claimed, were wrong. James G. Randall wrote an article referring to them as "The Blundering Generation." Writers in this school of thought included Avery O. Craven, Roy Nichols, Kenneth Stampp, Albert J. Beveridge, and Philip Auchampaugh.

It is more difficult to define scholarship on the Civil War since World War II and the Cold War. One modern school has emerged since the beginning of the Civil Rights movement and has come to defend the South to the last extremity, lashing out against each and every person who attacks the proper Southern memory of the war. This group has a plethora of websites, issues a wide range of literature, and has used the old Confederate battle flag as a symbol of the South.

In brief, given the ever-increasing number of sources available to modern historians, writing about the war has become more detailed, wide ranging, and critical. Since the 1960s, the military history of the war has become very popular—visit any bookstore to see the plethora of titles available on just about any battle or leader. Gettysburg alone has been the subject of more than 50 books over the past few years. Regimental histories, originally written by veterans' committees in the decades after the war, have again become popular. Many have been reprinted, and modern buffs continue to compile and author scores of unit histories. A number of new magazines have been launched in the past decade or so, demonstrating that the Civil War continues to be a hot topic for history buffs and scholars alike.

Winfield S. Hancock, commander of the 2nd Corps, Army of the Potomac, returned to the Gettysburg battlefield several years after the battle as part of a reunion called by historian John B. Bachelder so he could speak with veterans and record their recollections about the 1863 battle. In this scene, Bachelder, easily spotted by his long white sideburns, stands second from left. Hancock is sixth from left, standing near where he was wounded during Pickett's Charge on July 3, 1863.

Virginian Fitzhugh Lee, Robert E. Lee's nephew, was an 1856 West Point graduate who resigned his commission to join the Confederacy. After serving as a staff officer in Virginia, he led the 1st Virginia Cavalry and, as a result of gallantry in action, was eventually promoted to major general. After the war, Fitz Lee became governor of Virginia and president of one of that state's railroads. President Grover Cleveland appointed him consul general to Cuba in 1896. Lee was in Havana when the USS Maine exploded in the harbor. He served briefly in the Spanish-American War and was military governor of Havana afterward.

Civil War Veterans

By the late 1870s, soldiers from both sides were beginning to write about their wartime experiences. The Philadelphia *Weekly Times* published the "Annals of the War" series, which featured first-person accounts of the war. From 1877 until the late 1880s, the series included more than 800 articles. In the mid-1880s, the Century Company in New York issued a series of articles titled "Battles and Leaders" in *The Century Magazine*. This series proved so popular that the articles were collected and published as a four-volume set.

The growing wave of Civil War literature continued as the aged generals wrote their mem-

These two former Union soldiers enjoy a friendly game of cards during the 75th anniversary encampment at Gettysburg in 1938. The camp hosted 1,845 former Union and Confederate soldiers from 47 states, the District of Columbia, and Canada.

NOVEMBER 1
The Mississippi Plan takes effect in that state, instituting literacy tests and poll taxes to qualify for the vote, and disenfranchising most African Americans.

1894
SEPTEMBER 10
The United Daughters of the Confederacy is formed.

1894–1922
The U.S. Naval War Records Office publishes the 30-volume *Official Records of the Union and Confederate Navies in the War of the Rebellion.*

On July 3, 1913, these aged veterans moved across the same farm fields they had marched across 50 years earlier as part of Pickett's Charge at Gettysburg. This time, however, when they reached the stone wall on the crest of Cemetery Ridge they were met not by gunfire but by elderly Union veterans who reached across the wall to shake hands with their erstwhile enemies.

oirs. Soldiers from privates to colonels also contributed their accounts to a ready audience. Popular interest in the war waned as these veterans died out and America took a greater part in world affairs, but in the late 1950s, as the centennial of the conflict neared, magazines devoted entirely to the war began to appear. Since that time, popular interest in the Civil War keeps rising as new magazines are published, specialized dealers and publishers reprint older works on the war, and a new generation of professional historians and informed buffs keep readers inundated with new material.

Postwar reunions beginning in the 1880s added to the idea of national reconciliation. A few tentative reunions of former adversaries blossomed into more frequent joint get-togethers. Survivors of the Philadelphia Brigade and Pickett's division held a joint reunion at Gettysburg in 1887, the aged veterans shaking hands across the stone wall where 24 years earlier they had shot and stabbed at each other in fury. Pennsylvania veterans of the Ringgold Cavalry held joint reunions with their previous adversaries in West Virginia, McNeill's Rangers. In both 1913 and 1938, on the 50th and 75th anniversaries of Gettysburg, thousands of venerable survivors of the war gathered on the great battlefield to hold massive reunions covered in depth by the national press.

1895
Stephen Crane publishes his Civil War novel, *The Red Badge of Courage.*

FEBRUARY 11
The Gettysburg battlefield is transferred from a private association to the federal government.

APRIL 29
The state of Tennessee transfers the Shiloh battlefield park to the federal government.

Preservation of Civil War Sites

Even before the fighting ended in 1865, a privately held Pennsylvania corporation was formed to acquire property at Gettysburg in order to mark the most important points of that battle. At other noted war sites, private individuals and small corporations bought property in an effort to protect what they saw as the sacred soil on which the war had been fought. At Gettysburg and elsewhere, veteran societies erected monuments to honor the memory of their units and what they did on each battlefield. But private money was limited, and the government eventually became involved in the process. Beginning in the 1890s, the government began to acquire these private battlefields and improve access and interpretation. At first administered by the War Department, the federal system of national battlefield and military parks was turned over to the Department of the Interior in 1933. Today, the National Park Service administers a number of sites, while a few private foundations, such as Pamplin Park near Petersburg, Virginia, and the Cedar Creek Foundation in the Shenandoah Valley, preserve yet more acres.

Burgeoning interest in the Civil War has also led to a rising historic preservation movement. As the population grew and cities and towns expanded, some relatively important Civil War sites were lost to development. The 1960s centennial spurred interest in preservation by the federal government and private groups, as well as by individuals. Preservationists included a wide range of devotees, from those who would try to save every last square inch of a battlefield to others who wished to preserve core areas. These groups, such as the Association for the Preservation of Civil War Sites, alert supporters when danger threatens, issue their own publications, raise money, and lead the fight to preserve this part of America's heritage. Most notably, concerned citizens and supporters banded together in 1988 to repel an office complex that would have threatened the integrity of the Manassas National Battlefield. The problems associated with preserving Gettysburg have generated national headlines.

Much of this interest in preservation stemmed from the postwar activities of the veterans themselves, especially the former soldiers in blue. In 1866, a veterans' organization called the Grand Army of the Republic (GAR) was organized in Illinois

This imposing monument to General Ulysses S. Grant stands at Vicksburg, the scene of one of his major triumphs in the war. Grant started his campaign against Vicksburg in the fall of 1862 and was rebuffed in all of his early attempts to outflank the fortress. Finally, in May 1863, he outmaneuvered the enemy and put the city under siege. Its July 4 surrender resulted in 30,000 prisoners, a loss the Confederacy could ill afford.

SEPTEMBER 18–20
The Chickamauga and Chattanooga battlefield is officially dedicated.

1896
JANUARY 27
The Supreme Court, in a case involving Gettysburg National Military Park, establishes the precedent that the government can acquire private property by right of eminent domain.

MAY 18
The Supreme Court rules in *Plessy* v. *Ferguson* that "separate but

and quickly spread across the country. Membership was open to any soldier or sailor who had served honorably in the war. Local members organized themselves into posts, which were numbered separately in each state based on the date of organization. The GAR became the most powerful veterans' lobby the United States had ever seen. By the 1890s, its membership had peaked at 400,000. Presidents courted the GAR vote. Among its many activities, the GAR lobbied for liberal pension benefits. Its affiliated newspapers, such as the *National Tribune,* kept veterans informed of pension news and provided a forum for memoirs of the war. The GAR also worked to protect battlefields.

Other organizations, such as the Military Order of the Loyal Legion of the United States (MOLLUS), helped veterans with comradeship, provided a group for lobbying Congress, and ensured that the war would not be forgotten. The United Confederate Veterans performed much the same role for former Confederate soldiers and sailors. Today, the Sons of Union Veterans of the Civil War and the Sons of Confederate Veterans continue the proud traditions of their parent organizations.

Present-Day Reverberations

Modern-day commemoration of the Civil War has become a big business. Reenacting is on the rise as more and more recruits enter existing units or form new units to relive the days of the soldiers 150 years ago. A number of businesses cater to the reenactor community, providing firearms, clothing, equipment, and food, all painstakingly recreated from original patterns or recipes. Reenactments of battles or even simple living history camps bring in tourists by the thousands, helping local economies. This renewed interest in the war has spurred historic preservation of Civil War sites, whether they be isolated earthworks, battlefields, period structures, or reflected in artifacts in local museums. New Civil War museums, such as those at Pamplin Historical Park near Petersburg, Virginia, and the National Civil War Museum in Harrisburg, Pennsylvania, are constant reminders of how important the war yet remains to a signifi-

A monument to the soldiers of New York state looks down on these cannons at the Antietam battlefield. It is one of 94 monuments at Antietam National Battlefield. Some, like this one, have been erected by states honoring the soldiers that fought here. Others have been built by veterans themselves to commemorate their regiments and fallen comrades. The vast majority of monuments were built to memorialize Northern subjects—the South has only six monuments on the battlefield. Southern poverty after the war may have contributed to this dearth.

equal" train facilities fall within the Constitution, opening the door for separate but equal treatment for African Americans at all levels of society.

1897
APRIL 27
Grant's Tomb is dedicated in New York City's Riverside Park on what would have been the 75th birthday of Ulysses S. Grant.

1898
APRIL–DECEMBER
The United States fights in the Spanish-American War, with the participation of many Union and Confederate veterans.

cant segment of the American public. A steady production of books and magazines related to the war also illustrates its continuing popularity.

Modern controversy relating to the Civil War lives on, as well. Problems such as the struggle over how the conflict should be presented by the National Park Service, which maintains most Civil War battlefields, and the controversy over a statue of Abraham Lincoln unveiled in Richmond, Virginia, in 2003 illustrate that the war remains a divisive issue. But the most acrimonious disputes involve the Confederate battle flag. Its use by white supremacist groups has tarnished the flag carried into numerous battles by brave Confederate soldiers. Its political use has enraged activist African American leaders, who see the flag as a painful reminder of their race's enforced servitude prior to the war. When the state of South Carolina at first refused to haul down the Confederate flag over its state house, the NAACP and other related organizations organized a boycott of the state, which helped force its removal, to the anger of its defenders.

And so the legacy of the American Civil War continues. Conflict over battlefield preservation, arguments over slavery and the causes of the war, and anger over the old symbology of the war—as well as a steady outpouring of books, reenacting, and heritage tourism—are all vivid reminders that the Civil War was indeed a pivotal event in American history.

Reenacting became bigger and better in the 1970s. Large-scale reenactments in the 1980s and 1990s sometimes involved more than 10,000 participants. The reenacting community includes participants from all walks of life who portray generals and privates alike, civilians, chaplains, Christian Commission and Sanitary Commission workers, funeral workers, and more. Specialized businesses supply them with everything they need, including period eyeglasses with prescription lenses and hardtack, the staple of army food.

NOVEMBER 10
Racial tensions surrounding an election two days earlier erupt in white rioting directed toward African Americans in Wilmington, North Carolina. In the violence, the office of a black newspaper is burned and Republican officeholders in the city are deposed.

1899
FEBRUARY 21
Congress establishes the Vicksburg National Military Park.

Above: *James A. Garfield served in the Union Army, rising to major general before his retirement in December 1863 to serve in the House of Representatives. The 1880 Republican convention made him its presidential candidate. He defeated former Union General Winfield S. Hancock in the fall election but served only four months in office before he was mortally wounded by an assassin.*

Above: *Robert Todd Lincoln was President Lincoln's only son to survive into adulthood. He had the bitter duty of having his mother, Mary Todd Lincoln, declared insane and committed to an asylum when her behavior became erratic. Lincoln was secretary of war under Presidents James A. Garfield and Chester A. Arthur and minister to Britain for President Benjamin Harrison. Lincoln performed unremarkably but competently in each of these duties. He later became president of the Pullman Company. After his death in 1926, Robert willed his father's papers to the Library of Congress, where they remained sealed until 1947.*

Frank and Jesse James (sitting and standing at right) were brothers from Missouri who joined the Confederacy during the Civil War. Serving under notorious guerrilla leader William C. Quantrill, they took part in the vicious fighting in Kansas and Missouri, where irregulars of both sides used the conflict as an excuse for robbery and murder. They are seen here with Fletch Taylor, another of Quantrill's raiders. In 1866, the James brothers joined another former rebel, Cole Younger, to begin a 16-year rampage of bank and train robberies and related violence in the West. Jesse was slain by one of his gang members in 1882. Frank surrendered later that year, was tried for crimes and acquitted, and spent the rest of his life living as a respected farmer.

Associate Supreme Court Justice John Marshall Harlan, a former Kentucky slaveholder, became a vocal proponent for civil rights after the war. Appointed to the Supreme Court in 1877, Harlan became the only dissenter in the 1883 decision overturning the Civil Rights Act of 1875 and in the 1896 Plessy v. Ferguson *case. In his* Plessy *dissent, he wrote, "In view of the Constitution, in the eye of the law, there is in this country no superior, dominant, ruling class of citizens. There is no caste here."*

Samuel Langhorne Clemens, better known as Mark Twain, put blame for the war on Scottish writer Sir Walter Scott, author of Ivanhoe *and* Rob Roy. *"Sir Walter had so large a hand in making Southern character, as it existed before the war, that he is in great measure responsible for the war." Born in Missouri, Twain was a member of a Confederate cavalry for a short time before deserting.*

1905
President Theodore Roosevelt authorizes the return of captured Confederate flags.

1906
SEPTEMBER 22–26
After newspapers allege African American attacks on white women, whites in Atlanta riot, seeking to kill African Americans.

Police offer little protection. After a few days the official death count is about a dozen, although unofficial estimates are higher.

Names for the Conflict

Though widely known today as the Civil War, this conflict has had other names. When the government began publishing *The Official Records* in the 1880s, it used the name "War of the Rebellion" to denote the conflict. Later, the name "War Between the States" crept into public usage, generally as a result of Southern hatred of the term *rebellion*. To many Southerners, the war was—and still is—"The War of Northern Aggression" or "The War for Southern Independence," to use but two such titles. Some Yankees have called it "The War for the Preservation of the Union" or "The War of Secession." Others have used more of a euphemism than a name: "The Late Unpleasantness." In the 20th century, the federal government settled on the generic term "Civil War" as the generally accepted title for the conflict.

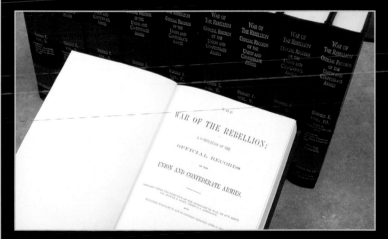

The Official Records is a publication of the U.S. government that brings together reports, orders, and correspondence from both sides of the conflict.

In this 1886 cartoon, President Grover Cleveland stands guard at the Treasury, protecting it from calls for Civil War pensions. Pensions began before the end of the war and became more liberal in the decades afterward. Congress, wary of the GAR's political power, tended to give that organization what it requested. Cleveland found some requests fraudulent and vetoed them. This was not the only issue on which he differed with the GAR, and the group may have been responsible for his loss in the 1888 election.

A frieze of Civil War units goes completely around the structure built for the Pension Bureau in the 1880s. The bureau was established to handle pensions for Union veterans. Today the Pension Building in Washington, D.C., is home to the National Building Museum.

1908
AUGUST 14–16
A white mob in Springfield, Illinois, rampages through black business and residential areas. The violence is ultimately stopped by state troops.

1909
FEBRUARY 12
W.E.B. DuBois, Ida Wells-Barnett, and others found what will become the National Association for the Advancement of Colored People (NAACP).

1910
The site of Andersonville Prison is given to the federal government.

This wartime photograph shows William Mahone, a Virginian who started the Civil War as colonel of the 6th Virginia Infantry. He soon led a brigade, and in 1864 he was promoted to division command. He proved instrumental in defeating the Union attack at the Crater and was present at the Appomattox surrender. After the war, Mahone went back to the railroad business and was elected to the Senate in 1880. He became a Republican supporter who was able to retain the confidence of his state. He remained active in Virginia politics until his death in 1895.

The advertising icon Aunt Jemima was created by mill owner Chris Rutt, who invented the country's first pancake mix. Rutt, a white man, got the idea for the character after visiting a minstrel show in 1889. He appropriated both the name and the cook's attire in an effort to link his product to "good Southern cooking." By 1893, Nancy Green (above), a former slave, had been cast in the part. By the 1960s, as a result of complaints about her stereotypical image, Aunt Jemima began to change. Most obviously, the character lost the kerchief covering her head and began to lose weight.

Booker T. Washington was a former slave who became educated and eventually founded Tuskegee Institute in Alabama in 1881. By the time of his death in 1915, Washington was regarded as one of America's preeminent African American spokespersons, arguing that African Americans should not rock the boat by demanding social equality. Instead, he believed they should become model citizens and keep to themselves. His 1901 autobiography, Up from Slavery, is a classic work.

W.E.B. DuBois is perhaps one of the best-known scholars of African American history. The Massachusetts-born DuBois earned a Ph.D. at Harvard University and was a prolific writer. His two most famous works are The Philadelphia Negro in 1899 and The Souls of Black Folk in 1903. DuBois opposed Booker T. Washington's concept of gradualism and was an early proponent of what would become the NAACP. DuBois gradually became more radical, joining the U.S. Communist Party and leaving the country for Ghana in 1961. He died there in 1963.

1913
Gettysburg hosts the 50th anniversary encampment of thousands of surviving Civil War veterans.

1915
FEBRUARY 8
D. W. Griffith's *The Birth of a Nation* premieres under its original name, *The Clansman*. It is the first significant Civil War motion picture.

NOVEMBER
William Simmons and others organize a new incarnation of the Ku Klux Klan at Stone Mountain, Georgia.

Veterans' Pensions

Returning Union veterans clamored for government assistance to offset losses caused by the war. Thousands of soldiers were maimed for life by the loss of arms or legs, while thousands more were racked by debilitating diseases. Although Congress had passed a simple bill in 1862 to provide for such cases, it was not enough.

Congress tinkered with pension legislation for decades. An arrears bill that was passed in 1868 made disability awards retroactive to the date of discharge from military service. A second such bill was passed in 1879—a year later, more than 130,000 new claims for pensions besieged the Pension Office.

The 23rd Ohio pose next to their monument at Woodland Cemetery in Cleveland, Ohio, in 1865. The 23rd included two future presidents—Rutherford B. Hayes and William McKinley. This is their last meeting, as the regiment is mustered out of service. They paid to build this monument, one of the first of the war, after the regiment took heavy losses at Antietam.

This 1895 cartoon illustrates the reaction of much of the public to increased income taxes so the government could balance its budget and dispense pension payments to Union veterans. The pension system was the largest single drain on the treasury during the decades following the Civil War.

Former veterans who sympathized with their less fortunate comrades made up a third of the Congress. As a result, pension laws became more and more liberal—and more and more open to fraud. Even the GAR pension committee admitted that the 1890 act "was calculated to place upon the pension rolls all survivors of the war whose conditions of health are not practically perfect." Between 1879 and 1924, veterans and their dependents received $5.7 trillion from the government. Indeed, in the years after the war until at least 1900, pension money was one of the government's highest expenditures.

Former Confederate veterans received state-sponsored pensions for their services during the Civil War. Today a handful of offspring of Civil War veterans continue to draw compensation from the government.

In this postwar scene, freed slaves work in cotton fields, little changed from their prewar status. The chaos of the struggling postwar economy meant that the former slaves had to obtain supplies and land from their former masters and then rely on themselves to survive.

A group of former prisoners of war gathers for a reunion at the place of their misery, Andersonville, Georgia. This spot is Providence Spring, which received its name from an action that many perceived as providential. After a particularly heavy storm, water bubbled from the ground here, providing fresh water for the prisoners to drink.

This drawing shows the Grand Army of the Republic parading through Washington, D.C. Rank upon rank of proud Union veterans march with their regiments, making sure the Civil War remained more than a simple memory. Thanks to the efforts of veterans such as these, Memorial Day was established as a national holiday. Many of the former Confederate states celebrate a Confederate Memorial Day, which falls on a different day in different states, as well.

1917
The Kennesaw Mountain battlefield is acquired by the federal government.

1919
JULY 27
Several days of rioting sparked by segregated beaches break out in Chicago, leaving 38 dead. This was just one incident in 1919's

"Red Summer," so called because of the amount of blood spilled by more than 20 race riots throughout the nation.

After the Civil War, the U.S. Army included segregated regiments of African American soldiers. In 1898, two black cavalry regiments—the 9th and 10th, the so-called "Buffalo Soldiers" from the days of fighting American Indians—took part in the Cuban campaign. Two regiments of African American foot soldiers also landed in Cuba.

After the war, both sides formed numerous veterans associations to honor different units or campaigns. This badge was issued to attendees of the 1904 reunion of the Burnside, Roanoke, and New Berne Association, dedicated to preserving the memory of the Burnside Expedition to North Carolina in 1862.

William McKinley enlisted in the 23rd Ohio infantry in 1861, was present at Antietam and several more battles, and ended the war as brevet major of his regiment. He became a lawyer after the war, served for almost 14 years in Congress, and followed that with two terms as governor of Ohio. McKinley was elected president in 1896 and led the country until assassinated in Buffalo, New York, in 1901.

Foundry owner Richard Smith funded the erection of this huge Civil War memorial in Philadelphia's Fairmount Park between 1897 and 1912. Four statues and eight busts honor famous Pennsylvania officers who fought in the Civil War, while the names of others are carved into the memorial's walls.

1920
AUGUST 26
The 19th Amendment to the Constitution, which grants women the right to vote, is declared ratified.

1922
MAY 30
The Lincoln Memorial is dedicated in Washington, D.C.

1925
AUGUST 8
An estimated 40,000 hooded members of the Ku Klux Klan march down Pennsylvania Avenue in Washington, D.C.

In this scene from The Birth of a Nation, *Colonel Ben Cameron leads the local troops in gray through Piedmont, South Carolina, to fight the invading Yankees. Sweethearts and families cheer, and flags flap in the breeze. The orchestra accompanying the film in the theater would play "When Johnny Comes Marching Home."*

During a reunion in June 1917, Virginia Confederates march with their old rifles, reproduction uniforms, and assistance from the United Daughters of the Confederacy. Note the veteran with an artificial leg on the left.

Marcus Garvey was nicknamed the Black Moses because of his ideal of uniting all black peoples of the world in one country. The Jamaican-born Garvey came to New York in 1916 and built up membership in the Universal Negro Improvement Association. Accused of mail fraud in 1922, Garvey was deported from the United States five years later. The flashy Garvey often dressed in a military-style uniform, as shown here in a Harlem parade.

This African American man takes his possessions to safety, fleeing the Chicago riots of 1919. The trouble began when an African American boy swimming in Lake Michigan drifted into the segregated white area of the beach. Whites on the beach threw rocks at the boy, causing him to drown.

1926
The Petersburg National Battlefield is established.

1927
Buster Keaton stars in the silent film comedy *The General*, based on Andrews's Raid of 1862.

FEBRUARY 14
Congress votes to establish a military park to commemorate the battles of Fredericksburg, Spotsylvania, the Wilderness, and Chancellorsville.

The Grand Army of the Republic

Even though the federal Army was huge, not all Northern men and boys joined the military. In fact, most did not, and when the troops returned home in 1865, not everyone welcomed them with open arms. Many employers believed that army life had corrupted the soldiers with alcohol, swearing, and prostitutes. Veterans found themselves out of jobs and facing discrimination when they tried to find work. For the thousands of maimed former soldiers, life was even tougher.

As a result, veterans banded together in fraternal and political organizations. The largest and most influential of these groups was the Grand Army of the Republic (GAR). Founded in 1866 by Benjamin F. Stephenson, General John A. Logan, and Richard J. Oglesby, the GAR promoted veterans' benefits, aided needy soldiers and their widows, and encouraged public allegiance to the government. The GAR organized local posts that used a system of ritual and secrecy. The posts were organized into departments for each state, which met in a national convention each year. By 1890, membership totaled more than 400,000 veterans.

The GAR proved very effective in using its considerable political clout. Every president through the turn of the century courted the GAR vote or risked the organization's wrath. When President Grover Cleveland vetoed some pension legislation and had the nerve during his first term in office to suggest captured Confederate flags be returned, the GAR withdrew its support, and he was defeated for reelection in 1888. Four years later, after Cleveland had mended his rift with the veterans, he was reelected back into the office.

Among the accomplishments of the GAR was the establishment of the national holiday Decoration Day (now called Memorial Day), the passage of liberal pension bills that benefited all Union veterans and cost the government more than $1 billion by 1900, the establishment of a series of soldiers' homes to house elderly veterans who could no longer care for themselves, patriotic exercises in schools—such as the Pledge of Allegiance— and the use of "proper" history textbooks in schools. The GAR conventions ceased in 1949, when only 16 members were still alive.

In this scene from the 1938 Memorial Day parade in New York City, surviving GAR members press forward, undaunted by age and infirmity. Relics of a bygone era, they were nevertheless still honored by their fellow citizens for their past deeds.

United Confederate Veterans

The postwar tribulations of former Confederate veterans were similar to those suffered by their Yankee counterparts. And although Union veterans received the largesse of pension benefits from Congress, their erstwhile foes were not entirely forgotten. The former Confederate states eventually passed their own pension laws to aid impoverished and disabled veterans, and in 1958, Congress, believing a few former Confederate soldiers still survived, passed pension legislation to help them.

In 1889, representatives of several state veterans' groups met in New Orleans and established the United Confederate Veterans (UCV). Local posts were called camps, and they eventually totaled more than 1,800, with more than 160,000 members. The UCV held annual meetings from 1890 until 1951, when only three members were able to attend. Pleasant Crump, the last surviving authenticated Confederate veteran, died in 1951.

United Confederate Veterans camps functioned at the local level, lobbying for pensions for veterans and widows, raising money for monuments, and encouraging their view of the Civil War to oppose the prevailing Northern view of the conflict. Former Confederate general Clement L. Evans, supported by UCV money, edited the 12-volume *Confederate Military History* in 1899.

The official voice of the Southern veterans was the magazine *Confederate Veteran*, published from 1893 to 1932. This monthly periodical contained biographies, memoirs, obituaries, monument news, UCV news, and information on the South in general.

In June 1917, Confederate veterans convened in Washington, D.C., for their annual reunion. A group from Texas, marching in one of the parades, proudly displayed both the American and Confederate flags.

In 1922, Anna Glud revealed a secret for her 68th birthday. When she was ten years old, she had posed as a boy to join the Union Army as a drummer boy. Her parents had disagreed about the war, so she had kept this secret to herself all those years.

These men are veterans of the Hawkins Zouaves, 9th New York Infantry, photographed at the 1922 New York Memorial Day parade. The soldiers at the right are wearing the distinctive baggy trousers of the Zouave uniform.

This image shows members of the Ku Klux Klan participating in some sort of ceremony. The KKK enjoyed phenomenal growth during the early 1920s. Scandal rocked the organization, and it officially disbanded in 1944. A third KKK emerged a few years later to oppose both communism and the civil rights movement.

As a demonstration of their size, an estimated 40,000 members of the Ku Klux Klan march down Pennsylvania Avenue away from the Capitol on August 8, 1925.

1931
MARCH 25
Nine African Americans ranging in age from 12 to 20 are arrested and accused of the gang rape of two white women. Within two weeks, all but the youngest boy are tried in Scottsboro, Alabama, found guilty, and sentenced to death. They will be known as the Scottsboro Boys.

1933
AUGUST 10
Civil War battlefields are transferred from the War Department to the Department of the Interior.

These masked women are part of the Dixie Protestant Women's Political League, an organization closely modeled after the Ku Klux Klan. This picture was taken in Atlanta, Georgia, in 1922.

Josephine Baker had experienced some success as a performer in the United States, but when she took her act to Paris during the 1920s, her career exploded, and she became one of the most famous women in the world.

Zora Neale Hurston, a key figure in the Harlem Renaissance of the 1920s, grew up in Florida. In addition to writing fiction, she studied anthropology and wrote widely in that field, as well.

Langston Hughes was a poet from Missouri who also worked as a columnist for African American newspapers in Chicago and New York. He helped focus attention on the struggles of black residents of Harlem, New York, often through works of fiction that centered on a character named Jesse B. Semple.

A brilliant actor, opera singer, and athlete, Paul Robeson graduated from Rutgers University as a member of Phi Beta Kappa in 1919. Playwright Eugene O'Neill cast Robeson in the lead role in his 1925 play The Emperor Jones. For a period of time, his acting career soared, and Robeson became one of the most sought-after artists on Broadway. However, he was outspoken on equal rights for African Americans and was a critic of American foreign policy. For most of the 1950s, the U.S. government denied him a passport to travel abroad. Public backlash undermined his career.

1935
Congress authorizes the establishment of a recreated village of Appomattox Court House to tell the story of Lee's surrender.

1936
MARCH 2
The Richmond National Battlefield Park is created.

1938
Gettysburg's 75th anniversary sees the last major encampment of Civil War veterans. President Franklin D. Roosevelt dedicates the Eternal Light Peace Memorial on the Gettysburg battlefield.

Louis Armstrong was born in New Orleans at the turn of the 20th century and grew up listening to the city's music. He taught himself to play the trumpet while in reform school and eventually became one of America's great jazz musicians. In later life, he made numerous goodwill tours abroad at the behest of the U.S. State Department.

When the Mississippi River flooded in 1927, it forced 700,000 people from their homes in the Mississippi Delta. When the waters receded, many African Americans left their ruined homes behind and migrated north.

In 1927, the state of Massachusetts returned captured Confederate flags to their rightful states as an act of reconciliation. Although the federal government returned all such flags in 1905, many Northern states still own captured flags that are on display in various museums. Some have been returned, but some have not. In more recent years, Virginia has asked Minnesota to return a flag captured at Gettysburg, but the official Minnesota response has been to keep the flag because scores of the state's troops in blue died defending the Union at Gettysburg.

Buster Keaton played a Southern engineer whose train is stolen by Yankee spies in 1927's The General. This film was based on Daring and Suffering: A History of the Great Railway Adventure, a book about Andrews's Raid written by William Pittenger, one of the Union spies who participated.

1939
APRIL 9
Marian Anderson sings to 75,000 people at the Lincoln Memorial.

December 15
Gone With the Wind, based on Margaret Mitchell's novel of the same name, premieres in Atlanta and becomes a Hollywood box office hit.

1940
FEBRUARY 29
Hattie McDaniel wins an Academy Award for Best Supporting Actress for playing Mammy in Gone With the Wind. She is the first African American to win an Oscar.

This is perhaps the most famous Lincoln photo ever taken. Mathew Brady, or possibly his assistant, A. Berger, captured this image in Brady's Washington studio on February 9, 1864. It later appeared on the five dollar bill. Lincoln also sat for a profile photograph during this same sitting. His profile taken that day would later appear on the penny.

In 1931, nine young black men were arrested in Scottsboro, Alabama, and charged with raping two white prostitutes. Although there was no evidence of the involvement of these men, an all-white jury found otherwise. Eight were sentenced to death and the ninth, 13 years old, was sent to prison. Years of appeals eventually led to freedom for all, although none were ever acquitted.

Established in 1909, the National Association for the Advancement of Colored People (NAACP) is an organization dedicated to the establishment of equal rights for African Americans and education of all races about the need for equality. In this picture, NAACP members march to protest lynchings. Southern members of Congress fought against the establishment of antilynching laws as a federal invasion of states' rights.

Mary M. Bethune graduated from Chicago's Moody Bible Institute in 1895. Nine years later, she founded Bethune-Cookman College in Daytona, Florida, which became a model school for African American women. Bethune became known widely as a preeminent black educator, and in 1935 she was appointed by President Franklin Roosevelt to direct the Division of Negro Affairs of the National Youth Administration, a position she held until 1944.

MAY 10
The Manassas battlefield is transferred to the federal government.

1942
APRIL
The Congress of Racial Equality (CORE), a civil rights organization dedicated to using nonviolent protest to fight for civil rights, is founded.

1943
JUNE 20–21
Racial tensions in Detroit explode as white and African American mobs face off against each other, leaving 25 African Americans and 9 whites dead.

Civil War Veterans in the Spanish-American War

When war broke out with Spain in 1898, many aged veterans of the Civil War were in positions of leadership in the American military. General Nelson A. Miles, a decorated Civil War veteran who began that war as a junior officer in a New York regiment, was the Army's general in chief. His boss, Secretary of War Russell A. Alger, was colonel of a Michigan cavalry regiment that served in George A. Custer's brigade. The American envoy in Havana, Cuba, prior to the war was former Confederate General Fitzhugh Lee.

The general who led the American expeditionary force to Cuba, William R. Shafter, also fought in the Civil War. The commander of his cavalry division was none other than former Confederate General Joseph Wheeler. Upon his return to battle, Wheeler, who was in his 60s at the time, reportedly became over-excited after a successful skirmish against Spanish

Joseph Wheeler, shown here in the uniform of a Confederate general, graduated 19th of 22 in the West Point class of 1859. A Georgian by birth, he joined the Confederacy and started the war as an artillery and infantry officer. After a transfer to the cavalry under orders from Braxton Bragg, Wheeler quickly displayed brilliance as a mounted commander. He served in the Army of Tennessee and led its cavalry until the war's end, becoming known as one of the South's best cavalry officers.

When war with Spain broke out in 1898, Joseph Wheeler was appointed a brigadier general of volunteers and donned a blue uniform to lead the cavalry in the expedition to Cuba. He remained in the Regular Army and was a department commander when he retired. After his death in 1906, he became one of the very few former rebels to be buried in Arlington National Cemetery.

troops, shouting, "We've got the damn Yankees on the run!" Other Union veterans among the chief commanders included Generals John R. Brooke, James H. Wilson, and Wesley Merritt. The top naval commanders—George Dewey, Winfield S. Schley, and William T. Sampson—were all Civil War veterans.

In 1936, 90-year-old R. D. Parker played the drum in the final parade of the remaining members of the GAR in Washington, D.C. Parker represented the stamina of the few aging veterans who remained alive in the 1930s. His generation of veterans was extremely proud of its efforts to keep the Union together. Many continued to visit schools and talk to children about the war as long as they were able to do so.

One of the terror tactics used by white supremacists after the Civil War was lynching to intimidate blacks. Between 1882 and 1964, some 4,742 persons, mostly African Americans, were lynched in this country, most frequently in the South and Midwest. The Ku Klux Klan was responsible for some of this, but unrestrained white mobs often took the law into their own hands and were generally not held back by local law enforcement officers.

Teenagers Abram Smith (left) and Thomas Shipp (right) were lynched in Marion, Indiana, on August 7, 1930, after being arrested and accused of the murder of 23-year-old Claude Deeter and the rape of his girlfriend, Mary Ball. This photo is notable for capturing the high spirits and enthusiasm of the mob after it took the pair from their jail cells. A third suspect, 16-year-old James Cameron, was later taken from his cell, as well, but was ultimately spared, becoming the only known survivor of a lynching.

1946
DECEMBER 5
President Harry S. Truman appoints the President's Committee on Civil Rights. The committee will issue its report, *To Secure These Rights,* in October 1947.

1948
JULY 26
President Truman orders complete desegregation of the armed forces.

1951
Medal of Honor winner Audie Murphy stars in *The Red Badge of Courage,* the film version of Stephen Crane's classic war story.

Artwork

The Civil War spawned an entire genre of related artwork to commemorate the conflict. Contemporary views of the fighting reached civilians on both sides by means of the popular illustrated newspapers of the day, such as *Harper's Weekly*, *Frank Leslie's Illustrated Newspaper*, *The Southern Illustrated News*, and the English *London Illustrated News*. Woodcuts appearing in these papers gave people a view of their leaders, soldiers, weapons, and battles.

After the war, paintings by a number of prominent artists specializing in the Civil War were reproduced and became known to many Americans. Winslow Homer worked as an artist for *Harper's Weekly* during the war and afterward executed a number of now-famous oil paintings, some of which were based on his wartime pencil sketches. Gilbert Gaul painted Civil War scenes exclusively after he graduated from the National Academy of Design. Julian

Conrad Wise Chapman's Sunset at Fort Sumter depicts the fort after being bombarded by federal guns in 1863. Chapman, the son of an artist, trained in Rome, but when war broke out, returned to his home country to join the Confederate Army. Serving much of his duty in Charleston, he recorded the city under siege in a series of paintings.

Scott, a Vermont drummer boy, used his wartime experiences to capture a host of battle scenes.

On the Confederate side, Conrad Wise Chapman, son of distinguished American artist John Gadsby Chapman, joined the Confederate Army but became better known for a series of paintings commissioned by General P.G.T. Beauregard to show the siege operations at Charleston, South Carolina. Allen C. Redwood, a thrice-wounded Southern veteran, worked as an artist after the war, contributing to the Century Company's "Battles and Leaders" series and illustrating many memoirs by veterans of both the Union and the Confederacy.

A couple of postwar series of prints popularized the war in the public mind. Lithographers Louis Kurz and Alexander Allison teamed to produce a series of three dozen stylized prints depicting famous Civil War battles. Still in print today, these scenes, although ridden with errors and overly rigid in style, were cheap and readily available when introduced in the 1880s and 1890s. Another lithographer, Louis Prang, commissioned a series of prints that competed with Kurz and Allison. This series of 18 prints has appeared in countless books ever since.

Civil War battles also became the subject of several circular paintings called cycloramas that were still in vogue after the conflict had ended. Only two, which are at Gettysburg and Atlanta, remain in existence. But in their heyday, several more cycloramas entertained the paying public, including scenes such as the Second Battle of Bull Run, the *Monitor-Virginia* battle, and the battle of Chattanooga. Extremely large and expensive to move around, many of these interesting artworks simply succumbed to time and deterioration.

With the resurgence of interest in the Civil War in recent decades, a number of contemporary artists have made scores of war-related prints available to the public. These artist-historians include Don Troiani, Keith Rocco, Mort Kunstler, Dale Gallon, and a number of others who provide a modern smorgasbord of Civil War scenes.

Hollywood and the War

Since the advent of moving pictures in the late 19th century, the Civil War has been the subject of perhaps 800 silent and sound pictures. Hollywood's involvement with the war has generally mirrored the tendencies of the country at large, especially in portraying the war as a national unifier. Until recent decades, African Americans were given few film roles, and their activities in the war were largely ignored or portrayed very inaccurately. When shown on screen in the early movies, African Americans were portrayed as docile servants, overweight mammies, or lazy and irresponsible workers.

The first major motion picture to feature the war was director D. W. Griffith's 1915 *The Birth of a Nation*. The Kentucky-born Griffith adapted Thomas Dixon's novel *The Clansman*, which made heroes of the Ku Klux Klan and portrayed black soldiers of Reconstruction as savages. In spite of NAACP protests, the picture was shown across the nation to rave reviews and became a staple of the Civil War film cannon.

In 1939, Margaret Mitchell's novel *Gone With the Wind* appeared on the big screen, also to sterling reviews. Never mind that the large plantations shown in the movie were extremely rare and happy slaves were largely a myth. *Gone With the Wind* influenced

Actor Jeff Daniels, playing Colonel Joshua Chamberlain of the 20th Maine, gives the order to launch a bayonet charge down the slopes of Little Round Top in this scene from Gettysburg. *The real Chamberlain issued just such an order on the afternoon of July 2, 1863, in a desperate bid to push back attacking Confederate troops. Low on ammunition and in danger of being outflanked, Chamberlain's risky decision indeed drove the Alabamans back and preserved the Union line.*

an entire generation with its depiction of the Civil War. Hollywood has generally characterized rabid abolitionists as the cause of the Civil War—secession is never mentioned, and the South is always shown to be gallantly defending its way of life. Once freed, movie slaves are usually shown as rapacious savages bent on destroying whites. This "moonlight and magnolias" school of thought has beautiful Southern belles, a gallant war, a saintly Abraham Lincoln devoid of the great political skills he actually had, and happy and obedient servants toiling in the fields.

In the past couple of decades, movies have become more accurate. Reenactors have been used extensively in movies such as 1993's *Gettysburg* to ensure better combat scenes. The contributions of African Americans were finally recognized in the 1989 hit *Glory*, an account of the 54th Massachusetts and its failed attack on Battery Wagner. But Hollywood has yet to produce a movie that accurately portrays the origins of the war, its course, and what happened from 1865 to 1877.

Rhett Butler and Scarlett O'Hara, portrayed by Clark Gable and Vivien Leigh, are in each other's arms in this famous staged publicity scene from Gone With the Wind. *Gable and Leigh brought Margaret Mitchell's classic novel of the South to life to the cheers of throngs of moviegoers nationwide.*

Hollywood's View of the War

GERALD. We've borne enough insults from the meddling Yankees. It's time we made them to understand we'll keep our slaves with or without their approval. 'Twas the sovereign right of the State of Georgia to secede from the Union!

AD LIB. That's right–

GERALD. The South must assert herself by force of arms. After we've fired on the Yankee rascals at Fort Sumter, we've got to fight! There's no other way!

AD LIB. Fight! That's right. Fight! Let the Yankees be the ones to ask for peace!

KENNEDY. We'll have Abe Lincoln on his knees.

BRENT. They can't start this war too quick to suit me.

GERALD. The situation is very simple. The Yankees can't fight and we can.

STUART. There won't even be a battle—that's what I think. They'll just turn and run every time.

CHARLES. One Southerner can lick twenty Yankees.

STUART. We'll finish them off in one battle. Gentlemen always fight better than rabble.

A group of Southern gentlemen in Gone With the Wind

Marian Anderson, one of the world's great contraltos, was born in Philadelphia in 1897 and began singing in a church choir at age six. Her career took off after she won a national voice contest in 1925. In 1939, the Daughters of the American Revolution (who owned the venue) refused to give Anderson permission for a concert in Constitution Hall because of her race. In response, First Lady Eleanor Roosevelt arranged for Anderson to sing on the steps of the Lincoln Memorial. The crowd of 75,000 gave her a thundering ovation.

Scarlett O'Hara, played by Vivien Leigh, passes water to thirsty wounded Confederates in this scene from Gone With the Wind. *Hundreds of extras, many working with dummies laying next to them, staged this massive hospital scene. In the film, the heroine was more interested in seeking medical help for her sister-in-law Melanie Wilkes than in helping the wounded.*

Billie Holiday was the premier jazz singer of the 1930s and 1940s, singing with the bands of Benny Goodman, Count Basie, and Artie Shaw. Her phrasing and delivery are still emulated today.

DECEMBER 31
Pleasant Crump, the last Confederate veteran, dies.

1954
MAY 17
The Supreme Court releases its decision in *Brown* v. *Board of Education,* putting an end to the doctrine of "separate but equal."

1955
AUGUST 28
Emmitt Till, a 14-year-old African American boy, is brutally murdered in Mississippi. An all-white jury will acquit his killers.

The U.S. Health Service, in conjunction with Tuskegee Institute, began an experiment to study the effects of syphilis in African American men in 1932. Most of the 500 men who took part had the disease but were never told. Even after penicillin became available to treat syphilis in 1947, it was kept from the subjects. The study lasted 40 years.

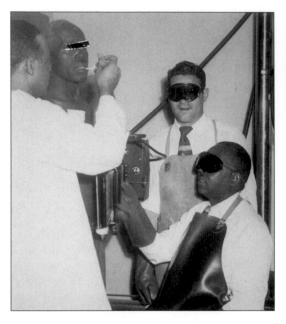

Another "Tuskegee Experiment" had loftier results. When World War II started, African Americans were thought to lack the abilities necessary to pilot planes. With the Army Air Corps, Tuskegee Institute began to train air personnel in 1941. The Tuskegee Airmen entered combat in 1943 and never lost a plane to enemy fire.

Novelist Richard Wright was born in poverty in Mississippi and drifted from place to place as a laborer. After working for a government agency in Chicago, Wright moved to New York City in 1937, then to Paris in 1946. His novels, which include Native Son, Black Boy, Uncle Tom's Children, and The Outsider, depict life in black America and its desperation and violence.

In the summer of 1948, President Harry S. Truman struck a blow for civil rights when he ordered the ban of segregation within the armed forces. Although some officers tried to avoid following through, Truman made clear that he intended the complete integration of the military.

DECEMBER 1
African American seamstress Rosa Parks is arrested when she refuses to give her seat on a bus in Montgomery, Alabama, to a white man.

1956
The Montgomery bus boycott, sparked by Rosa Parks's arrest, lasts most of the year.

AUGUST 2
Albert Woolson, the last Union veteran, dies.

1957
SEPTEMBER 25
After being prevented from

In 1947, Jackie Robinson broke major league baseball's color barrier when he became the first African American player in the modern major leagues. When the Brooklyn Dodgers promoted him to the majors, Robinson rose to all-star status and was named rookie of the year. After his career was over, he was elected to the Baseball Hall of Fame.

Democratic Governor Strom Thurmond of South Carolina was one of the South's champions of segregation and states' rights. During the 1948 presidential race, Thurmond was nominated by the States' Rights party, also known as the Dixiecrats, a block of Southern Democrats who left the main party. Thurmond won 39 electoral votes—from Alabama, Louisiana, Mississippi, and South Carolina, with one from Tennessee— but Harry Truman won the election.

An older Southern woman proudly waves the Confederate flag in support of Strom Thurmond's racist policies at a Dixiecrat campaign rally in Birmingham, Alabama.

Plessy v. Ferguson stood from 1896 until 1954, when the Supreme Court acted on an appeal and unanimously declared the idea of "separate but equal" unconstitutional. The challenge came from the NAACP on behalf of 11-year-old Linda Brown (at left), who was forced to attend an exclusively African American school on orders from the school board of Topeka, Kansas. The court's decision began a long, difficult process of desegregation and civil rights, not only in the South but across the country, which was met with widespread social and racial unrest in the 1960s.

attending Little Rock Central High School by the Arkansas National Guard and the threat of violence, nine African American students enter the school under the protection of the U.S. Army.

1960
FEBRUARY 1
Four African American students begin a sit-in at a Woolworth lunch counter in Greensboro, North Carolina.

1961
MAY 4
Seven African Americans and six whites leave Washington, D.C., to begin their Freedom Ride.

In 1955, Rosa Parks declined to give up her seat on a bus in Montgomery, Alabama, to a white rider. This act was illegal, and Parks was arrested. With the backing of the Montgomery Improvement Association, headed by Dr. Martin Luther King Jr., African Americans boycotted the city's buses for 381 days. In spite of racial tensions, police antagonism, and legal struggles, King's policy of nonviolence prevailed. In 1956, the U.S. Supreme Court ruled that segregated buses were unconstitutional. King received national attention, and a new civil rights policy had been initiated.

Rosa Parks, seen here on a bus after the boycott had ended, defied the norm in Montgomery by sitting in a whites-only part of a city bus. Her arrest resulted in national attention to the city ordinance, and the ensuing boycott essentially started the nonviolence campaign of Martin Luther King Jr.

The woman in this 1950s photograph has dressed her son in Klan attire, demonstrating how the Klan could sometimes be a family affair. The original Ku Klux Klan had effectively ceased to exist by the late 1870s. It was reorganized in Georgia in 1915 by William Simmons, who added anti-Catholicism, anti-Semitism, and militant patriotism to the group's original purpose. The new Klan spread quickly throughout the South, the North, and the Midwest. After years of declining membership, the Klan again grew during the 1950s as unrest over civil rights developed.

A week after arriving in Mississippi from Chicago, Illinois, to visit his uncle, 14-year-old Emmitt Till was kidnapped and murdered for allegedly whistling at a white woman. Roy Bryant and J. W. Milam were arrested for the crime and stood trial but were acquitted by a white jury. Milam later confessed to Look magazine.

Ralph Ellison released his first novel, Invisible Man, in 1952. The allegorical story of an African American man searching for truth, the book became a best seller and won the National Book Award.

1961–65
The centennial of the Civil War is marked by battle reenactments and other observances.

1962
OCTOBER 1
Backed by a court order and accompanied by federal law enforcement officials, James Meredith is the first African American to enroll in the University of Mississippi.

1963
JUNE 11
Alabama Governor George Wallace personally blocks an entrance at the University of Alabama to prevent two African Americans from enrolling.

Albert Woolson, the Last Veteran

Tradition has it that the last Civil War veteran was Walter Williams, a Texan who allegedly fought with John B. Hood's brigade during the war. Williams died in 1959, ostensibly at the age of 117, but recent research has proven his claim untrue. According to census records, Williams was born in 1855. Another self-identified Southern vet who also died in 1959, John Salling, was likewise not old enough to have served, having been born only in 1858. These two men, along with ten others, all claimed their status as Civil War soldiers during the Depression, some 70 years after the conflict ended. Records unable to be accessed in the 1950s, however, indicate that none of them had been Confederate soldiers.

Once the wheat was separated from the chaff, the last bona fide Civil War veteran appears to have been Albert Woolson, who died at 108 on August 2, 1956. Woolson enlisted as a drummer boy in the 1st Minnesota Heavy Artillery during the last year of the war. This unit saw no active combat service but garrisoned Chattanooga from late 1864 until mid-1865.

Woolson lived in Duluth, Minnesota, until his death. Even in old age, he proudly wore his uniform into school classrooms, carrying his drum and telling youngsters in the 1950s about his experiences in the Civil War.

Albert Woolson spent a year in Union uniform as a drummer boy. Before he died in 1956 in Duluth, Minnesota, he was the last surviving veteran of the war.

James Baldwin grew up in Harlem and became a novelist whose main theme was how African Americans are victimized by white imagination and its associated hates and longings. His first novel was Go Tell It on the Mountain in 1953. A nonfiction book in 1963, The Fire Next Time, warned of forthcoming racial violence. Baldwin was also a playwright.

In 1957, Arkansas Governor Orval Faubus failed to ensure the safety of nine African American students when they tried to enter the all-white Central High School in Little Rock, Arkansas, going so far as to send in the Arkansas National Guard to keep them away. The students were forced to flee when a white mob formed. Enraged, President Dwight D. Eisenhower sent in troops from the 101st Airborne Division to enforce desegregation.

The Preservation Movement

Gettysburg was the first battlefield on which a plethora of monuments was erected to tell the story of the Union regiments and batteries that fought there. By the time the private Gettysburg Battlefield Memorial Association transferred its approximately 800 acres to the federal government in 1895, more than 300 monuments, markers, and plaques had been erected by veterans, often with state support. With the establishment of other federal parks, such as Shiloh and Chickamauga, veterans continued to memorialize the late conflict. At first restricted to Union memorials, the battlefields honored the Confederate units by erecting plaques for brigades, divisions, and corps to mark battle lines. A few Southern veterans associations occasionally erected monuments to specific units.

An upsurge of public interest in Civil War battlefields occurred after World War I, when isolationism, the advent of a shorter work week, and the rise of the automobile meant people could spend more of their leisure time traveling. Congress continued to add parcels of land to existing parks and occasionally funded new federal parks.

The 1960s centennial again brought renewed interest in battlefield parks. The National Park Service updated its land acquisition policy and undertook boundary surveys of the Civil War parks, determining that any land within the authorized boundaries could be acquired without Congressional approval. Land outside these park boundaries that was donated or up for sale would need Congressional assent before it could be acquired by the National Park Service.

This decision, unfortunately, was far from perfect. The acquisition of a farm outside the Gettysburg boundary by the private Gettysburg Battlefield Preservation Association brought new problems for

Reminiscent of the type of large plantation house made famous by Tara in Gone With the Wind, *this photo shows the Rosedown Plantation, located close to the Mississippi River in St. Francisville, Louisiana. Houses such as this are now museums, displaying the antebellum way of life of the privileged few who owned such magnificent mansions.*

this park. The GBPA wanted to donate the farm to the park, but the local Congressional representative refused to see this land taken off the local tax roles. The end result was a series of lively, sometimes acrimonious, hearings that in 1987 resulted in the donation of the farm along with a required survey and report on the park's final boundary. Similar issues beset other parks as increased population and the lure of commercial development brought preservationists and businesspeople into conflict at Manassas, Fredericksburg, and a number of other battlefields. More recently, a lack of adequate funding by the National Park Service has resulted in the formation of a number of private groups to assist in raising money for general funds and specific projects at a number of Civil War sites.

A new wave of African American protests began in Greensboro, North Carolina, in February 1960. Local African American college students asked for service at an all-white lunch counter in the Woolworth store and were refused. They then staged a sit-in and refused to leave the lunch counter, which touched off a wave of similar protests across the South. Here, African Americans sit at a lunch counter in Miami, Florida, after the waitstaff has refused to serve them.

To test a recent Supreme Court decision outlawing segregation on interstate buses, several African American and white riders sponsored by the Congress of Racial Equality (CORE) set out on a bus from Washington, D.C., into the Deep South. In Anniston, Alabama, a bus was attacked and set on fire. As Freedom Riders exited the bus into the waiting crowd, they were beaten. The ride continued and was met with further violence in Birmingham and Montgomery, Alabama.

Alabaman George Wallace was elected governor of his native state in 1962. He vowed "segregation forever" and bitterly opposed desegregation. Wallace attracted national attention when he symbolically stood in the doorway of Foster Auditorium at the University of Alabama to keep two African American students from enrolling. He was not successful. Wallace later organized the American Independent party and received almost 10 million votes for president in the 1968 election.

Medgar Evers was Mississippi's first field secretary for the NAACP. He set up local chapters of the organization around the state and focused on civil rights issues. His position alone made him a controversial figure in the state, but his activist style in matters such as helping to arrange James Meredith's enrollment at the University of Mississippi raised his profile. On June 12, 1963, Evers was gunned down outside of his house. A veteran of World War II, Evers was buried in Arlington National Cemetery.

Byron De La Beckwith, a member of Mississippi's White Citizens Council, was arrested and charged with the murder of Medgar Evers. However, despite finding Beckwith's fingerprints on the rifle that killed Evers, two trials in 1964 ended with all-white hung juries. Thirty years later, the 74-year-old Beckwith was tried for the murder again, and this time the jury found him guilty.

AUGUST 28
A combination of African American and white civil rights groups lead 250,000 people on a march on Washington. Martin Luther King Jr. addresses the crowd from the steps of the Lincoln Memorial.

1964
FEBRUARY 4
The 24th Amendment to the Constitution, which makes poll taxes illegal, is officially declared ratified.

JULY 2
President Lyndon Johnson signs the Civil Rights Act of 1964, the first far-reaching civil rights legislation in 89 years. A previous weak but precedent-setting Civil Rights Act had been passed in 1957.

The Mississippi Summer Project began in 1964, as hundreds of volunteers, mostly college students, came to the state to register African American voters. Michael Schwerner had come from New York to work for CORE and had hired James Chaney, a local African American, to work with him. The two, along with Andrew Goodman, a friend from Queens College in New York City who had only arrived in the state the day before, were murdered by a sheriff's deputy and a number of other members of the Ku Klux Klan. This poster was released by the FBI after the three had gone missing but before they were known to be dead.

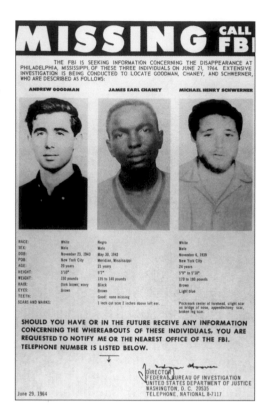

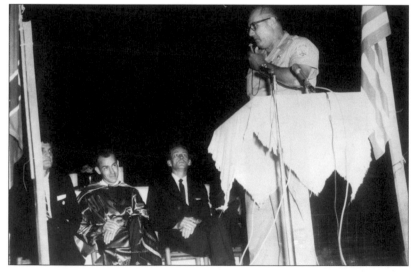

Lawrence Rainey was the sheriff of Neshoba County, Mississippi, where the three civil rights workers were killed by the Ku Klux Klan. Although he was arrested for the murder with a number of other people in December 1964, he was acquitted. His deputy, Cecil Price, and six others were found guilty. Rainey is seen here addressing a Klan rally a few months after his arrest.

On August 28, 1963, a crowd estimated at more than a quarter of a million people marched into Washington, D.C., in support of racial equality. Among the speakers was Martin Luther King Jr., whose "I Have a Dream" speech from the steps of the Lincoln Memorial electrified the crowd gathered on the National Mall.

1965
FEBRUARY 21
Malcolm X is assassinated by followers of Elijah Muhammad, his former mentor.

MARCH 7
Civil rights protesters begin a march from Selma to Montgomery, Alabama. When they reach the Edmund Pettus Bridge, not even at Selma's city limits, they are met by violent state troopers.

AUGUST 6
The Voting Rights Act of 1965 is signed by President Johnson. It picks up where the Civil Rights Act of 1964 left off, ensuring all citizens the right to vote.

Images such as this one taken by news photographers helped build support for African American demonstrators in the South. Police turned their dogs on peaceful demonstrators, a tactic that led to violence and, unintentionally, more support for racial harmony and equality.

Thurgood Marshall, born in 1908, spent more than 25 years as a civil rights attorney for the NAACP before President Lyndon Johnson appointed him to the U.S. Supreme Court, the first African American to be given that honor. Marshall was also the attorney in the decision of Brown v. Board of Education, *which struck down separate but equal laws.*

In 1965, President Lyndon Johnson pushed the Voting Rights Act through Congress to enforce the Civil Rights Act signed into law the year before. The Voting Rights Act authorized the federal government to send examiners with authority to expedite registrations into counties where less than 50 percent of eligible voters were registered. This law also suspended literacy tests in such cases where they could be judged discriminatory. As a result, the number of African American voters in the South rose sharply.

President Lyndon Johnson became one of the nation's most influential senators in the 1950s, credited with maneuvering the Civil Rights Act of 1957 through Congress. As president, Johnson engineered the Civil Rights Act of 1964 and the Voting Rights Act of 1965. Upon signing the Civil Rights Act, he is said to have predicted that Democrats had "just lost the South for a generation."

1970
MAY 9
The Confederate Memorial Carving of Jefferson Davis, Robert E. Lee, and Stonewall Jackson at Stone Mountain, Georgia, is dedicated.

1973
The wreck of the USS *Monitor* is discovered off Cape Hatteras.

1975
AUGUST 5
President Gerald Ford restores Robert E. Lee's citizenship.

In August 1965, the arrest of a black man for drunken driving resulted in a riot in the Los Angeles neighborhood of Watts, an overcrowded, poor section of town inhabited mostly by African Americans. When the riot was finally quelled, 28 African Americans had died, and estimates of property damage ran into tens of millions of dollars.

Malcolm X (born Malcolm Little) came to national prominence in the 1960s as a black nationalist and spokesman for the Nation of Islam, led by Elijah Muhammad. Muhammad was a black separatist who disapproved of the civil rights movement, and Malcolm eventually split with him. Although Malcolm went on to found the Organization for Afro-American Unity, he was assassinated by followers of Muhammad on February 21, 1965. Malcolm's autobiography, published posthumously, became a best seller.

Lawyer Edward W. Brooke became Massachusetts attorney general in 1962. Four years later, he won election to the U.S. Senate, the first African American to win a senate election by popular vote, and the first to sit in that body since Reconstruction.

One reaction to court-directed school desegregation in the 1970s was the forced busing of students from one school to another within school districts to achieve a racial balance, leaving no school all white or all African American. Here, students in Boston, Massachusetts, require a police escort to ride safely to and from their new school. Threats of violence against forced integration were not relegated only to the South.

The initiation of Martin Luther King Jr. Day as a national holiday has continued to draw sporadic protests across the former Confederacy. In this image, Ku Klux Klan members proudly fly the Confederate flag in Lawrenceburg, Tennessee, to protest King's day. Until the year 2000, the holiday for celebrating King was also shared with celebrations for Robert E. Lee and Stonewall Jackson, who also had birthdays in mid-January. Mississippi commemorates King's and Lee's birthdays together.

1977
ABC's television miniseries *Roots*, based on Alex Haley's book, brings widespread recognition to the pre-Civil War slavery system in the South. It also leads to an increase in genealogical research.

1982
CBS telecasts an 8-hour Civil War miniseries, *The Blue and the Gray*.

1986–90
The 125th anniversary of the Civil War witnesses the largest reenact-

ments yet held. The 1988 Gettysburg event includes more than 10,000 participants.

1987
The Association for the Preservation of Civil War Sites is formed.

The Confederate Flags

The Confederacy had a number of flags during its four years of existence. At the national level, its first banner was the Stars and Bars, a rectangular banner with seven stars representing the first seven seceded states. On May 1, 1863, the Confederate Congress adopted the Stainless Banner as its flag. This white rectangular flag contained a red field in the upper left corner upon which was emblazoned a blue cross with 13 stars. This banner remained as the Confederacy's official flag until March 4, 1865, when a vertical red stripe was added to the fly edge of the banner to ensure that the Stainless Banner would no longer be mistaken for a white flag of surrender.

The more familiar flag used by Confederate armies and more recently appropriated by white supremacist groups is the square red flag with a blue cross containing 13 stars. This battle flag was first used in Virginia and then spread to other Southern armies. Units of the Army of Tennessee also carried a variety of other flags, as did troops in the Trans-Mississippi Department. The Confederate Navy had a variation of the battle flag as well as other pennants and jacks. The individual states, of course, each had their own flags, many of which are still in use today without change.

This is the common Confederate battle flag carried by many infantry units during the Civil War. The 11th Mississippi Infantry carried this color. One company of this regiment, known as the University Grays, had left the University of Mississippi to fight for the Confederacy. The University Grays took part in Pickett's Charge at Gettysburg, but most did not survive the day.

1988
A dispute over the building of a business park near the battlefield of Manassas/Bull Run becomes "The Third Battle of Bull Run." Preservation wins a victory when the government intervenes.

1989
The film *Glory* portrays the African American 54th Massachusetts Regiment.

OCTOBER 3
The United States and France reach an accord over the sunken wreck of the CSS *Alabama*.

Reenacting the Civil War

With the Civil War centennial in 1961 came the beginnings of reenacting the conflict. Early reenactors wore a variety of authentic and modern uniforms of the appropriate colors. Spectators viewed recreations of battles, many held on National Park Service land. However, the inaccuracy of these battles, coupled with accidents, led the NPS to ban firearms at future events.

By the late 1970s, however, the reenacting hobby had begun to change for the better. Specialized companies now offered exacting reproductions of uniforms, weapons, and equipment. Fresh research into the original 1860s units being recreated lent more credibility to the hobby, many of whose participants wished to be called "living his-

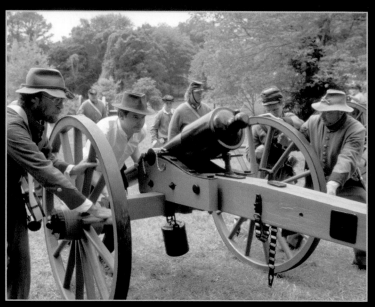

Many reenactment cannons are working full-scale reproductions operated by crews, such as these Confederates, who faithfully conduct original gun drills.

torians." Unit commanders immersed themselves into the study of Civil War tactical and drill manuals. Units began drilling according to period regulations. Many units banned modern comforts from camp—thousands of participants now slept in canvas tents that leaked and endured mud, frost, snow, and scorching sun.

The war's 125th anniversary from 1986 to 1990 saw even larger reenactments. The 1988 Gettysburg event included more than 10,000 participants. Many national parks now authorize specific reenactor units to set up living history camps for visitors. Other "living historians" visit schools nationwide to show eager youngsters how Civil War soldiers lived and died.

During multiday reenactments, most participants remain in period camps, keeping warm by rolling in wool blankets, cooking over campfires, and sometimes being soaked during sudden rainstorms.

1990–92
Controversy erupts at Gettysburg over a secret land swap between Gettysburg College and the National Park Service that results in destruction of part of the battlefield.

1993
The film *Gettysburg* is released in theaters across the nation.

1994
The Walt Disney Corporation announces plans for a history theme park near Manassas National Battlefield Park. The company backs away from the idea after meeting widespread opposition from preservation groups.

When Douglas Wilder was sworn in as governor of the state of Virginia in 1990, he became the first African American elected to the governor's office not only of that state but of any state in U.S. history. Wilder had previously served as state senator and lieutenant governor.

The CSS H. L. Hunley *rises from the sea off Charleston, South Carolina, on August 8, 2000. Since the submarine was retrieved, the bones of the ill-fated crew have been buried, and the vessel is slowly but surely being cleaned and examined to determine what might have sent it to its grave.*

On March 3, 1991, Los Angeles police officers stopped a car driven by Rodney King, who was then stunned and beaten by the officers. The incident was caught on videotape, and the officers were taken to court. After a jury found them not guilty of using excessive force in April 1992, Los Angeles experienced five days of deadly riots, the worst the country had seen since the New York City draft riots of 1863.

The idea of financial reparations to African Americans for slavery has been raised since slavery was abolished in the United States. John Conyers (above), a member of Congress from Michigan, has introduced a bill for a commission to study the issue in every Congress since 1989 but has yet to bring it to a vote. In the courts, lawsuits have been filed against companies that profited from slavery in the past. Opponents argue that slavery's victims and beneficiaries are no longer living.

1995
JANUARY 14
A white 19-year-old driving a pickup truck with a rebel flag the weekend before Martin Luther King Jr. Day is killed in Tennessee by African American youths.

1996
NOVEMBER 12
The Shenandoah Valley Battlefields National Historic District is created by Congress to protect its encompassed sites against modern encroachment.

2000
JULY 3
The controversial Gettysburg National Tower is destroyed, providing preservationists with a major victory.

More than 17,000 Union soldiers are buried at Vicksburg National Cemetery in Mississippi's Vicksburg National Military Park. The Confederate soldiers are buried in a cemetery in the town of Vicksburg.

The War Department appropriated General Robert E. Lee's Arlington estate as a burial ground for Union dead. Today, it is the famous Arlington National Cemetery, which includes the graves of numerous Civil War officers, the Tomb of the Unknown Soldier, and President Kennedy's grave site.

On June 13, 2005, the Senate passed a resolution apologizing for its history of inaction against lynching. James Cameron, 91 years old and the only known survivor of a lynching attempt, was on hand for the occasion. Here he's greeted by Senator Mark Pryor as Senator Mary Landrieu stands by.

General Lewis A. Armistead, played by Richard Jordan, leads his troops over the stone wall at Gettysburg in this scene from Gettysburg, the 1993 film based on the novel The Killer Angels by Michael Shaara. Gettysburg used thousands of reenactors to ensure the battle scenes were as authentic as possible. In fact, many of the actors said they were very much surprised at the dedication of those they led into the staged battles.

AUGUST 8
The submarine CSS *H. L. Hunley* is raised from its underwater grave off Charleston, South Carolina.

2003
APRIL 5
A controversial statue of Abraham Lincoln is dedicated in Richmond, Virginia. It is the first statue of Lincoln to be erected in the South.

2005
APRIL 19
The Abraham Lincoln Presidential Library and Museum holds its dedication ceremony with President George W. Bush in Springfield, Illinois.

In July 1974, the Gettysburg National Tower, a 307-foot observation tower located on private land adjacent to the national park, opened for business. Maryland developer Thomas Ottenstein had financed its construction, which was delayed for several years by litigation, including opposition from the Commonwealth of Pennsylvania. The tower marred the historic landscape until it was condemned and purchased by the federal government. On July 3, 2000, the tower was brought down by a controlled explosion. Pieces were sold to souvenir hunters, with profits going to help finance battlefield preservation.

South Carolina attracted national attention after it continued to fly the Confederate flag beneath the American and state flags on its state capitol. The flag was first raised in that position in 1962. Although it was ostensibly intended to commemorate the Civil War's centennial, the decision was widely seen at the time as a response to the growing civil rights movement. The flag was still flying in the 1990s when the NAACP organized boycotts and protests, which culminated in a massive march and protest in Columbia in April 2000. After much debate, the legislature authorized that the flag be taken down, although it continued to fly at Confederate cemeteries and monuments across the state.

Barack Obama, Democratic senator from Illinois, took office as President of the United States on January 20, 2009. The son of a black father from Kenya and a white mother from Kansas, he became the first African American to hold the office of the nation's leader. Obama campaigned on a program of change for America, and in his first years in office his administration fulfilled some long sought-after Democratic goals, but the election and his term in office also had a polarizing effect on the country.

2008
SEPTEMBER
Gettysburg National Military Park opens a new tour center with the restored 1884 cyclorama.

NOVEMBER 4
Barack Obama is the first African American elected president of the United States. He wins 53 percent of the popular vote and carries the Southern states of North Carolina, Virginia, and Florida.

2011
APRIL 12
The 150th anniversary of the firing on Fort Sumter—the first shots of the Civil War—is commemorated.

Index

Photo Credits

Front cover: Library of Congress (top left center, top right, bottom center, bottom right center, bottom right); MOLLUS - Mass & USAMHI (top left); National Archives (top right center); PIL Collection (top & bottom left)

Back cover: National Archives (top right); PIL Collection (background, top left, bottom left & bottom right)

Alamy Images: P-59 Photos, 431 (bottom); **AP Images:** 429 (top right), 430 (bottom left); **Art Resource, NY:** Newark Museum, 225 (bottom); Smithsonian American Art Museum, Washington, DC, 313, 362 (bottom); Snark, 335 (bottom right); **Boston Public Library:** 166 (top left); **Brown Brothers:** 21, 40 (top), 43 (bottom left), 100 (bottom left), 142 (right), 146, 148 (right center), 172 (bottom left), 198 (bottom right), 272 (bottom left), 273 (bottom right), 292 (left center), 341 (top left), 356, 362 (top left), 367 (top), 373 (top right), 412 (top left); **Susan & Mark Carlson:** 80 (bottom), 350; **Chicago Historical Society:** 232, 293; **Chicago Public Library, Special Collections and Preservation Division:** 339 (bottom); **The Clements Library, University of Michigan:** 104 (top), 150; **www.civilwarprints. com:** 148 (top), 154 (bottom), 181, 203 (top right), 228, 265 (top), 275 (bottom), 290 (top), 294 (bottom left), 297 (top), 298 (top), 299 (top), 318 (top); **Courtesy of Colorado Historical Society:** 148 (left center), 159 (bottom), 301 (top); **Corbis:** contents, 12 (top), 15, 16, 19, 22, 23, 25, 28 (bottom left), 29 (left & right), 30, 31 (top), 32 (top left & center), 34, 35 (bottom), 36 (bottom right), 37 (bottom), 38 (top), 39 (bottom left & bottom right), 40 (bottom right), 43 (top left), 44 (right), 48, 49, 52 (bottom right), 53 (bottom), 54, 55, 56 (bottom), 57 (bottom left), 58 (top left & bottom), 59 (top right & bottom), 62, 63, 64, 66, 69 (right), 71, 72, 79, 81 (top left & top right), 82 (top & bottom right), 85 (top left, top right & bottom right), 90, 91 (top left, top right & bottom right), 92 (top right, bottom left & bottom right), 93, 94 (top left, top center & right center), 95 (left center), 100 (bottom right), 101 (bottom left), 104 (bottom left & bottom right), 119 (top), 130, 138 (bottom), 139 (top & bottom), 142 (bottom left), 143 (top right), 144 (top right), 149, 152, 153 (center & right), 154 (top right), 156 (top left), 158 (top left), 160 (top right & bottom right), 166 (top center), 167 (top right & left center), 170 (top & bottom left), 173 (top right), 180, 190, 194 (top & bottom right), 199 (left center), 203 (bottom left), 205 (top & right center), 210, 222, 226 (top right & bottom right), 230 (top left), 234 (bottom right), 242, 244 (bottom), 254 (bottom), 255 (top), 260 (top right & top left), 261 (top left, top right & bottom left), 262 (top left), 263 (top right), 268 (bottom left), 271 (top right), 275 (top right), 276 (top right & bottom left), 277 (top left & top right), 280 (top), 284 (top right), 286 (top right), 287 (bottom right), 288, 293 (top left), 295 (bottom), 298 (bottom), 300 (top & bottom left), 306, 311, 316, 320 (top), 322, 323 (top), 324 (top), 331, 335 (top right), 336 (top left), 337 (top), 339 (top right), 343 (bottom left), 346, 348, 351 (bottom), 354 (top & right), 359 (bottom), 361 (top right & bottom right), 362 (top right), 364 (top right), 367 (bottom right), 368, 370 (top left & bottom right), 371, 372 (top left & top right), 373 (bottom left), 374 (top & bottom right), 375 (bottom left), 376 (top left), 377, 378 (top left & top right), 379 (top), 380, 381 (bottom right), 382, 384 (top & bottom left), 385 (left & bottom right), 389 (top right), 390 (top & bottom right), 395 (top right & bottom), 400 (top left, top center, bottom left & bottom right), 402 (bottom left & bottom right), 404 (top right), 405 (top left), 406 (top left & top right), 407, 408, 410 (bottom left & bottom center), 411 (top right & bottom left), 412 (bottom center & bottom right), 413 (top), 418 (top right & bottom left), 428 (top); AFP, 431 (right); Bettmann, 10–11, 20, 24, 27, 31 (right center), 32 (top right), 33, 34, 35 (top left & top right), 36 (top & bottom left), 39 (top), 40 (bottom left), 42, 43 (right center, bottom center & bottom right), 46 (top), 47 (top left & top right), 52 (left & top right), 53 (top right), 58 (top right), 60–61, 83 (left center), 111 (bottom), 112–113, 116, 119 (bottom), 160 (bottom left), 162, 166 (top right & bottom left), 170 (bottom right), 176–177, 187, 194 (bottom left), 197, 206 (top left), 214 (bottom right), 215, 216 (top), 231 (top right & bottom right), 252, 274 (bottom right), 309 (left), 318 (bottom), 329 (bottom right), 344–345, 347 (left), 349, 353, 354 (bottom), 358, 359 (top left), 360 (left center), 363 (top right & bottom left), 364 (bottom), 365, 366, 372 (bottom), 373 (top left), 374 (bottom left), 375 (bottom right), 376 (top right), 378 (bottom left), 379 (bottom left), 381 (top left), 390 (bottom left & bottom center), 393 (bottom), 400 (bottom right), 402 (top right), 403 (bottom), 405 (bottom left), 406 (bottom right), 409 (top left, top right & bottom right), 411 (bottom right), 412 (top right), 415, 416 (bottom), 417 (top), 419, 420, 421 (bottom left), 423, 424, 425, 426, 429 (bottom right); David Butow/SABA, 397, 430 (top left); Collection of The Corcoran Gallery of Art, 34; Michael Freeman, 87 (bottom right); David J. & Janice L. Frent Collection, 373 (bottom right), 412 (bottom left); Historical Picture Archive, 41; Robert Holmes, 422; Hulton-Deutsch Collection, 417 (bottom right); Howard Jacqueline/Sygma, 416 (top), 430 (bottom right); John Springer Collection, 417 (bottom left); Joseph Schwartz Collection, 393 (top); William Manning, 430 (top right); Francis G. Mayer, 101 (bottom right); Medford Historical Society Collection, 101 (top left), 145 (top right), 153 (top), 204 (top right), 234 (bottom left), 271 (bottom right), 276 (bottom right), 333 (top right), 375 (top right), 381 (top right); Minnesota Historical Society, 230 (bottom); David Muench, 51 (left); National Archives, 327 (bottom right); Richard T. Nowitz, 401 (bottom right); Profiles in History, 411 (top left); Reuters, 431 (left); Lee Snider, 398; Sygma, 370 (bottom left), 418 (top left); Bequest of Mrs. Benjamin Ogle Tayloe, Collection of The Corcoran Gallery of Art, 34; Peter Turnley, 421 (top), 429 (bottom left); Underwood & Underwood, 384 (bottom right), 406 (bottom left), 410 (top left, top right & bottom right); Oscar White, 355; Tim Wright, 429 (top left); **Edward G. Miller Library, University of Rochester:** 289; **Eleanor S. Brockenbrough Library/ Museum of the Confederacy, Richmond, Virginia:** 107 (bottom right); **F. Forbes:** 106 (top); **Getty Images:** 264 (bottom); Hulton|Archive: 141, 160 (top left), 167 (top left), 168 (bottom), 201, 204 (bottom left), 207, 219 (top), 220 (bottom), 230 (top right), 234 (top), 235, 236 (top), 334, 336 (bottom), 343 (bottom right), 359 (top right), 364 (top left), 379 (bottom right), 383, 404 (bottom); Time Life Pictures, 259; **The Granger Collection, New York:** 195 (bottom), 229 (bottom), 335 (bottom left), 427; **Courtesy of Hagley Museum & Library:** 110 (bottom); **The Harvard Theatre Collection, The Houghton Library:** 300 (bottom right); **Illinois State Historical Library:** 86; **Independence National Historical Park:** 13; **Jim Crow Museum of Racist Memorabilia, Ferris State University:** 391; **Kansas State Historical Society, Topeka:** 45, 229 (top right); Kean Archives, 50; **Library Company of Philadelphia:** 104 (bottom center); **Library of Congress:** contents, 9, 78 (bottom), 94 (left center), 95 (top), 97 (top), 98 (bottom), 100 (top left & top right), 110 (top), 118, 134 (top left), 156 (bottom left), 163 (bottom), 164 (top left), 165 (bottom left), 172 (bottom right), 173 (top left), 195 (top), 198 (top), 206 (bottom), 212 (top & bottom right), 217 (top left), 218 (top left), 226 (bottom left), 231 (top left), 233 (bottom left & bottom right), 237 (bottom), 238, 243, 249 (top), 266, 267, 274 (top right & bottom left), 277 (bottom left & bottom right), 280 (bottom), 281 (top left, top right & bottom right), 282 (bottom right), 284 (top left, bottom left & bottom right), 285 (top left, left center & right center), 286 (bottom right), 287 (top right & right center), 291 (top left & top right), 292 (bottom left), 295 (top), 299 (bottom), 301 (bottom left), 305, 307, 312, 314, 315 (top), 323 (bottom right), 324 (bottom left), 327 (top right), 328 (bottom), 330 (bottom right), 336 (top right), 337 (bottom right), 338 (right center), 339 (top left), 340, 388, 413 (bottom); George N. Barnard, 5, 196 (top), 236 (bottom right), 250, 255 (bottom), 257, 293 (bottom right), 294 (bottom right); George N. Barnard & James F. Gibson, 140 (top); Brady Gallery, 76 (left), 84 (top right & left center), 123 (right), 131, 139 (left center), 140 (right center), 142 (top left), 156 (top right), 164 (bottom right), 199 (right center), 218 (top right), 220 (top right), 223 (top), 224 (top right), 233 (top right), 272 (right), 273 (bottom left), 278, 294 (top left), 309 (right), 351 (top), 360 (top left); Mathew B. Brady, contents, 317, 341 (bottom); George S. Cook, 91 (bottom left); Alexander Gardner: 134 (bottom), 171 (top), 186, 211, 231 (bottom left), 310, 332 (top right & bottom), James Gardner, 213 (top), 264 (top left), 272 (top left); James F. Gibson, 7, 131, 133, 138 (top), 164 (top right), 214 (bottom left), 282 (bottom left); Timothy H. O'Sullivan, contents, 8, 133, 154 (top left), 169 (bottom right), 172 (top right), 204 (bottom right), 206 (top right), 213 (bottom right), 214 (top), 217

(top right), 218 (bottom), 220 (top left), 245, 248, 264 (top right), 286 (top left), 327 (bottom left), 335 (top left); William M. Smith, 159 (top), 286 (bottom left), 342 (top right & bottom); David B. Woodbury, 163 (top left); **The Lincoln Museum:** 283; **Lloyd Ostendorf Collection:** 325; **Minnesota Historical Society:** 166 (bottom right); **MOLLUS – Mass & USAMHI:** 37 (top left), 78 (center), 84 (bottom), 105 (top right), 144 (bottom left), 169 (bottom left), 236 (bottom left), 320 (center & bottom), 328 (top), 403 (top); **National Archives:** contents, 8 (bottom), 34 (bottom), 38 (bottom right), 46 (right), 47 (bottom right), 53 (top left), 57 (top left), 67, 68, 76 (right), 80 (top), 81 (left center), 82 (bottom left), 83 (bottom right), 84 (right center), 85 (bottom left), 92 (top left), 95 (right center), 96, 98 (top right), 107 (top & bottom left), 115, 129, 132, 143 (top left & bottom), 145 (top left), 169 (top), 171 (bottom right), 175 (bottom left), 182, 184, 185, 199 (top), 200, 208 (bottom), 209 (bottom), 219 (bottom), 224 (bottom), 226 (top left), 227, 246, 265 (bottom left & bottom right), 271 (left), 274 (top left), 276 (top left), 281 (bottom left), 282 (top left & top right), 294 (top right), 298 (left), 304, 333 (top left), 338 (top & bottom left), 341 (top right), 343 (top), 361 (left center), 376 (bottom right), 378 (bottom right), 389 (top left), 402 (top left); **Ohio Historical Society:** 151; **Pennsylvania Historical & Museum Commission Drake Well Museum Collection, Titusville, PA:** 57 (right); **Pennsylvania State Archives:** 396; **Petersburg National Battlefield:** 327 (top left); **PictureHistory:** 56 (top left), 69 (left), 98 (top left), 123 (left), 199 (bottom right), 209 (top right), 323 (bottom left), 337 (bottom left), 363 (top left), 367 (bottom left), 385 (top right), 386–387, 392, 401 (top right), 404 (top left), 418 (bottom right); **Richard A. Sauers:** 168 (top left & top right), 172 (top left), 175 (top right & bottom right), 192, 198 (bottom left), 225 (top), 347 (right), 399, 405 (bottom right), 428 (bottom); Courtesy of Gettysburg NMP and Lane Studios, 395 (top left); **Seymour Library:** 44 (left); **Courtesy of Special Collections and Archives, Furman University:** 59 (top left); **Stock Montage, Inc.:** 26, 124, 165 (top), 174, 321 (top left), 360 (right), 370 (top right), 375 (top left); **SuperStock:** 14, 17, 28 (bottom right), 31 (left center), 37 (top right), 43 (top right), 46 (bottom), 56 (top right), 144 (bottom right), 196, 302–303, 321 (top right), 326 (bottom), 333 (bottom), 338 (bottom left), 342 (top left), 409 (bottom left); Jamie Abecasis, contents, 38 (bottom left); Bridgeman Art Library, London, 127; Alan Briere, 28 (top right); Christie's Images, 376 (bottom left); Newberry Library, 369; **U.S. Naval Academy Museum:** 73; **Valentine Richmond History Center:** 12 (bottom), 65, 111 (top left), 158 (bottom left), 352; **Virginia Military Institute:** 268 (bottom right); **Frank Vizetelly pfMS Am 1585 (8), (15), (18) By permission of the Houghton Library, Harvard University:** 128 (top), 229 (top left), 275 (top left); **Wadsworth Atheneum Museum of Art:** 290 (bottom); **West Point Museum:** 87 (top); **West Virginia State Archives:** 205 (left center); **White House Historical Association:** 326 (top left); **Courtesy of Frank & Marie-Therese Wood Print Collection, Alexandria, VA:** 158 (top right), 217 (bottom left), 262 (top right), 291 (bottom left), 293 (top right), 301 (bottom right), 308, 326 (top right), 330 (bottom left)